Lecture Notes in Artificial Intellig

Subseries of Lecture Notes in Computer Scienc
Edited by J. G. Carbonell and J. Siekmann

Lecture Notes in Computer Science
Edited by G. Goos, J. Hartmanis, and J. van Leeuwen

Springer
*Berlin*
*Heidelberg*
*New York*
*Barcelona*
*Hong Kong*
*London*
*Milan*
*Paris*
*Tokyo*

Céline Rouveirol Michèle Sebag (Eds.)

# Inductive Logic Programming

11th International Conference, ILP 2001
Strasbourg, France, September 9-11, 2001
Proceedings

Series Editors

Jaime G. Carbonell, Carnegie Mellon University, Pittsburgh, PA, USA
Jörg Siekmann, University of Saarland, Saarbrücken, Germany

Volume Editors

Céline Rouveirol
Université Paris Sud, LRI
bât. 490, 91405 Orsay Cedex, France
E-mail: Celine.Rouveirol@lri.fr

Michèle Sebag
Ecole Polytechnique, LMS
91128 Palaiseau, France
E-mail: Michele.Sebag@polytechnique.fr

Cataloging-in-Publication Data applied for

Die Deutsche Bibliothek - CIP-Einheitsaufnahme

Inductive logic programming : 11th international conference ; proceedings / ILP 2001, Strasbourg, France, September 9 - 11, 2001. Céline Rouveirol ; Michèle Sebag (ed.). - Berlin ; Heidelberg ; New York ; Barcelona ; Hong Kong ; London ; Milan ; Paris ; Tokyo : Springer, 2001
(Lecture notes in computer science ; Vol. 2157 : Lecture notes in artificial intelligence)
ISBN 3-540-42538-1

CR Subject Classification (1998): I.2.3, I.2, D.1.6, F.4.1, F.2.2

ISBN 3-540-42538-1 Springer-Verlag Berlin Heidelberg New York



Springer-Verlag Berlin Heidelberg New York
a member of BertelsmannSpringer Science+Business Media GmbH

http://www.springer.de


Printed in Germany

Typesetting: Camera-ready by author, data conversion by Steingräber Satztechnik GmbH, Heidelberg
Printed on acid-free paper SPIN: 10840266 06/3142 5 4 3 2 1 0

# Preface

The 11th international conference on Inductive Logic Programming, ILP 2001, was held in Strasbourg, France, September 9–11, 2001. ILP 2001 was co-located with the 3rd international workshop on Logic, Learning, and Language (LLL 2001), and nearly co-located with the joint 12th European Conference on Machine Learning (ECML 2001) and 5th European conference on Principles and Practice of Knowledge Discovery in Databases (PKDD 2001).

Continuing a series of international conferences devoted to Inductive Logic Programming and Relational Learning, ILP 2001 is the central annual event for researchers interested in learning structured knowledge from structured examples and background knowledge.

One recent one major challenge for ILP has been to contribute to the exponential emergence of Data Mining, and to address the handling of multi-relational databases. On the one hand, ILP has developed a body of theoretical results and algorithmic strategies for exploring relational data, essentially but not exclusively from a supervised learning viewpoint. These results are directly relevant to an efficient exploration of multi-relational databases.

On the other hand, Data Mining might require specific relational strategies to be developed, especially with regard to the scalability issue. The near-colocation of ILP 2001 with ECML 2001-PKDD 2001 was an incentive to increase cross-fertilization between the ILP relational *savoir-faire* and the new problems and learning goals addressed and to be addressed in Data Mining.

Thirty-seven papers were submitted to ILP, among which twenty-one were selected and appear in these proceedings. Several – non-disjoint – trends can be observed, along an admittedly subjective clustering.

On the theoretical side, a new mode of inference is proposed by K. Inoue, analog to the open-ended mode of Bayesian reasoning (where the frontier between induction and abduction wanes). New learning refinement operators are proposed by L. Badea, while R. Otero investigates negation-handling settings. Rule stretching (M. Eineborg and H. Boström) can also be considered a new inductive-deductive operator.

Several hybrid frameworks are proposed, either bridging the gap between ILP and other learning paradigms, e.g. Bayesian inference (K. Kersting and L. De Raedt), Neural Nets (R. Basilio, G. Zaverucha, and V. C. Barbosa) or Feature Selection (T. Ozabaki and K. Furukawa) – or exploiting other search paradigms, e.g. Constraint Satisfaction (J. Maloberti) or Genetic Algorithms (A. Braud and C. Vrain), to address particular ILP tasks.

Among the tasks addressed, changes of representation take an increasing importance, ranging from propositionalization (A. Braud and C. Vrain, already mentioned) and construction of structural features (S. Kramer), to aggregation-based transformations (M.-A. Krogel and S. Wrobel).

Committee-based and statistical machine learning interestingly pervade ILP through boosting-based approaches (S. Hoche and S. Wrobel), positive-only learning (F. Zelezny), and transductive inference (M. Eineborg and H. Boström, already mentioned). Last but not least, an efficient relational cross-validation procedure is proposed by J. Struyf and H. Blockeel.

The application papers deserve a special mention as they demonstrate when and how relational representations can make the difference. Language-related applications range from Natural Language (M. Nepil) to XML documents (A. Yamamoto, K. Ito, A. Ishino, and H. Arimura), and shell logs (N. Jacobs and H. Blockeel). Bio-informatics offers many challenging relational problems (A. Karwath and R. D. King), in the spirit of the founding ILP application, i.e. the mutagenesis problem[1]. Other applications are concerned with medical control (R. Quiniou, M.-O. Cordier, G. Carrault, and F. Wang) and spatial data mining (D. Malerba and F. A. Lisi).

The invited talks, one joint conference with LLL, given by D. Roth, Univ of Illinois, USA and one by H. T. T. Toivonen, Nokia, Finland, described the challenges a in two of the hottest fields for Machine Learning and ILP: Natural Language, and the Genome[2].

We wish to thank all researchers who submitted their papers to ILP 2001, all external referees whose kind help was very welcome, and the members of the Program Committee for their commitment to making ILP 2001 an open and lively high scientific venue.

July 2001

Céline Rouveirol and Michèle Sebag
Program Chairs

---

1 R.D. King, A. Srinivasan, and M.J.E. Sternberg, *Relating chemical activity to structure: an examination of ILP successes*, New Gen. Comput., 13, 1995.

2 Available at: `http://www.lri.fr/ ilp2001/`

# Organization

| | |
|---|---|
| Local chair: | Nicolas Lachiche (Univ. Robert Schuman - LSIIT, Strasbourg, France ) |
| Web chair: | Fabien Torre (Univ. Lille 3, France) |

## Program Committee

H. Blockeel, Belgium
J.-F. Boulicaut, France
H. Boström, Sweden
I. Bratko, Slovenia
J. Cussens, UK
L. Dehaspe, Belgium
S. Džeroski, Slovenia
F. Esposito, Italy
P. Flach, UK
A. Frisch, UK
K. Furukawa, Japan
J-U. Kietz, Switzerland
N. Lavrač, Slovenia
J. Lloyd, Australia
S. Kramer, Germany
S. Matwin, Canada
S. Muggleton, UK
D. Page, USA
B. Pfahringer, NZ
L. Saitta, Italy
C. Sammut, Australia
A. Srinivasan, UK
P. Tadepalli, USA
S. Wrobel, Germany
A. Yamamoto, Japan

## External Referees

A. Borgida, Ch. Giraud-Carrier, J.-F. Puget, L. de Raedt, V. Ventos, C. Vrain.

## Sponsoring Institutions

ILPNet2,
IUT Robert Schuman,
Université Robert Schuman,
Université Louis Pasteur,
Conseil général du Bas-Rhin
Région Alsace,
and the city of Strasbourg.

# Table of Contents

# A Refinement Operator for Theories

Liviu Badea

AI Lab, National Institute for Research and Development in Informatics
8-10 Averescu Blvd., Bucharest, Romania.
badea@ici.ro

**Abstract.** Most implemented ILP systems construct hypotheses clause by clause using a refinement operator *for clauses*. To avoid the problems faced by such greedy covering algorithms, more *flexible* refinement operators *for theories* are needed. In this paper we construct a syntactically monotonic, finite and solution-complete refinement operator for theories, which eliminates certain annoying redundancies (due to clause deletions), while also addressing the limitations faced by HYPER's refinement operator (which are mainly due to keeping the number of clauses constant during refinement).

We also show how to eliminate the redundancies due to the commutativity of refinement operations while preserving weak completeness as well as a limited form of flexibility. The refinement operator presented in this paper represents a first step towards constructing more efficient and *flexible* ILP systems with precise theoretical guarantees.

## 1 Introduction and Motivation

Although the research in Inductive Logic Programming (ILP) has concentrated on both implementations (e.g. [8,7]) and theoretical results [4] (such as correctness, completeness and complexity), there is still a significant gap between these aspects, mainly due to a poor understanding of the combinatorial aspects of the search for solutions. In this respect, correctness and completeness results are necessary but not sufficient for obtaining an *efficient* learner. On the other hand, ad-hoc search heuristics might prove effective in certain cases, but the lack of theoretical guarantees limits their applicability and the interpretation of their results.

With only a few notable exceptions (such as HYPER [3], or MPL [5]), most implemented ILP systems construct hypotheses clause by clause by employing a *refinement operator for clauses*. As shown by Bratko [3], such greedy covering algorithms face several problems such as: unnecessarily long hypotheses (with too many clauses), difficulties in handling recursion and difficulties in learning multiple predicates simultaneously. These problems are due to the fact that a good hypothesis is not necessarily assembled from locally optimal clauses. In fact, locally inferior clauses may reveal their (global) superiority only as a whole. And it is exactly this case (of mutually interacting clauses) that most implemented ILP systems do not deal with well.

C. Rouveirol and M. Sebag (Eds.): ILP 2001, LNAI 2157, pp. 1–14, 2001.

A solution to this problem would be to construct hypotheses as a whole (rather than on a clause by clause basis) by using a *refinement operator for entire theories*. But unfortunately, the combinatorial complexity of a refinement operator *for clauses* is high enough already, making a naive refinement operator *for theories* useless for all practical purposes.

The main problem encountered when constructing a refinement operator for theories is its redundancy, which heavily multiplies the size of an already huge search space. Sometimes, a good search heuristic can compensate for the size of such search spaces. However, very often, the failure in coping with the required search is attributed solely to the weakness (or maybe myopia) of the heuristic employed. In [2] we have argued that among the responsible factors for such failures one should also count the lack of *flexibility* of the refinement operator, its *redundancy*, as well as its *incompleteness*. While completeness and non-redundancy are desiderata that have been achieved in state-of-the art systems like Progol [7], flexibility has hardly been studied or even defined in a precise manner. (A precise definition of *flexibility* of refinement operators *for clauses* was given in [2].)

Flexibility becomes an issue especially in the case of (weakly) complete and non-redundant refinement operators, because redundancy is usually avoided by imposing a strict discipline on refinement operations, which usually relies on a predetermined (static) ordering of the literals, variables and even clauses. The resulting lack of flexibility can unfortunately disallow certain refinements, even in cases in which the search heuristic recommends their immediate exploration (These hypotheses will be explored eventually, but maybe with an exponential time delay.) The solution to this problem, proposed in [2], consists in enhancing the *flexibility* of the clausal refinement operator by using a dynamic literal ordering, constructed at search time. In this paper, we show how to construct a flexible refinement operator *for theories.*

Combining (weak) completeness and non-redundancy with flexibility has been studied in [2], but only for *clausal* refinement operators. Although *maximal* flexibility can only be achieved at the expense of intractability and exponential storage space, a limited form of flexibility can be achieved without significant additional costs, while preserving the completeness and non-redundancy of the refinement operator. This hints at a very general trade-off between (weak) completeness, non-redundancy, flexibility and tractability.[1]

---

[1] If we insist on (weak) completeness and non-redundancy, there is a fundamental trade-off between *flexibility* and *tractability*. For achieving non-redundancy, we have to store somehow a representation of the visited hypotheses space, so that every time a refinement of some $H_2$ to some $H'$ is considered, we can check that $H'$ hasn't been visited before. For tractability (of these checks), we cannot store a very fine grained representation of the visited space, so whenever visiting a hypothesis $H$ we will store a coarse grained representation $\tilde{H}$ of $H$. However, this will block (in the future) not only the refinements leading to $H$, but also all those $H' \in \tilde{H}$ that are indiscernible w.r.t. the coarse graining. This diminishes the flexibility of the refinement operator.

A natural question is "why don't we use the partial refinement tree as a sort of index structure for the visited hypotheses space?" Although the depth of the

At the level of clauses, FOIL [8], for example, gives up completeness for maximum flexibility. But if the heuristic fails to guide the search to a solution, the system cannot rely on a complete refinement operator to explore alternative paths. On the other hand, Progol [7] insists on completeness and non-redundancy at the expense of flexibility: some refinement steps are never considered because of the static discipline for eliminating redundancies. Finally, systems based on *ideal* refinement operators are complete and can be maximally flexible, but they are highly redundant.

At the level of theories, both FOIL and Progol construct clauses one by one (Progol does this for ensuring non-redundancy and weak completeness). MPL [5] has more flexibility, but is incomplete. HYPER is less incomplete and still performs surprisingly well, even if the search heuristic were not perfect. This is mainly due to its avoiding an overly complex refinement operator such as[2]

$$\rho_T(T) = \{(T \setminus \{C\}) \cup \rho(C) \mid C \in T\}$$

by keeping the number of clauses constant during refinement:

$$\rho_H(T) = \{(T \setminus \{C\}) \cup \{C'\} \mid C \in T,\ C' \in \rho(C)\}. \tag{1}$$

Therefore, HYPER has to start with theories containing *multiple copies* of certain very general clauses (corresponding to the predicates to be learned). Thus, the main reason for HYPER's success seems to be its avoidance of certain redundancies and combinatorial explosions by keeping the number of clauses constant. But there are still other redundancies, such as:

- redundancies due to the commutativity of the refinement operations
- redundant clauses within a theory (which are not removed in order to give them later the chance to be specialized).

Keeping a constant number of clauses in theories during refinement is especially problematical when the number of clauses in the target theory cannot be easily estimated. If this number is significant, HYPER will rediscover fragments of the target theory over and over again without being able to reuse an $k$-clause solution fragment in a larger $n$-clause theory ($n > k$).[3] This also significantly increases the search time. Even worse, when learning theories for $n$ predicates

refinement tree is typically logarithmic in the number of visited hypotheses, searching for a given hypothesis, for example a clause with literals $L_1 L_2 \ldots L_n$, involves in general searching along $n!$ paths (corresponding to all permutations of $L_1 L_2 \ldots L_n$). Of course, at most one such path will actually lead to our hypothesis (since the refinement tree belongs to a non-redundant operator), but the search along $n!$ paths *at each refinement step* cannot be avoided and is intractable in practice.

[2] Theories $T$ are viewed as sets of clauses $C$. $\rho$ is a complete refinement operator for clauses.

[3] In HYPER we also have redundancies between theories with different numbers of clauses, for example between $T_1 = T$ and $T_2 = T \wedge T_{rest}$ for a (very specific) $T_{rest}$ such that $\forall C_2 \in T_{rest}$, $\exists C_1 \in T$ with $C_1 \succeq C_2$. (This ensures that $T_1 \sim T_2$.)

$p_1, p_2, \ldots, p_n$ (while allowing at most $N$ clauses for each of them), HYPER will have to consider $N^n$ start theories.

In this paper we present a refinement operator for theories that solves most of the above-mentioned problems:

- it is complete and flexible (i.e. allows interleaving the refinement of clauses)
- it can exploit a good search heuristic by avoiding the pitfalls of a greedy covering algorithm
- it doesn't keep the number of clauses in a theory constant: it introduces new clauses exactly when these are needed
- it never deletes clauses (unlike MPL for example, where deleted clauses have to be marked to avoid adding them again later).

## 2 Refinement Operators for Theories

Refinement operators decouple the search heuristic from the search algorithm. Instead of the usual refinement operators for clauses, we will construct refinement operators for entire theories. For a top-down search, we deal with *downward* refinement operators, i.e. ones that construct theory *specialisations*. More precisely, we will consider refinement operators w.r.t. the *subsumption ordering* between theories.

In the following, we will regard *clauses* as sets of literals (connected by disjunction) and *theories* as sets of clauses (connected by conjunction). Clauses will be denoted by $C$, while theories by $T$ (possibly with super/sub-scripts).

**Definition 1.** *Clause $C_1$* subsumes *clause $C_2$, $C_1 \succeq C_2$ iff there exists a substitution $\theta$ such that $C_1\theta \subseteq C_2$ (the clauses being viewed as sets of literals).*

*Theory $T_1$* subsumes *theory $T_2$, $T_1 \succeq T_2$ iff $\forall C_2 \in T_2$. $\exists C_1 \in T_1$ such that $C_1 \succeq C_2$.*

*A hypothesis $H$ (either a clause or a theory)* properly subsumes *$H'$, $H \succ H'$ iff $H \succeq H'$ and $H' \not\succeq H$.*

*$H$ and $H'$ are* subsume-equivalent, *$H \sim H'$ iff $H \succeq H'$ and $H' \succeq H$.*

**Definition 2.** *A* downward refinement operator for theories *$\rho_T$ maps theories $T$ to sets of theories subsumed by $T$: $\rho_T(T) \subseteq \{T' \mid T \succeq T'\}$.*

**Definition 3.** *A refinement operator $\rho : HYP \to 2^{HYP}$ is called:*

- (locally) finite *iff $\rho(H)$ is finite and computable for all hypotheses $H$.*
- proper *iff for all $H$, $\rho(H)$ contains no $H' \sim H$.*
- complete *iff for all $H$ and $H'$, $H \succ H' \Rightarrow \exists H'' \in \rho^\star(H)$ such that $H'' \sim H'$.*
- weakly complete *iff $\rho^*(H_{TOP})$ covers the entire set of hypotheses $HYP$ ($H_{TOP}$ being the top hypothesis, for example the empty clause $\Box$ in the case of clauses, or the theory $\{\Box\}$ containing the empty clause in the case of theories).*

- solution complete *(for* theory *refinement operators only) iff for all* $H \succ H'$ *such that* $H$ *and* $H'$ *cover all positives,* $\exists H'' \in \rho^\star(H)$ *such that* $H'' \sim H'$.
- non-redundant *iff for all* $H_1, H_2$ *and* $H$, $H \in \rho^\star(H_1) \cap \rho^\star(H_2) \Rightarrow H_1 \in \rho^\star(H_2)$ *or* $H_2 \in \rho^\star(H_1)$.
- minimal *iff for all* $H$, $\rho(H)$ *contains only downward covers*[4] *and all its elements are incomparable* $(H_1, H_2 \in \rho(H) \Rightarrow H_1 \not\succeq H_2$ *and* $H_2 \not\succeq H_1)$.

Refinement operators have a dual nature. On the one hand, they make *syntactic* modifications to clauses and theories. On the other, these syntactic modifications have to agree with a *semantic* (generality) criterion (for a downward operator, the refinements have to be specialisations).

A refinement operator that never performs any deletions is called *syntactically monotonic* (however, such an operator may perform replacements). Syntactical monotonicity is important from a practical point of view since it avoids certain redundancies (the target of a deletion could also be reached without introducing the deleted element).

Downward refinement operators for clauses operate by adding literals and are therefore syntactically monotonic. (Adding literals to clauses produces even more specific clauses.)

However, adding clauses to theories makes these theories more general. Constructing a syntactically monotonic downward refinement operator for theories (i.e. one that doesn't delete clauses) is therefore not as simple as for clauses.

Let $\rho(C)$ be a finite and complete refinement operator for clauses. $\rho(C)$ induces the following finite and complete refinement operator for theories:

$$\begin{aligned} \rho_T(T) = \{(T \setminus \{C\}) \cup \rho(C) \mid C \in T\} \quad & \text{\% refinement} \\ \cup \, \{T \setminus \{C\} \mid C \in T\} \quad & \text{\% (clause) deletion} \end{aligned} \tag{2}$$

In other words, $\rho_T$ either replaces a clauses $C \in T$ by (the conjunction of) *all* its refinements $\rho(C)$, or deletes a clause $C \in T$. The latter alternative (clause deletion) is necessary for completeness, although it spoils the syntactic monotonicity of $\rho_T$, making it highly redundant and therefore impractical.

At this point, Bratko [3] severely restricts the refinement operator to reduce its non-redundancy by keeping the number of clauses constant during refinement (see (1) above). The resulting refinement operator is however incomplete. This leaves open the question of whether a syntactically monotonic and complete refinement operator can be constructed.

## 3 A Syntactically Monotonic Refinement Operator for Theories

In the following, we construct a *syntactically monotonic, finite and solution-complete refinement operator for theories.* (A solution-complete refinement operator may not generate all possible theories, but it will guarantee the generation

[4] $H'$ is a *downward cover* of $H$ iff $H \succ H'$ and no $H'' \in HYP$ satisfies $H \succ H'' \succ H'$.

of all *solutions*, i.e. theories covering all positive examples and no negative examples, while locally maximizing a certain covering heuristic.)

To start with, note that $\rho_T(T)$ replaces a clause $C$ by *all* its clause refinements $\rho(C)$. This produces in just a few refinement steps very long theories. These could be simplified by clause deletion, but it still begs for the following question: are all clauses from $\rho(C)$ really necessary in the refinement of $T$?

The answer is 'no', especially when strict subsets $\rho'$ of $\rho(C)$ are capable of covering (jointly with $T \setminus \{C\}$) all positives. Indeed, even if $(T \setminus \{C\}) \cup \rho(C)$ is in principle more general than $(T \setminus \{C\}) \cup \rho'$, the introduction of the *redundant* clauses $\rho(C) \setminus \rho'$ in the refinement of $T$ seems unjustified, especially since it only increases theory size without improving its coverage (since $(T \setminus \{C\}) \cup \rho(C)$ is more general, it could in fact cover more negative examples! On the other hand, both theories cover all positives.[5])

For obtaining *minimal* theories using a downward operator, we should therefore only add the smallest subsets $\rho'$ of $\rho(C)$ that preserve the covering of all positives:

$$\begin{aligned} \rho'_T(T) = \{T' = (T \setminus \{C\}) \cup \rho' \mid & \text{ for } C \in T \text{ and } \rho' \subseteq \rho(C) \textit{ minimal} \\ & \text{(w.r.t. set inclusion) such that } T' \text{ covers } \textit{all} \text{ positives}\} \end{aligned} \tag{3}$$

Considering a minimal[6] $\rho' \subseteq \rho(C)$ instead of the full $\rho(C)$ ensures that clauses which do not interact in (or *jointly* contribute to) covering the positives are not kept together, thereby minimizing the theory size (which is obviously important in learning).

Normally, if the clauses $C_i$ of $\rho(C) = \{C_1, \ldots, C_n\}$ do not "interact", we re-obtain HYPER's refinement operator

$$\rho'_T(T) = \{(T \setminus \{C\}) \cup \{C_i\} \mid C \in T,\ C_i \in \rho(C)\}.$$

However, in general, clauses $C_i \in \rho(C)$ do interact. These are the cases in which our new refinement operator increases the number of clauses in the theory. This is done only when the introduction of new clauses is necessary for preserving the coverage of all positives.

For example, when refining a theory $T$ (by refining one of its clauses $C \in T$), the number of clauses will increase only if some $C_i \in \rho(C)$ is not capable of covering[7] *all* positives by itself, so that at least some other $C_j \in \rho(C)$ is needed as well (see Figure 1): $T \mapsto (T \setminus \{C\}) \cup \{C_i, C_j\}$. Obviously, replacing $C$ by the more specific $C_i \wedge C_j$ may avoid covering some negative examples.

The unrestricted refinement operator $\rho_T$ makes *minimal* refinement steps (whenever it doesn't perform deletions) since $(T \setminus \{C\}) \cup \rho(C)$ is more general than $(T \setminus \{C\}) \cup \rho'$ for every $\rho' \subseteq \rho(C)$.

---

[5] When refining theories using a downward operator, we can safely discard any theory not covering all positives, since downward refinements are specialisations and therefore will not be able to extend their coverage.

[6] There can be several such minimal $\rho' \subseteq \rho(C)$.

[7] together with $T \setminus \{C\}$.

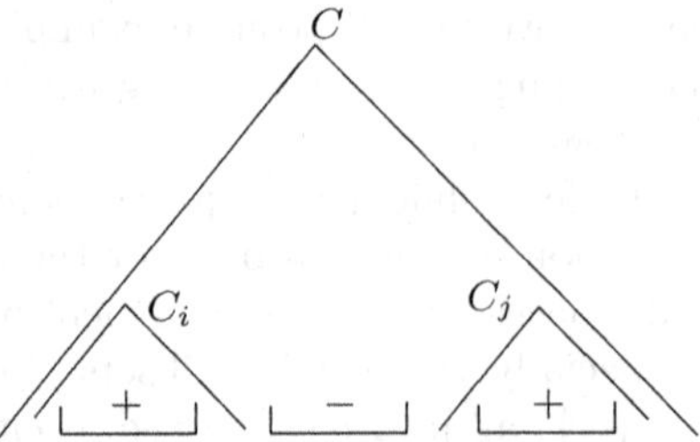


**Fig. 1.** $C$ is refined to $C_i \wedge C_j$. Refining $C$ separately to $C_i$ or $C_j$ would spoil the coverage of all positives, making the introduction of a new clause in the theory necessary.

However, the minimality of the refinement steps of $\rho_T$ also involves a *significant increase in theory size*[8], which is usually not justified by the examples.[9] To make this observation more precise, we introduce a *heuristic function* for evaluating the merit of a hypothesis:

$$f(T) = pos(T) - neg(T) - |T|$$

where $|T|$ is the size of theory $T$, while $pos(T)$ (respectively $neg(T)$) is the number of positive (negative) examples covered by $T$. ($f$ is to be maximized. Since all theories constructed by $\rho'_T$ cover *all* positives, $pos(T) = pos$ is a constant.)

We also introduce the notion of *"compression"* realized by a theory $T$ as

$$k(T) = pos(T) - |T|.$$

A *solution* $T$ covers no negative examples ($neg(T) = 0$) and its size should be smaller than the number of positive examples covered: $|T| \leq pos(T)$, i.e. $k(T) \geq 0$. (Note that the compression $k(T)$ is an upper bound on the merit function $f(T) \leq k(T)$, with equality only in the case of solutions.)

Very frequently, the unrestricted $\rho_T$ makes only very small[10] refinement steps and thus only increases the size $|T|$ without modifying the coverage $pos(T) - neg(T)$. This size increase would be justified only if the coverage would be improved. This is exactly what our improved $\rho'_T$ does: it tolerates a size increase only if all the newly introduced clauses are necessary for covering all positives.

More precisely, let $\rho'$ be a minimal subset of $\rho(C)$ such that $(T \backslash \{C\}) \cup \rho'$ still covers all positives. Then adding any additional (redundant) clause $C'' \in \rho(C) \backslash \rho'$ to a refinement $T' = (T \backslash \{C\}) \cup \rho'$ of $T$, i.e. considering $T'' = (T \backslash \{C\}) \cup \rho' \cup \{C''\}$, will not only increase the size of the resulting theory: $|T''| > |T'|$, but will also possibly increase the number of negative examples covered $neg(T'') \geq neg(T')$ (since $T''$ is more general than $T'$), thus leading to a theory that is *worse* (w.r.t. the heuristic function) than the original refinement: $f(T'') < f(T)$.

---

[8] which makes the resulting theories impractical in just a few refinement steps.

[9] There may be no difference in example coverage between $(T \setminus \{C\}) \cup \rho(C)$ and $(T \setminus \{C\}) \cup \rho'$. In other words, while the first theory is *intensionally* more general than the second, the two theories can be *extensionally* equivalent.

[10] small w.r.t. the generality order.

### 3.1 Implementing the Syntactically Monotonic Refinement Operator for Theories

The pseudo-code below, implementing $\rho'_T$ (3), avoids generating all subsets of $\rho(C)$ – it never generates supersets of the *minimal* subsets $\rho'$. This is realized by generating the subsets in increasing $|\rho'|$[11] and by blocking the generation of supersets of the minimal subsets covering all positives.

Subsets $S'$ covering all positives are never added to the candidate list $L$, so we will never generate supersets of $S'$ *from* $S'$ *itself*. However, since supersets of $S'$ could also be generated from sets that differ from $S'$, we use *nogoods* for avoiding the generation of such supersets.[12]

```
Compute ρ'_T(T)
  ρ'_T(T) := ∅
  forall C ∈ T
    L := ∅;   assume ρ(C) = {C_1, ..., C_n}
    while L is non-empty
      extract the first S = {i_1, ..., i_k} from L
      for j = i_k + 1, ..., n
        S' = S ∪ {j}
        if ∄ nogood(S'') such that S'' ⊆ S'        (⋆)
          if T' = (T \ {C}) ∪ {C_{i_1}, ..., C_{i_k}} covers all positives
            add T' to ρ'_T(T)  % return T'
            add nogood(S')
          else append S' to L
        end if
      end for
    end while
  end for
```

Instead of adding $T'$ to $\rho'_T(T)$, one could return $T'$ (as a refinement of $T$) immediately and rely on backtracking to obtain alternative refinements.

For $\rho(C) = \{C_1, \ldots, C_n\}$, the above algorithm computes the subsets $\rho' \subseteq \rho(C)$ that are *minimal* w.r.t. set inclusion such that $T' = (T \setminus \{C\}) \cup \rho'$ covers *all* positives.

For example, for $\rho(C) = \{C_1, C_2, C_3\}$, if $\rho'_1 = \{C_1\}$ and $\rho'_{23} = \{C_2, C_3\}$ cover all positives[13], but $\rho'_2 = \{C_2\}$ and $\rho'_3 = \{C_3\}$ do not, we will consider only the two theory refinements corresponding to $\rho'_1$ and $\rho'_{23}$. Note that we will *not* consider the refinement $\rho'_{12} = \{C_1, C_2\}$ since it is not minimal w.r.t. set inclusion ($\{C_1, C_2\} \supseteq \{C_1\}$, which covers all positives). See Figure 2.

---

[11] i.e. we first generate the refinements for which $\rho'$ is a singleton, then those where $\rho'$ contains 2, then 3, 4, ... clauses.

[12] The nogood test ($\star$) can be efficiently implemented (using a tree-like representation for nogood sets).

[13] together with $T \setminus \{C\}$.

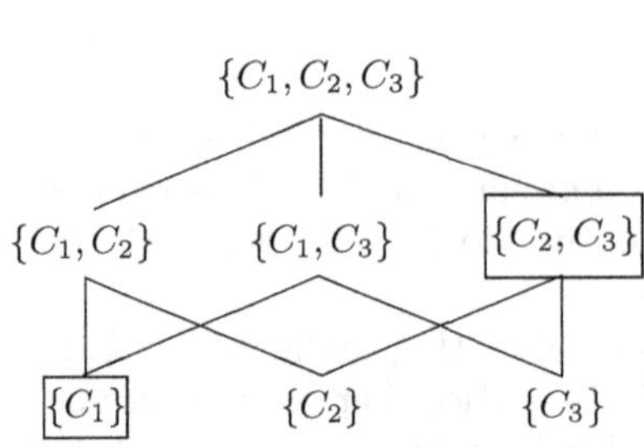


**Fig. 2.** Minimal subsets covering all positives.

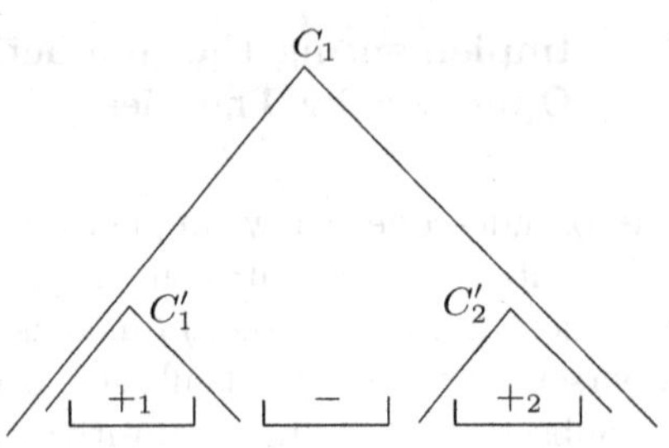


**Fig. 3.** $C_1$ is refined to $C'_1$ for avoiding the negatives $-$. $C'_2$ is introduced to cover the remaining positives $+_2$, but only when it is needed (i.e. as a refinement of $C_1$, and not before refining $C_1$).

Intuitively, considering $\{C_1, C_2\}$ (i.e. $C_1 \wedge C_2$) as a refinement would amount to considering a 2-clause theory containing $C_1$ even if $C_1$ covers by itself all positives. Now, it may be that a second clause $C'_2$ will be needed later to preserve the coverage of all positives (after having refined $C_1$ to a more specific $C'_1$ for avoiding negatives). However, this $C'_2$ need not be introduced now – it will be when needed (e.g. when refining $C_1$ to $C'_1 \wedge C'_2$ – see Figure 3).

Testing *all* subsets $\rho' \subseteq \rho(C)$ for minimality may pose efficiency problems due to the large number of such subsets. However, due to the syntactic monotonicity of $\rho'_T$, the size of theories increases during refinement, while their compression decreases monotonically. This imposes an upper bound on the size of subsets $\rho'$ that should be considered. More precisely, when replacing clause $C$ by some subset $\rho' \subseteq \rho(C)$ with $n$ clauses, $|T'| = |T| - |C| + n(|C|+1)$, since the clauses $C' \in \rho'$ are obtained from $C$ by adding a literal. For obtaining a positive compression: $0 \leq k(T') = pos - |T'| = k(T) + |C| - n(|C|+1)$,

$$n \leq \frac{k(T) - k(T') + |C|}{|C| + 1} \tag{4}$$

The upper bound (4) on the size of subsets $\rho'$ we have to consider is not very useful in the case of high compression rates. However, we can use it in a more sophisticated implementation in which the subsets $\rho'$ are subject to *lazy evaluation* (instead of being generated all at once).

More precisely, we can first construct only the refinements $\rho'$ that guarantee a given (high) compression rate $K$ ($k(T') = K$)[14] and then gradually decrease $K$ until a solution is found.

*Example 1.* For simplicity, we consider a *propositional* example, where we can simply represent positive and negative examples for some predicate $p$ as:
$+a, b \quad + a, c \quad - a \quad - c$

[14] using (4) to impose an upper bound on the size $n$ of the subsets $\rho'$.

($+a, b$ denotes a positive example $e_1$, which would be represented in the usual ILP notation as $p(e_1).\ \ a(e_1).\ \ b(e_1).$
$+a, c$ represents $p(e_2).\ \ a(e_2).\ \ c(e_2).$
while $-a$ denotes the negative example $\neg p(e_3).\ \ a(e_3).$)

Figure 4 depicts the associated refinement tree for the starting theory $T_0 = \{p \leftarrow\}$. The refinements of clause $p \leftarrow$ are $\rho(p \leftarrow) = \{p \leftarrow a,\ p \leftarrow b,\ p \leftarrow c\}$ and the minimal subsets covering all positives make up the theory refinements: $T_1 = \{p \leftarrow a\}$ and $T_2 = \{p \leftarrow b,\ p \leftarrow c\}$.

Then, when refining $T_1$ with $\rho(p \leftarrow a) = \{p \leftarrow a, b,\ p \leftarrow a, c\}$, both refinements are needed for covering all positives thus producing theory $T_3$ (which is a solution).

On the other hand, refining $T_2$ produces $T_4$ and $T_5$, only $T_4$ being a solution.

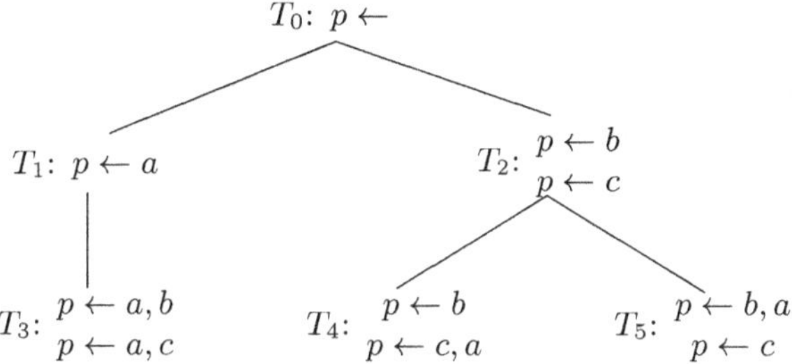


**Fig. 4.** A refinement tree

The search algorithm presented below uses a list of hypotheses (*Theories*), initialized with a starting theory (for example the one containing the empty clause).

<u>solution search</u>
  *Theories* $:= [\{\Box\}]$
  **while** *Theories* is nonempty
    extract $T$ from *Theories* (according to heuristic $f$)
    **if** $T$ is a solution **then** return $T$
    add $\rho'_T(T)$ to *Theories*
  **end while**

The refinement operator $\rho(C)$ for clauses used by $\rho'_T$ works by adding to clause $C$ either

- a positive literal $p(X_1, \ldots, X_n)$ (with new and distinct variables) involving a target predicate $p$ (in the case of Horn clauses, this is allowed only if $C$ contains no other positive literal), or
- a negative literal $\overline{p(X_1, \ldots, X_n)}$ (with new and distinct variables) involving either a target predicate or a predicate from the background theory, or
- a negative equality literal $\overline{X_i = X_j}$ involving variables $X_i$ and $X_j$ from $C$ (for properness, $X_i = X_j$ should not be deducible from the equality literals of $C$).

## 4 Reducing Redundancies

Although $\rho'_T$ eliminates certain redundancies of $\rho_T$, other redundancies still remain. These are mainly due to the *commutativity* of the refinement operations (such as adding a literal to a clause), since all the permutations of a set of operations will now produce the same hypothesis. As shown in [1,2], eliminating such redundancies amounts to destroying the commutativity of the refinement operations. This is equivalent to imposing a traversal discipline in the space of hypotheses and can be done by using order relations on literals, variables and clauses. As already hinted in the Introduction, a *flexible* refinement operator requires dynamic order relations (constructed at search time, rather than predetermined). [2] deals with such flexible refinement operators *for clauses*. In the following, we show how to construct flexible refinement operators *for theories* by extending the technique from [2]. Note that a straight-forward extension of the technique from [2] to theories would introduce order relations not only on variables and literals, but also on clauses. However, this would only allow constructing theories clause by clause, just like in implemented systems using refinement operators for clauses (like Progol or FOIL).

*Example 2.* Consider the 2 clause theory $T = \{C_1, C_2\}$ initially with $C_1 = a$, $C_2 = d$, which we want to refine first by adding literal $b$ to $C_1$, then $e$ to $C_2$ and finally $c$ to $C_1$.

If we have *separate* (dynamic) literal and *clause* orderings, then adding $b$ to $C_1$ induces the literal ordering $a < b$, then adding $e$ to $C_2$ induces not only $d < e$, but also the clause ordering $C_1 < C_2$. The latter ordering will now disallow a further refinement of $C_1$, such as adding $c$ to $C_1$. (We could have obtained the desired refinement only if all refinements of $C_1$, i.e. adding $b$ and $c$, would have preceded the refinements of $C_2$. This reduces the flexibility of the refinement operator for theories and in fact we re-obtain the usual clause by clause covering approach.)

To increase the flexibility of the theory refinement operator, we shall replace the two *separate* literal and clause orderings by a single order relation on the literals from *all* clauses. Thus, instead of ordering the literals within clauses and subsequently the clauses in their entirety, we introduce a finer grained ordering between the literals of all clauses.

More precisely, the ordering will involve literal occurrences of the form $L.id(C)$ (representing literal $L$ from clause $C$). Distinguishing the occurrences of the same literal in different clauses increases the flexibility of the resulting refinement operator. For example, refining $T = \{C_1, C_2\}$ with $C_1 = a$, $C_2 = b$ by adding $b$ to $C_1$ and $a$ to $C_2$ wouldn't be allowed if we hadn't made the above-mentioned distinction (since an inconsistent ordering $a < b$, $b < a$ would result). With literal occurrences, we obtain the consistent ordering $a.1 < b.1$, $b.2 < b.1$, $b.1 < a.2$ (where $id(C_1) = 1$, $id(C_2) = 2$).

However, this simple approach using literal occurrences $L.id(C)$ only works whenever clauses are not "split" and therefore have a well-defined identity $id(C)$, one that does not change under refinement (as for example in HYPER). We will therefore show in the following how the redundancy of HYPER's refinement operator (1) can be reduced by adding an ordering '$<$' between literal occurrences $L.id(C)$ and one '$\prec_{id(C)}$' between variable occurrences $X_i$. (See [2] for a justification of the treatment of the variable ordering.)

The following refinement operator $\tilde{\rho}_H$ eliminates not only the redundancies brought about by the commutativity of the refinements of a given clause (as in [2]), but also the redundancies arising from the commutativity of refinement operations on different clauses (of the theory being refined).[15]

$T' \in \tilde{\rho}_H(T)$ iff $T' = (T \setminus \{C\}) \cup \{C'\}$ for $C \in T$, $C' \in \tilde{\rho}(C, T)$, where

$C' \in \tilde{\rho}(C, T)$ iff either

(1) $C' = C \cup \{L^{(i)}\}$ for some background literal $L$[16] that occurs $i-1$ times in $C$ (i.e. $L^{(1)}, \ldots, L^{(i-1)} \in C$) and such that adding the global constraints $L^{(i)}.id(C) > T$[17] preserves the consistency of the global constraint store, $vars(C') = vars(C) \cup vars(L^{(i)})$,
(where $vars(L^{(i)})$ are the variables $\overline{X}^{(i)}$ of $L^{(i)} = p(\overline{X}^{(i)})$), or

(2) $C' = C \cup \{X_i = X_j\}$ with $X_i, X_j \in vars(C)$, such that adding the global constraints
  (a) $(X_i = X_j).id(C) > T$ and
  (b1) $X_i \prec_{id(C)} X_j$, $X_k \prec_{id(C)} X_j$ for each $X_k$ such that $(X_i = X_k) \in C$ or $(X_k = X_i) \in C$[18],
  (b2) $X_j \prec_{id(C)} X_i$, $X_k \prec_{id(C)} X_i$ for each $X_k$ such that $(X_j = X_k) \in C$ or $(X_k = X_j) \in C$

  preserves the consistency of the global constraint store.
  $vars(C') = vars(C) \setminus \{X_i\}$ if (b2) was applied,
  else $vars(C') = vars(C) \setminus \{X_j\}$.

In both cases, (1) and (2), $id(C') = id(C)$.

$\tilde{\rho}_H$ adds either a new ordinary literal, or a new equality literal. The order relation on literals is constructed dynamically, as literals are added during successive refinements. (Of course, the consistency of the global constraint store needs to be preserved.)

---

[15] Since the *order* of clauses is important in Prolog programs, we do not attempt to eliminate the redundancies due to *permutations* of clauses (in the theory being refined), such as $C_1 \wedge C_2 = C_2 \wedge C_1$. Eliminating such redundancies would involve technical complications that are outside the scope of this paper.

[16] For a literal $L = p(\overline{X})$ with variable tuple $\overline{X}$, we introduce a standardization for the variables $\overline{X}^{(i)}$ of the $i$-th occurrence $L^{(i)} = p(\overline{X}^{(i)})$ of the literal $L$ in some clause (the new and distinct variables $\overline{X}^{(i)}$ are the same for the $i$-th occurrence of $L$ *on all alternative paths*).

[17] Adding $L'.id(C') > T$ to the global constraint store ($L'$ being a literal, $id(C')$ a clause identifier and $T$ a theory) amounts to adding $L'.id(C') > L.id(C)$ for all $C \in T$ and all $L \in C$ (or, more practically, for all *maximal* $L \in C \in T$).

[18] We add $X_i \prec_{id(C)} X_j$ only if such an $X_i = X_k$ or $X_k = X_i$ exists in $C$.

Special care has to be taken for allowing multiple occurrences of a given background literal $L$ in a clause $C$. For ensuring the compatibility of the induced (literal and variable) orderings on the various alternative search paths, we have to use the same variable names $\overline{X}^{(i)}$ for the $i$-th occurrence $L^{(i)} = p(\overline{X}^{(i)})$ of literal $L$ *on all paths*.

Adding equalities is trickier to a certain extent due to the transitivity of equality. First, we have to avoid the trivial redundancies that would appear if we allowed adding $X_i = X_j$ for $X_i$ and $X_j$ already belonging to the same *cluster* of variables. (A cluster is a set of variables already unified with each other.) We do this by keeping in the set of variables candidates for unification $vars(C)$ just one representative of each variable cluster.

The constraints introduced at step *(2b)* ensure that a variable cluster $X_1 = X_2 = \ldots = X_n$ can be generated with only one sequence of refinements of type *(2)*, for example $X_1 = X_2$, followed by successively adding $X_3, X_4, \ldots, X_n$ to the growing cluster.

*Example 3.* For the theory $T = \{C_1, C_2\}$, the following sequence of refinements:

> add literal $a$ to $C_1$, add $b$ to $C_1$, add $c$ to $C_2$, add $d$ to $C_1$, add $e$ to $C_2$, add $f$ to $C_2$

produces the literal ordering: $\mathbf{a}.1 < b.1 < c.2 < \mathbf{d}.1 < e.2 < f.2$, which will disallow the re-generation of the same theory by a permutation of the above operations.

Reducing the redundancies of our more general $\rho'_T$ operator is even more complicated, mainly because of the difficulty in assigning identities to clauses obtained by "splitting". Due to space limitations, it will be the subject of a separate paper.

## 5 Conclusions

The refinement operator *for theories* $\rho'_T$ presented in this paper represents a first step towards constructing more efficient and *flexible* ILP systems with precise theoretical guarantees.

Its main properties are syntactical monotonicity, solution completeness and flexibility. Flexibility allows interleaving the refinements of clauses, and thus exploiting a good search heuristic by avoiding the pitfalls of a greedy covering algorithm. On the other hand, syntactical monotonicity is important for eliminating certain annoying redundancies due to clause deletions.

We also show how to eliminate (for HYPER's refinement operator) the redundancies due to the commutativity of refinement operations while preserving a limited form of flexibility.

The paper [6] also deals with theory refinement, but the main focus is on other aspects, such as constructing bottom theories.[19] Unfortunately, the paper has several problems, which, for lack of space, cannot be discussed here.

**Acknowledgments**

I am grateful to Monica Stanciu for several helpful discussions on the topics of this paper.

## References

1. Badea Liviu, Stanciu M. *Refinement Operators can be (weakly) perfect.* Proceedings ILP-99, pp. 21-32, LNAI 1634, Springer Verlag, 1999.
2. Badea Liviu. *Perfect Refinement Operators can be Flexible.* In Werner Horn, editor, Proceedings ECAI-2000, pp. 266–270. IOS Press, August 2000.
3. Bratko I. *Refining Complete Hypotheses in ILP.* Proceedings ILP-99, pp. 44-55, LNAI 1634, Springer Verlag, 1999.
4. Nienhuys-Cheng S.H., de Wolf R. *Foundations of Inductive Logic Programming.* LNAI 1228, Springer Verlag 1997.
5. De Raedt L., Lavrac N., Dzeroski S. *Multiple Predicate Learning.* In R. Bajcsy, editor, Proceedings IJCAI-93, pages 1037–1043. Morgan Kaufmann, 1993.
6. Midelfart H. *A Bounded Search Space of Clausal Theories.* Proc. ILP-99, 210–221.
7. Muggleton S. *Inverse entailment and Progol.* New Generation Computing Journal, 13:245-286, 1995.
8. Quinlan J.R. *Learning Logical Definitions from Relations.* Machine Learning 5:239-266, 1990.

[19] While bottom *clauses* are very useful for a covering approach (since they contain the literals that *can* appear in a hypothesis), bottom *theories* are less useful, since they play the role of constraints (they specify which clauses *have to appear* in a hypothesis).

# Learning Logic Programs with Neural Networks

Rodrigo Basilio, Gerson Zaverucha, and Valmir C. Barbosa

Programa de Engenharia de Sistemas e Computação—COPPE
Universidade Federal do Rio de Janeiro
Caixa Postal 68511, 21945-970, Rio de Janeiro, RJ, Brasil
{rbasilio, gerson, valmir}@cos.ufrj.br

**Abstract.** First-order theory refinement using neural networks is still an open problem. Towards a solution to this problem, we use inductive logic programming techniques to introduce FOCA, a First-Order extension of the Cascade ARTMAP system. To present such a first-order extension of Cascade ARTMAP, we: a) modify the network structure to handle first-order objects; b) define first-order versions of the main functions that guide all Cascade ARTMAP dynamics, the choice and match functions; c) define a first-order version of the propositional learning algorithm to approximate Plotkin's least general generalization. Preliminary results indicate that our initial goal of learning logic programs using neural networks can be achieved.

## 1 Introduction

The Cascade ARTMAP system [21] is a knowledge-based neural network (KBNN) [20], like KBANN [22], RAPTURE [11], and C-IL$^2$P [6], that has been shown to outperform other purely analytical or inductive systems in the task of propositional theory refinement: a prior incomplete and/or partially correct propositional symbolic knowledge about a problem domain is given to a theory refinement system and it is revised by training the system with examples.

Three main advantages of Cascade ARTMAP over other KBNN systems are: a) the initial rule structure of the network created by the insertion algorithm is preserved during training (this is a major problem when using backpropagation training for the task of theory refinement), which facilitates rule extraction by allowing a direct comparison of the extracted rules to the originally inserted rules; b) it is an incremental learning system; c) it combines instance-based learning with rule induction[1].

All these characteristics are inherited from the fuzzy ARTMAP system [4], of which Cascade ARTMAP is an extension that allows the representation of intermediate attributes of rule-based knowledge and multi-step inference (rule chaining).

Inductive Logic Programming (ILP) [10] augments the expressive power of inductive learning and theory refinement tasks to (first-order) logic programming [23]. This has allowed ILP systems to handle problems like mutagenicity, carcinogenicity, drug design, language learning [15], and benchmark problems like The east-west train problem [12].

[1] This characteristic is shared by the Rule Induction from a Set of Exemplars (RISE) system [5].

C. Rouveirol and M. Sebag (Eds.): ILP 2001, LNAI 2157, pp. 15–26, 2001.

Most ILP systems, such as FOIL [17], GOLEM [13], TIM [9], and PROGOL [14], use a covering algorithm to generate hypotheses. However, as pointed out by Bratko (whose HYPER is a recent exception [3]), systems that use a covering algorithm have difficulties in learning multiple predicates and recursive definitions, and will have unnecessarily long clauses for hypotheses. Cascade ARTMAP, by contrast, uses a non-covering algorithm to generate each hypothesis as whole, like other KBNN systems.

Our main goal is to combine ILP techniques with Cascade ARTMAP, defining a unified hybrid first-order KBNN system, named FOCA, which takes advantage of its parent methodologies while attempting to overcome their limitations. In order to present such a first-order extension of Cascade ARTMAP, we: a) modify the network structure to handle first-order objects; b) define first-order versions of the choice (similarity) function and of the vigilance criterion (functions that guide all Cascade ARTMAP dynamics); c) define a first-order version of the learning algorithm (the weight update), which is related to [8] and approximates Plotkin's least general generalization (lgg) [16].

Related work includes the following. The ILP systems GOLEM and TIM are also bottom-up systems that use and approximate lgg, but not combined with incremental clustering. The work in [1] uses the ILP system LINUS [10] that transforms a first-order learning task to attribute-value form, and applies a neural network as its attribute-value learning algorithm. This can only be done to a restricted class of problems. The work in [2] presents a first-order KBNN based on radial-basis networks. The learning algorithm only deals with the numeric part of the theory, which has no rule chaining and is recursion-free. The work in [7] shares the same objectives with this work, but the learning part is still being developed and uses a backpropagation-based KBNN.

The remaining sections of this paper are organized as follows. Section 2 presents an introduction to Cascade ARTMAP, Section 3 describes the FOCA system, Section 4 presents preliminary experimental results, and Section 5 contains conclusions and directions for future work.

## 2 Cascade ARTMAP

We only review Fuzzy ARTMAP [4], since Cascade ARTMAP is an extension of it that allows rule insertion and rule cascading (chaining), and these are done similarly in FOCA.

Fuzzy ARTMAP (see Fig. 1) incorporates two Fuzzy ART modules, $\mathrm{ART}_a$ and $\mathrm{ART}_b$, which are linked together via an inter-ART map field $\mathrm{F}^{ab}$. Each ART module is an unsupervised clustering system. We can view each example presented to Fuzzy ARTMAP as a rule, the input part being the body (antecedent) and the output part (class) being the head (consequent) of the rule. $\mathrm{ART}_a$ receives the examples' bodies and constructs a clustering scheme, aggregating similar bodies in the same cluster (a node in the $\mathrm{F}_2^a$ layer). Each cluster has a prototype (a weight vector $\mathbf{w}_j$ connecting cluster $j$ to all nodes in $\mathrm{F}_1^a$) that is the generalization of the bodies that belong to that cluster. $\mathrm{ART}_b$ receives examples' heads and similarly constructs a clustering scheme in $\mathrm{F}_2^b$. The map field links each category formed in each ART module consistently. Each Fuzzy ART module has three layers:

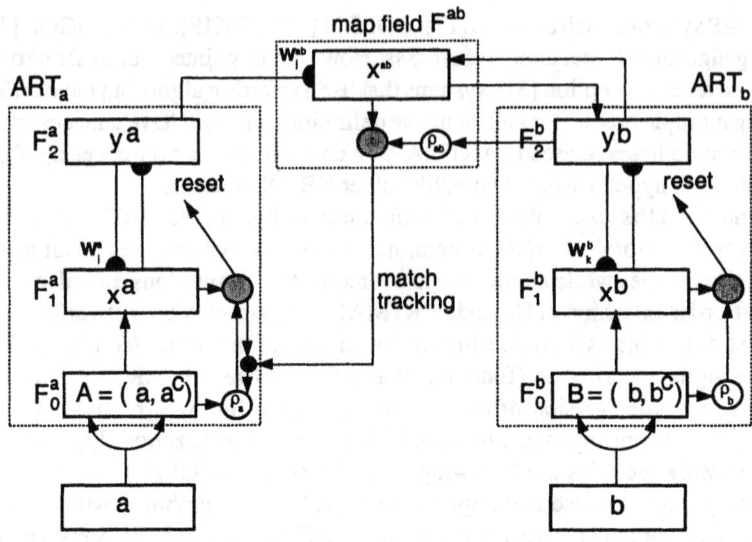


**Fig. 1.** The Fuzzy ARTMAP system [4]

1. $F_0$, with the same number of nodes as the module's input vector (unless we use a normalization scheme like complement coding, as in Fig. 1). Vector **I** denotes the activation of $F_0$ (**A** in $ART_a$ and **B** in $ART_b$);
2. $F_1$, with the same number of nodes as $F_0$. The nodes in these two layers are linked together by one-to-one weights. Vector **x** denotes the activation of $F_1$;
3. $F_2$, which is fully connected with $F_1$. The most important weights in the ART network are the weights between one node $j$ in $F_2$ and all nodes in $F_1$, denoted by $\mathbf{w}_j$, because they contain information about the prototypes of the network. Vector **y** denotes the activation of $F_2$.

The dynamics of Fuzzy ART depends on a choice parameter $\alpha > 0$, a learning rate parameter $\beta \in [0,1]$, and a vigilance parameter $\rho \in [0,1]$. For Fuzzy ARTMAP, there are two additional parameters: the minimum value of the vigilance parameter of $ART_a$, called the baseline parameter $\overline{\rho_a}$, and the vigilance parameter of the map field, $\rho_{ab}$.

We can view the Fuzzy ARTMAP dynamics as a propositional inductive learning system: for each example presentation (see step 1 of the algorithm below), the most similar rule already encoded in the Fuzzy ARTMAP (steps 2 and 3) satisfying the vigilance criterion is chosen to generalize with this example (step 4a); if there is no rule satisfying the criterion, a new one is created from the example.

The following is the Fuzzy ARTMAP learning algorithm for a set $E$ of examples.

**Algorithm**

For each example $e = (a, b) \in E$, do:

**step 1 (Input presentation):** Let $\rho_a = \overline{\rho_a}$, $\mathbf{A} = a$, $\mathbf{B} = b$, (here a normalization scheme is applied as in Fig. 1), $\mathbf{x}^a = \mathbf{A}$ and $\mathbf{x}^b = \mathbf{B}$.

**step 2 (Category selection): 2.1)** For each ART module, calculate the choice function $\mathbf{T}_j(\mathbf{I})$ (the degree to which $\mathbf{w}_j$ is a subset of the input $\mathbf{I}$) for each node $j$ in $F_2$, and select the node $J$ that has the greatest value. The choice function $\mathbf{T}_j(\mathbf{I})$ is defined by:

$$\mathbf{T}_j(\mathbf{I}) = \frac{|\mathbf{I} \wedge \mathbf{w}_j|}{\alpha + |\mathbf{w}_j|}$$

where input $\mathbf{I}$ is $\mathbf{A}$ in $\text{ART}_a$ and $\mathbf{B}$ in $\text{ART}_b$, $\wedge$ is the fuzzy intersection defined by $(p \wedge q)_i = \min(p_i, q_i)$, and the norm $|.|$ is defined by

$$|\mathbf{p}| = \sum_i |\mathbf{p}_i|$$

**2.2)** For each node pre-selected in 2.1 ($J$ in $F_2^a$ and $K$ in $\mathbf{F}_2^b$), calculate the match function $\mathbf{m}_j(\mathbf{I})$ (the degree in which the input is a subset of the prototype $\mathbf{w}_j$), defined as

$$\mathbf{m}_j(\mathbf{I}) = \frac{|\mathbf{I} \wedge \mathbf{w}_j|}{|\mathbf{I}|}$$

If the match function for node $J$ and/or $K$ is greater than or equal to $\rho$ (vigilance criterion), we say that *resonance* happens and then the respective $F_2$ layer is activated; for $\text{ART}_a$: $\mathbf{y}_J = 1$ and $\mathbf{y}_j = 0$ for $j \neq J$ (winner-take-all activation, and similarly for $\text{ART}_b$). Otherwise, shutdown the actual chosen node (the node cannot be selected during the presentation of the actual example), and go to 2.1 to select a new node in the respective module. If no category can be chosen, let $J$ and/or $K$ be the new nodes created dynamically, with $\mathbf{w}_J^a = 1$, $\mathbf{w}_J^{ab} = 1$, $\mathbf{y}_J^a = 1$, and $\mathbf{y}_j^a = 0$ for $j \neq J$, and/or, $\mathbf{w}_K^b = 1$, $\mathbf{y}_K^b = 1$, $\mathbf{y}_k^b = 0$, for $k \neq K$.

**step 3 (Verification in the map field):** In the map field, $\mathbf{x}^{ab} = \mathbf{w}_J^{ab} \wedge \mathbf{y}^b$. If $|\mathbf{x}^{ab}|/|\mathbf{y}^b| \geq \rho_{ab}$ then go to step 4a, otherwise go to step 4b.

**step 4a (Learning):** Let

$$\mathbf{w}_J^{a(new)} = \beta_a(\mathbf{I} \wedge \mathbf{w}_J^{a(old)}) + (1 - \beta_a)\mathbf{w}_J^{a(old)}$$

$$\mathbf{w}_K^{b(new)} = \beta_b(\mathbf{I} \wedge \mathbf{w}_K^{b(old)}) + (1 - \beta_b)\mathbf{w}_K^{b(old)}$$

and $\mathbf{w}_J^{ab}$ will be updated :

$$\mathbf{w}_j^{ab(new)} = \beta^{ab}(\mathbf{y}^b \wedge \mathbf{w}_j^{ab(old)}) + (1 - \beta^{ab})\mathbf{w}_j^{ab(old)} \tag{1}$$

(fast learning corresponds to setting $\beta$=1).

**step 4b (Match Tracking):** Let $\rho_a = \mathbf{m}_J^a(\mathbf{A}) + \epsilon$, $\mathbf{T}_J = 0$, and go back to step 2.

## 3 The FOCA System

A logic program is a set of clauses: $h \leftarrow b_1, \ldots, b_n$ where $h$ is an atom and $b_1, \ldots, b_n$ are literals (positive or negative atoms). The general learning framework [15] from ILP is: given an initial domain theory (background knowledge) $B$, a set of positive examples $E^+$, and a set of negative examples $E^-$, the goal is to build a hypothesis $H$, where $B$, $E^+$, $E^-$, and $H$ are logic programs satisfying the following conditions:

- **Necessity:** $B \not\models E^+$ ($B$ does not cover $E^+$);
- **Sufficiency:** $B \wedge H \models E^+$ ($B$ and $H$ cover $E^+$);
- **Weak Consistency:** $B \wedge H \not\models$ false;
- **Strong Consistency:** $B \wedge H \wedge E^- \not\models$ false.

In systems that handle noise, sufficiency and strong consistency are not required.

Generally in ILP, an example is a ground instance $p(c_1, \ldots, c_n)$ of a target concept $p(V_1, \ldots, V_n)$ and its description is logically encoded in $B$. The hypothesis space is generally ordered by $\theta$-subsumption. Some ILP bottom-up (specific to general) systems search the hypothesis space using the relative least general generalization operator for two clauses (rlgg$(e_1, e_2)$) [16], which can be calculated in two steps [9]: first calculate the saturation (bottom-clause) of $e_1$ and $e_2$, $\bot_1$ and $\bot_2$, respectively, and then calculate lgg$(\bot_1, \bot_2)$ [16].

The FOCA system is a relational bottom-up system that works with clauses (the bottom-clauses) as examples, clustering separately the bodies and the heads of those clauses, and makes a consistent linking between body and head clusters. Each bodies or heads cluster is represented by a prototype that $\theta$-subsumes all elements in that cluster and holds the information necessary to calculate the pertinence of a new element in the cluster. FOCA also uses the same language bias of PROGOL, like mode declarations, to restrict the size of a bottom-clause [14].

Before presenting the FOCA algorithm in Section 3.4, we describe its architecture in Section 3.1, the new choice and match functions in Section 3.2 and the lgg-based operator that we use in Section 3.3.

### 3.1 Architecture

The architecture of the FOCA system is shown in Fig. 2

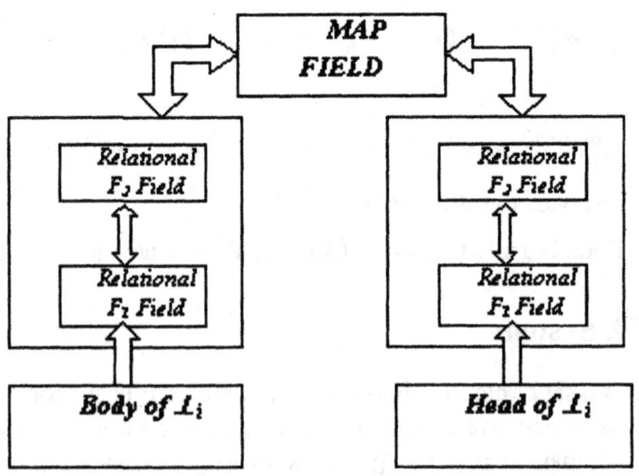


**Fig. 2.** Overview of the FOCA system

In Cascade ARTMAP, information flows through the links as numbers. In FOCA, this information is a set of tuples of terms, each tuple having a number associated to it. The bottom-clause's body is the input to $\text{ART}_a$ and its head is the input to $\text{ART}_b$.

Each neuron in $F_1$ represents a predicate symbol of the problem. Let *predicate*$(k)$ be the predicate symbol that neuron $k$ represents. The activation of each neuron $k$ in $F_1$ is the set $\mathbf{A}_k$, consisting of tuples of terms of *predicate*$(k)$ that appear in the input of an ART module. For instance, for the input $\mathbf{I} = \{\texttt{father}(Z,S), \texttt{father}(Z,D), \texttt{mother}(Q,S), \texttt{mother}(Q,D)\}$ we have $\mathbf{A}_k = \{(Z,S),(Z,D)\}$ and $\mathbf{A}_j = \{(Q,S), (Q,D)\}$, where *predicate*$(k)$ = *father* and *predicate*$(j)$ = *mother*.

Let the union of all $\mathbf{A}_k$ with the respective predicate symbol applied to each tuple be $\mathbf{X} = \{p(V_1,\ldots,V_n) \mid (V_1,\ldots,V_n) \in \mathbf{A}_k$, where *predicate*$(k) = p$, for each $k \in F_1\}$ ($\mathbf{X}$ is $\mathbf{X}^a$ in $\text{ART}_a$ and $\mathbf{X}^b$ in $\text{ART}_b$). In Cascade ARTMAP, the vector $\mathbf{x}^a$ represents a working memory: the input and all attributes activated by the rule chaining. Here, similarly, the set $\mathbf{X}^a$ will also hold all literals inferred during the rule chaining. Steps 4b and 5a of the algorithm show how $\mathbf{X}^a$ is updated with the literals activated in rule chaining.

Each cluster $j$ in the $F_2$ layer has a set $\mathbf{W}_{jk}$ associated to each link with a neuron $k$ in $F_1$. $\mathbf{W}_{jk}$ holds all tuples of terms from *predicate*$(k)$ that belongs to the relational prototype, defined as $\mathbf{W}_j = \{p(t_1,\ldots,t_n) \mid (t_1,...,t_n) \in \mathbf{W}_{jk}$, where *predicate*$(k) = p$, for each $k \in F_1\}$. If a cluster $j$ encodes more than one example, $\mathbf{W}_j$ can be viewed as an approximate rlgg of all saturations of examples encoded by $j$. Associated with each literal $p$ there is a number, named *Fuzzy*$(p) \in [0,1]$, that represents its fuzzy information. Initially, if a literal does not have such a number the default value is one.

### 3.2 The First-Order Choice and Match Functions

The choice and match functions were developed based on [18], but having the goal that in the propositional case they be reduced to their propositional versions.

Given a category $J$ in $F_2^a$ and the set $\mathbf{X}^a$, the first-order equations of choice and match functions are defined below

$$\mathbf{T}_j(\mathbf{X}^a) = \frac{\sum_{(w,x)\in INT_{WX}} \mathit{Fuzzy}(w) \wedge \mathit{Fuzzy}(x)}{\sum_{(w,x)\in INT_{WX}} \mathit{Fuzzy}(w) + \alpha} \tag{2}$$

and

$$\mathbf{m}_j(\mathbf{X}^a) = \frac{\sum_{(w,x)\in INT_{WX}} \mathit{Fuzzy}(w) \wedge \mathit{Fuzzy}(x)}{\sum_{(w,x)\in INT_{WX}} \mathit{Fuzzy}(x)}, \tag{3}$$

where $INT_{WX} \subseteq \mathbf{W}_j \times \mathbf{X}^a$ is the relational intersection, defined as

$$INT_{WX} = \{(w,x) \mid m \in m_{OP}, w = m\theta_w, x = m\theta_x\}$$

with

$$m_{OP} = O \cap P$$

such that

$$\max_{\theta_w, \theta_x} |O \cap P|,$$

where $O\theta_w = \mathbf{W}_j$, $P\theta_x = \mathbf{X}^a$, $\theta_w$ and $\theta_x$ being renaming substitutions. If we have more than one candidate for $INT_{WX}$, we choose arbitrarily. The choice and match functions in $F_2^b$ are calculated similarly.

### 3.3 Learning

For a cluster $J$ in $ART_a$ and the working memory $\mathbf{X}^a$, the learning operator is defined as

$$\mathbf{W}_j = algg(\mathbf{W}_j, \mathbf{X}^a), \tag{4}$$

where the operator *algg* is defined as

$$algg(\mathbf{W}_j, \mathbf{X}^a) = \{lgg(w, x) \mid (w, x) \in INT_{WX}\}.$$

The *algg* operator, unlike *lgg*, is dependent on the order: two different sequences of calculations can produce two different clauses. This learning definition only supports the fast learning setting, because we eliminate every literal in $\mathbf{W}_j$ that is not in $INT_{WX}$.

The fuzzy information is updated by

$$Fuzzy(w) = \beta \min(Fuzzy(w), Fuzzy(x)) + (1 - \beta) Fuzzy(w), \tag{5}$$

where $(w, x) \in INT_{WX}$. In $F_2^b$, the prototype set and fuzzy information are also updated similarly.

### 3.4 Algorithm

The algorithm of FOCA, shown below, is similar to the Cascade ARTMAP algorithm. The notion of the $\psi(J)$ set is defined similarly to [21].

For each example $e \in E$, do

**step 1 (Bottom-Clause generation):** Calculate bottom-clause $\bot_e$ from example $e$. The body of $\bot_e$ is presented to $ART_a$ and the head of $\bot_e$ to $ART_b$.

**step 2 (Show $\bot_e$):** Let $\rho_a = \overline{\rho_a}$. In $F_1^a$, Let $\mathbf{X}^a$ be the body of $\bot_e$.

**step 3 (Cluster selection): 3.1)** Calculate $\mathbf{T}_j^a(\mathbf{X}^a)$ (eq. 2) for each node $j$ in $F_2^a$. **3.2)** Let $J$ be the node chosen in step 3.1. If $J$ passes the vigilance criterion $\mathbf{m}_j^a(\mathbf{X}^a) \geq \rho_a$, go to step 4b else shutdown the chosen node and go to step 3.1 to choose a new node. If no category can be chosen in $F_2^a$, go to step 4a.

**step 4a (New node):** Let $J$ be a new node created dynamically. In $ART_b$, $\mathbf{X}^b$ is the head of $\bot_e$. **4a1)** Calculate the choice function for each node $k$ in $F_2^b$ and let $K$ be the node chosen. **4a2)** If $K$ pass in the vigilance criterion $\mathbf{m}_j^b(\mathbf{X}^b) \geq \rho_b$ then go to step 4a3 else shutdown $K$ and go to step 4a1 to choose a new node. If no category can be chosen in

$F_2^b$, let $K$ be a new node in $F_2^b$. **4a3)** Each node in $\psi(J)$ and node $K$ in $F_2^b$ will be updated like defined in Section 3.3 using eqs. 4 and 5. The weight $\mathbf{w}_j^{ab}$ is updated using eq. 1.

**step 4b (Inference):** $\mathbf{x}^{ab} = \mathbf{w}_j^{ab}$ and the map field is activated. The one-to-one weights between $F^{ab}$ and $F_2^b$ activate $F_2^b$. For each node $k$ in $F_2^b$, the choice function is such that $\mathbf{T}_k^b = \mathbf{x}_k^{ab}$. The winning node $K$ is such that $\mathbf{T}_K^b = \max\{\mathbf{T}_k^b \mid k \in F_2^b\}$. When $K$ is chosen, $\mathbf{y}_K^b = 1$ and $\mathbf{y}_k^b = 0$ for each $k \neq K$. $\mathbf{X}^b = \mathbf{W}_k^b\theta$, where $\theta = \theta_w^{-1}\theta_x$, and $\theta_w$, $\theta_x$ are the renaming substitutions used to calculate $INT_{WX}$ for the cluster $J$ in $F_2^a$ in step 3. If $\mathbf{X}^b$ holds a target atom then go to step 5b, else go to step 5a.

**step 5a (Update):** Let $\mathbf{X}^a = \mathbf{X}^a \cup \mathbf{X}^b$. Go to step 3.

**step 5b (Matching):** Let $\mathbf{X}^b$ be the head of $\perp_e$ and calculate $\mathbf{m}_k^b(\mathbf{X}^b)$, imposing for the variables in the body that appear in the head the same substitutions in $\theta_w$ and $\theta_x$ used to calculate $INT_{WX}$ for the cluster $J$ in $F_2^a$ in step 3. If $\mathbf{m}_k^b(\mathbf{X}^b) \geq \rho_b$ then go to step 6a, else go to step 6b.

**step 6a (Resonance):** Update each activated node in $\psi$(J) and $K$ in $F_2^b$ like defined in Section 3.3, using eqs. 4 and 5.

**step 6b (Mini-Match Tracking):** Let $\rho_a = \mathbf{m}_z^a(\mathbf{X}^a) + \epsilon$, where $\mathbf{m}_z^a(\mathbf{X}^a) = \{\min(\mathbf{m}_k^a(\mathbf{X}^a) \mid k \in \psi(J)\}$, $\mathbf{T}_z^a = 0$. Go back to step 3.

**Example.** We present a simple trace of the algorithm above for the east-west train problem [12]. Consider that we have already presented two examples. Therefore, there are already in each module two clusters: clusters 1 and 2 in $\text{ART}_a$ associated with clusters 1 and 2 in $\text{ART}_b$, respectively. The $F_2$ layer of each ART module is shown in table 1.

**Table 1.** $F_2^a$ and $F_2^b$ Layer

| | $F_2^a$ Layer ($\text{ART}_a$) |
|---|---|
| Cluster 1 | $W_1^a$= {*has_car(X,V), open(V), long(V),shape(V,rectangle), has_car(X,W), not long(W), not open(W), shape(W, rectangle), has_car(X,Z), not long(Z),open(Z),shape(Z,rectangle)*} |
| Cluster 2 | $W_2^a$= {*has_car(A,B), not open(B), long(B),shape(B,rectangle), has_car(A,C), not long(C), open(C), shape(C,rectangle)*} |

| | $F_2^b$ Layer ($\text{ART}_b$) |
|---|---|
| Cluster 1 | $W_1^b$={*eastbound(X)*} |
| Cluster 2 | $W_2^b$= {*not eastbound(A)*} |

Let $\overline{\rho_a} = 0$, $\alpha_a = \alpha_b = 0.001$ and $\rho_{ab} = \rho_b = 1$. Now consider the presentation of the following example $e$ = *eastbound(east3)* in step 1. The bottom-clause $\perp_3$ generated is:

$\bot_3$={*eastbound(E)* ← *has_car(E,F), not long(F), open(F), shape(F, u_shaped), has_car(E, G), open(G), not long(G), shape(G, bucket), has_car(E, H), not open(H), not long(H), shape(H, rectangle)*}

In step 2, $\mathbf{X}^a$ is the body of $\bot_3$. In step 3, we calculate the choice and match functions for each node:

For cluster 1, the relational intersection $INT_{WX}$ is

$INT_{WX}$ = {*(has_car(X,V), has_car(E,F)), (open(V), open(F)), (has_car(X, Z), has_car(E,G)), (open(Z), open(G)), (not long(Z), not long(G)), (has_car(X, W), has_car(E, H)), (not open(W), not open(H)), (not long(W), not long(H)), (shape(W,rectangle),shape(H,rectangle)*}

using substitutions $\theta_w$ ={*E/X, H/W,G/Z, F/V*} and $\theta_x = \emptyset$. Since $Fuzzy(w) = Fuzzy(x) = 1$, for each $(w, x) \in INT_{WX}$, then $\mathbf{T}_1^a(\mathbf{X}^a) = 9/(12+\alpha) \approx 0.75$ and $\mathbf{m}_1^a(\mathbf{X}^a) = 9/12 = 0.75$.

For cluster 2, the relational intersection $INT_{WX}$ is

$INT_{WX}$ = {*(has_car(A, C), has_car(E,G)), (open(C), open(G)), (not long(C), not long(G)), (has_car(A, B), has_car(E, H)), (not open(B), not open(H)), (shape(B, rectangle), shape(H, rectangle)*}

using substitutions $\theta_w$ = {*E/A,H/B,G/C*} and $\theta_x = \emptyset$.

Then $\mathbf{T}_2^a(\mathbf{X}^a) = 6/(8+\alpha) \approx 0.75$ and $\mathbf{m}_2^a(\mathbf{X}^a) = 6/12 = 0.5$.

Therefore, node 1 is chosen and passes the vigilance criterion (step 3.2). In step 4b, we calculate the choice function in $F_2^b$: $\mathbf{X}^{ab} = \mathbf{w}_1^{ab}$=(10), $\mathbf{T}_1^b$= 1 and $\mathbf{T}_2^b$ = 0. Then node 1 in $F_2^b$ is chosen and $\mathbf{X}^b = W_1^b \theta_w^{-1} \theta_x$ = {*eastbound(E)*}. $\mathbf{X}^b$ holds a target atom, so we go to step 5b, and calculate

$INT_{WX}$ = {*(eastbound(X), eastbound(E))*}

using substitutions $\theta_w$ = {*E/X, H/W,G/Z, F/V*} and $\theta_x = \emptyset$. Then, $\mathbf{m}_1^b(\mathbf{X}^b) = 1/1 = 1$.

In step 6a, the nodes 1 in each module are updated using eqs. 4 and 5. The final state of the $F_2^a$ and $F_2^b$ layer is shown in table 2.

### 3.5 Performance Evaluation

To classify a test example, we only execute steps 1, 2, 3 (in case it needs to go to 4a, we stop and return 'no'), 4b, 5a, 5b (here, if $\mathbf{m}_k^b(\mathbf{X}^b) \geq \rho_b$, then we return 'yes' else 'no') of the algorithm.

## 4 Preliminary Experiments

The system has been tested on some machine learning domain problems. The first three problems are defined in [10]: learning the concept of an arch, family relationships, and

**Table 2.** Final state of the $F_2^a$ and $F_2^b$ layers

| | $F_2^a$ Layer ($ART_a$) |
|---|---|
| Cluster 1 | $W_1^a$={*has_car(M,N), open(N), has_car(M,O), not long(O), not open(O), shape(O, rectangle), has_car(M,P), not long(P), open(P)*} |
| Cluster 2 | $W_2^a$= {*has_car(A,B), not open(B), long(B),shape(B,rectangle), has_car(A,C), not long(C), open(C), shape(C,rectangle)*} |

| | $F_2^b$ Layer ($ART_b$) |
|---|---|
| Cluster 1 | $W_1^b$={*eastbound(M)*} |
| Cluster 2 | $W_2^b$= {*not eastbound(A)*} |

the Eleusis problem (layouts 1, 2 and 3). The fourth problem is the east-west train problem with 10 examples [12]. They do not have a test set and, for each problem, the theory extracted from FOCA is equal the correct known theory.

The Illegal KRK endgames problem [10] has a test set. We use the same experimental methodology for the purpose. The rules extracted from FOCA yielded 97.92% accuracy, with 0.005% of standard deviation. Other ILP systems' performances are presented for comparison in table 3.

**Table 3.** Results on the KRK problem

| SYSTEMS | ACC. (5 Sets of 100 Exs.) |
|---|---|
| FOIL | 90.8% sd 1.7% |
| LINUS-ASSISTANT | 98.1% sd 1.1% |
| LINUS-NEWGEM | 88.4% sd 4.0% |
| FOCA | 97.92% sd 0.005% |

## 5 Conclusions

This work contributes to bridge the gap between symbolic and connectionist learning systems. A first-order extension of the neural network Cascade ARTMAP, the FOCA system, was presented, by extending to first-order the structure of the network, the choice and match functions, and the learning algorithm. Since (Fuzzy) ARTMAP is composed of two (Fuzzy) ART modules, this work can be also be seen as presenting a first-order (Fuzzy) ART, a first-order clustering system.

The preliminary experimental results show that FOCA can learn first-order theories as an ILP system. Nevertheless, they have not yet explored FOCA's main advantage as a first-order theory refinement system. We are now in process of applying FOCA on such problems and other real-world ILP applications: mutagenicity, drug design, language learning [15], and character recognition [24]. This could not be done because the relational intersection defined here is intractable in general case. We plan to enhance FOCA with stochastic matching [19] to solve this problem.

Like the ART family, FOCA is also sensitive to the order of example presentation. We can overcome this problem by using an ensemble, as in [4].

**Acknowledgements**

We acknowledge supported by the Brazilian agencies CAPES and CNPq, the PRONEX initiative of Brazil's MCT, and a FAPERJ BBP grant. We would like to thank Jude Shavlik, David Page and Ah-Hwee Tan for useful discussions.

## References

1. Basilio R., Zaverucha, G., and Garcez, A.: Inducing Relational Concepts with Neural Networks Via the LINUS System, In Proc. Fifth International Conference on Neural Information Processing (ICONIP'98), Vol. 3, Japan, 1998, pp. 1507-1510.
2. Botta M., Giordana A., and Piola, R.: FONN: Combining First Order Logic with Connectionist Learning. Proc. of the 14th International Conference on Machine Learning ICML-97, Morgan Kaufmann, 1997, pp. 46-56.
3. Bratko, I.: Refining Complete Hypotheses in ILP. ILP-99, LNAI 1634, Springer-Verlag, 1999, pp. 44-55.
4. Carpenter, G. A., Grossberg, S., Reynolds, J.H., Markuzon, N., Rosen, D.B.: Fuzzy ARTMAP: A neural network architecture for incremental supervised learning of analog multidimensional maps. IEEE Trans. Neural Networks 3, 1992, pp. 698-713.
5. Domingos, P.: Rule Induction and Instance-Based Learning: a Unified Approach, IJCAI, vol. 2, 1995, pp. 1226-1232.
6. Garcez, A. S., Zaverucha G.: The Connectionist Inductive Learning and Logic Programming System. Applied Intelligence Journal, F. Kurfess (editor), Vol. 11, Number 1, 1999, pp. 59-77.
7. Hallack, N. A.,Zaverucha, G., and Barbosa, V. C.: Towards a hybrid model of first-order theory refinement. In Hybrid Neural Systems. LNAI 1778, Springer-Verlag, 2000.
8. Haussler, D.: Learning Conjunctive concepts in structural domains. Machine Learning 4, 1989, pp. 7-40.
9. Idestam-Almquist, P.: Efficient Induction of Recursive Definitions by Structural Analysis of Saturations. Advances in Inductive Logic Programming. Ed. Luc De Raedt, IOS Press, 1996, pp. 192-205.
10. Lavrac, N., and Dzeroski, S.: Inductive Logic Programming: Techniques and Applications. Ellis Horwood Series in Artificial Intelligence,1994.
11. Mahoney, J.J., and Mooney, R. J.: Combining Connectionist and Symbolic Learning Methods to Refine Certainty-factor Rule-bases. Connection Science 5, 1993, pp. 339-364.
12. Michie, D. , Muggleton, S., Page, D., Srinivasan, A.: To the international computing community: a new East-West Challenge. Technical Report, Oxford University Computing Laboratory, Oxford, UK, 1994.

13. Muggleton, S., and Feng, C.: Efficient Induction of Logic Programs. In Muggleton, S. (Eds) Inductive Logic Programming, Academic Press, London, 1992, pp. 453-472.
14. Muggleton, S.: Inverse Entailment and Progol. In New Generation Computing 13, 1995, pp. 245-286.
15. Muggleton, S.: Inductive logic programming: issues, results and the LLL challenge. Artificial Intelligence 114, pp. 283-296, December 1999, pp. 283-296.
16. Plotkin, G.: A further note on inductive generalization. Machine Intelligence, v.6. University Press, 1971.
17. Quinlan, J. R.: Learning logical definitions from relations. Machine Learning 5, 1990, pp. 239-266.
18. Ramon, J. and Bruynooghe, M.: A framework for defining distances between first-order logic objects. ILP-98, LNAI 1446. Springer-Verlag, 1998, pp. 271-280.
19. Sebag, M. and Rouveirol, C.: Tractable Induction and Classification in First-Order Logic Via Stochastic Matching. Proc. of the 15th International Join Conference on Artificial Intelligence IJCAI-97, Morgan Kaufmann, 1997, pp. 888-892.
20. Shavlik, J.: Framework for Combining Symbolic and Neural Learning. Machine Learning 14, 1994, pp. 321-331.
21. Tan, Ah-Hwee: Cascade ARTMAP: Integrating Neural Computation and Symbolic Knowledge Processing. IEEE Trans.on Neural Networks vol. 8, n.2, 1997, pp. 237-250.
22. Towell, G., and Shavlik, J.: Knowledge-Based Artificial Neural Networks. Artificial Intelligence, vol. 70, 1994, pp. 119-165.
23. Wrobel, S.: First Order Theory Refinement. Advances in Inductive Logic Programming. Ed. Luc De Raedt, IOS Press, 1996, pp. 14-33.
24. Kijsirikul, B. and Sinthupinyo, S.: Approximate ILP Rules by Backpropagation Neural Network: A Result on Thai Character Recognition. 9th International Workshop on Inductive Logic Programming, LNAI 1634, Springer-Verlag, 1999, pp. 162-173.

# A Genetic Algorithm for Propositionalization

Agnès Braud and Christel Vrain

LIFO, Université d'Orléans,
rue Léonard de Vinci, BP 6759,
F-45067 Orléans Cedex 2, France
{Agnes.Braud,Christel.Vrain}@lifo.univ-orleans.fr

**Abstract.** Nowadays, propositionalization is an important method that aims at reducing the complexity of Inductive Logic Programming, by transforming a learning problem expressed in a first order formalism into an attribute-value representation. This implies a two steps process, namely finding an interesting pattern and then learning relevant constraints for this pattern. This paper describes a novel genetic approach for handling the second task.

The main idea of our approach is to consider the set of variables appearing in the pattern, and to learn a partition of this set. Numeric constraints are directly put on the equivalence classes involved by the partition rather than on variables. We have proposed an encoding for representing a partition by an individual, and general set-based operators to alter one partition or to mix two ones. For propositionalization, operators are extended to change not only the partition but also the associated numeric constraints.

## 1 Introduction

Propositionalization (LINUS [9], STILL [15], REPART [17], [1], ...) enables to restrict the search space of traditional Inductive Logic Programming (ILP) systems, by limiting the number of relations that could appear in a rule to those defined in a pattern. This pattern has to be carefully chosen to allow the discovery of an interesting rule; it can be learned or given by the user. The system has to specialize it by learning either symbolic constraints or numeric ones on its variables. Solving an ILP problem by propositionalization thus implies a two steps process, namely finding an interesting pattern and then learning relevant constraints for this pattern. We are interested in the second step, and we propose an approach based on a Genetic Algorithm (GA) to realize it. Our GA performs generalization and specialization, but also operations that enable to explore new points of the search space. This avoids the drawback of some deterministic methods that can explore unfruitful path without backtracking.

At first, we have concentrated our work on learning only equality relations between variables occurring in the pattern [4]. The idea is to consider the set of variables and to learn a partition of this set defining which variables are equal. For this purpose, we have proposed an encoding for representing a partition of a set of variables by an individual, and several set-based operators to alter

C. Rouveirol and M. Sebag (Eds.): ILP 2001, LNAI 2157, pp. 27–40, 2001.

a partition or to mix two ones. The resulting GA goes beyond the scope of propositionalization: it enables to learn genetically an optimal partition of a set of objects, and can be applied to other problems that can be reformulated as learning a partition.

In this paper, the approach is extended to achieve other propositionalization requirements, namely learning numeric constraints on variables at the same time as equality relations between them. Numeric constraints are thus directly put on equivalence classes involving numeric variables, and the genetic operators are extended to change not only the partition but also the associated constraints.

This paper is organized as follows. Section 2 is dedicated to the presentation of our approach, in particular the encoding we propose to represent a partition of variables by an individual, and a set of operators to generate new individuals. Then Sect. 3 gives some interesting properties of these operations for learning a rule. Sect. 4 presents preliminary experiments. In Sect. 5, some related works are presented; and finally conclusions are given in Sect. 6.

## 2 From Learning Rules to Learning Partitions with Constraints

Let us recall that in propositionalization, a pattern expressing the general form of the rule we are looking for is given.

Let us now recall that GAs are stochastic optimization algorithms that make evolve a population of individuals representing potential solutions for the problem at hand. This is done by selecting good individuals in the current population and applying them genetic operators. The basic algorithm works as follows:

```
initialize the population
do
   evaluate population
   select good individuals
   apply genetic operators
until end criterion
```

This requires to find a suitable encoding to represent a potential solution as an individual in a way that enables potentially good solutions to be crossed.

### 2.1 The Pattern

In our work, the pattern is a Horn clause, in which all occurrences of variables are distinct (it is thus the most general clause based on the given relations), except when some equality relations are fixed at the beginning. For the time being, our approach allows to learn equality relations between variables occurring in the pattern, and minimum and maximum thresholds on the values of the numeric ones. The equality relations involve a partition of the set of variables into equivalence classes. An individual encodes such a partition and constraints on numeric variables are directly put on the equivalence class $\mathcal{C}$ to which they belong.

There may exist or not constraints on the minimum and maximum values of a class of numeric variables.

### 2.2 Individuals Encoding

Let us denote by $\mathcal{S} = \{X_1, \ldots, X_n\}$ the set of variables occurring in the pattern.

As already stated, an individual, in our approach, encodes a partition of $\mathcal{S}$, together with the constraints put on numeric classes.

Each class is identified by a label. Our encoding represents an individual as an array $Ind$ indexed from 1 to $n$, where $n$ is the cardinality of $\mathcal{S}$. For $i \in \{1, \ldots, n\}$, $Ind[i]$ is associated to the variable $X_i$ of $\mathcal{S}$ and gives information about the class this variable belongs to in the partition (label, minimum value, maximum value). For labelling a class, we consider the variables it contains and take the lowest index among them. This rule ensures the uniqueness of the representation of a partition by an individual. Our search space is thus restricted to valid and non redundant potential solutions.

Figure 1 shows an example of the representation of a rule by an individual, based on a given pattern. In this example, $R$ and $S$ are two relations of arity 2; $X_4$ and $X_6$ are numeric variables of the same type, while the others are symbolic ones with the same type.

Let us notice that encoding partitions as strings of group numbers has already been done in the field of clustering, and this is known as group-number encoding [8]. Nevertheless, as far as we know, none of the works in this field imposes that a group number is the lowest index among the objects it contains.

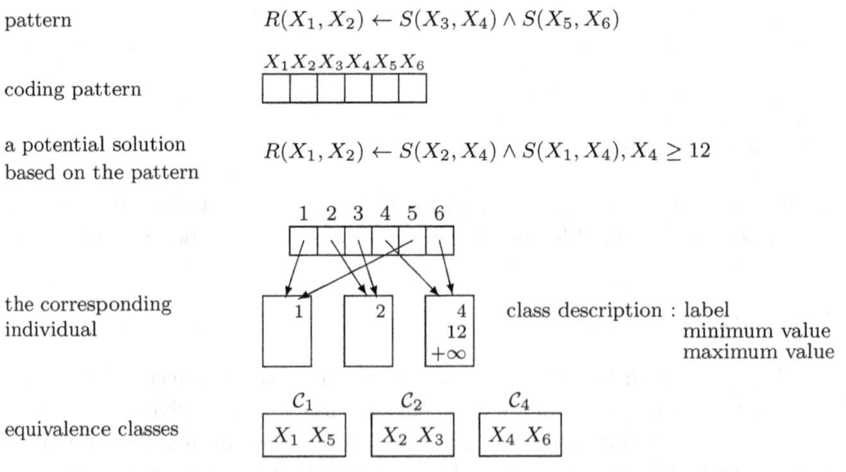


**Fig. 1.** An example of encoding

## 2.3 Operations on Equivalence Classes and Numeric Constraints

Let us now describe the genetic operations we have defined. For each operation, we describe its effects on the partitions coded by the individuals concerned. A more detailed description of how it is achieved in the more general context of learning a partition of a set of objects is given in [4].

We focus in this paper on the application of our approach to propositionalization, and to the extension to deal with numeric constraints.

Let us note that

- variables are typed,
- all the variables of an equivalence class must have the same type,
- a class has the type of its variables.

Two classes involved in an operation must have the same type. Moreover, in case of classes with numeric variables, numeric operations are applied to put appropriate constraints on them. In most cases, several treatments are possible to modify constraints on the numeric classes concerned by a genetic operation, or to set some on the new ones. In the next section, we will study the effects of these operations in terms of generalization or specialization of the underlying rule.

For clarity purpose, we only consider numeric variables with the same type in the illustrating examples, so that all classes can be mixed.

**Operations Involving One Individual.**
Let us denote by $Ind$ the individual concerned, $Ind'$ its child, by $\mathcal{C}$ the class of $Ind$ on which the operation is performed, and in case of a numeric class by $min_{\mathcal{C}}$ and $max_{\mathcal{C}}$ its bounds.

On the figures, we denote by $\mathcal{C}_l$ a class labelled by $l$ in the parent and by $\mathcal{C}'_l$ a class labelled by $l$ in its child.

Let us notice that when there is no lower bound $min_{\mathcal{C}} = -\infty$ (or 0 for positive values), and when there is no upper bound $max_{\mathcal{C}} = +\infty$.

*Isolating a Variable.* A variable $V$ is selected, $V \in \mathcal{C}$. $V$ is removed from $\mathcal{C}$ and put alone in a new class $\mathcal{C}'$ in $Ind'$, while the rest of the partition is kept unchanged.
For this operation, if $V$ is a numeric variable, two possibilities can be considered to put constraints on $\mathcal{C}'$:

- constraints on $\mathcal{C}$ are propagated to $\mathcal{C}'$ ($min_{\mathcal{C}'} = min_{\mathcal{C}}$ and $max_{\mathcal{C}'} = max_{\mathcal{C}}$);
- constraints on $\mathcal{C}'$ are fired at random.

In Fig. 2, $V = X_3$ is removed from the class $\mathcal{C}_3$ of $Ind$. This leads to two classes $\mathcal{C}'_3$ and $\mathcal{C}'_4$ in $Ind'$, with $\mathcal{C}'_3$ containing only $X_3$ and $\mathcal{C}'_4$ the other variables of $\mathcal{C}_3$. In this example, the constraint on $\mathcal{C}'_3$ is obtained by propagating this of $\mathcal{C}_3$ (treatment 1).

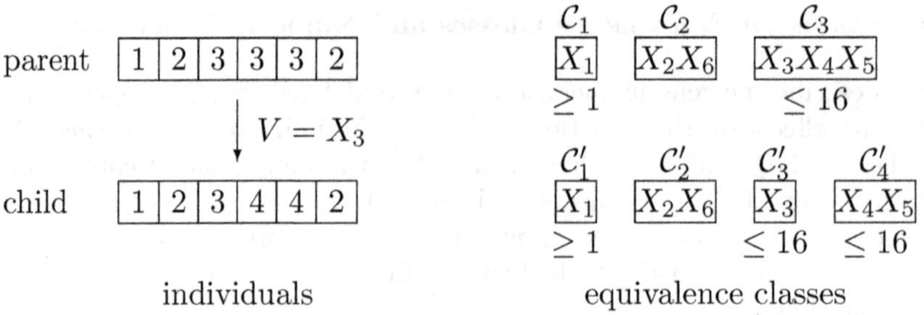

**Fig. 2.** Isolating a variable

*Moving a Variable across Classes.* A variable $V$ and an equivalence class $\mathcal{C}$ containing variables of the same type as $V$ are selected in $Ind$. $V$ is added to $\mathcal{C}$ in $Ind'$, and the rest of the partition is kept unchanged.
$\mathcal{C}$ keeps its numeric constraints.

Figure 3 gives an example where $X_2$ is added to the class labelled 3.

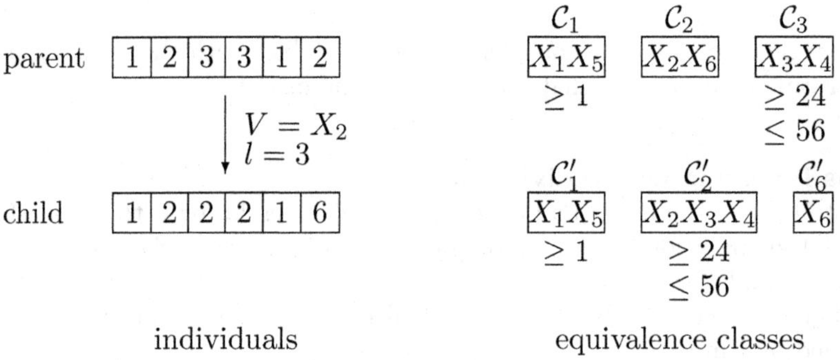

**Fig. 3.** Moving a variable across classes

*Splitting a Class into Two Ones.* A class $\mathcal{C}$ is selected in $Ind$. $Ind'$ has the same equivalence classes as $Ind$, except that $\mathcal{C}$ is divided into two classes, $\mathcal{C}'_{split_1}$ and $\mathcal{C}'_{split_2}$, which contain the variables of $\mathcal{C}$, randomly distributed between them. Two cases are possible to treat numeric constraints:

- constraints put on $\mathcal{C}$ are propagated to $\mathcal{C}'_{split_1}$ and $\mathcal{C}'_{split_2}$,
- $\mathcal{C}'_{split_1}$ has the same constraints as $\mathcal{C}$, and those of $\mathcal{C}'_{split_2}$ are fired at random.

In the example given in Fig. 4, the class $\mathcal{C}_2$ is selected in $Ind$ and is split into $\mathcal{C}'_2$ and $\mathcal{C}'_3$ in $Ind'$. Constraints on $\mathcal{C}'_2$ are those of $\mathcal{C}_2$, while constraints on $\mathcal{C}'_3$ are fired at random (treatment 2).

Let us note that isolating a variable is a special case of splitting a class. Nevertheless, it often breaks fewer equality relations in $\mathcal{C}$, so that it can be interesting when few changes are necessary in the partition to achieve a better solution.

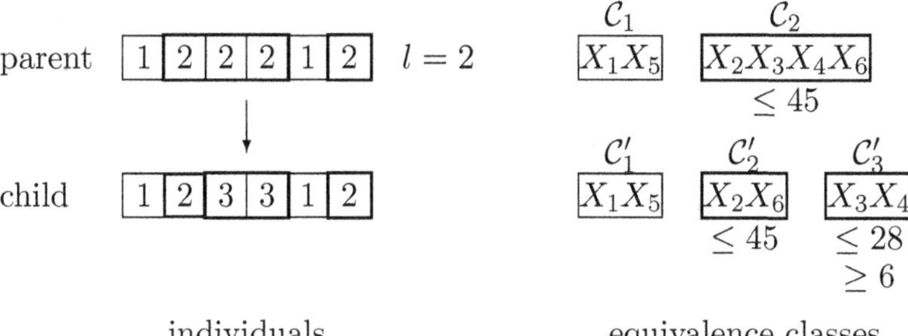


**Fig. 4.** Splitting a class

*Merging Two Classes.* Two classes $\mathcal{C}_i$ and $\mathcal{C}_j$ $(i \neq j)$ with the same type are selected in $Ind$; $Ind'$ encodes the same partition as $Ind$, except that the variables of $\mathcal{C}_i$ and $\mathcal{C}_j$ are gathered into a same class $\mathcal{C}'_{merge}$.
In case of numeric variables, three cases can be considered to put numeric constraints on $\mathcal{C}$:

- $min_{\mathcal{C}'_{merge}} = \min(min_{\mathcal{C}_i}, min_{\mathcal{C}_j})$ and $max_{\mathcal{C}'_{merge}} = \max(max_{\mathcal{C}_i}, max_{\mathcal{C}_j})$,
- $min_{\mathcal{C}'_{merge}} = \max(min_{\mathcal{C}_i}, min_{\mathcal{C}_j})$ and $max_{\mathcal{C}'_{merge}} = \min(max_{\mathcal{C}_i}, max_{\mathcal{C}_j})$,
- $min_{\mathcal{C}'_{merge}} = min_{\mathcal{C}_i}$ and $max_{\mathcal{C}'_{merge}} = max_{\mathcal{C}_i}$.

On Fig. 5, the two classes $\mathcal{C}_2$ and $\mathcal{C}_3$ of $Ind$ are merged into $\mathcal{C}'_2$ in $Ind'$. The treatment on constraints corresponds to the first one described.

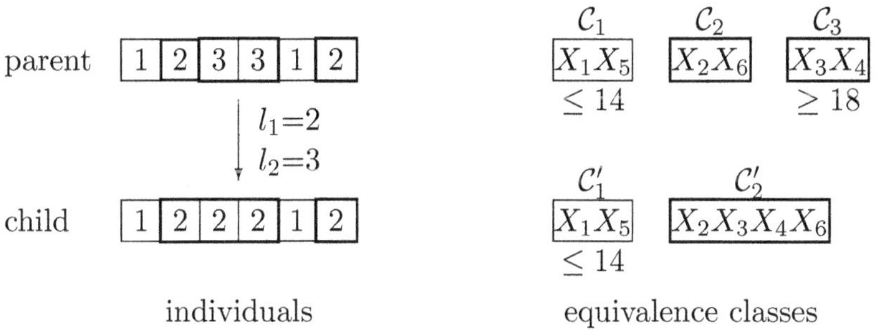

parent
1 2 3 3 1 2
$l_1$=2
$l_2$=3
child
1 2 2 2 1 2
$\mathcal{C}_1$ $X_1X_5$ $\leq 14$
$\mathcal{C}_2$ $X_2X_6$
$\mathcal{C}_3$ $X_3X_4$ $\geq 18$
$\mathcal{C}'_1$ $X_1X_5$ $\leq 14$
$\mathcal{C}'_2$ $X_2X_3X_4X_6$
individuals
equivalence classes

**Fig. 5.** Merging two classes

**Operations Involving Two Individuals.**

Let us denote by $Ind_1$ and $Ind_2$ the individuals concerned, by $Ind'_1$ and $Ind'_2$ their children.

In the figures, we denote by $C_{il}$ a class labelled by $l$ in Parent $i$ and by $C'_{il}$ a class labelled by $l$ in Child $i$.

*Union.* A class $C_{1i}$ is selected in $Ind_1$, and another class $C_{2j}$ in $Ind_2$ such that $C_{1i}$ and $C_{2j}$ have a common variable. After the operation, $Ind'_1$ and $Ind'_2$ encode the same partition as $Ind_1$ and $Ind_2$ respectively, except that variables of $C_{1i}$ and $C_{2j}$ are gathered in a unique class $C_{union}$. Numeric constraints on $C_{union}$ are determined as in the case of merging two classes.

In Fig. 6, Class $C_{12}$ is selected in $Ind_1$; only two classes have a common variable with $C_{12}$ in $Ind_2$, namely $C_{22}$ and $C_{24}$, and we choose $C_{24}$. The resulting children encode the same partitions as their parents, except that variables of $C_{12}$ and $C_{22}$ are gathered in a same class. In this example, treatment on numeric constraints is the first one described.

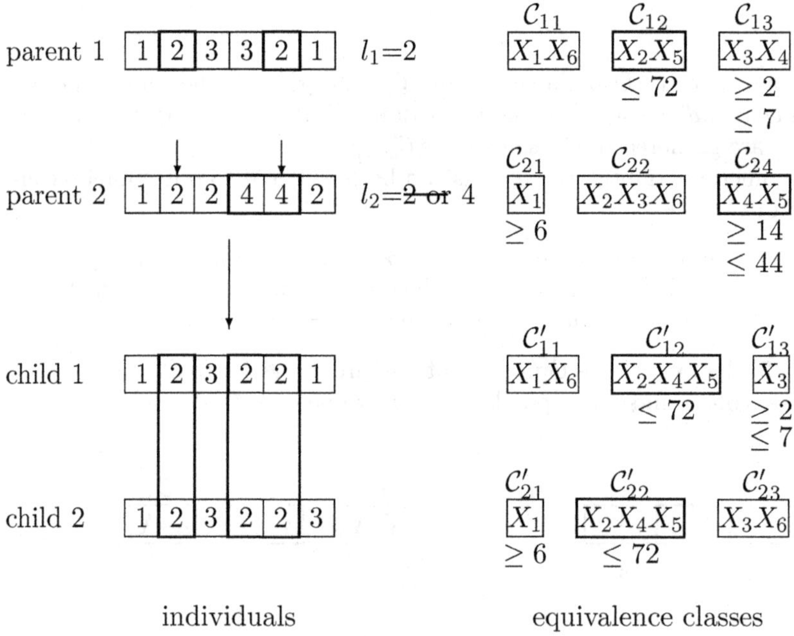


**Fig. 6.** Union

*Intersection.* A class $C_{1i}$ is selected in $Ind_1$, and another class $C_{2j}$ in $Ind_2$ such that $C_{1i}$ and $C_{2j}$ have a common variable. After the operation, $Ind'_1$ and $Ind'_2$ encode the same partition as $Ind_1$ and $Ind_2$ respectively, except that variables common to $C_{1i}$ and $C_{2j}$ are gathered into a class $C'_{inter}$. Numeric constraints on

$\mathcal{C}'_{inter}$ are determined according to one of the cases described for the merging two classes operation.

Figure 7 gives an example where Class $\mathcal{C}_{12}$ is selected in $Ind_1$; only two classes have a common variable with $\mathcal{C}_{12}$ in $Ind_2$, namely $\mathcal{C}_{22}$ and $\mathcal{C}_{23}$, and we choose $\mathcal{C}_{22}$. The resulting children encode the same partitions as their parents, except that variables of $\mathcal{C}_{12}$ and $\mathcal{C}_{22}$ are gathered in a unique class. For this example, treatment on numeric constraints is the second described.

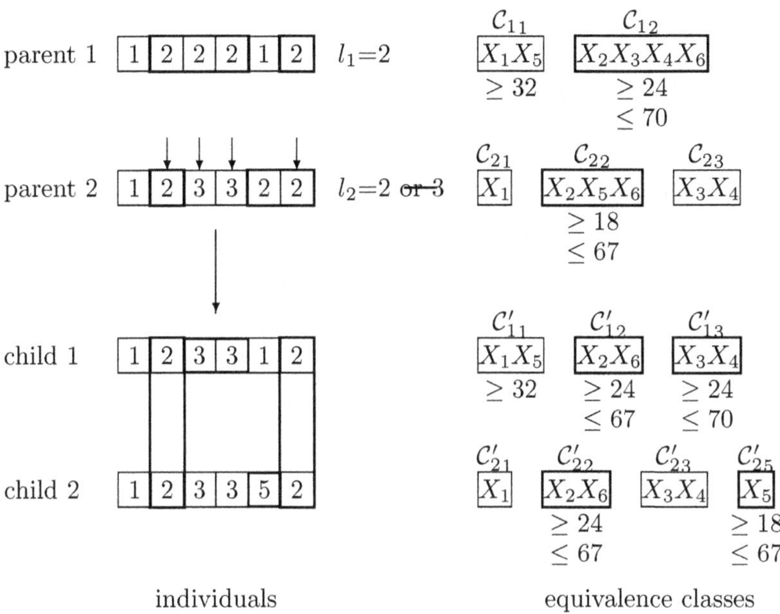


**Fig. 7.** Intersection

For these two operators, we require a common variable between the two classes involved. As $\mathcal{C}_{1i}$ and $\mathcal{C}_{2j}$ belong to individuals selected for their quality, they induce equality relations potentially good for the problem, and we hope to gather interesting links connected by this variable. In the case of intersection this requirement is necessary to have an effect. In the case of union this avoids to have too many side effects. For example, if we had chosen Classes $\mathcal{C}_{11}$ and $\mathcal{C}_{24}$ in Fig. 6, every class would have been disturbed, with nothing indicating in $Ind_1$ or $Ind_2$ that Variables $X_1, X_6$ and $X_4, X_5$ could be advantageously gathered.

**Operations on Constraints.**
These operations involve one individual and consist in altering constraints put on a given numeric class, to reinforce or relax them. For each of them, the minimum and maximum values can be altered or not depending on probabilities.

*Reinforcing Constraints on a Class.* If altered, the minimum (resp. maximum) takes a value greater (resp. lower) than the previous one.

*Relaxing Constraints on a Class.* If altered, the minimum (resp. maximum) takes a value lower (resp. greater) than the previous one.

## 3 Operators Properties

In Inductive Logic Programming the most current definition of generalization between clauses is $\theta$-subsumption [13], defined as follows:

**Definition 1 ($\theta$-subsumption between clauses).** *Let $C : h_C \leftarrow B_C$ and $D : h_D \leftarrow B_D$ be two clauses. $C$ $\theta$-subsumes $D$ (or $C$ is more general than $D$ by $\theta$-subsumption), written $C \succeq D$, when there exists a substitution $\theta$ such that $\theta(h_C) = h_D$ and $\theta(B_C) \subseteq B_D$.*

Nevertheless, this definition must be extended to handle numeric data: with $\theta$-subsumption two relations $X = 3$ and $X = 5$ are generalized into $X = Y$, whereas the expected relation would be $3 \leq X \leq 5$. To deal with this, several works [14,2,10] have suggested to model learning with symbolic and numeric data in the framework of Constraint Logic Programmming, and have proposed a new definition of generalization between constrained clauses [14,2].

**Definition 2 (ce-subsumption between constrained clauses).** *Let $C$ and $D$ be two constrained clauses $h_C \leftarrow c_C, B_C$ and $h_D \leftarrow c_D, B_D$ where $c_C$, $c_D$ are conjunctions of constraints, $h_C$, $h_D$ are atoms and $B_C$, $B_D$ are conjunctions of atoms. The clause $C$ ce-subsumes $D$, written $C \succeq D$, iff there exists a substitution $\theta$ such that $\models_D \widetilde{\forall}(c_D \rightarrow c_C\theta)$, $\theta(h_C) = h_D$ and $\theta(B_C) \subseteq B_D$.*

In this paper, we are mainly interested in numeric constraints, expressed by $X$ *comp* $\alpha$, with *comp* $\in \{\leq, \geq\}$.

We call *operator* the combination of an operation on equivalence classes and a corresponding operation on the constraints associated to the numeric classes possibly involved, or an operation on constraints only. Some of these operators enable to specialize or generalize a rule under ce-subsumption, while the others do not have a determined effect but enable to explore the search space, being partly guided by the information contained in the parents.

Let us denote by $\mathcal{V}(c_i)$ the set of variables occurring in a clause $c_i$, $c$ the clause coded by $Ind$ and $c'$ the clause coded by $Ind'$. Let us notice that the variables of $Ind$ are those of the pattern, whereas $\mathcal{V}(c)$ is composed of representatives of the equivalence classes coded in $Ind$.

**Proposition 1.** *Isolating a variable together with treatment 1 on numeric constraints generalizes a rule.*

*Proof.* Let us denote by $V$ the isolated variable of $Ind$ with $V \in C$. If $V$ is not a numeric variable:

- If $\mathcal{C} = \{V\}$: nothing is done and $Ind' = Ind$.
- If $\mathcal{C} \neq \{V\}$:
  - if $V \in \mathcal{V}(c)$ ($V$ is the representative of Class $\mathcal{C}$ in $c$), there exists $U$ such that $U \in \mathcal{C}$, $U \in \mathcal{V}(c')$ and $U \neq V$. More precisely, $V$ occurs in $c'$ as the representative of the new class, and a new variable $U \in \mathcal{C}$ represents the class $\mathcal{C} - \{V\}$.
    Denoting $\sigma = \{U/V\}$, we obtain $c'\sigma = c$.
  - if $V \notin \mathcal{V}(c)$, there exists $U$ such that $U \in \mathcal{C}$, $U \in \mathcal{V}(c)$ and $U \neq V$.
    Denoting $\sigma = \{V/U\}$, we obtain $c'\sigma = c$.

So $c'$ $\theta$-subsumes $c$.

If $V$ is a numeric variable, the same applies but the constraint $a \leq V \leq b$ in $c$ is transformed into $a \leq V \leq b \wedge a \leq U \leq b$ in $c'$. Applying the substitution $\sigma$ to $(a \leq V \leq b \wedge a \leq U \leq b)$ leads to $a \leq V \leq b \wedge a \leq V \leq b$ which is equivalent to $a \leq V \leq b$. Therefore $\models c \rightarrow c'\theta$. So $c'$ ce-subsumes $c$.

**Proposition 2.** *Splitting a class together with treatment 1 on numeric constraints generalizes a rule.*

*Proof.* If the class does not contain numeric variables:

- If $\mathcal{C}'_{split_1} = \{\}$ or $\mathcal{C}'_{split_2} = \{\}$: nothing is done and $Ind' = Ind$.
- If $\mathcal{C}'_{split_1} \neq \{\}$ and $\mathcal{C}_{split_2} \neq \{\}$: there exists $U$ and $V$ such that $U, V \in \mathcal{C}$, $U \in \mathcal{V}(c)$, $V \notin \mathcal{V}(c)$ and $U, V \in \mathcal{V}(c')$ ($U$ is the representative of Class $\mathcal{C}$ that occurs in $c$, $V$ does not occur in $c$; $U$ is the representative of Class $\mathcal{C}'_{split_1}$ in $c'$, $V$ is the representative of Class $\mathcal{C}'_{split_2}$ in $c'$).
  Denoting $\sigma = \{V/U\}$, we obtain $c'\sigma = c$.

So $c'$ $\theta$-subsumes $c$.

If the class contains numeric variables, the proof is similar to that of Prop. 2. So $c'$ ce-subsumes $c$.

**Proposition 3.** *Merging two classes together with treatment 2 on numeric constraints specializes a rule.*

*Proof.* Let us assume that the representative that is kept is $U$ and thus belongs to $\mathcal{C}_1$.

There exist $U$ and $V$ such that $U \in \mathcal{C}_1$, $U \in \mathcal{V}(c)$ and $U \in \mathcal{V}(c')$, $V \in \mathcal{C}_2$, $V \in \mathcal{V}(c)$ and $V \notin \mathcal{V}(c')$.

If $U$ and $V$ are not numeric variables: denoting $\sigma = \{V/U\}$, we obtain $c\sigma = c'$. So $c\,\theta$-subsumes $c'$.

If $U$ and $V$ are numeric variables with constraints $a \leq U \leq b$ and $d \leq V \leq e$ in $c$, then the new constraints on $U$ in $c'$ are $\max(a, d) \leq U \leq \min(b, e)$. Applying the substitution $\sigma$ to $a \leq U \leq b$ and $d \leq V \leq e$ leads to $a \leq U \leq b$ and $d \leq U \leq e$ and $\max(a, d) \leq U \leq \min(b, e)$ implies $a \leq U \leq b$ and $d \leq U \leq e$. Therefore $\models c' \rightarrow c\theta$. So $c$ ce-subsumes $c'$.

**Proposition 4.** *Intersection together with treatment 1 on numeric constraints generalizes a rule.*

*Proof.* Let us now denote by $c_1$ the clause encoded by $Ind_1$, $c_2$ the clause encoded by $Ind_2$, $c'_1$ the clause encoded by $Ind'_1$ and $c'_2$ the clause encoded by $Ind'_2$.

Let $U$ be the variable that occurs in $c_1$ and represents Class $\mathcal{C}_{1i}$. Class $\mathcal{C}_{1i}$ is split into $\mathcal{C}_{inter}$ and a class containing the other variables of $\mathcal{C}_{1i}$.

Let us denote by $V$ and $W$ the representatives of the two classes. We have either $U = W$ or $V = W$.

If $V$ is not a numeric variable, the proof is the same as for the splitting case, and $c'_1$ $\theta$-subsumes $c_1$.

If $V$ is a numeric variable: let us denote by $U$ the representative of Class $\mathcal{C}_{1i}$ in $c_1$, by $V$ the representative of Class $\mathcal{C}_{2j}$ in $c_2$ and by $W$ the representative of Class $\mathcal{C}_{inter}$ in $c'_1$ (it may happen that $U = V$ or $U = W$ or $V = W$).

If $a \leq U \leq b$ (resp. $c \leq V \leq d$) is the constraint linked to $U$ (resp. $V$) in $Ind_1$ (resp. $Ind_2$) then the constraint linked to $W$ is $\min(a, c) \leq W \leq \max(b, d)$. It is easy to show that substitution $\sigma$ satisfies $(a \leq U \leq b \wedge c \leq V \leq d) \vdash (\min(a, c) \leq W \leq \max(b, d))\sigma)$. So $c'_1$ ce-subsumes $c_1$.

The proof is the same for $c'_2$ ce-subsumes $c_2$.

**Proposition 5.** *Reinforcing constraints specializes a rule.*

**Proposition 6.** *Relaxing constraints generalizes a rule.*

For the two last propositions, proofs are similar to the previous ones.

## 4 Preliminary Experiments

We have implemented this approach in C++, and used the Database Management System PostgreSQL. Tests have been performed on two classical datasets, namely a family dataset with $grand\_father$ as the target concept and Michalski 10 trains dataset [11].

For the time being, we are only searching for a conjunctive description of the concept, that covers at least one example and rejects many counter-examples. Our fitness function thus gives a null quality to an individual that does not cover any example. If any is covered, it gives more weight to the rejection of counter-examples than to the coverage of examples, so that we favour consistent solutions. The probabilities used for the operators in our experiments are the following:

- union: 0.3,
- intersection: 0.3,
- isolating a variable: 0.05,
- moving a variable across classes: 0.05,

- splitting a class: 0.1,
- merging two classes: 0.1.

During the initialization step, for each individual, all variables are considered in the order they appear, and a parameter indicates whether it is put alone or in an existing class (if there exists one, else a new class is however created). In our experiments, we create individuals with a large amount of classes, and this parameter is set to 0.9.

Results are encouraging. For the family example, our database is composed of 4 tables: one for the relation *father*, one for the relation *mother*, one for storing the examples and one for storing the counter-examples. For instance, we provide our program with 4 relations: *grand_father*, *mother*, *father* and *mother*, and set the population size to 20 individuals. Consistent definitions for *grand_father* rapidly emerge, as for instance the solution 0 1 2 1 0 2 6 7 which corresponds to one of the possible definitions of a maternal grandfather. Providing it with 8 relations, with a population of 30 individuals, we also obtain the results very quickly.

For our tests on the 10 trains dataset, we have worked on a database composed of 25 relations. Indeed, we have converted relations such as *lhshape*, which indicates the form of a given load, into 4 relations, one for each shape, because we do not learn constraints on symbolic classes at the moment. For instance, we have provided it with 14 relations (the target concept *east* and 13 others, all different), leading to individuals composed of 30 genes which correspond to the 30 variables appearing in the pattern. With a population of 30 individuals, the system has converged rapidly towards, for example, the consistent description which states that a train goes east if it has a rectangular wagon whose position is equal to the number of wheels of a wagon. This description covers two examples and our algorithm has to be embedded in a complete system in order to learn a set of rules that covers all the examples.

## 5 Related Works

Our work can be compared to the approach presented in [16], since both works address the same task of searching the subsumption lattice by means of Genetic Algorithms. Nevertheless, we propose a more compact representation of the individuals: the links between $N$ variables are represented in our approach by an individual of length $N$, whereas it is represented in [16] by the top triangle of a matrix. The operators we propose are based on set operations whereas in their framework they are based on binary matrixes operations.

Many works have dealt with applying GA to Concept Learning in an attribute-value representation. Some attempts have been made in first order representations. Nevertheless, the problem is much more complicated than with attribute-value representation. Indeed, when learning in an attribute-value context, the pattern on which a rule is based is known and can be represented by a fixed-length individual. When the description of the concept has to be expressed in first order logic, we cannot determine in advance the form of the optimal rule (which literal occurs in, which variables of these literals are equal, ...). In some genetic relational concept learners, a model for the rule is provided to the system: it is given by the user (REGAL [6], G-NET [7]) or based on a seeding example (SIAO1 [3]). In REGAL, as described in [6], a pattern (called a template) is a conjunction of literals in which an argument is replaced by a domain. It fixes the links between the variables in the literals, and the system only learns the values allowed among those of the given domains. For example, the template $P(X, Y, [v_{p1}, \ldots, v_{pm}]) \wedge Q(Y, [v_{q1}, \ldots, v_{qn}]))$ indicates that the second variable of $P$ and the first variable of $Q$ are linked, that the third argument of $P$ can take the values $v_{p1}, \ldots, v_{pm}$ and the second argument of $Q$ the values $v_{q1}, \ldots, v_{qn}$.

Let us notice that by the use of a pattern, such works can be seen as based on propositionalization.

In SIAO1, relations between variables are modified either by mutations when changing a gene to a variable (and replacing with probability the other occurrences of the past symbol by the new one in the individual), or when applying a one-point crossover (but its effect on the exploitation of relations between variables seems more limited) or a generalization operator. For example, the seeding example $P(a, b) \wedge Q(b)$ could be generalized by mutation in $P(a, Y) \wedge Q(Y)$ or $P(a, Y) \wedge Q(b)$. In this approach relations between variables evolve, but the operators realize only generalization.

## 6 Conclusion

In this paper, we have mainly focused on the subtask of learning symbolic and numeric constraints in a pattern by means of a GA. Such a work could then be embedded in a propositionalization framework. A possible way of achieving this is for instance to use a star approach [12], as follows:

1. choose a seed example $e$
2. define a starting pattern $P$ that covers $e$
3. refine $P$ by learning symbolic links or numeric constraints
4. if some examples are not covered, then iterate at Step 1

Propositionalization is an interesting solution to the complexity problems linked to the size of the search space. Nevertheless, once a pattern is given, the database of positive and negative instantiations of this pattern must be built, and this leads to complexity problems comparable in some degree to that of Data Mining systems flattening a relational database into a single one. We have previously studied the interests of parallelizing GAs [5], and we have shown that under some conditions it was interesting to distribute the database on several processors. Some approaches have been proposed to deal with this problem as for instance stochastic sampling [15].

The genetic approach that we present is original in the sense that instead of representing in an individual whether two variables are equal or not, we encode the equivalence classes involved by these equality relations, and we define genetic operators that manipulate equivalence classes and their associated numeric constraints.

Preliminary results are encouraging. A difficult part for testing our algorithm is the setting of the different parameters, mainly probabilities linked to the application of operators. We plan to make experiments on artificial examples, to study the influence of these parameters according to the expected form of the clause (number of linked variables, numeric variables, ...).

## References


1. E. Alphonse. Propositionnalisation sélective en apprentissage relationnel. In *Conférence d'Apprentissage CAp'2000*, Saint-Etienne, June 2000.
2. S. Anthony and A. M. Frisch. Generating numerical literals during refinement. In *Proceedings of ILP*, volume 1297, pages 61–76. Springer-Verlag, 1997.
3. S. Augier, G. Venturini, and Y. Kodratoff Learning first order logic rules with a genetic algorithm. In *Proceedings of KDD'95*, pages 21–26. AAAI Press, 1995.
4. A. Braud and C. Vrain. Learning constraints between variables in inductive logic programming. Research report, LIFO, 2001.
5. A. Braud and C. Vrain. A study of the scalability of a data mining genetic algorithm on a distributed database. In *Proceedings of GECCO-2001*. Morgan Kaufmann, 2001, to appear. Note: Poster.
6. A. Giordana and F. Neri. Search-intensive concept induction. *Evolutionary Computation Journal*, 3(4):375–416, 1996.
7. A. Giordana, L. Saitta, and G. Lo Bello. A coevolutionary approach to concept learning. In *Proceedings of ISMIS-97*, volume 1325 of *LNAI*, pages 257–266. Springer, 1997.
8. D. A. Jones and M. A. Beltramo. Solving partitioning problems with genetic algorithms. In L. B. Belew, R. K. Booker, editor, *Proceedings of ICGA-91*, pages 442–449, San Diego, CA, July 1991. Morgan Kaufmann.
9. N. Lavrac and S. Dzeroski. *Inductive Logic Programming: Techniques and Applications*. Artificial Intelligence. Ellis Horwood (Simon & Schuster), 1994.
10. L. Martin and C. Vrain. Learning linear constraints in inductive logic programming. In *Proceedings of the ECML*, volume 1224 of *LNAI*, pages 162–169. Springer, 1997.
11. R. S. Michalski. Pattern recognition as rule-guided inductive inference. In *Proceedings of IEEE Transactions on Pattern Analysis and Machine Intelligence*, pages 349–361, 1980.
12. R. S. Michalski. A theory and methodology of inductive inference. In *Machine Learning Vol 2*, pages 215–244. Morgan Kaufmann, 1986.
13. G. D. Plotkin. A note on inductive generalization. In *Machine Intelligence 5*, pages 153–163. Elsevier North Holland, New York, 1970.
14. C. Rouveirol and M. Sebag. Constraint inductive logic programming. In L. De Raedt, editor, *Proceedings of ILP-95*, pages 181–198. Department of Computer Science, Katholieke Universiteit Leuven, 1995.
15. M. Sebag and C. Rouveirol. Tractable induction and classification in first order logic via stochastic matching. In *Proceedings of IJCAI-97*, pages 888–893, San Francisco, August 23–29 1997. Morgan Kaufmann Publishers.
16. A. Tamaddoni-Nezhad and S. Muggleton. Searching the subsumption lattice by a genetic algorithm. In *Proceedings of ILP-2000*, volume 1866 of *LNAI*, pages 243–252. Springer-Verlag, 2000.
17. J.-D. Zucker and J.-G. Ganascia. Learning structurally indeterminate clauses. In David Page, editor, *Proceedings of ILP-98*, volume 1446 of *LNAI*, pages 235–244, Berlin, July 22–24 1998. Springer.

# Classifying Uncovered Examples by Rule Stretching

Martin Eineborg[1] and Henrik Boström[1,2]

[1] Machine Learning Group, Department of Computer and Systems Sciences, Stockholm University/Royal Institute of Technology, Electrum 230, Stockholm, Sweden, {eineborg,henke}@dsv.su.se

[2] Virtual Genetics Laboratory, 171 77 Stockholm, Sweden Henrik.Bostrom@vglab.com

**Abstract.** This paper is concerned with how to classify examples that are not covered by any rule in an unordered hypothesis. Instead of assigning the majority class to the uncovered examples, which is the standard method, a novel method is presented that minimally generalises the rules to include the uncovered examples. The new method, called Rule Stretching, has been evaluated on several domains (using the inductive logic programming system Virtual Predict for induction of the base hypothesis). The results show a significant improvement over the standard method.

## 1 Introduction

One major distinction between methods for induction of classification rules is whether they treat the hypothesis as an ordered or unordered set of rules. In the ordered case, there is no need for resolving classification conflicts among the rules, since the first applicable rule is used (such an hypothesis is commonly referred to as a decision list [15]). Furthermore, a decision list always includes a default rule at the end, which means that any example that may have passed through the previous rules without being covered will still be assigned a class. It should be noted that the standard inductive logic programming setting with two classes (positive and negative examples) and where a hypothesis is searched for that covers all positive examples but none of the negative, in fact is a special case of the ordered case, since it implicitly assumes that any example that is not covered by the rules should be classified as negative. In the case with unordered hypotheses, rules need to be generated for all classes and some strategy has to be adopted for resolving conflicts among the rules (e.g., [5]). Furthermore, it may very well happen that none of the rules is applicable when trying to classify new examples. A common strategy for handling such examples is to classify them as belonging to the majority class (e.g., [8]).

In this paper we present a new method for classifying examples that are not covered by any of the rules in an (unordered) hypothesis. The method, Rule

C. Rouveirol and M. Sebag (Eds.): ILP 2001, LNAI 2157, pp. 41–50, 2001.

Stretching, is applied after the hypothesis has been induced, during the classification phase. Rule Stretching works by generalising the rules in a hypothesis to cover the previously uncovered examples. The method is not targeted at any special inductive logic programming system but is a general method for assigning classes to uncovered examples.

The paper is organised as follows. In the next section, we present a general algorithm for Rule Stretching. This algorithm is specialised in Section 3 with respect to a specific learning paradigm and a system called Virtual Predict, which is used for induction of base hypotheses. The setup of the experiments and the results are presented in Section 4. The work presented in this paper has some ideas in common with Analogical Prediction [11], which are discussed in Section 5. The paper ends with concluding remarks in Section 6. The reader is assumed to be familiar with basic concepts of logic programming [9].

## 2 Rule Stretching

Examples that are not covered by an unordered hypothesis are usually classified as belonging to a default class (usually the majority class). The work in this paper is instead based on the idea that unordered rules of an induced hypothesis can be 'stretched out' to cover previously uncovered examples. Rule Stretching is used in the following way:

1. Induce an unordered set of rules using an inductive logic programming system
2. Classify new examples using the induced rules
3. Examples that are not covered by any of the rules are given to the Rule Stretching system for classification

A new, more general, hypothesis that is ensured to cover a previously uncovered example, can be formed by computing the minimal generalisation of the example and each rule in the hypothesis. The rules of the new hypothesis has to be evaluated since, by generalising the rules to cover the example, the accuracy of the rules may have been changed (important conditions could have been removed by the generalisation making it possible for a rule to cover more examples of other classes than it did before the generalisation).

An example on how Rule Stretching works is illustrated in Figure 1 where there are two classes $a$ and $b$, two rules, $R1$ and $R2$, and an uncovered example denoted '?'. In the picture to the left, the two rules and their coverage can be seen as well as the uncovered example. In the picture to the right the two rules have been generalised so that they cover the unclassified example and the class of the example can be determined by, for example, selecting the most probable class for the most accurate rule, which in this case means class $a$. Note that when generalising rule $R2$ it covers not only examples of class $b$ but also two examples of class $a$ (thus decreasing its accuracy).

A general algorithm for Rule Stretching is presented in Figure 2. The algorithm takes a hypothesis $H$, background knowledge $B$, examples $E$, an uncovered

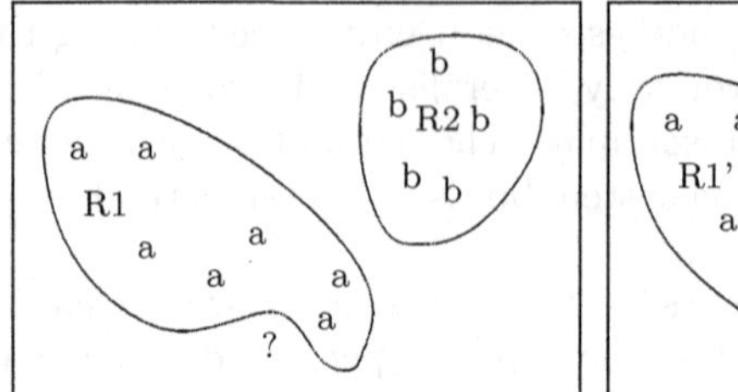


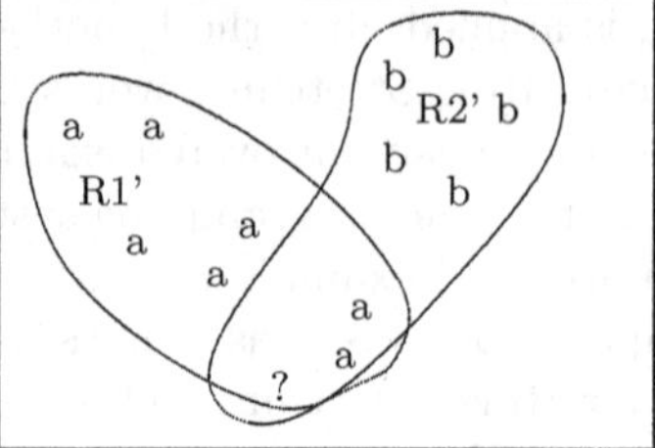


**Fig. 1.** Rule Stretching

example $e \in E$ such that $H \wedge B \not\models e$, and returns a class label. Three functions are used by the algorithm: the *minimal_generalisation* function, which returns the minimal generalisation of a rule and an example, the *coverage* function, which takes a rule and a set of examples and returns the number of examples of the different classes it covers, and the *classify* function, which returns a class label given a set of pairs of generalised rules and their coverage.

**Input:** hypothesis $H$, background knowledge $B$, examples $E$, an uncovered example $e$
**Output:** a class label $c$

1. $H' = \{r' \mid r \in H \wedge r' = minimal\_generalisation(r, e)\}$
2. $V = \{(r, v) \mid r \in H' \wedge v = coverage(r, E)\}$
3. $c = classify(V)$

**Fig. 2.** Rule Stretching Algorithm (general version)

## 3 Rule Stretching Using Least General Generalisations

The general version of the Rule Stretching algorithm should be specialised with respect to the theoretical foundation of the inductive logic programming system that is used. In this study we consider the framework of the system Virtual Predict, which is described in Section 3.1. A special version of the Rule Stretching algorithm that takes advantage of the properties of this particular system is given in Section 3.2.

### 3.1 Virtual Predict

Virtual Predict [2] is an inductive logic programming system that is a successor of Spectre 3.0 [3]. The system can be viewed as an upgrade of standard decision tree and rule induction systems in that it allows for more expressive hypotheses to be generated and more expressive background knowledge (i.e., logic programs) to be incorporated in the induction process. The major design goal has been to achieve this upgrade in a way so that it should still be possible to emulate the standard techniques with lower expressiveness (but also lower computational cost) within the system if desired. As a side effect, this has allowed the incorporation of several recent methods, such as bagging, boosting and randomisation, that have been developed for standard machine learning techniques into the more powerful framework of Virtual Predict.

Like its predecessor, Virtual Predict uses resolution as a specialisation operator [4]. This means that each rule generated by the system is the result of repeatedly applying resolution to some overly general clause. For reasons of efficiency, the system internally represents rules on the same format as it represents proofs of examples, namely as *derivation terms.*

A derivation term is a term on the form $c_i(t_1, \ldots, t_n)$, where $c_i$ is an identifier of some input clause in the derivation of the rule (or the proof of the example), and $t_1, \ldots, t_n$ are derivation terms corresponding to the sub-derivations (or sub-proofs) for the $n$ literals in the body of the clause $c_i$.

For example, given the following overly general theory:

```
(c1) target(Size,Shape,Weight):-
        size(Size), shape(Shape), weight(Weight).
(c2) size(A):- A = small.
(c3) size(A):- A = medium.
(c4) size(A):- A = large.
(c5) shape(A):- regular(A).
(c6) shape(A):- irregular(A).
(c7) regular(A):- A = circular.
...
(c15) weight(A):- A = low.
```

the proof of the example `target(small,circular,low)` would be represented by the derivation term $c1(c2, c5(c7), c15)$. The derived rule

```
target(Size,Shape,Weight):-
        Size = small, regular(Shape), weight(Weight).
```

is represented by the derivation term $c1(c2, c5(\_), \_)$.

It should be noted that a derivation term for a derived rule typically is non-ground, while a derivation term for a proof of an example always is ground[1]. By finding the proofs of all examples in advance of the induction process and by representing the proofs together with derived rules as derivation terms, the coverage check of a derived rule and an example is reduced to unification, i.e. no theorem proving is needed. This has led to an order of magnitude speedup in Virtual Predict compared to its predecessor.

---

[1] It should also be noted that some built-in predicates (such as arithmetic predicates) need special treatment, but this falls outside the scope of the paper.

### 3.2 A Specialised Rule Stretching Method

Since Virtual Predict represents the rules of a hypothesis as terms it is possible to compute the minimal generalisation of a rule and the proof of an example by computing the least general generalisation [13].

**Definition 1.** *An atom $c$ is a generalisation of atoms $a$ and $b$ if there exists substitutions $\theta_1$ and $\theta_2$ such that $c\theta_1 = a$ and $c\theta_2 = b$.*

**Definition 2.** *A generalisation $c$ for two atoms $a$ and $b$ is a least general generalisation (lgg) if for each other generalisation $c_i$ of $a$ and $b$ there exists a substitution $\theta_i$ such that $c = c_i\theta_i$.*

A new more specific version of the general Rule Stretching algorithm, was formed by replacing the *minimal_generalisation* function with a function, *lgg*, that computes the least general generalisation of a rule and the proof of an example. Furthermore, the *classify* function was replaced with a function, *use_best_rule*, that given a set of evaluated rules returns the class of the rule that has the highest accuracy (with Laplace-correction). The lgg version of the Rule Stretching algorithm can be seen in Figure 3.

**Input:** hypothesis $H$, background knowledge $B$, examples $E$, an uncovered example $e$
**Output:** a class label $c$

1. $H' = \{r' \mid r \in H \wedge r' = lgg(r, e)\}$
2. $V = \{(r, v) \mid r \in H' \wedge v = coverage(r, E)\}$
3. $c = use\_best\_rule(V)$

**Fig. 3.** Rule Stretching Algorithm (lgg version)

## 4 Empirical Evaluation

A number of experiments were conducted in order to find out whether the Rule Stretching method performs better than choosing the majority class for uncovered examples. In all of the experiments the base hypotheses were induced by Virtual Predict. In Section 4.1, we describe how Virtual Predict was configured and the domains used. The experimental results are given in Section 4.2.

### 4.1 Experimental Setting

There are a number of parameters that can be set when defining learning methods in Virtual Predict, allowing a very wide range of methods to be defined, including the emulation of standard techniques, such as decision tree induction and naive Bayes classification. The parameters include the search strategy to use (separate-and-conquer or divide-and-conquer), optimisation criterion (e.g. information gain), probability estimate (e.g. m estimate), whether an ordered or unordered hypothesis should be induced, inference method (how to apply the resulting hypothesis), post-pruning (using e.g. an MDL criterion or a prune set) as well as ensemble learning methods (bagging, boosting, and randomisation). There are also a number of parameters that have to be set when defining experiments in Virtual Predict, such as what experimental methodology to use (e.g. n-fold cross validation).

The parameters and their values were in this study set according to Table 1. A covering (separate and conquer) approach to rule induction was used together with incremental reduced error pruning [6], by which a generated rule is immediately pruned back to some ancestor in the derivation sequence (the pruning criterion was in this experiment set to accuracy on the entire training set, but other options in Virtual Predict include accuracy on a validation set and most compressive ancestor).

In case an example was covered by more than one rule this conflict was resolved by computing the most probable class using naive Bayes, by maximising the following expression:

$$P'(C|R_1 \wedge \ldots \wedge R_n) = P(C)P(R_1|C)\ldots P(R_n|C) \quad (1)$$

where $C$ is a class and $R_1 \ldots R_n$ are the rules that cover a particular example. It should be noted that in case a particular example is not covered by any rule, maximising the above expression leads to assigning the example the most probable class *a priori*, which is the standard method for classifying uncovered examples.

**Table 1.** Virtual Predict settings

| Parameter | Value |
|---|---|
| Strategy | Separate and Conquer |
| Optimisation criterion | Information Gain |
| Probability estimate | M Estimate, with M=2 |
| Measure | Information Gain |
| Incremental Reduced Error Pruning | Most Accurate on Training Set |
| Inference method | Naive Bayes |
| Experiment type | 10-Fold Cross Validation |

Rule Stretching was tested on the seven problems that can be seen in Table 2 along with some statistics about the number of classes, the distribution of the classes, the number of examples that were not covered by the base hypothesis, and the total number of examples in the domain. Four of the domains were collected from the UCI Machine Learning Repository: the Balance Scale Database, the Car Evaluation Database, the Congressional Voting Records Database, and the Student Loan Relational Database. The data for the problem of recognising illegal positions on a chess endgame with a two kings and a rook, KRKI, and the problem of predicting the secondary structure of proteins (described in [12]) were available from the web page of the Machine Learning Group at the University of York. The Alzheimers toxicity domain was available from Oxford University Computing Laboratory. The domain was described in [7].

In the secondary protein structure domain the hypothesis was restricted to looking at properties for only three positions at a time (i.e., the predicate `alpha_triplet/3` was used).

**Table 2.** Domain statistics

| Domain | Classes | Class Distribution (%) | Uncovered Examples (%) | Total Examples |
|---|---|---|---|---|
| Balance | 3 | 7.84; 46.08; 46.08 | 19.04 | 625 |
| Car | 4 | 3.76; 3.99<br>22.22; 70.02 | 3.36 | 1728 |
| House Votes | 2 | 38.62; 61.38 | 2.53 | 435 |
| KRKI | 2 | 34.2; 65.8 | 2.6 | 1000 |
| Alzheimers tox. | 2 | 50; 50 | 6.54 | 886 |
| Secondary Protein Structure | 2 | 43.4; 56.6 | 27.61 | 1014 |
| Student Loan | 2 | 35.7; 64.3 | 5.4 | 1000 |

### 4.2 Experimental Results

Two methods for classifying uncovered examples were compared in the seven domains: selecting the majority class and Rule Stretching. The same base hypotheses were used in conjunction with the two methods, and these were produced by Virtual Predict using the settings shown in the previous section. In all but one of the domains, 10-fold cross validation was employed. Due to long computation time for the secondary protein structure domain only a single run was made, using a single training and test set.

The null hypothesis was that Rule Stretching is not more accurate than selecting the majority class. The results of using the two methods is shown in Table 3. One can see that in seven out of seven cases, Rule Stretching results in more accurate classifications than when assigning uncovered examples the majority class. The one sided binomial tail probability of this number of successes, given that the probability of success is 0.5, is approximately 0.0078, which allows for a rejection of the null hypothesis at the 1% level.

## 5 Related Work

The idea of including the example to be classified in the formation of the hypothesis is shared with Analogical Prediction [11]. Analogical Prediction uses

**Table 3.** Results

| Domain | Majority Class | Rule Stretching |
|---|---:|---:|
| Balance | 76.32% | 84.64% |
| Car | 93.98% | 94.16% |
| House Votes | 94.25% | 95.4% |
| KRKI | 97.1% | 99.4% |
| Alzheimers Tox. | 88.26% | 90.18% |
| Secondary Protein Structure | 57.99% | 61.14% |
| Student Loan | 92.2% | 92.7% |

background knowledge, training examples, and the example to be classified to form a hypothesis which is used to classify the example. For every new example that is to be classified, a new hypothesis is formed. This leads to a different behavior when classifying examples than the normal setting of inductive logic programming does.

The main difference between Rule Stretching and Analogical Prediction is that Analogical Prediction forms a new hypothesis for every example that is to be classified whereas in Rule Stretching a previously induced hypothesis is used to classify examples that it covers, and rules of the hypothesis are minimally generalised to cover the remaining examples. This results in that Rule Stretching only evaluates as many candidate rules as there are rules in the original hypothesis, while Analogical Prediction performs a costly search for each example to be classified, typically evaluating a large number of candidate rules.

Another related work, although not specifically aimed at the problem of classifying uncovered examples, was described in [1] where a two-layered system for handling imprecise definitions was presented. The rules of the first layer are supposed to capture the basic properties of the concepts while the second layer defines possible modifications of the basic properties which makes it possible to classify examples not covered by the rules of the first layer.

## 6 Concluding Remarks

A novel method for classifying examples that are not covered by an unordered hypothesis has been presented. The method, Rule Stretching, is based on the assumption that a more accurate classification can be made by generalising rules of a base hypothesis to cover the uncovered examples than using the standard method of assigning the examples to the majority class. The experiments, in which the inductive logic programming system Virtual Predict was used for the induction of a base hypothesis, showed that Rule Stretching performs significantly better than the standard method.

There are several directions for future research. One is to alter the least general generalisation version of the Rule Stretching algorithm, by replacing the *use_best_rule* function with some other, more elaborate, function. For example, all of the generalised rules could contribute to the decision of the correct class label to return, by using naive Bayes to find the most probable class given all of the generalised rules and their coverage. Another alternative is to replace the *classify* function with a CN2 type of function [5].

Another interesting direction for future research would be to formulate a version of Rule Stretching for some other system, such as Progol [10]. Since rules and examples are not represented as terms in Progol, it is not possible to compute the minimal generalisation by computing the least general generalisation. Instead, rules in a hypothesis could be stretched out to include uncovered examples by using relative least general generalisation [14]. However, one major drawback of using relative least general generalisation (compared to computing the least general generalisation of a pair of atoms as done in this study) is that the computational cost is significantly higher.

Yet another direction for future research would be to relax the condition in Rule Stretching that each rule is generalised minimally. One possibility is to allow the system to search in the lattice formed by the rule to be stretched and the most general rule. This would however be significantly more costly than the current approach. Another possibility would be to let the generalisation process continue after having classified an uncovered example by computing the minimal generalisations of the generalised hypothesis and a new uncovered example and stop this process only when the accuracy of the rules in the hypothesis significantly decreases.

## References

1. F. Bergadano, S. Matwin, R.S. Michalski, and J. Zhang. Learning Two-Tiered Descriptions of Flexible Concepts: The POSEIDON System. *Machine Learning*, 8(1):5–43, 1992.
2. H. Boström. Virtual Predict User Manual. Virtual Genetics Laboratory, 2001.
3. H. Boström and L. Asker. Combining divide-and-conquer and separate-and-conquer for efficient and effective rule induction. In *Proceedings of the 9th International Workshop on Inductive Logic Programming*, volume 1634, pages 33–43. Springer-Verlag, 1999.
4. H. Boström and P. Idestam-Almquist. Induction of logic programs by example-guided unfolding. *Journal of Logic Programming*, 40(2–3):159–183, 1999.
5. P. Clark and R. Boswell. Rule induction with CN2: Some recent improvements. In *Proceedings of the Fifth European Working Session on Learning*, pages 151–163, Berlin, 1991. Springer Verlag.
6. W. W. Cohen. Fast effective rule induction. In *Proceedings of the 12th International Conference on Machine Learning.* Morgan Kaufmann, 1995.
7. R.D. King, A.Srinivasan, and M.J.E. Sternberg. Relating chemical activity to structure: an examination of ilp successes. *New Generation Computing*, 13(3–4):411–433, 1995.
8. W. Van Laer, L. De Raedt, and S. Dzeroski. On multi-class problems and discretization in inductive logic programming. In *Proceedings of the 10th International Symposium on Methodologies for Intelligent Systems*. Springer-Verlag, 1997.
9. J.W. Lloyd. *Foundations of Logic Programming.* Springer-Verlag, 1987.
10. S. Muggleton. Inverse entailment and Progol. *New Generation Computing Journal*, 13:245–286, 1995.

11. S. Muggleton and M. Bain. Analogical prediction. In *Proceedings of the 9th International Workshop on Inductive Logic Programming*, volume 1634, pages 234–244. Springer-Verlag, 1999.
12. S. Muggleton, R. King, and M. Sternberg. Protein secondary structure prediction using logic-based machine learning. *Protein Engineering*, 5:647–657, 1992.
13. G. D. Plotkin. A note on inductive generalisation. *Machine Intelligence 5*, pages 153–163, 1970.
14. G.D. Plotkin. A further note on inductive generalization. In *Machine Intelligence*, volume 6, pages 101–124. Edinburgh University Press, 1971.
15. R.L. Rivest. Learning decision lists. *Machine Learning*, 2(3):229–246, 1987.

# Relational Learning Using Constrained Confidence-Rated Boosting

Susanne Hoche and Stefan Wrobel

Magdeburg University, Magdeburg, Germany,
{hoche,wrobel}@iws.cs.uni-magdeburg.de

**Abstract.** In propositional learning, boosting has been a very popular technique for increasing the accuracy of classification learners. In first-order learning, on the other hand, surprisingly little attention has been paid to boosting, perhaps due to the fact that simple forms of boosting lead to loss of comprehensibility and are too slow when used with standard ILP learners. In this paper, we show how both concerns can be addressed by using a recently proposed technique of constrained confidence-rated boosting and a fast weak ILP learner. We give a detailed description of our algorithm and show on two standard benchmark problems that indeed such a weak learner can be boosted to perform comparably to state-of-the-art ILP systems while maintaining acceptable comprehensibility and obtaining short run-times.

## 1 Introduction

In recent years, the field of Machine Learning has seen a very strong growth of interest in a class of methods that have collectively become known as ensemble methods. The general goal and approach of such methods is to increase predictive accuracy by basing the prediction not only on a single hypothesis but on a suitable combination of an entire set of hypotheses. *Boosting* is a particularly attractive class of ensemble methods since on the one hand it has originated in theoretical studies of learnability, but on the other hand has also been developed into practical algorithms that have demonstrated superior performance on quite a broad range of application problems. Boosting constructs multiple hypotheses by first calling a "weak" learner on the given examples to produce a first hypothesis. During each subsequent round of boosting, the weight of examples correctly handled by the hypothesis induced in the previous round is decreased, while the weight of examples incorrectly handled is increased. In the resulting set of hypotheses, each hypothesis gets a voting weight corresponding to its prediction confidence, and the total prediction is obtained by summing up all these votes.

Given the set of boosting approaches in propositional learning, it is somewhat surprising that boosting has not received comparable attention within ILP, with a notable exception of Quinlan's [8] initial experiments. There are two possible reasons for this situation which appear especially relevant. Firstly, understandability of results has always been a central concern of ILP researchers beyond accuracy. Unfortunately, if, as in Quinlan's study, one uses the classic form of

C. Rouveirol and M. Sebag (Eds.): ILP 2001, LNAI 2157, pp. 51–64, 2001.

confidence-rated boosting (Adaboost.M1) the result will be quite a large set of rules each of which in addition has an attached positive or negative voting weight. To understand the behaviour of one rule in this rule set, it is necessary to consider all other rules and their relative weights, making it quite difficult to grasp the results of the learner. Secondly, in propositional learning, boosting is often applied simply by using an unchanged existing propositional learner as a basis. If one carries this over to ILP (e.g. Quinlan simply used FFOIL as a base learner), the run-times of such a boosted ILP learner clearly would be problematic due to the high effort already expended by a typical ILP system.

In this paper, we show that both of these concerns can be addressed by suitably combining recent advances in boosting algorithms with a fast weak learner. In particular, we show how *constrained confidence-rated boosting* (CCRB), which is our denomination and interpretation of the approach described in [2], can be used to significantly enhance the understandability of boosted learning results by restricting the kinds of rule sets allowed. We combine this with a greedy top-down weak learner based on the concept of *foreign links* introduced in Midos [14] which uses a limited form of look-ahead and optimizes the same heuristic criterion as used in [2]. In an empirical evaluation on two known hard problems of ILP, the well-studied domains of mutagenicity and Qualitative Structure Activity Relationships (QSARs), we show that indeed such a simple weak learner together with CCRB achieves accuracies comparable to much more powerful ILP systems, while maintaining acceptable comprehensibility and obtaining short run-times.

The paper is organized as follows. In section 2, we review boosting, and motivate the basic ideas of constrained confidence-rated boosting based on [2]. In section 3, we briefly describe our foreign link based weak learner and give a more detailed account of the heuristic evaluation functions employed to guide the search in the constrained hypothesis space. Section 4 details how the hypotheses generated by the weak learner are used in the framework of CCRB. Our experimental evaluation of the approach is described and discussed in section 5. In section 6, we discuss related work in more detail. Section 7 contains our conclusions and some pointers to future work.

## 2 Boosting

Boosting is a method for improving the predictive accuracy of a learning system by means of combining a set of classifiers constructed by a weak learner into a single, strong hypothesis [10,8,7]. It is known to work well with most unstable classifier systems, i.e. systems where small changes to the training data lead to notable changes in the learned classifier. The idea is to "boost" a weak learning algorithm performing only slightly better than random guessing into an arbitrarily accurate learner by repeatedly calling the weak learner on changing distributions over the training instances and combining the set of weak hypotheses into one strong hypothesis. In the resulting set of hypotheses, i.e. the strong hypothesis, each hypothesis gets a voting weight corresponding to its prediction confidence, and the total prediction is obtained by summing up all these votes.

A probability distribution over the set of training instances is maintained. The probabilities model the weights associated with each training instance and indicate the influence of an instance when building a classifier. Initially, all instances have equal influence on the construction of the weak hypotheses. In each iterative call of the learner, a weak hypothesis is learned, which computes a prediction confidence for each example. How this confidence is determined is a design issue of the weak learning algorithm and will, for our approach, be discussed in detail in section 3.2.

On each round of boosting, the distribution over the training instances is modified in accordance with the learned weak hypothesis, i.e. in dependence of its assigned prediction confidence and the examples covered by it. The weights of misclassified instances are increased and, in analogy, those of correctly classified instances are decreased according to the confidence of the learned weak hypothesis. Thus, correctly classified instances will have less influence on the construction of the weak hypothesis in the next iteration, and misclassified instances will have a stronger influence. That way, the learner is confronted in each new round of boosting with a modified learning task and forced to focus on the examples in the training set which have not yet been correctly classified. Finally, all weak hypotheses learned are combined into one strong hypothesis. An instance $x$ is classified by the strong hypothesis by adding up the prediction confidence of each weak hypothesis covering $x$ and predicting the class $y$ of $x$ as positive if the sum of confidences of all hypotheses covering $x$ is positive, otherwise predicting $y$ as negative.

The classic form of (unconstrained) confidence-rated boosting (Adaboost.M1) yields quite a large set of rules each of which in addition has an attached positive or negative voting weight. Moreover, each weak hypothesis may vote with different confidences for different examples. This way, rules inferring the target predicate are learned as well as rules for the negation of the target predicate.

In our ILP setting, we will, in contrast, firstly assume that the weak learner produces on each iteration a hypothesis in form of a single Horn clause $H \leftarrow L_1, L_2, \cdots, L_n$ $[c]$ with an associated real number $c$, where $H$ is the atom $p(X_1, \cdots, X_{a(p)})$ and $p$ the target predicate of arity $a(p)$, the $L_i$ are atoms with background predicates $p_i$, and $c$ represents the prediction confidence of the hypothesis. This prediction confidence is used as the voting weight of the hypothesis on all examples covered by it, where large absolute values indicate high confidence. Moreover, we will restrict the weak hypothesis to vote "0" to abstain on all examples not covered by it.

Thereby, the semantics of a rule is, as opposed to usual ILP practice, determined by the sign of its attached prediction confidence. A hypothesis $H \leftarrow L_1, L_2, \cdots, L_n$ $[c]$ such that $c > 0$ implies that $H$ is true. It is interpreted as classifying all instances covered by it as positive with prediction confidence $c$. $H$ $[c]$ such that $c < 0$ implies that $H$ is false and is interpreted as classifying each instance as negative.

Here is an example of a boosting result consisting of 7 weak hypotheses when learning a target predicate $p$.

| | | |
|---|---|---|
| 1. p(X) ← q(X,a). [0.2] | 4. p(X) ← q(X,Y), v(Y). | [-0.6] |
| 2. p(X) ← q(X,Y), r(Y). [0.9] | 5. p(X) ← r(X). | [-0.5] |
| 3. p(X) ← s(X). [0.1] | 6. p(X) ← q(X,b). | [-0.3] |
| | 7. p(X) ← t(X). | [-0.9] |

In order to classify a new instance about which we know q(1,a), v(a), t(1), s(1), we need to check which hypotheses cover this example. Here, we find that 1,3,4,7 cover the example, so we compute the sum of their confidences, yielding $0.2+0.1-0.6-0.9 = -1.2 < 0$, and the instance is classified as negative. In other words, to understand the behaviour of one rule in this rule set, it is necessary to consider all other rules and their relative weights, making it quite difficult to grasp the results of the learner.

In our approach of *constrained confidence-rated boosting*, which is our interpretation of the ideas in [2], we will restrict each hypothesis to either of two forms. A hypothesis is either positively correlated, i.e. predicting the positive class, and equipped with a positive prediction confidence, or it is the default hypothesis $p(X_1, \cdots, X_{a(p)})$ with an assigned negative confidence. Constraining the hypotheses to either of these two forms ensures that the resulting set of hypotheses can be more easily interpreted. Namely, in order to appraise the quality of a hypothesis, it suffices to consider its assigned prediction confidence in proportion to just the weight of the default hypothesis, instead of having to consider all other hypotheses and their assigned weights.

Using the additional restrictions, we see for the above example that with CCRB only results of the following form would be allowed, making learning harder but guaranteeing better understandability:

| | | |
|---|---|---|
| 1. p(X) ← q(X,a). | [0.2] | 4. p(X). [-0.3] |
| 2. p(X) ← q(X,Y), r(Y). | [0.9] | |
| 3. p(X) ← s(X). | [0.1] | |

Since the same weak hypothesis might be generated more than once by the weak learner, we can further simplify the set of resulting hypotheses by summarizing hypotheses $H\ [c_1], \cdots, H\ [c_n], 1 \leq i \leq n$, which only differ with regard to their assigned confidences. A set of such identical hypotheses can be replaced by a single hypothesis $H'\ [c], H' = H_i, 1 \leq i \leq n$, with $c = \sum_{1 \leq i \leq n} c_i$.

The constraint on the weak hypotheses requires the weak learner to employ a search strategy guaranteeing that only positively correlated hypotheses with a positive prediction confidence are learned, or that the default hypothesis is opted for if no such positive correlated hypothesis can be induced from the training instances. [2] offer a theoretically well founded heuristics for this problem which will be discussed in more detail in the following sections.

## 3 The Weak Relational Learner

Our greedy top-down weak learner is using a refinement operator based on the concept of *foreign links* introduced in Midos [14]. This refinement operator is elucidated in detail in the following section. We will then discuss in section 3.2 the heuristics guiding the search of the greedy weak learner based on this refinement operator in the hypothesis space. In Table 1, we give a more concise description of the weak greedy learner embedded into the framework of constrained confidence-rated boosting. In the following, references to steps in Table 1 will be indicated by "T1._".

### 3.1 The Refinement Operator

The refinement operator $\rho$ is based on the concept of *foreign links* introduced in Midos [14]. The hypothesis space consists of non-recursive, function-free Horn clauses $C = H \leftarrow B$, where $H$ is the atom $p(X_1, \cdots, X_{a(p)})$ and $p$ the target predicate of arity $a(p)$. In order to constrain the complexity of the hypothesis space, our weak learner employs a foreign literal restriction [14] as declarative bias which is a constrained form of linkedness of clauses. When specializing a clause $C$ by adding a new literal $L$, $L$ must share at least one variable with previous literals in $C$. The foreign literal restriction further confines the set of alternative literals by means of an explicit definition of those literals and variable positions that are to be considered for refinement. Hypotheses are only refined along link paths designated by these definitions, or so called foreign links. For a clause $C = L_1, \cdots, L_n$, a foreign link between a variable $V$ first occurring at position $p_i$ in literal $L_i$ with predicate name $r$, and a different variable $U$ first occurring at position $p_j$ in $L_j$ with predicate name $s$ is defined as $r[p_i] \rightarrow s[p_j]$.

Furthermore, we employ a limited form of look-ahead in our refinement operator in order to avoid the shortsightedness problem with respect to existential variables in the hypotheses generated by the greedy weak relational learner. Merely introducing new existential variables in a clause will probably not lead to notable changes, and the greedy learner is apt to rather select a literal that restricts existing variables. Thus, when specializing a clause $C$ into $C' = C, L$ by means of adding a new literal $L$ to $C$, we concurrently add to the set $\rho(C)$ of refinements of $C$ all specializations of $C'$ obtained by successively instantiating the new variables in $L$.

Given, for example, a target predicate active/1, a predicate atm/3, and a foreign link declaration active[1] $\rightarrow$ atm[1], applying $\rho$ on $C = \text{active}(X_1)$ would result in the specializations

$$\begin{array}{l}
\text{active}(X_1) \leftarrow \text{atm}(X_1, X_2, X_3), \\
\text{active}(X_1) \leftarrow \text{atm}(X_1, c, X_3), \\
\text{active}(X_1) \leftarrow \text{atm}(X_1, cl, X_3), \\
\text{active}(X_1) \leftarrow \text{atm}(X_1, X_2, X_3), X_3 \leq -0.782, \\
\text{active}(X_1) \leftarrow \text{atm}(X_1, X_2, X_3), X_3 > -0.782, \\
\text{active}(X_1) \leftarrow \text{atm}(X_1, X_2, X_3), X_3 \leq \phantom{-}1.002, \\
\text{active}(X_1) \leftarrow \text{atm}(X_1, X_2, X_3), X_3 > \phantom{-}1.002,
\end{array}$$

if $X_2$ is a nominal variable with the domain $\{c, cl\}$, and $X_3$ is a continuous variable with discretization $\mathcal{D} = [-0.782, 1.002]$.

More generally, let $L = r(V_1, \cdots, V_{a(r)})$ be a literal with predicate name $r$ of arity $a(r)$, and let $Vars(L)$ denote the variables in $L$ not occurring in the clause

$C$ to be specialized. Then, adding $C' = C, L$ to $\rho(C)$ results in additionally adding to $\rho(C)$ the following refinements:

1. $C, L\theta_i^j, 1 \leq i \leq a(r), 1 \leq j \leq |Val(V_i)|$, such that $V_i \in Vars(L)$ and $V_i$ is a variable with nominal values, where $Val(V_i)$ denotes the domain of variable $V_i$ and $L\theta_i^j = r(V_1, \cdots, V_{i-1}, V_i/c_j, V_{i+1}, \cdots, V_{a(r)}), c_j \in Val(V_i)$
2. $C, L, \rho(V_i), 1 \leq i \leq a(r)$ such that $V_i \in Vars(L)$ and $V_i$ is a variable with continuous values. $\rho(V_i)$ is defined for variables $V_i$ with continuous values as follows. If $\mathcal{D} = \{d_1, \cdots, d_n\}$ is the discretization of the values of $V_i$, then for any $d_k$ in $\mathcal{D}$ $V_i \leq d_k$ and $V_i > d_k$ are in $\rho(V_i)$.

Let $C = L_1, \cdots, L_n$ be a clause to be specialized, and let $U_1, \cdots, U_{k-1}, U_{k+1}, \cdots, U_{a(s)}$ be new variables not occurring in $C$. Let $a(r)$ denote the arity of a literal with predicate name $r$, and let $Val(V)$ denote the domain of a variable $V$. Furthermore, let $F$ be the set of all foreign links defined for the literals at hand. Then the refinement operator $\rho$ can be defined as follows: for any $L_i = r(V_1, \cdots, V_{a(r)})$ in $C$ such that $r[m] \rightarrow s[k] \in F$,

1. $L_1, \cdots, L_n, s(U_1, \cdots, U_{k-1}, V_m, U_{k+1}, \cdots, U_{a(s)}) \in \rho(C)$
2. $L_1, \cdots, L_n, s(U_1, \cdots, U_{k-1}, V_m, U_{k+1}, \cdots, U_{a(s)})\theta_l^j \in \rho(C)$ for $1 \leq l \leq a(s), 1 \leq j \leq |Val(U_l)|, U_l$ a variable with nominal values
3. $L_1, \cdots, L_n, s(U_1, \cdots, U_{k-1}, V_m, U_{k+1}, \cdots, U_{a(s)}), \rho(U_l) \in \rho(C)$ for $1 \leq l \leq a(s), U_l$ a variable with continuous values.

### 3.2 Search Strategy

Our weak first-order inductive learner accepts as input instances from a set $E = E^+ \cup E^-$ of training examples along with a probability distribution $D$ over the training instances. The background knowledge is provided in form of a set $B$ of ground facts over background predicates. However, we will sometimes write $E^+$ and $E^-$ somewhat differently than used in ILP, and will say that $E = \{(x, 1) \mid x \in E^+\} \cup \{(x, -1) \mid \neg x \in E^-\}$.

To avoid overfitting in the weak learner, the training instances are randomly split into two sets, $\mathcal{G}, \mathcal{P}$, used to specialize clauses and to prune these refinements later on, respectively. Starting with the target predicate, the weak learner greedily generates specializations which are positively correlated with the training instances and thus have a positive prediction confidence on the training set.

When thinking about strategies to guide the search of a greedy learner, entropy based methods like information gain represent an obvious choice. However, the theoretical framework of boosting provides us with a guiding strategy based on one of the specific features of boosting, namely the probability distribution being modified in each iterative call of the weak learner.

As suggested by [2], the training error can be minimized by searching in each round of boosting for a weak hypothesis maximizing the objective function

$$z(C) =_{def.} \left(\sqrt{w_+(C, \mathcal{G})} - \sqrt{w_-(C, \mathcal{G})}\right)^2 \quad (1)$$

which is based on the collective weight of all positive and negative instances in $\mathcal{G}$ covered by clause $C$. For a clause $C$ and a set $\mathcal{S}$, the two weight functions $w_+, w_-$ are defined by

$$w_+(C,\mathcal{S}) =_{def.} \sum_{(x_i,y_i)\in\mathcal{S} \text{ covered by } C, y_i=1} D_i^t \tag{2}$$

$$w_-(C,\mathcal{S}) =_{def.} \sum_{(x_i,y_i)\in\mathcal{S} \text{ covered by } C, y_i=-1} D_i^t.$$

Since clauses $C$ maximizing $z(C)$ may be negatively correlated with the positive class, we restrict, as proposed in [2], the search to positively correlated clauses, i.e. to clauses maximizing the objective function $\tilde{z}$ defined as

$$\tilde{z}(C) =_{def.} \sqrt{w_+(C,\mathcal{G})} - \sqrt{w_-(C,\mathcal{G})}. \tag{3}$$

The refinement operator $\rho$ of the weak relational learner iteratively refines, as described in detail in section 3.1, the clause $C$ currently maximizing the objective function $\tilde{z}$ until either a clause $C'$ is found with hitherto maximal $\tilde{z}(C')$ that covers only positive examples, or until the objective function $\tilde{z}$ can not be further maximized (T1.2d).

The positively correlated clause $C$ resulting from this greedy refinement process is subject to overfitting on the training instances, and is thus immediately examined to see whether it can be pruned. Namely, all generalizations of $C$ resulting from deleting single literals and constants in $C$ from right to left are generated (T1.2e).

The objective function (3) is only maximized on the set $\mathcal{G}$ based on which rules are generated by the weak learner. However, the evaluation of the prediction confidence of a weak hypothesis is based on the entire set of training examples. Thus, it is possible for the weak learner to learn a hypothesis $C'[c], c < 0$, which is, on the entire training set, negatively correlated with the positive class. Such hypotheses are not considered in order to ensure the constraint for a weak hypothesis to be either positively correlated or to be the default hypothesis. Thus, generalizations of $C$ which have a non-positive prediction confidence on the whole training set are ruled out (T1.2f). If no generalization of $C$ with a positive prediction confidence exists, the default hypothesis is chosen as current weak hypothesis (T1.2g). The prediction confidence of a clause $C$ on a set $\mathcal{S}$ is defined as

$$c(C,\mathcal{S}) =_{def.} \frac{w_+(C,\mathcal{S}) + \frac{1}{2N}}{w_-(C,\mathcal{S}) + \frac{1}{2N}}, \tag{4}$$

where $N$ is the number of training instances and $\frac{1}{2N}$ is a smoothing constant applied to avoid extreme estimates when $w_-(C,\mathcal{S})$ is small.

All generalizations of $C$ with a positive prediction confidence on the entire training set are then evaluated with respect to their confidence on the set $\mathcal{G}$ and their coverage and accuracy on the set $\mathcal{P}$. This kind of evaluation is proposed by [2] who define, based on the definition of the loss of a clause $C$ with associated confidence $c(C, \mathcal{G})$ of [2], a loss function for a clause $C$ as

$$loss(C) =_{def.} (1 - (w_+(C, \mathcal{P}) + w_-(C, \mathcal{P}))) + w_+(C, \mathcal{P}) \cdot e^{(-c(C,\mathcal{G}))} + w_-(C, \mathcal{P}) \cdot e^{(c(C,\mathcal{G}))}. \tag{5}$$

This loss function is minimized over all generalizations of $C$ with a positive prediction confidence (T1.2(h)i).

In a last step, the positively correlated generalization $C'$ of $C$ with minimal $loss(C')$ is compared to the default hypothesis with respect to the expected training error (T1.2(h)ii). Since a positively correlated clause is compared to the default hypothesis predicting the negative class, the objective function to be maximized is in this case $z$ as defined in equation (1). Whichever of these two hypotheses maximizes $z$ is chosen as the weak hypothesis of the current iteration of the greedy learner.

## 4 Constrained Confidence-Rated Boosting of a Weak Relational Learner

In this section, following [2], we explain how the weak hypotheses generated in each iteration of the weak greedy learner are used in the framework of CCRB [2]. The weak learner is invoked $T$ times. Let $C_t$ denote the weak hypothesis generated in the $t$-th iteration based on the refinement operator and the heuristic search strategy described in the previous section.

$C_t$ is used in function $h_t : X \to \Re$,

$$h_t(x) = \begin{cases} c(C_t, E) & \text{if e = (x, y) is covered by } C_t \\ 0 & \text{else,} \end{cases}$$

mapping each instance $x$ to a real-valued number, i.e. to the prediction confidence of $C_t$ on the entire training set if $x$ is covered by $C_t$, and to 0 otherwise (T1.2i).

Before starting the next round of boosting, the probability distribution over the training instances, which is initially uniform, is updated by means of $h_t$, namely by determining

$$D_i^{t'} = \frac{D_i^t}{e^{(y_i \cdot h_t(x_i))}}. \tag{6}$$

This way, the weights of all instances $x$ not covered by the weak hypothesis $C_t$, i.e. such that $h_t(x) = 0$, are not modified, whereas the weights of all positive and negative instances covered by $C_t$ are decreased and increased, respectively, in proportion to the prediction confidence of $C_t$ (T1.2j) by means of $h_t$.

Then, the sum of the resulting weights is normalized

$$D_i^{t+1} = \frac{D_i^{t'}}{\sum_i D_i^{t'}}, 1 \leq i \leq N, \tag{7}$$

so as to serve as the probability distribution of the next iteration.

**Table 1.** Constrained Confidence-Rated Boosting Algorithm

---

Let $N$ denote the number of training instances $e = (x_i, y_i) \in E = E^+ \cup E^-$, $p$ the target predicate of arity $a(p)$, and let $T$ denote the total number of iterations of the weak learner. Furthermore, let $w_+, w_-$ denote the weight functions defined according to equation (2), $c(C, \mathcal{S})$ the prediction confidence of a clause $C$ on a set $\mathcal{S}$ defined according to equation (4), and $\tilde{z}$ the objective function defined according to equation (3).

1. **Set** $D_i^1 := \frac{1}{N}$ for $1 \leq i \leq N$
2. **For** $t = 1 \ldots T$
   (a) **Split** training set $E$ randomly into $\mathcal{G}$ and $\mathcal{P}$ according to $D_t$ such that $\sum_{(x_i,y_i)\in\mathcal{G}} D_i^t \approx \frac{2}{3}$
   (b) $C := p(X_1, \cdots, X_{a(p)})$
   (c) $\tilde{Z} := 0$
   (d) **While** $w_-(C, \mathcal{G}) > 0$
      i. **Let** $C' := argmax_{C'' \in \rho(C)}\{\tilde{z}(C'')\}$
      ii. **Let** $\tilde{Z}' := \tilde{z}(C')$
      iii. **If** $\tilde{Z}' - \tilde{Z} \leq 0$ exit loop
      iv. **Else** $C := C'$, $\tilde{Z} := \tilde{Z}'$
   (e) $Prunes(C) := \{p(X_1, \cdots, X_{a(p)}) \leftarrow B \mid C = p(X_1, \cdots, X_{a(p)}) \leftarrow BB'\}$
   (f) **Remove** from $Prunes(C)$ all clauses $C'$ where $c(C', E) \leq 0$
   (g) **If** $Prunes(C) = \emptyset$ let $C_t := p(X_1, \cdots, X_{a(p)})$
   (h) **Else**
      i. $C' := argmin_{C'' \in Prunes(C)}\{loss(C'')\}$, where $loss(C'')$ is defined according to equation (5)
      ii. **Let** $C_t := argmax_{C'' \in \{C', p(X_1, \cdots, X_{a(p)})\}}\{\left(\sqrt{w_+(C'', \mathcal{G})} - \sqrt{w_-(C'', \mathcal{G})}\right)^2\}$
   (i) $h_t : X \to \Re$ is the function

$$h_t(x) = \begin{cases} c(C_t, E) & \text{if e = (x, y) is covered by } C_t \\ 0 & \text{else} \end{cases}$$

   (j) **Update** the probability distribution $D_t$ according to

$$D_i^{t'} = \frac{D_i^t}{e^{(y_i \cdot h_t(x_i))}}$$

$$\begin{cases} = D_i^t & \text{if } e = (x_i, y_i) \text{ not covered by } C_t \\ > D_i^t & \text{if } e \text{ covered by } C_t \text{ and } e \in E^- \\ < D_i^t & \text{if } e \text{ covered by } C_t \text{ and } e \in E^+ \end{cases}$$

$$D_i^{t+1} = \frac{D_i^{t'}}{\sum_i D_i^{t'}}, 1 \leq i \leq N$$

3. **Construct** the strong hypothesis

$$H(x) := sign\left(\sum_{C_t:(x,y) \text{ covered by } C_t} c(C_t, E)\right)$$

---

After the last iteration of the weak learner, the strong hypothesis is defined by means of all weak hypotheses induced by the training instances. For each instance $x$ the prediction confidences of all hypotheses covering $x$ are summed up. If this sum is positive, the strong hypothesis classifies $x$ as positive, otherwise $x$ is classified as negative:

$$H(x) := sign\left( \sum_{C_t:(x,y) \text{ covered by } C_t} c(C_t, E) \right) \tag{8}$$

## 5 Empirical Evaluation

We conducted an empirical evaluation of our approach to CCRB on two domains, namely on the domain of mutagenicity [13], which is a thoroughly investigated benchmark problem for ILP learners, and on the domain of Quantitative Structure Activity Relationships (QSARs), another important test-bed for ILP-systems [4,5]. The weak learner is invoked $T = 100$ times. Although the number $T$ of iterations can be automatically determined by cross-validation [2], we treat $T$ as fixed in our experiments.

**Mutagenicity:** The task is to predict the mutagenicity of a set of small, highly structurally heterogeneous molecules (aromatic and heteroaromatic nitro compounds). Mutagenic compounds are often known to be carcinogenic and to cause damage to DNA. Not all compounds can be empirically tested for mutagenesis, and the prediction of mutagenicity is vital to understanding and predicting carcinogenesis. A molecule is described by its atoms, the bonds between them, global properties of and chemical structures present in the molecule.

Several relational descriptions of the domain are available [12], ranging from a weakly structured description $\mathcal{B}_2$ only involving the atoms and bonds of the molecules, to a strongly structured description $\mathcal{B}_4$ also involving high level chemical concepts present in the molecules. We conducted our experiment with $C^2$RIB, which stands for **C**onstrained **C**onfidence-**R**ated **ILP** **B**oosting, on the strongly structured description $\mathcal{B}_4$ restricted to a subset of 188 so called regression-friendly compounds 125 of which are classified as having positive levels of mutagenicity. The predictive accuracy is estimated by 10-fold-cross-validation, where we used the same folds as [12] for their experiments with Progol. The accuracy obtained in our experiment with $C^2$RIB is displayed in Table 2 together with reference results on the 188–dataset using background knowledge $\mathcal{B}_4$ and the sources from which the results are reported. Runtime[1] of $C^2$RIB averages to 7 minutes for 100 iterations, as compared to 307 minutes for Progol on all 188 compounds (the run-time for Progol was determined in experiments we performed on our sparc SUNW, Ultra-4, in which we obtained the same accuracy as [13]).

In Table 2, we show only results obtained on the most comprehensive set of background knowledge, $\mathcal{B}_4$, which we have worked with.[2] As can be seen

[1] All run-times are referring to results obtained on a sparc SUNW, Ultra-4.

[2] Additional results have been obtained by other authors on the $\mathcal{B}_3$ dataset [12], in particular by STILL [11] ($87 \pm 8$) and G-Net [1] ($91 \pm 8$).

from the table, $C^2$RIB performs on par with other ILP learners on the 10-fold-cross-validation data sets of the mutagenicity domain. Moreover, the results are obtained in reasonable time, and the final hypotheses represent fairly comprehensible results. The number of literals in the final hypothesis averages to 64 (32 clauses on average, where the body of each clause averagely comprises two literals), as compared to the result of averagely 46 literals in the hypotheses obtained by FOIL as published in [12]), and 28 literals on average in the hypotheses obtained by Progol. A final hypothesis obtained by $C^2$RIB is displayed in Table 3 in the appendix.

**QSARs:** The task is to construct a predictive theory relating the activity of chemical compounds to their molecular structure. Often, these so called Qualitative Structure Activity Relationships cannot be derived solely from physical theory, and experimental evidence is needed. Again, not all compounds can be empirically evaluated, and machine learning methods offer a possibility to investigate QSARs. We conducted our experiments on a 5-fold-cross-validation series of 55 pyramidine compounds as described in [5]. A pyramidine compound is described by chemical groups that can be added at three possible substitution positions. A chemical group is an atom or a set of structurally connected atoms each of which is described by a set of chemical properties. QSARs problems are in general regression problems, i.e. not a class but real numbers must be predicted. To get around this problem for ILP, the greater activity relationship between pairs of compounds is learned. Rules learned for this relationship can then be employed to rank drugs by their activity. As opposed to [4,5], we restrict our experiments to the prediction of the greater activity relationship between pairs of the 55 compounds.

We conducted experiments on the same data sets with the systems Progol [6] and FOIL [9] in order to obtain reference results on this domain (Table 2). The predictive accuracy obtained by $C^2$RIB on the 5-fold-cross-validation data sets of QSARs domain is slightly higher than the ones obtained with the other two systems (however still within the range of the standard deviations). Runtime of $C^2$RIB averages to 57 minutes for 100 iterations, as compared to 372 and 0.7 minutes for Progol and FOIL, respectively. The number of literals in the final hypotheses obtained by $C^2$RIB averages to 142 (71 clauses on average, where the body of each clause averagely comprises two literals), as compared to 140 and 154 literals on average in the hypotheses obtained by FOIL and Progol, respectively. The fact that FOIL yields good results in very short run-times suggests to investigate why FOIL's heuristics are so successful and how elements of FOIL could be incorporated in our weak learner.

## 6 Related Work

The work described in this paper is based on recent research in the area of propositional boosting, and centrally builds on Cohen and Singer's [2] approach to constrained confidence-rated boosting. However, the properties of the weak learner embedded in the boosting framework, namely the declarative bias em-

**Table 2.** Accuracy, standard deviation, average run-time and number of literals in the final hypotheses on the $188 - \mathcal{B}_4$ mutagenicity dataset and the QSARs dataset

| | | $C^2$RIB | FOIL | Fors | Progol |
|---|---|---|---|---|---|
| Mutagenicity | Accuracy ± StdDev | $88.0 \pm 6.0$ | $82.0 \pm 3.0$ [13] | $89.0 \pm 6.0$ [3] | $88.0 \pm 2.0$ [13] |
| | ⊘ Runtime (minutes) | 7 | n/a | n/a | 307 |
| | ⊘ Number of literals | 64 | 46 | n/a | 28 |
| QSARs | Accuracy ± StdDev | $83.2 \pm 3.0$ | $82.9 \pm 2.7$ | n/a | $79.8 \pm 3.7$ |
| | ⊘ Runtime (minutes) | 57 | 0.7 | n/a | 372 |
| | ⊘ Number of literals | 142 | 140 | n/a | 154 |

ployed in form of a foreign literal restriction, the application of look-ahead, and the preclusion of hypotheses negatively correlated with the positive class, distinguish our work from the approach of [2].

The ILP work probably closest related to our approach is that of Quinlan [8]. However, Quinlan uses, in conjunction with Adaboost.M1, a standard ILP learner (FFOIL), so that the boosted ILP learner can be expected to produce fairly large run-times due to the high effort already expended by FFOIL. Moreover, FFOIL itself generates as the first-order learner embedded into the boosting framework weak hypotheses each of which comprises a set of clauses. Thus, the resulting strong hypothesis is apt to be highly complex. Lastly, this approach works, due to the absence of a confidence measure, with equal voting weights for all weak hypotheses, and, instead of a probability distribution over the training instances a re-sampling procedure is used to approximate the weights of the examples.

The weak learner employed in our approach is based on the refinement operator and declarative bias in form of *foreign links* introduced in Midos [14]. Additionally, a limited form of look-ahead has been employed in order to avoid the shortsightedness problem with respect to existential variables in the hypotheses generated by the greedy weak relational learner.

## 7 Conclusion

In this paper, we have presented an approach to boosting in first order learning. Our approach, which we have termed *constrained confidence rated boosting*, builds on recent advances in the area of propositional boosting; in particular, it adapts the approach of Cohen and Singer [2] to the first order domain. The primary advantage of constrained confidence rated boosting is that the resulting rule sets are restricted to a much simpler and more understandable format than the one produced by unconstrained versions, e.g. AdaBoost.M1, as it has been used in the only prior work on boosting in ILP by Quinlan [8]. On two standard benchmark problems, we have shown that by using an appropriate first order weak learner with look-ahead, it is possible to design a learning system that produces results that are comparable to much more powerful ILP-learners both in accuracy and in comprehensibility while achieving short run-times due to the simplicity of the weak learner.

These encouraging results need to be substantiated in future work, in particular in the direction of examining other points in the power/run-time trade-off of the weak learner. The current weak learner has short run-times and already reaches comparable results to other non-boosted systems, but it appears possible to make this weak learner slightly more powerful by adding in more of the standard elements of "full-blown" ILP-learners. While this would certainly slow down the system, it would be an interesting goal of further research to determine exactly the right balance between speed and accuracy of the weak learner.

This work was partially supported by DFG (German Science Foundation), project FOR345/1-1TP6.

## References

1. C. Anglano, A. Giordana, G. Lo Bello, and L. Saitta. An experimental evaluation of coevolutive concept learning. In J. Shavlik, editor, *Proceedings of the 15th ICML*, 1998.
2. W. Cohen and Y. Singer. A Simple, Fast, and Effective Rule Learner. *Proc. of 16th National Conference on Artificial Intelligence*, 1999.
3. A. Karalic. *First Order Regression.* PhD thesis, University of Ljubljana, Faculty of Computer Science, Ljubljana, Slovenia, 1995.
4. R.D. King, S. Muggleton, R.A. Lewis, and M.J.E. Sternberg. Drug design by machine learning: The use of inductive logic programming to model the structure activity relationships of trimethoprim analogues binding to dihydrofolate reductase. *Proceedings of the National Academy of Sciences of the United States of America* 89(23):11322-11326, 1992.
5. R.D. King, A. Srinivasan, and M. Sternberg. Relating chemical activity to structure: An examination of ILP successes. *New Generation Computing, Special issue on Inductive Logic Programming* 13(3-4):411-434, 1995.
6. S. Muggleton. Inverse Entailment and Progol. *New Generation Computing*, 13:245-286, 1995.
7. J.R. Quinlan. Bagging, boosting, and C4.5. In *Proc. of 14th National Conference on Artificial Intelligence*, 1996.
8. J.R. Quinlan. Boosting First-Order Learning. *Algorithmic Learning Theory*, 1996.
9. J.R. Quinlan and R. M. Cameron-Jones. FOIL: A Midterm Report. In P. Brazdil, editor, *Proceedings of the 6th European Conference on Machine Learning*, volume 667, pages 3-20. Springer-Verlag, 1993.
10. R.E. Schapire. Theoretical views of boosting and applications. In *Proceedings of the 10th International Conference on Algorithmic Learning Theory*, 1999.
11. M. Sebag and C. Rouveirol. Resource-bounded Relational Reasoning: Induction and Deduction through Stochastic Matching. *Machine Learning* , 38:41-62, 2000.
12. A. Srinivasan, S. Muggleton, and R. King. Comparing the use of background knowledge by inductive logic programming systems. *Proceedings of the 5th International Workshop on Inductive Logic Programming*, 1995.
13. A. Srinivasan, S. Muggleton, M.J.E. Sternberg, and R.D. King. Theories for mutagenicity: A study in first-order and feature-based induction. *Artificial Intelligence*, 85:277-299, 1996.
14. S. Wrobel. An algorithm for multi-relational discovery of subgroups. In J. Komrowski and J. Zytkow, editors, *Principles of Data Mining and Knowledge Discovery: First European Symposium - Proceedings of the PKDD-97*, pages 78-87, 1997.

# A Sample Output from $C^2$RIB

**Table 3.** A strong hypothesis obtained from $C^2$RIB

DEFAULT RULE:
active(A). [-1.40575]

POSITIVE RULES:
active(A) ← logp(A,C),C>2.0,logp(A,D),D≤4.0. [0.00082336]
active(A) ← lumo(A,C),C> -2.0,lumo(A,D),D≤ -1.2. [0.0210132]
active(A) ← logp(A,C),C>2.0. [0.115733]
active(A) ← lumo(A,C),C> -2.0,logp(A,D),D≤3.0,atm(A,E,F,29,G). [0.175073]
active(A) ← atm(A,C,D,35,E). [0.176489]
active(A) ← atm(A,C,D,1,E). [0.197106]
active(A) ← ringSize5(A,C). [0.215675]
active(A) ← atm(A,C,D,27,E). [0.231689]
active(A) ← lumo(A,C),C≤ -1.2. [0.283592]
active(A) ← lumo(A,C),C> -2.0,atm(A,D,E,29,F). [0.355777]
active(A) ← logp(A,C),C>5.0. [0.470995]
active(A) ← bond(A,C,D,5). [0.582912]
active(A) ← atm(A,C,D,26,E),atm(A,F,G,1,H),lumo(A,I),I≤ -1.2. [0.584057]
active(A) ← atm(A,C,cl,D,E),bond(F,C,G,H). [0.763684]
active(A) ← atm(A,C,D,26,E),logp(A,F),F>3.0. [0.778605]
active(A) ← atm(A,C,D,27,E),logp(A,F),F>2.0,logp(A,G),G≤3.0. [0.832673]
active(A) ← atm(A,C,D,27,E),ringSize5(A,F). [0.925553]
active(A) ← atm(A,C,D,230,E). [0.977438]
active(A) ← logp(A,C),C>3.0,ringSize5(A,D). [1.00485]
active(A) ← atm(A,C,D,16,E). [1.01437]
active(A) ← atm(A,C,D,32,E),bond(F,G,C,2). [1.1001]
active(A) ← carbon5aromaticRing(A,C). [1.4434]
active(A) ← bond(A,C,D,3). [1.46341]
active(A) ← lumo(A,C),C≤ -2.0. [1.64408]
active(A) ← ringSize5(A,C),logp(A,D),D>4.0. [1.69492]
active(A) ← atm(A,C,D,28,E). [1.69956]
active(A) ← anthracene(A,C). [2.21461]
active(A) ← carbon6Ring(A,C). [3.06628]
active(A) ← phenanthrene(A,C). [3.55481]

# Induction, Abduction, and Consequence-Finding

Katsumi Inoue

Department of Electrical and Electronics Engineering
Kobe University
Rokkodai, Nada, Kobe 657-8501, Japan
inoue@eedept.kobe-u.ac.jp

**Abstract.** This paper shows a sound and complete method for inverse entailment in inductive logic programming. We show that inverse entailment can be computed with a resolution method for consequence-finding. In comparison with previous work, induction via consequence-finding is sound and complete for finding hypotheses from full clausal theories, and can be used for inducing not only definite clauses but also non-Horn clauses and integrity constraints. We also compare induction and abduction from the viewpoint of consequence-finding, and clarify the relationship and difference between the two.

## 1 Introduction

Both *induction* and *abduction* are ampliative reasoning, and agree with the logic to seek hypotheses to account for given observations and examples. That is, given a background theory $B$ and observations (or positive examples) $E$, the task of induction and abduction is common in finding hypotheses $H$ such that

$$B \wedge H \models E, \tag{1}$$

where $B \wedge H$ is consistent [9,5,8,14]. While the logic is in common, they differ in the usage in applications. According to Peirce, abduction infers a cause of an observation, and can infer something quite different from what is observed. On the other hand, induction infers something to be true through generalization of a number of cases of which the same thing is true. The relation, difference, similarity, and interaction between abduction and induction are extensively studied by authors in [6].

Compared with automated abduction, one of the major drawbacks of automated induction is that computation of inductive hypotheses require a large amount of search that is highly expensive. General mechanisms to construct hypotheses rely on *refinement* of current hypotheses, which has a lot of alternative choices unless good heuristics is incorporated in search. We thus need a logically principled way to compute inductive hypotheses. One such a promising method to compute hypotheses $H$ in (1) is based on *inverse entailment*, which transforms the equation (1) into

$$B \wedge \neg E \models \neg H. \tag{2}$$

C. Rouveirol and M. Sebag (Eds.): ILP 2001, LNAI 2157, pp. 65–79, 2001.

The equation (2) says that, given $B$ and $E$, any hypothesis $H$ *deductively* follows from $B \wedge \neg E$ in its negated form. For example, given $B_1 = \{human(s)\}$ and $E_1 = \{mortal(s)\}$, $H_1 = \{\forall x(human(x) \supset mortal(x))\}$ satisfies (1). In fact, $B_1 \wedge \neg E_1 = \{human(s), \neg mortal(s)\} \models \exists x(human(x) \wedge \neg mortal(x)) = \neg H_1$. The equation (2) is seen in literature, e.g., [11] for abduction and [17] for induction.

While the equation (2) is useful for computing abductive explanations of observations in abduction, it is more difficult to apply it to compute inductive hypotheses. In abduction, without loss of generality, $E$ is written as a ground atom, and each $H$ is usually assumed to be a conjunction of literals. These conditions make abductive computation relatively easy, and *consequence-finding* algorithms [11,4,16] can be directly applied.

In induction, however, $E$ can be clauses and $H$ is usually a general rule. Universally quantified rules for $H$ cannot be easily obtained from the negation of consequences of $B \wedge \neg E$. Then, Muggleton [17] considered the so called *bottom clause*:

$$\bot(E, B) = \{\neg L \mid L \text{ is a literal and } B \wedge \neg E \models L\}.$$

A hypothesis $H$ is then constructed by generalizing a sub-clause of $\bot(E, B)$, i.e.,

$$H \models \bot(E, B).$$

While this method is adopted in Progol, it is incomplete for finding hypotheses satisfying (1). Then, several improvements have been reported to make inverse entailment complete [18,7,23] or to characterize inverse entailment precisely [21,22,19]. However, such improved inductive procedures are not very simple when compared with abductive computation. More seriously, some improved procedures are unsound even though they are complete. Another difficulty in the previous inductive methods lies in the facts: (i) each constructed hypothesis in $H$ is usually assumed to be a Horn clause, (ii) the example $E$ is given as a single Horn clause, and (iii) the background theory $B$ is a set of Horn clauses. Finding full clausal hypotheses from full clausal theories have not been received much attention so far.

In this paper, we propose a simple, yet powerful method to handle inverse entailment (2) for computing inductive hypotheses. Unlike previous methods based on the bottom clause, we do not restrict the consequences of $B \wedge \neg E$ to literals, but consider the *characteristic clauses* of $B \wedge \neg E$, which were originally proposed for AI applications (including abduction) of consequence-finding [11]. Using our method, sound and complete hypothesis-finding from full clausal theories can be realized, and not only definite clauses but also non-Horn clauses and integrity constraints can be constructed as $H$. In this way, inductive algorithms can be designed with deductive procedures, which reduce search space as much as possible like computing abduction. In this paper, we also clarify the relationship and difference between abductive and inductive computation.

This paper is organized as follows. Section 2 introduces the theoretical background in this paper. Section 3 reviews a consequence-finding method for abduction. Section 4 provides the basic idea called *CF-induction* to construct inductive hypotheses using a consequence-finding method. Section 5 compares induction with abduction in the context of consequence-finding. Section 6 discusses related work, and Section 7 is the conclusion. The proof of the main theorem is given in the appendix.

## 2 Background

### 2.1 Inductive Logic Programming

Here, we review the terminology of inductive logic programming (ILP). A *clause* is a disjunction of literals, and is often denoted as the set of its disjuncts. A clause $\{A_1, \ldots, A_m, \neg B_1, \ldots, \neg B_n\}$, where each $A_i, B_j$ is an atom, is also written as $B_1 \wedge \cdots \wedge B_n \supset A_1 \vee \cdots \vee A_m$. Any variable in a clause is assumed to be universally quantified at the front. A *definite clause* is a clause which contains only one positive literal. A *positive* (*negative*) *clause* is a clause whose disjuncts are all positive (negative) literals. A negative clause is often called an *integrity constraint.* A *Horn clause* is a definite clause or negative clause; otherwise it is *non-Horn.* A *clausal theory* $\Sigma$ is a finite set of clauses. A clausal theory is *full* if it contains non-Horn clauses.

A (*universal*) *conjunctive normal form* (CNF) formula is a conjunction of clauses, and a *disjunctive normal form* (DNF) formula is a disjunction of conjunctions of literals. A clausal theory $\Sigma$ is identified with the CNF formula that is the conjunction of all clauses in $\Sigma$. We define the *complement* of a clausal theory, $\Sigma = C_1 \wedge \cdots \wedge C_k$ where each $C_i$ is a clause, as the DNF formula $\neg C_1\sigma_1 \vee \cdots \vee \neg C_k\sigma_k$, where $\neg C_i = B_1 \wedge \cdots \wedge B_n \wedge \neg A_1 \wedge \cdots \wedge \neg A_m$ for $C_i = (B_1 \wedge \cdots \wedge B_n \supset A_1 \vee \cdots \vee A_m)$, and $\sigma_i$ is a substitution which replaces each variable $x$ in $C_i$ with a Skolem constant $sk_x$. This replacement of variables reflects the fact that each variable in $\neg C_i$ is existentially quantified at the front. Since there is no ambiguity, we write the complement of $\Sigma$ as $\neg\Sigma$.

Let $C$ and $D$ be two clauses. $C$ *subsumes* $D$ if there is a substitution $\theta$ such that $C\theta \subseteq D$. $C$ *properly subsumes* $D$ if $C$ subsumes $D$ but $D$ does not subsume $C$. For a clausal theory $\Sigma$, $\mu\Sigma$ denotes the set of clauses in $\Sigma$ not properly subsumed by any clause in $\Sigma$.

Let $B$, $E$, and $H$ be clausal theories, representing a *background theory, (positive) examples*, and *hypotheses*, respectively. The most popular formalization of concept-learning is *learning from entailment* (or *explanatory induction*), in which the task is: given $B$ and $E$, find $H$ such that $B \wedge H \models E$ and $B \wedge H$ is consistent. Note that we do not consider *negative examples* in this paper.

### 2.2 Consequence-Finding

For a clausal theory $\Sigma$, a *consequence* of $\Sigma$ is a clause entailed by $\Sigma$. We denote by $Th(\Sigma)$ the set of all consequences of $\Sigma$. The *consequence-finding* problem was firstly addressed by Lee [15] in the context of resolution principle. Lee proved that, for any consequence $D$ of $\Sigma$, the resolution principle can derive a clause $C$ from $\Sigma$ such that $C$ entails $D$. In this sense, the resolution principle is said *complete for consequence-finding.* In Lee's theorem, "$C$ entails $D$" can be replaced with "$C$ subsumes $D$". Hence, the consequences of $\Sigma$ that are derived by the resolution principle includes $\mu Th(\Sigma)$. The notion of consequence-finding is used as the theoretical background for discussing the completeness of ILP systems [20].

By extending the notion of consequence-finding, Inoue [11] defined *characteristic clauses* to represent "interesting" clauses for a given problem. Each characteristic clause is constructed over a sub-vocabulary of the representation language called a *production field*. In this paper, for the sake of simplicity, a production field $\mathcal{P}$ is defined as a set of distinguished literals. Let $Th_{\mathcal{P}}(\Sigma)$ be the clauses in $Th(\Sigma)$ all of whose literals belong to $\mathcal{P}$. Then, the *characteristic clauses* of $\Sigma$ with respect to $\mathcal{P}$ are defined as:

$$Carc(\Sigma, \mathcal{P}) = \mu\, Th_{\mathcal{P}}(\Sigma)\,.$$

Here, we do not include any tautology $\neg L \vee L$ ($\equiv True$) in $Carc(\Sigma, \mathcal{P})$ even when both $L$ and $\neg L$ belong to $\mathcal{P}$. Note that the empty clause $\Box$ is the unique clause in $Carc(\Sigma, \mathcal{P})$ if and only if $\Sigma$ is unsatisfiable. This means that proof-finding is a special case of consequence-finding. In the propositional case, each characteristic clause of $\Sigma$ is a *prime implicate* of $\Sigma$.

When a new clause $C$ is added to a clausal theory $\Sigma$, some consequences are newly derived with this new information. Such a new and "interesting" clause is called a "new" characteristic clause. Formally, the *new characteristic clauses* of $C$ with respect to $\Sigma$ and $\mathcal{P}$ are:

$$\begin{aligned} NewCarc(\Sigma, C, \mathcal{P}) &= \mu\,[\,Th_{\mathcal{P}}(\Sigma \wedge C) - Th(\Sigma)\,] \\ &= Carc(\Sigma \wedge C, \mathcal{P}) - Carc(\Sigma, \mathcal{P}). \end{aligned}$$

When a new formula is not a single clause but a CNF formula $F = C_1 \wedge \cdots \wedge C_m$, where each $C_i$ is a clause, $NewCarc(\Sigma, F, \mathcal{P})$ can be decomposed into $m$ $NewCarc$ operations each of whose added new formula is a single clause [11]:

$$NewCarc(\Sigma, F, \mathcal{P}) = \mu\,[\,\bigwedge_{i=1}^{m} NewCarc(\Sigma_i, C_i, \mathcal{P})\,]\,, \tag{3}$$

where $\Sigma_1 = \Sigma$, and $\Sigma_{i+1} = \Sigma_i \wedge C_i$, for $i = 1, \ldots, m-1$. This incremental computation can be applied to get the characteristic clauses of $\Sigma$ with respect to $\mathcal{P}$ as follows.

$$Carc(\Sigma, \mathcal{P}) = NewCarc(True, \Sigma, \mathcal{P}). \tag{4}$$

Several procedures have been proposed to compute (new) characteristic clauses. For example, *SOL resolution* [11] is an extension of the Model Elimination (ME) calculus to which the Skip rule is introduced. In computing $NewCarc(\Sigma, C, \mathcal{P})$, SOL resolution treats a newly added clause $C$ as the *top clause* input to ME, and derives those consequences relevant to $C$ directly. With the Skip rule, SOL resolution focuses on deriving only those consequences belonging to the production field $\mathcal{P}$. Various pruning methods are also introduced to enhance the efficiency of SOL resolution in a *connection-tableau* format [12].

Instead of ME, *SFK resolution* [4] is a variant of ordered resolution, which is enhanced with the Skip rule for finding characteristic clauses. An extensive survey of consequence-finding algorithms in propositional logic is given by Marquis [16].

## 3 Abduction as Consequence-Finding

Abduction is elegantly characterized by consequence-finding as follows. We here denote the set of all literals in the representation language by $\mathcal{L}$, and a set $\Gamma$ of candidate hypotheses (*abductive bias*) is defined as a subset of $\mathcal{L}$. Any subset $H$ of $\Gamma$ is identified with the conjunction of all elements in $H$. Also, for any set $T$ of formulas, $\overline{T}$ represents the set of formulas obtained by negating every formula in $T$, i.e., $\overline{T} = \{ \neg C \mid C \in T \}$.

Let $E_1, \ldots, E_n$ be a finite number of observations, and suppose that they are all literals. We want to explain the observations $E = E_1 \wedge \cdots \wedge E_n$ from an *abductive theory* $(B, \Gamma)$, where $B$ is a clausal theory representing a background theory and $\Gamma$ is a set of ground literals representing an abductive bias. Then, $H = H_1 \wedge \cdots \wedge H_k$ is an *(abductive) explanation* of $E$ from $(B, \Gamma)$ if:

1. $B \wedge (H_1 \wedge \cdots \wedge H_k) \models E_1 \wedge \cdots \wedge E_n$ ,
2. $B \wedge (H_1 \wedge \cdots \wedge H_k)$ is consistent,
3. Each $H_i$ is an element of $\Gamma$.

These are equivalent to the following three conditions:

1′. $B \wedge (\neg E_1 \vee \cdots \vee \neg E_n) \models \neg H_1 \vee \cdots \vee \neg H_k$ ,
2′. $B \not\models \neg H_1 \vee \cdots \vee \neg H_k$ ,
3′. Each $\neg H_i$ is an element of $\overline{\Gamma}$.

By 1′, a clause derived from the clausal theory $B \wedge \neg E$ is the negation of an explanation of $E$ from $(B, \Gamma)$, and this computation can be done as automated deduction over clauses in a way of "inverse entailment". By 2′, such a derived clause must not be a consequence of $B$ before adding $\neg E$. By 3′, every literal appearing in such a clause must belong to $\overline{\Gamma}$. Moreover, $H$ is a minimal explanation from $(B, \Gamma)$ if and only if $\neg H$ is a minimal consequence from $B \wedge \neg E$. Therefore, we obtain the following result.

**Theorem 31** *Let $(B, \Gamma)$ be an abductive theory. The set of minimal explanations of an observation $E$ from $(B, \Gamma)$ is:*

$$\overline{NewCarc(B, \neg E, \mathcal{P})} ,$$

*where the production field $\mathcal{P}$ is $\overline{\Gamma}$.*

In the above setting, $E$ is assumed to be a conjunction of literals. Extending the form of each example $E_i$ to a clause, let $E = E_1 \wedge \cdots \wedge E_n$ be a CNF formula, where each $E_i$ is a clause. Then, $\neg E$ is a DNF formula. By converting $\neg E$ from DNF into the CNF formula $F$, $NewCarc(B, F, \mathcal{P})$ can be computed by (3).

In Theorem 31, explanations obtained by a consequence-finding procedure are not necessarily ground and can contain variables. In implementing resolution-based abductive procedures, however, each variable in the CNF formula $E$ is replaced with a new constant in the complement $\neg E$ through Skolemization. Then, to get a universally quantified explanation by negating each new characteristic clause containing Skolem constants, we need to apply the *reverse Skolemization* algorithm [2]. For example, if $\neg P(x, sk_y, u, sk_v)$ is a new characteristic clause where $sk_y, sk_v$ are Skolem constants, we get the explanation $\forall y \forall v \exists x \exists u\, P(x, y, u, v)$ by reverse Skolemization.

## 4 Induction as Consequence-Finding

In this section, we characterize explanatory induction by consequence-finding. Suppose that we are given a background theory $B$ and examples $E$, both of which are clausal theories (or CNF) possibly containing non-Horn clauses. Recall that explanatory induction seeks a clausal theory $H$ such that:

$$B \wedge H \models E,$$
$$B \wedge H \text{ is consistent.}$$

These two are equivalent to

$$B \wedge \neg E \models \neg H, \tag{5}$$
$$B \not\models \neg H. \tag{6}$$

Like inverse entailment, we are interested in some formulas derived from $B \wedge \neg E$ that are not derived from $B$ alone. Here, instead of the bottom clause $\perp(B, E)$ in [17], we consider some clausal theory $CC(B, E)$. Then, the equation (5) can be written as

$$B \wedge \neg E \models CC(B, E), \tag{7}$$
$$CC(B, E) \models \neg H. \tag{8}$$

The latter (8) is also written as

$$H \models \neg CC(B, E). \tag{9}$$

Also, by (6) and (8), we have

$$B \not\models CC(B, E). \tag{10}$$

By (7), $CC(B, E)$ is obtained by computing the characteristic clauses of $B \wedge \neg E$ because any other consequence of $B \wedge \neg E$ can be obtained by constructing a clause that is subsumed by a characteristic clause. Hence,

$$Carc(B \wedge \neg E, \mathcal{P}) \models CC(B, E), \tag{11}$$

where the production field $\mathcal{P}$ ($\subseteq \mathcal{L}$) is defined as some set of literals reflecting an *inductive bias*. When no inductive bias is considered, $\mathcal{P}$ is just set to $\mathcal{L}$, which is the set of all literals in the first-order language. The other requirement for $CC(B, E)$ is the equation (10), which is satisfied if at least one of the clauses in $CC(B, E)$ is not a consequence of $B$; otherwise, $CC(B, E)$ is entailed by $B$. This is realized by including a clause from $NewCarc(B, \neg E, \mathcal{P})$ in $CC(B, E)$.

In constructing hypotheses $H$ from the clausal theory $CC(B, E)$, notice that $\neg CC(B, E)$ is entailed by $H$ in (9). Since $\neg CC(B, E)$ is DNF, we convert it into the CNF formula $F$, i.e., $F \equiv \neg CC(B, E)$. Then, $H$ is constructed as a clausal theory which entails $F$, i.e., $H \models F$. There are several methods to perform such an inverse of entailment in ILP. Such a procedure to construct a new clausal theory that entails a given clausal theory is called a *generalizer* [23].[1] In some case, reverse Skolemization in abduction works as a generalizer, but there exist other techniques to generalize clauses such as anti-instantiation (i.e., replacement of terms with variables), dropping literals from clauses, inverse resolution, addition of clauses, and Plotkin's least generalization of multiple clauses. Note that applying arbitrary generalizer to $F$ may cause an inconsistency of $H$ with $B$. To ensure that $B \wedge H$ is consistent, the clauses of $H$ must keep those literals that are generalizations of the complement of at least one clause from $NewCarc(B, \neg E, \mathcal{P})$.

Now, the whole algorithm to construct inductive hypotheses is as follows.

**Definition 41** Let $B$ and $E$ be clausal theories. A clausal theory $H$ is derived by a *CF-induction* from $B$ and $E$ if $H$ is constructed as follows.

---

**Step 1.** Compute $Carc(B \wedge \neg E, \mathcal{P})$;[2]
**Step 2.** Construct $CC(B, E) = C_1 \wedge \cdots \wedge C_m$, where each $C_i$ is a clause satisfying the conditions:
(a) Each $C_i$ is an instance of a clause in $Carc(B \wedge \neg E, \mathcal{P})$;
(b) At least one $C_i$ is an instance of a clause from $NewCarc(B, \neg E, \mathcal{P})$;
**Step 3.** Convert $\neg CC(B, E)$ into the CNF formula $F$;
**Step 4.** $H$ is obtained by applying a generalizer to $F$ under the constraint that $B \wedge H$ is consistent.

---

**Example 41** The following theory is a variant of an example in [1], and is often used to illustrate how the bottom clause is used in inverse entailment [21,22]. Consider

$$\begin{aligned} B_2 = {} & (cat(x) \supset pet(x)) \wedge \\ & (small(x) \wedge fluffy(x) \wedge pet(x) \supset cuddly\_pet(x)), \\ E_2 = {} & (fluffy(x) \wedge cat(x) \supset cuddly\_pet(x)). \end{aligned}$$

[1] If "entailment" is replaced with "subsumption" here, the completeness in Theorem 41 does not precisely hold.

[2] Since the number of characteristic clauses may be large or infinite in general, this step should be interleaved on demand with construction of each $C_i$ at Step 2 in practice.

Then, the complement of $E_2$ is

$$\neg E_2 \;=\; \mathit{fluffy}(sk_x) \wedge \mathit{cat}(sk_x) \wedge \neg \mathit{cuddly\_pet}(sk_x)),$$

and $\mathit{NewCarc}(B_2, \neg E_2, \mathcal{L})$ is

$$\neg E_2 \wedge \mathit{pet}(sk_x) \wedge \neg \mathit{small}(sk_x).$$

Let $CC(B_2, E_2) = \mathit{NewCarc}(B_2, \neg E_2, \mathcal{L})$. In this case, $F_2 = \neg CC(B_2, E_2) = \bot(B_2, E_2)$ hold. By applying reverse Skolemization to $F_2$, we get the hypothesis $H_2$:

$$\mathit{fluffy}(x) \wedge \mathit{cat}(x) \wedge \mathit{pet}(x) \supset \mathit{cuddly\_pet}(x) \vee \mathit{small}(x).$$

While in the above cited reference the subclause

$$\mathit{fluffy}(x) \wedge \mathit{cat}(x) \supset \mathit{small}(x)$$

is adopted for a definite clause, $H_2$ is the most-specific hypothesis in the sense of [17].

**Example 42** [21] This example illustrates the incompleteness of inverse entailment based on the bottom clause in [17]. Consider the background theory and the example:

$$B_3 = \mathit{even}(0) \wedge (\neg \mathit{odd}(x) \vee \mathit{even}(s(x))),$$
$$E_3 = \mathit{odd}(s(s(s(0)))).$$

Then, $\mathit{Carc}(B_3 \wedge \neg E_3, \mathcal{L}) = B_3 \wedge \neg E_3$. Suppose that $CC(B_3, E_3)$ is chosen as:

$$\mathit{even}(0) \wedge (\neg \mathit{odd}(s(0)) \vee \mathit{even}(s(s(0)))) \wedge \neg \mathit{odd}(s(s(s(0)))),$$

where the second clause is an instance of the latter clause in $B_3$, and the third clause belongs to $\mathit{NewCarc}(B_3, \neg E_3, \mathcal{L})$. By converting $\neg CC(B_3, E_3)$ into CNF, $F_3$ consists of the clauses:

$$\neg \mathit{even}(0) \vee \mathit{odd}(s(0)) \vee \mathit{odd}(s(s(s(0)))),$$
$$\neg \mathit{even}(0) \vee \neg \mathit{even}(s(s((0))) \vee \mathit{odd}(s(s(s(0)))).$$

Considering the single clause:

$$H_3 = \neg \mathit{even}(x) \vee \mathit{odd}(s(x)),$$

$H_3$ subsumes both clauses in $F_3$, so is the hypothesis. On the other hand, the bottom clause is

$$\bot(B_3, E_3) = \neg \mathit{even}(0) \vee \mathit{odd}(s(s(s(0)))),$$

from which $H_3$ cannot be obtained by any generalizer. In fact, $H_3 \not\models \bot(B_3, E_3)$.

Below is the correctness result for clausal theories derived using CF-induction. The result implies not only the completeness but the soundness of CF-induction.

**Theorem 41** *Let $B$, $E$ and $H$ be clausal theories. $H$ is derived by a CF-induction from $B$ and $E$ if and only if $B \wedge H \models E$ and $B \wedge H$ is consistent.*

In Theorem 41, both $B$ and $E$ may contain non-Horn clauses and integrity constraints. Also, the derived hypotheses $H$ may be non-Horn. This result is an answer to the open question posed by [18], as to whether a generalization of inverse entailment would be complete for arbitrary clausal background theories.

## 5 Abduction vs. Induction

CF-induction is realized by abductive computation. In fact, computing $Carc(B \wedge \neg E, \mathcal{P})$ at Step 1 can be implemented by calling *NewCarc* operations incrementally in (3) and (4), each of which can be regarded as computing abduction by Theorem 31.

Conversely, computing abduction is regarded as a special case of CF-induction.

**Theorem 51** *Let $(B, \Gamma)$ be an abductive theory. A conjunction $H$ of literals is a minimal explanation of an observation $E$ from $(B, \Gamma)$ if and only if $H$ is derived by a CF-induction from $B$ and $E$ in which the size of $CC(B, E)$ at Step 2 is 1 ($m = 1$) and reverse Skolemization is used as the generalizer at Step 4.*

The set of all minimal explanations is characterized by Theorem 31, and can also be obtained by slightly modifying CF-induction. Namely, every clause of $CC(B, E)$ is taken from $NewCarc(B, \neg E, \mathcal{P})$ at Step 2, and we do not have to convert $\neg CC(B, E)$ into CNF at Step 3, and reverse Skolemization is used as the generalizer at Step 4. By Theorem 51, each single conjunction $\neg C_i$ obtained in this way is a minimal explanation of $E$. Then, the disjunction $\neg CC(B, E)$ of every $\neg C_i$ is also an explanation. Such DNF explanations are used in AI applications such as *diagnosis* [13] and computing *circumscription* [10].

Thus, abduction and induction are very similar if we allow arbitrary form of clausal theories as hypotheses. There are three differences between them. First, the form of hypotheses in induction is CNF, while it is usually DNF in abduction. Second, at least one of the clauses in $CC(B, E)$ is from $NewCarc(B, \neg E, \mathcal{P})$ in induction, while all clauses in $CC(B, E)$ must be in $NewCarc(B, \neg E, \mathcal{P})$ in abduction. Third, reverse Skolemization is used as a generalizer in abduction, while other generalizers can be used in induction. No other difference exists between abduction and induction as long as their implementation is concerned in the context of consequence-finding. The next example illustrates the similarity between induction and abduction.

**Example 51** [23] Let

$$B_4 = (dog(x) \wedge small(x) \supset pet(x)),$$
$$E_4 = pet(c).$$

be the background theory and the example. Then,

$$NewCarc(B_4, \neg E_4, \mathcal{L}) = \neg pet(c) \wedge (\neg dog(c) \vee \neg small(c)).$$

Now, put $CC(B_4, E_4) = NewCarc(B_4, \neg E_4, \mathcal{L})$. Then,

$$\neg CC(B_4, E_4) = pet(c) \vee (dog(c) \wedge small(c)),$$

which is exactly the same as the minimal abductive explanations. Converting $\neg CC(B_4, E_4)$ into CNF, we have

$$F_4 = (dog(c) \vee pet(c)) \wedge (small(c) \vee pet(c)).$$

By applying anti-instantiation, we get the clausal theory

$$H_4 = \{\, dog(x) \vee pet(x),\ \ small(x) \vee pet(x) \,\}.$$

On the other hand, the next example shows the main difference between abduction and induction, which is the second one in the above differences. Namely, induction often utilizes consequences of $B$ before adding $\neg E$ in the construction of $CC(B, E)$. This operation is essential to associate observations with the background theory in induction. Abduction does not need such consequences because they are redundant in virtue of the *minimality* of explanations.

**Example 52** [17] Let us consider the background theory and the example:

$$B_5 = white(swan1), \quad E_5 = \neg black(swan1).$$

Then, $NewCarc(B_5, \neg E_5, \mathcal{L}) = \neg E_5 = black(swan1)$. Hence, $\neg black(swan1)$ is the unique minimal abductive explanation of $E_5$. In induction, on the other hand, let

$$CC(B_5, E_5) = white(swan1) \wedge black(swan1),$$

in which the first conjunct is the clause of $B_5$. By anti-instantiating $F_5 = \neg CC(B_5, E_5)$, we can learn the integrity constraint:

$$\neg white(x) \vee \neg black(x).$$

## 6 Related Work

CF-induction is obviously influenced by previous work on inverse entailment (IE), which was initiated by Muggleton [17]. The original IE allows Horn clauses for $B$ and a single Horn clause for each of $B$ and $E$. Even in this setting, however, the method based on $\bot(B, E)$ is incomplete for finding $H$ such that $B \wedge H \models E$ [21]. Muggleton [18] considers an enlarged bottom set to make IE complete, but the revised method is unsound. Furukawa [7] also proposes a complete algorithm, but it is relatively complex. Yamamoto [22] shows that a variant of SOL resolution can be used to implement IE based on $\bot(B, E)$. However, he computes positive and negative parts in $\bot(B, E)$ separately, where SOL resolution is used only for computing positive literals. Muggleton and Bryant [19] suggest the use of Stickel's PTTP for implementing theory completion using IE, which seems inefficient since PTTP is not a consequence-finding procedure but a theorem prover. Compared with these previous works, CF-induction proposed in this paper is simple, yet sound and complete for finding hypotheses from full clausal theories. Instead of the bottom clause, CF-induction uses the characteristic clauses, which strictly include the literals in $\overline{\bot(B, E)}$.

Yamamoto and Fronhöfer [23] firstly extend IE to allow for full clausal theories for $B$ and $E$, and introduce the *residue hypothesis* for ground instances of $B \wedge \neg E$. Roughly speaking, a residue hypothesis corresponds to the enumeration of all paths in the matrix in Bibel's Connection method. By contrast, CF-induction is realized by a resolution-based consequence-finding procedure, which naturally extends most previous work on IE, and can easily handle non-ground clauses. Compared with the procedure by [23], a merit of CF-induction is the existence of a *production field* $\mathcal{P}$, which can be used to guide and restrict derivations of clauses by reflecting an *inductive bias*.

## 7 Concluding Remark

In this paper, we put emphasis on the completeness of inverse entailment in full clausal theories. To this end, we proposed CF-induction, which is sound and complete for finding hypotheses from full clausal theories. CF-induction performs induction via consequence-finding, which enables us to generate inductive hypotheses in a logically principled way. CF-induction can be implemented with existing systematic consequence-finding procedures such as SOL resolution [11] and SFK resolution [4]. We also clarified the similarity and difference between abduction and induction in the context of consequence-finding.

There exist formalizations of induction other than explanatory induction in the literature on ILP, such as *learning from interpretations (or satisfiability)* [3], and *descriptive induction* [9,14]. De Raedt [3] proposes a translation of learning from interpretations into learning from entailment, but the method requires the notion of *negative examples.* Lachiche [14] discusses various forms of descriptive induction, which can also be characterized by deduction from completed theories. The precise relationships between these different formalisms and consequence-finding need to be addressed in the future.

**Acknowledgements**

The author thanks reviewers for helpful comments and Akihiro Yamamoto for fruitful discussion on the topic of this paper.

## A Proof of Theorem 3.1

We prove the correctness of CF-induction by giving its soundness and completeness. Let $B$, $E$ and $H$ be clausal theories. Section A.1 shows that for any $H$

derived by a CF-induction from $B$ and $E$, it holds that $B \wedge H \models E$ and $B \wedge H$ is consistent. Section A.2 shows the converse, that is, if $B \wedge H \models E$ and $B \wedge H$ is consistent then $H$ is derived by a CF-induction from $B$ and $E$.

In the following, we assume the language $\mathcal{L}_H$ for all hypotheses $H$'s. Usually, $\mathcal{L}_H$ is given as the set of all clauses constructed from the first-order language, but we can restrict the form of hypotheses by considering an inductive bias with a subset of literals/predicates. The following proofs can be applied to the case with any inductive bias. Then, the production field $\mathcal{P}$ is set to the complement of $\mathcal{L}_H$. When $\mathcal{L}_H$ is the set of all clauses, $\mathcal{P}$ is given as $\mathcal{L}$. We also assume the existence of a sound and complete generalizer at Step 4 of a CF-induction.

### A.1 Soundness of CF-Induction

Let $H$ be a hypothesis obtained by a CF-induction from $B$ and $E$. Then, by the definition of a CF-induction, there is a DNF formula $CC(B,E) = C_1 \wedge \cdots \wedge C_m$ such that [a] $H$ is obtained by applying a generalizer to the CNF representation of $\neg CC(B,E)$; [b] every $C_i$ $(i = 1, \ldots, m)$ is an instance of a clause from $Carc(B \wedge \neg E, \mathcal{P})$; and [c] there is a $C_j$ $(1 \leq j \leq m)$ that is an instance of a clause from $NewCarc(B, \neg E, \mathcal{P})$. Then, by [b], for any $C_i$ $(i = 1, \ldots, m)$, there is a clause $D_i \in Carc(B \wedge \neg E, \mathcal{P})$ such that $B \wedge \neg E \models D_i$ and $D_i \models C_i$. Obviously, it holds that $B \wedge \neg E \models C_i$. Also, by [c], it holds that $B \not\models C_j$. Hence,

$$B \wedge \neg E \models C_1 \wedge \cdots \wedge C_m \quad \text{and} \quad B \not\models C_1 \wedge \cdots \wedge C_m.$$

Now, let

$$F \equiv \neg CC(B,E) \equiv \neg C_1 \vee \cdots \vee \neg C_m.$$

Then,

$$B \wedge \neg E \models \neg F \quad \text{and} \quad B \not\models \neg F,$$

which are equivalent to

$$B \wedge F \models E \quad \text{and} \quad B \wedge F \text{ is consistent.}$$

Finally, $H \models F$ holds by [a], which implies that $B \wedge H \models E$. The condition that $B \wedge H$ is consistent is included in Step 4 of a CF-induction. □

### A.2 Completeness of CF-Induction

Suppose that $B \wedge H \models E$ and $B \wedge H$ is consistent. Then, $B \wedge \neg E \models \neg H$ and $B \not\models \neg H$. We first show that $\neg H$ is entailed by $Carc(B \wedge \neg E, \mathcal{P})$. Suppose not, i.e., $Carc(B \wedge \neg E, \mathcal{P}) \not\models \neg H$. Then, $H$ is consistent with $Carc(B \wedge \neg E, \mathcal{P})$. Here, by the definition of the characteristic clauses, $Carc(B \wedge \neg E, \mathcal{P}) \subseteq Th(B \wedge \neg E)$. Also, $Carc(B \wedge \neg E, \mathcal{P})$ belongs to the production field $\mathcal{P}$. On the other hand, $H$ belongs to $\mathcal{L}_H$ that is the complement of $\mathcal{P}$. Hence, $H$ does not belong to $\mathcal{P}$. Then, $H$ is consistent with $B \wedge \neg E$. This contradicts the fact that $B \wedge \neg E \models \neg H$. Therefore,

$$Carc(B \wedge \neg E, \mathcal{P}) \models \neg H.$$

Hence, $Carc(B \wedge \neg E, \mathcal{P}) \wedge H$ is unsatisfiable. Now, there are two ways to prove the completeness of CF-induction.

[A] *Using Herbrand's theorem,* there is a finite set $S$ of ground instances of clauses from $Carc(B \wedge \neg E, \mathcal{P})$ such that $S \wedge H$ is unsatisfiable. This set $S$ can actually be constructed by a CF-induction. In fact, we can set $S$ as $CC(B, E)$. In other words, let us construct $CC(B, E) = C_1 \wedge \cdots \wedge C_m$ at Step 2 of a CF-induction such that

(a) each $C_i$ $(i = 1, \ldots, m)$ is a ground instance of a clause from $Carc(B \wedge \neg E, \mathcal{P})$,
(b) $C_1 \wedge \cdots \wedge C_m \wedge H$ is unsatisfiable.

Then, there is a $C_j$ $(1 \leq j \leq m)$ that is a ground instance of a clause from $NewCarc(B, \neg E, \mathcal{P})$ (for this, see the discussion below the equation (11) in Section 4). Finally, at Steps 3 and 4, $H$ can be obtained by applying a generalizer (including anti-instantiation) to the CNF representation of $\neg CC(B, E)$. □

[B] *Using the compactness theorem,* there is a finite subset $S$ of $Carc(B \wedge \neg E, \mathcal{P})$ such that $S \wedge H$ is unsatisfiable. In this case, $S$ can also be constructed at Step 2 of a CF-induction as $CC(B, E) = C_1 \wedge \cdots \wedge C_m$, where

(a) every $C_i$ $(i = 1, \ldots, m)$ is a variant of a clause from $Carc(B \wedge \neg E, \mathcal{P})$, and
(b) $C_1 \wedge \cdots \wedge C_m \wedge H$ is unsatisfiable.

Then, there is a $C_j$ $(1 \leq j \leq m)$ that is a variant of a clause in $NewCarc(B, \neg E, \mathcal{P})$ as in the proof of [A]. In this case, however, we have to take care of variables in $C_i$'s. Taking the complement of a $C_i$, each variable $x$ in $C_i$ becomes a Skolem constant $sk_x$ in $\neg C_i$, in which $x$ is interpreted as existentially quantified. Sometimes we need multiple "copies" of $\neg C_i$ in $\neg CC(B, E)$ using different constants like $sk_x^1$, $sk_x^2$, etc, depending on how many times $C_i$ is used to derive $\neg H$ from $B \wedge \neg E$. Then, at Steps 3 and 4, $H$ can be obtained by applying a generalizer to the CNF representation of $\neg CC(B, E)$. □

**Example A1** We now verify the completeness proof [B] by applying it to the theory in Example 42, while the proof [A] can easily be checked by following the way shown in Example 42. This time, we choose a non-ground characteristic clause as

$$CC'(B_3, E_3) \ = \ even(0) \wedge (\neg odd(x) \vee even(s(x))) \wedge \neg odd(s(s(s(0)))).$$

Then, the complement of $CC'(B_3, E_3)$ becomes

$$\begin{gathered}(\neg even(0) \vee odd(sk_x) \vee odd(s(s(s(0))))) \\ \wedge\ (\neg even(0) \vee \neg even(s(sk_x)) \vee odd(s(s(s(0))))).\end{gathered}$$

Here, we need only one copy of $\exists x(odd(x) \wedge \neg even(s(x)))$. The hypothesis $H_3 = \neg even(x) \vee odd(s(x))$ entails $\neg CC'(B_3, E_3)$ because $H_3$ entails

$$\exists y[(\neg even(0) \vee odd(y)) \wedge (\neg even(s(y)) \vee odd(s(s(s(0)))))].$$

To see this, take the substitution $y/s(0)$ in the above formula. Then, $H_3$ subsumes both $\neg even(0) \vee odd(s(0))$ and $\neg even(s(s(0))) \vee odd(s(s(s(0))))$, and thus entails $\neg CC'(B_3, E_3)$.

## References


1. Wray Buntine. Generalized subsumption and its applications to induction and redundancy. *Artificial Intelligence*, 36:149–176, 1988.
2. P.T. Cox and T. Pietrzykowski. Causes for events: their computation and applications. In: *Proceedings of the 8th International Conference on Automated Deduction*, LNCS, 230, pages 608–621, Springer, 1986.
3. Luc De Raedt. Logical settings for concept-learning. *Artificial Intelligence*, 95:187–201, 1997.
4. Alvaro del Val. A new method for consequence finding and compilation in restricted languages. In: *Proceedings of AAAI-99*, pages 259–264, AAAI Press, 1999.
5. Yannis Dimopoulos and Antonis Kakas. Abduction and inductive learning. In: Luc De Raedt, editor, *Advances in Inductive Logic Programming*, pages 144–171, IOS Press, 1996.
6. Peter A. Flach and Antonis C. Kakas, editors. *Abduction and Induction: Essays on their Relation and Integration.* Kluwer, 2000.
7. Koichi Furukawa. On the completion of the most specific hypothesis computation in inverse entailment for mutual recursion. In: *Proceedings of Discovery Science '98*, LNAI 1532, pages 315–325, Springer, 1998.
8. Éric Grégoire and Lakhdar Saïs. Inductive reasoning is sometimes deductive. In: *Proceedings of ECAI-96 Workshop on Abductive and Inductive Reasoning*, 1996.
9. Nicolas Helft. Induction as nonmonotonic inference. In: *Proceedings of KR '89*, pages 149–156, Morgan Kaufmann, 1989.
10. Nicolas Helft, Katsumi Inoue and David Poole. Query answering in circumscription. In: *Proceedings of IJCAI-91*, pages 426–431, 1991.
11. Katsumi Inoue. Linear resolution for consequence finding. *Artificial Intelligence*, 56:301–353, 1992.
12. Koji Iwanuma, Katsumi Inoue, and Ken Satoh. Completeness of pruning methods for consequence finding procedure SOL. In: *Proceedings of the 3rd International Workshop on First-Order Theorem Proving*, pages 89–100, 2000.
13. Kurt Konolige. Abduction versus closure in causal theories. *Artificial Intelligence*, 53:255–272, 1992.
14. Nicolas Lachiche. Abduction and induction from a non-monotonic reasoning perspective. In: [6], pages 107–116.
15. Char-Tung Lee. A completeness theorem and computer program for finding theorems derivable from given axioms. Ph.D. thesis, Department of Electrical Engineering and Computer Science, University of California, Berkeley, CA, 1967.
16. Pierre Marquis. Consequence finding algorithms. In: D. Gabbay and P. Smets, editors, *Handbook for Defeasible Reasoning and Uncertain Management Systems*, Volume 5, Kluwer, 2000.
17. Stephen Muggleton. Inverse entailment and Progol. *New Generation Computing*, 13:245–286, 1995.
18. Stephen Muggleton. Completing inverse entailment. In: D. Page, editor, *Proceedings of the 8th International Conference on Inductive Logic Programming*, LNAI 1446, pages 245–249, Springer, 1998.
19. Stephen Muggleton and Christoper Bryant. Theory completion and inverse entailment. In: J. Cussens and A. Frisch, editors, *Proceedings of the 10th International Conference on Inductive Logic Programming*, LNAI 1866, pages 130–146, Springer, 2000.
20. Shan-Hwei Nienhuys-Cheng and Ronald de Wolf. *Foundations of Inductive Logic Programming.* LNAI, 1228, Springer, 1997.

21. Akihiro Yamamoto. Which hypotheses can be found with inverse entailment? In: N. Lavrač and S. Džeroski, editors, *Proceedings of the 7th International Workshop on Inductive Logic Programming*, LNAI 1297, pages 296–308, Springer, 1997.
22. Akihiro Yamamoto. Using abduction for induction based on bottom generalization. In: [6], pages 267–280.
23. Akihiro Yamamoto and Bertram Fronhöfer. Hypotheses finding via residue hypotheses with the resolution principle. In: *Proceedings of the 11th International Conference on Algorithmic Learning Theory*, LNAI 1968, pages 156–165, 2000.

# From Shell Logs to Shell Scripts

Nico Jacobs and Hendrik Blockeel

Katholieke Universiteit Leuven,
Department of Computer Science,
Celestijnenlaan 200A, B-3001 Leuven
tel +32 16327550
fax +32 16327996
{Nico.Jacobs, Hendrik.Blockeel}@cs.kuleuven.ac.be

**Abstract.** Analysing the use of a Unix command shell is one of the classic applications in the domain of adaptive user interfaces and user modelling. Instead of trying to predict the next command from a history of commands, we automatically produce scripts that automate frequent tasks. For this we use an ILP association rule learner. We show how to speedup the learning task by dividing it into smaller tasks, and the need for a preprocessing phase to detect frequent subsequences in the data. We illustrate this with experiments with real world data.

**Keywords**: sequences, adaptive user interface

## 1 By Your Command

For many years now, the Unix command shell[1] is used by experienced and inexperienced users to interact with their system. Although this shell exists for many years, it can still be considered a flexible and customisable user interface: aliases allow you to give easier names for certain commands, with scripts you can build new commands by combining existing commands, et cetera. Many users do not fully utilise the power of the shell, either because they do not know all the tools the shell can provide or they do not want to go through the effort of using the tools.

Since the shell is such a complex and powerful user interface many people have investigated how users use this shell. Greenberg [6] collected logs from 168 different users, classified in four categories: computer scientists, experienced programmers, novice programmers and users performing no programming tasks (such as people from the administration et cetera). He used the standard statistical techniques to analyse e.g. which history mechanism is most useful.

Later on, people start using machine learning techniques to automatically analyse logs of shell use. One way to help people using the shell is by predicting the next command they will type, given the history of previous typed commands.

[1] although there exist a large number of different Unix shells, the differences between these shells are not relevant for this paper. Therefore we will talk about 'the' Unix command shell

C. Rouveirol and M. Sebag (Eds.): ILP 2001, LNAI 2157, pp. 80–90, 2001.

These predictions (most techniques present a list of the n most likely commands, with n small) are presented to the user, who can accept the prediction or type another command. A simple but useful prediction technique is building a probability table which stores for each command A and B the probability that the next command will be B given that the last command was A. Many variations on this technique have been investigated: using the n last commands instead of just the last one or using a decay factor in updating the probabilities to make the most recent information more important than older observations [3]. Other approaches for predicting the next command use decision trees [2] or combine different techniques [9].

These techniques predict up to 75% of the commands correctly, and about 50% when also the extra parameters of the command (switches, filenames et cetera) are predicted. The accuracy is even higher when multiple predictions are shown. Although this looks promising, there are some drawbacks:

- the user often uses short commands [6]. For those commands, it is as little effort to type the command as to select or verify a prediction, so nothing is gained.
- long commands are difficult to predict correctly. Verifying and correcting the prediction can take as much time as typing the command (or even more).
- a special shell is necessary to integrate the results of the prediction, but users often want to keep using the shell they are used to.

As a result, these techniques may be very useful to help people who have difficulties with typing (physically impaired or while performing other tasks), but for 'normal' shell users, although it may result in less keystrokes, the time gained will probably be low.

## 2 Automating the Automation

Another way of helping shell users is by suggesting scripts that automate frequent performed tasks. The advantages over the previous approach are:

- the user has to verify the proposed script only once, and can then used it as often as he likes without the need to verify or edit the script.
- even a script that consist of only short commands can still reduce the users effort.
- a system that suggests these scripts can be independent from the shell, so that the user can keep on using his familiar shell.
- it is easy to exchange such proposed scripts with other users.
- users can become more aware of their own behaviour.

This approach also has some drawbacks: probably it does not save you as many keystrokes as the first approach and it takes a large history of typed commands to extract meaningful scripts. Both approaches can be combined, which eliminates some of the drawbacks of the scripting approach, but introduces some drawbacks of the predicting the next command approach.

To the best of our knowledge, only very few implementations of this scripting approach exist. Graph based induction is used in [11] to analyse which files are used as input or are produced as output by Unix commands. In this way, sequences of commands that operate on one file (or files produced from this file) are detected and transformed into scripts. This allows them e.g. to detect edit-compile-run sequences, but they are not able to detect sequences of commands that are not related by common file use such as `lpr -P<printer> <file> ; lpq -P<printer>` or sequences of commands that are not related by any resource at all such as starting a set of common applications right after logging in.

Macro operators [7,8] are also related to the approach we presented above. When solving problems one starts from a start state and tries to get to a solution state by applying operators. Macro operators are a sequence of such operators, and the goal is to find a set of such macro operators such that solving the task with the basic operators and the macro operators takes less time than with the basic operators only. This relates to our approach: we look for sequences of actions, and we face the same length consideration: longer sequences solve bigger tasks, but can be used less often. However, there are some major differences between these macro operators and the shell scripts: a script can contain gaps (see section 3.2) and more important the actions in scripts have parameters, which makes this a relational problem.

Why can this be seen as a relational learning problem? Commands are interrelated by their execution order (or time), and each command is possible related to one or more parameters. This allows us to represent a shell log as a set of logical ground atoms. We translate these as follows:

- commands are translated to `stub/3` predicates, where the first argument is the order of execution (which is also a unique identifier), the second argument is the time of execution (expressed as the number of seconds past a certain fixed moment in time) and the third is the command itself.
- parameters are translated to `parameter/3` predicates, where the first argument is the identifier of the command, the second argument is the order of the parameter within that command, and the third is the parameter itself.

For example, the shell log

```
cp /etc/skel/.bashrc ~/.mybashrc
emacs ~/.mybashrc
```

would be translated to

```
stub(1,987882636,'cp').
parameter(1,1,'/etc/skel/.bashrc').
parameter(1,2,'~/.mybashrc').
stub(2,987882639,'emacs').
parameter(2,1,'~/.mybashrc').
```

Notice that this representation has difficulties representing piped commands. Either such commands must be represented as two separate commands where the first one writes to a imaginary named pipe and the second reads from this named pipe or as one command that has the second command as a parameter. We could also introduce a new predicate to handle this, but this will increase the search space.

We can also represent a parameterised script as a logical conjunction. For instance a script for copying a file and then start editing that copy could be represented as

```
stub(A,_,'cp'), parameter(A,1,F1), parameter(A,2,F2),
  B is A + 1, stub(B,_,'emacs'), parameter(B,1,F2).
```

In the next section we present how inductive logic programming can be used to detect such scripts and the problems we faced when applying them to real world data. In section 4 we evaluate the resulting system by analysing shell logs and conclude in section 5.

## 3 Generating Scripts with WARMR

WARMR [4] is an upgrade of the propositional APRIORI algorithm to an algorithm that can detect association rules expressed in a subset of first order logic. WARMR does this in two phases: first it searches for all frequent patterns (i.e. legal conjunctions of literals as defined in a language) in the dataset, and in a second phase it combines these frequent patterns into association rules. This first phase can more formally be expressed as follows:

**Definition 1.** *Given a set of ground atoms (examples) $\mathcal{E}$, a set of datalog clauses (background knowledge) $\mathcal{B}$, a language $\mathcal{L}$ defining all legal patterns and $m \geq 1$ (minimal occurrence), find all $l \in \mathcal{L}$ such that the query $l$ succeeds for at least $m$ examples in $\mathcal{E} \cup \mathcal{B}$.*

The scripts we are looking for can be found with this first phase of the WARMR algorithm. The examples consist of the logs represented as facts as discussed in the previous section, the language allows the `stub/3` and `parameter/3` predicates (where these arguments can be constants as well as variables). An additional predicate is added that allows two commands to link to each other. This predicate specifies when two commands are considered next to each other in a sequence. This can be that one command B must be executed right after command A (such as in the example above) but it can also be that B is executed at most n commands after A or at most n time units after A. Because we can also provide background knowledge to the system, we can e.g. tell the system that `ls -a` and `ls -all` are exactly the same command or tell the system that it should not distinguish between different editor commands. We can also use background knowledge to split up filenames (provided as parameter) into directory, filename root and filename extension.

In this way we can use WARMR to find the same sequences as those that could be found using the graph induction algorithm, but it has some advantages over the graph induction algorithm:

- additional information can be incorporated via the use of background knowledge (aliases, hierarchies,...),
- any relation between parameters of any command in the sequence can be expressed or learned; not just equality between parameters of two consecutive commands

The major drawback however is the execution time of this algorithm. For a small shell log of 500 commands, this algorithm needs more than 10 hours[2] of CPU time to find all sequences that occur at least 5 times. For larger logs the algorithm was even unable to finish due to lack of resources. However we can speedup this algorithm by splitting up the learning task and by using a better algorithm for one of the learning tasks.

### 3.1 Speedup by Splitting Up the Learning Task

WARMR builds its frequent patterns levelwise: the list of frequent patterns of level 1 contains all frequent atoms in $\mathcal{L}$. Each run each pattern $P$ in the frequent set is extended to a pattern $P \wedge A$ for each atom $A \in \mathcal{L}$ if there exists no infrequent pattern $Q$ that is more general than $P \wedge A$. This means that WARMR will build patterns that include `parameter/3` atoms for commands in incomplete frequent sequences or commands that will never belong to a frequent sequence. This problem can be solved by first constructing all frequent sequences of commands without taking the parameter information into account and then transform each of these sequences into a separate pattern discovery task to find the frequent parameter patterns. Usually the user is not interested in a script for each frequent pattern, but only in frequent patterns that are not part of a longer frequent pattern, so we filter these out before we start searching for the frequent parameter patterns.

This split up dramatically reduces the size of the search space. Finding the frequent parameter patterns for a given frequent command pattern only takes a few seconds because frequent command patterns only contain few commands (compared with the total set of commands) and so the search space is small. Most of the time still goes into finding frequent command patterns. But since this is a propositional task, more efficient algorithms can be found.

### 3.2 Speedup by Using the Minimal Occurrence Algorithm

The way in which WARMR extends a frequent pattern is not optimised for finding frequent sequences in which the order of the items is important. We illustrate this with an example. Suppose that our dataset contains the frequent sequence `a b c d`. When WARMR has reached its second level, it has constructed these frequent patterns:

[2] all timings in this paper are on a Pentium III 800 MHz computer with 256 Mb memory, running linux and the Ace version of WARMR running ilProlog[1]

```
a -> b
b -> c
c -> d
```

However, when WARMR extends the first pattern `a -> b`, it will extend it to

```
a -> b -> a
a -> b -> b
a -> b -> c
a -> b -> d
```

and test each of these patterns on the dataset, to see that only the third succeeds. However, since we are looking for subsequent commands, we know that only `a -> b -> c` can be a valid extension. Moreover, if we know the identifiers at which the sequences `a -> b` and `b -> c` start, we can calculate from this the number of occurrences of `a -> b -> c` (together with the identifiers of `a` on which these sequences start) without looking into the dataset.

The above idea is implemented in the minimal occurrence algorithm [10]. We use an algorithm based on this minimal occurrence algorithm to find all maximal frequent sequences, where we add identifiers for left and right parents to efficiently combine elements into longer sequences.

**Definition 2.** *Let $s$ be a sequence of $n$ elements: $e_{s,1}e_{s,2}e_{s,3}...e_{s,n-1}e_{s,n}$. A sequence $s'$ ($e_{s',1}e_{s',2}...e_{s',p-1}e_{s',p}$) of length $p$ is a subsequence of the sequence $s$ of length $n$ if*
$1 \leq p \leq n$
*and* $\forall i 1 \leq i \leq p, \exists j 1 \leq j \leq n : e_{s',i} = e_{s,j}$
*and* $\forall i, j 1 \leq i < j \leq p \exists k, l 1 \leq k < l \leq n : e_{s',i} = e_{s,k}$ *and* $e_{s',j} = e_{s,l}$.
*The frequency of a subsequence in a sequence is the number of different mappings from elements of $s'$ into the elements of $s$ such that the previous conditions hold.*

Notice that this a general definition, usually we will restrict the sequence by introducing a maximal gap size in the third requirement:
$\forall i 1 \leq i < p \exists k, l 1 \leq k < l \leq n, l - k \leq gapsize + 1 : e_{s',i} = e_{s,k}$ and $e_{s',i+1} = e_{s,l}$

**Definition 3.** *A sequence $s'$ is a maximal subsequence of frequency $f$ of a sequence $s$ if $s'$ is a subsequence of the sequence $s$ with a frequency of at least $f$ and there is no sequence $s''$, subsequence of $s$ with frequency at least $f$, such that $s'$ is a subsequence of $s''$.*

Each sequence $s$ of length $n > 1$ has 2 frequent subsequences of length $n-1$. We call this first subsequence $leftparent(s)$ and the second $rightparent(s)$. To extend a sequence $s$ of length 2 or longer, one just combines this sequence with a sequence $t$ where the right parent of $s$ is the left parent of $t$. However for sequences $p$ and $q$ of length one, there are no restrictions in combining them, except that $p$ should occur before $q$ (and the maximal gap size if defined). Because of this, for constructing the second level, we can do no better than just trying all combinations of 2 sequences from level one. The algorithm is shown in figure 1.

We give each sequence a unique identifier and we store and index the identifiers from left and right parents for each sequence. This allows us to retrieve possible extensions for a frequent subsequence very efficient.

```
length = 2
let S(1) be the set of all frequent subsequences of s of length 1
Output = ϕ
foreach t, u ∈ S(1)
        if e_{t,1} , e_{u,1} is frequent in s w.r.t. maximal gap size
                add e_{t,1}, e_{u,1} to S(2)
while S(length) ≠ ϕ do
        S(length+1) = ϕ
        foreach t ∈ S(length)
                foreach u ∈ S(length) such that leftparent(u) = rightparent(t)
                        if e_{t,1}e_{t,2}...e_{t,length}e_{u,length} is frequent
                                add it to S(length+1)
        foreach t ∈S(length)
                if t is not part of any element in S(length+1)
                        add t to Output
        length = length + 1
return Output
```

**Fig. 1.** Calculating all frequent maximal subsequences of s

This algorithm is also related to the cSPADES algorithm [12] which can search for sequences in large databases in an efficient way. However, we combine elements based on their left and right parent instead of combining elements with identical tails because this last approach results in a less efficient search when using maximal gap size constraints as we do.

### 3.3 Gluing Everything Together

How do we use all this information to transform a shell log into a set of shell scripts? First we remove from the logs all commands that are useless in scripts because they can not change the state of the computer: `ls, more, date` et cetera. Of course, when the aim of the analysis is to get an insight in the behaviour of the user instead of producing scripts, this step can be skipped.

Next we use our variant of the minimal occurrences algorithm on the altered log file. By varying the maximal gap size and the minimal frequency for a subsequence to be considered frequent one can control the number of frequent sequences. We also add to the algorithm the possibility do define constraints on the subsequences. These constraints allow us for example to reject sequences that use a command more than $n$ times. We output the frequent subsequences as a set of `freqep/4` predicates, where the first argument is the identifier of the subsequence, the second is the identifier of the mapping (the highest identifier for a given subsequence is the frequency of that subsequence), the third argument is the element identifier within the subsequence and the fourth argument is the element identifier within the input sequence. We use this representation because it is independent of the ILP program that is going to use this subsequence information.

```
freqep(1,1,1,28).    freqep(1,1,2,30).
freqep(1,2,1,72).    freqep(1,2,2,73).
```

This could be such a result from this algorithm, specifying that it found only one frequent subsequence, that occurred twice: element number 28 in the input sequence is the first element in the first occurrence of the subsequence, element 30 is the second (so there is a gap of size 1). The second occurrence of the sequence is at position 72 and 73.

In the next step we add the subsequence output to the log data that we transform to the representation discussed in section 2. We do not allow `stub/3` atoms to be used in the language (WARMR would again start looking for frequent sequences this way) but force the use of `freqep/4` instead. The `parameter/3` and other predicates defined in background knowledge are also added to the language. We then let WARMR search for frequent patterns. An example of such a pattern is:

```
freqep(1,Occ,1,Pos1), parameter(Pos1,1,Param1), base(Param1,Base1),
 ext(Param1,'tex'), freqep(1,Occ,2,Pos2), parameter(Pos2,1,Param2),
 ext(Param2,'dvi'), base(Param2,Base1).
```

Since WARMR outputs all frequent patterns, we first have to make sure we remove all redundant rules. For instance together with the above rule, WARMRwould also produce next rules:

```
freqep(1,Occ,1,Pos1), parameter(Pos1,1,Param1), base(Param1,Base1),
 ext(Param1,Ext1), freqep(1,Occ,2,Pos2), parameter(Pos2,1,Param2),
 ext(Param2,Ext2), base(Param2,Base1).
freqep(1,Occ,1,Pos1), parameter(Pos1,1,Param1), base(Param1,Base1),
 ext(Param1,'tex'), freqep(1,Occ,2,Pos2), parameter(Pos2,1,Param2),
 ext(Param2,'dvi').
freqep(1,Occ,1,Pos1), parameter(Pos1,1,Param1), base(Param1,Base1),
 ext(Param1,'tex'), freqep(1,Occ,2,Pos2), parameter(Pos2,1,Param2).
```

et cetera.

Next the most specific frequent rules are translated to scripts: the commands are looked up in the input sequence and the remaining of the rules is parsed and written as a Unix function. Our first rule would be translated to:

```
function giveyourownname() {
  latex $1.tex
  xdvi $1.dvi
}
```

Now we sort the resulting scripts. Although length and frequency are important attributes of a script, we sort the scripts according to the frequency divided by the expected frequency of this subsequence in a sequence where the elements are put in random order. The higher this number, the more 'exceptional' the sequence is.

## 4 Experiments

We compare these approaches on the Greenberg dataset [5]. Table 1 shows the timings of finding frequent subsequences for 5 user logs from the Greenberg dataset with the default minimal frequency of 0.01. We see that, as the number of commands grows, the execution time of both algorithms (expressed in seconds) increases. The number of maximal frequent subsequences found does not seem to influence the execution time. The minimal occurrences algorithm is about 7 times faster than WARMR .

**Table 1.** Timing results with maximal gap size 0

| file | #commands | #frequent seq. | max. length seq. | time Warmr | time minocc |
|---|---|---|---|---|---|
| non-5 | 216 | 4 | 6 | 1.2 | 0.5 |
| non-16 | 590 | 26 | 6 | 13.8 | 1.8 |
| non-23 | 962 | 21 | 3 | 21.7 | 2.0 |
| non-11 | 1537 | 13 | 4 | 30.4 | 4.5 |
| non-4 | 3608 | 16 | 4 | 83.7 | 13.1 |

However, when we set the maximal gap size to 1, this changes the timings dramatically (see table 2). It takes WARMR almost 200 times as long as with gap size 0 to find the sequences for non-5. For non-16 this is nearly a factor 800 slower. For larger datasets, WARMR was not able to compute all sequences due to lack of resources. The minimal occurrences algorithm does not suffer from this problem, it does not even double the execution time.

**Table 2.** Timing results with maximal gap size 1

| file | #frequent seq. | max. length seq. | time Warmr | time minocc |
|---|---|---|---|---|
| non-5 | 8 | 6 | 236 | 0.7 |
| non-16 | 70 | 9 | 9975 | 2.6 |
| non-23 | 31 | 6 | - | 2.4 |
| non-11 | 63 | 8 | - | 6.9 |
| non-4 | 39 | 6 | - | 18.2 |

When we raise the maximal gap size to 2 (see table 3) WARMR is not able to find all frequent subsequences for even the smallest log file. While the other algorithm finishes in about a minute or less, we see that not only the length of the input but also the number of frequent subsequences found influences the execution time.

**Table 3.** Timing results with maximal gap size 2

| file | #frequent seq. | max. length seq. | time minocc |
|---|---|---|---|
| non-5 | 35 | 9 | 1.6 |
| non-16 | 607 | 13 | 27.1 |
| non-23 | 99 | 9 | 5.6 |
| non-11 | 401 | 11 | 40.6 |
| non-4 | 173 | 10 | 63.6 |

Just for illustration purpose we show some of the scripts found:

```
lpr -P $1 $2
lpq -P $1
```

```
cd ..
rmdir $1
```

```
mkdir $1
cd $1
```

## 5 Conclusion

In this paper we tackled the problem of creating shell scripts (a sequence of commands together with their (variable) parameters) from shell logs. Since this task can be formulated as a relational pattern discovery task, we used the WARMR algorithm. To speed up this task we separate the propositional subtask (detecting frequent subsequences of command stubs) from the relational task (detecting frequent patterns in the parameters of a frequent subsequence of commands). We also presented a version of the minimal occurrences algorithm to find frequent subsequences in an efficient way.

We compared WARMR with this new system on real world data. WARMR is considerably slower, and often fails to find all sequences due to lack of computing resources. These experiments also show that shell logs do contain frequent subsequences, and even frequent subsequences of considerably length.

Other possible applications for this technique are other sequence analysing tasks, such as analysing traces of visits to a website where each click is annotated with extra information. This can help the designer in understanding how users visit the site or allow for automatic site modification. The system can also be used in analysing other user interfaces: a prototype of the user interface is built and testers try this interface. All their annotated actions are logged and analysed. If important long subsequences of actions are found, the developer can consider redesigning the interface in such a way that these actions can be performed more easily. All applications were sequential annotated data is involved and were frequent subsequences provide important knowledge are potential application domains for this technique.

But not only in applications where detecting sequences is the main task, also other applications can make use of efficient subsequence detection algorithms.

Analysis of molecular data is such an example: sequences of atoms can be important features in such applications.

**Acknowledgements**

The authors thank Jan Ramon for his help with the WARMR system, Luc De Raedt for the discussions on this subject and Saul Greenberg for providing the test data. Hendrik Blockeel is a post-doctoral fellow of the Fund for Scientific Research of Flanders (FWO-Vlaanderen).

## References

1. H. Blockeel, B. Demoen, L. Dehaspe, G. Janssens, J. Ramon, and H. Vandecasteele. Executing query packs in ILP. In J. Cussens and A. Frisch, editors, *Proceedings of the 10th International Conference in Inductive Logic Programming*, volume 1866 of *Lecture Notes in Artificial Intelligence*, pages 60–77, London, UK, July 2000. Springer.
2. Brian D. Davison and Haym Hirsch. Experiments in UNIX command prediction. In *Proceedings of the 14th National Conference on Artificial Intelligence and 9th Innovative Applications of Artificial Intelligence Conference (AAAI-97/IAAI-97)*, pages 827–827, Menlo Park, July 27–31 1997. AAAI Press.
3. Brian D. Davison and Haym Hirsh. Predicting sequences of user actions. In *Predicting the Future: AI Approaches to Time Series Problems*, pages 5–12. AAAI Press, July 1998. WS-98-07.
4. L. Dehaspe. *Frequent Pattern Discovery in First-Order Logic.* PhD thesis, Department of Computer Science, Katholieke Universiteit Leuven, 1998. `http://www.cs.kuleuven.ac.be/~ldh/`.
5. Saul Greenberg. Using unix: collected traces of 168 users. Technical report, University of Calgary, 1988.
6. Saul Greenberg. *The Computer User as Toolsmith: The Use, Reuse, and Organization of Computer-Based Tools.* Cambridge Series on Human-Computer Interaction. Cambridge University Press, 1993. QA76.9H85G73.
7. Glenn A. Iba. A heuristic approach to the discovery of macro-operators. *Machine Learning*, 3:285–317, 1989.
8. R. E. Korf. *Learning to Solve Problems by Searching for Macro-Operators.* Research Notes in Artificial Intelligence. Pitman, London, 1985.
9. Benjamin Korvemaker and Russell Greiner. Predicting UNIX command lines: Adjusting to user patterns. In *Adaptive User Interfaces: Papers from the 2000 AAAI Spring Symposium*, pages 59–64, 2000.
10. Heikki Mannila and Hannu Toivonen. Discovering generalized episodes using minimal occurrences. In Evangelos Simoudis, Jia Wei Han, and Usama Fayyad, editors, *Proceedings of the Second International Conference on Knowledge Discovery and Data Mining (KDD-96)*, page 146. AAAI Press, 1996.
11. Hiroshi Motoda and Kenichi Yoshida. Machine learning techniques to make computers easier to use. *Artificial Intelligence*, 103(1–2):295–321, 1998.
12. Mohammed Javeed Zaki. Sequence mining in categorical domains: Incorporating constraints. In Arvin Agah, Jamie Callan, and Elke Rundensteiner, editors, *Proceedings of the 2000 ACM CIKM International Conference on Information and Knowledge Management (CIKM-00)*, pages 422–429, N.Y., November 6–11 2000. ACM Press.

# An Automated ILP Server in the Field of Bioinformatics

Andreas Karwath and Ross D. King

Department of Computer Science, University of Wales
Aberystwyth, SY23 3DB, Ceredigion, UK

**Abstract.** The identification of evolutionary related (homologous) proteins is a key problem in molecular biology. Here we present a inductive logic programming based method, *Homology Induction* (HI), which acts as a filter for existing sequence similarity searches to improve their performance in the detection of remote protein homologies. HI performs a PSI-BLAST search to generate positive, negative, and uncertain examples, and collects descriptions of these examples. It then learns rules to discriminate the positive and negative examples. The rules are used to filter the uncertain examples in the "twilight zone". HI uses a multi-table database of 51,430,710 pre-fabricated facts from a variety of biological sources, and the inductive logic programming system Aleph to induce rules. Hi was tested on an independent set of protein sequences with equal or less than 40 per cent sequence similarity (PDB40D). ROC analysis is performed showing that HI can significantly improve existing similarity searches. The method is automated and can be used via a web/mail interface.

## 1 Introduction

The identification of evolutionary related (homologous) proteins is a key problem in molecular biology. Knowledge of a homologous relationship between two proteins, one of known function and the other of unknown function, allows the probabilistic inference that the proteins have the same function (as evolution generally conserves function). Such inferences are the basis of most of our knowledge of sequenced genomes.

### 1.1 Homology Searches

Protein homology is usually inferred by using computer programs to measure the similarity of two or more proteins. This is almost always done by comparing the two amino-acid strings of the proteins under consideration, and measuring the character-wise similarity between them. *However there is generally much more information available which is ignored.*

Initially, sequence homology searches were done using dynamic programming [32,24]. Due to the rapid growth of the sequence databases, dynamic programming became too time consuming and more efficient heuristic approaches were

C. Rouveirol and M. Sebag (Eds.): ILP 2001, LNAI 2157, pp. 91–103, 2001.

developed. The most common programs are FASTA [28,19], BLAST [1] and PSI-BLAST [2,18], as well as hidden Markov-model approaches such as SAM-T98 [13]. Such programs consume more CPU time than all other bioinformatic programs put together. Although, these algorithms perform well for closely related homologous sequences, the results for more distantly related proteins are less reliable [26], detecting only $\sim 50\%$ of all possible homologies.

Here, we describe a procedure using background knowledge together with the protein's amino acid sequence to induce homology. The basic idea is to collect as much information as possible for a protein and its likely homologous proteins, and then to infer homology using discriminatory inductive logic programming (ILP). We call this approach *Homology Induction* (HI).

Related work to HI are BLAST PRINTS [37] and PrePRINTS BLAST Search [38]. PrePRINTS is a tool to aid biologists filter BLAST results by "decorating" the output of BLAST with keywords. A score is given based on a statistical analysis of the frequency of keyword pairs. A similar approach is taken by SAWTED - structure assignments with text descriptions [20], retrieving remote homologues using annotations in the SWISS-PROT database based on a text-similarity measure. A different approach was used by Jaakola *et. al* employing the Fisher kernel method on top of a HMM as a discriminative method for detecting remote homologues [12]. HI is distinguished from these approaches by its ability to use all available background knowledge, its more general learning ability, and by its more comprehensive experimental validation.

## 2 Methods

### 2.1 Homology Induction

The HI approach is based on the following steps: (a) collection of possible homologous proteins using an existing method of sequence similarity search (SSS); (b) accumulation of all available information for these proteins; (c) division of the possible homologues into closely related homologues (training set) and set of more remote homologues (twilight zone) and generation of negative examples; (d) induction of rules for the training set; and (e) application of these rules to a set od possible homologues in the twilight zone . The individual steps are explained in the following subsections.

**a) Similarity Search.** A similarity search is performed and the result collected, which becomes a set of examples of possible homologous proteins. PSI-BLAST, the most used homology search program [2,18], was employed as the similarity search algorithm. PSI-BLAST has state-of-the-art accuracy [26]. PSI-BLAST is essentially an iterative nearest-neighbour method (in sequence space). The result of a PSI-BLAST search is a list of *possible* homologues, sorted by their e-value [2,18]. The lower the e-value, the higher the probability that the match does *not* randomly occur in the database, which implies that the matches are evolutionary related.

**b) Data Accumulation and Data Preparation.** For each possible homologous protein all available data from the database of pre-fabricated facts is collected. The information stored in the database was selected for relevance to the detection of homology, originating from a wide variety of bioinformatic sources. For each protein in the SWISS-PROT database [3] we collected:

- Directly from SWISS-PROT: the description, keywords, organism's classification, molecular weight, and database references (Prosite, HSSP, EMBL, PIR - excluding SCOP classifications).
- The predicted secondary structure - we used the DSC method [14] on single sequences (as a multiple sequence method would require a homology search).
- The amino acid distribution for singlets and pairs of residues, as used by the PROPSEARCH algorithm [11].
- The predicted cleavage sites from the SignalIP [25].
- The total hydrophobic moment assuming secondary structure [9,14].
- The length and starting point of local PSI-BLAST alignments.

Assembling this information in one large table would, in principle, be possible, but access to the data would be highly complex and inefficient. However, the assembly of such a table is required as the staring point for statistical, neural networks, or standard machine learning. This limitation of standard learning techniques is known as the "multi-table problem", i.e. learning from multi-relational data stored in multiple tables [7,17]. We therefore chose to represent this information in form of a database of datalog facts.

To give an example of the database, we show how the predicted secondary structure was translated from a single string into a set of datalog facts. The secondary structure of a protein possesses three states: $\alpha$-helix, $\beta$-strand, and coil. If, for example a, protein has the following predicted secondary structure: $\alpha\alpha\alpha\alpha cccccc\alpha\alpha\alpha\alpha\alpha ccccccc\beta\beta\beta$, this would translate into: the 1st $\alpha$-helix secondary structure prediction is of length 4; the 1st coil secondary structure prediction is of length 6; the 2nd $\alpha$-helix secondary structure prediction is of length 5; the 2nd coil secondary structure prediction is of length 7; and the 1st $\beta$-strand structure prediction is of length 3.

The translated SWISS-PROT database (version 39) is 1.21 Gb and contains 51,430,710 facts for a total of 86,593 proteins.

**c) Division.** The result of the initial similarity search is divided into two subsets: a set of *positive* examples (proteins which are almost certainly homologous), and a set of *uncertain* examples. As a threshold for this division, the algorithm uses the inclusion e-value used in a). A third set is generated, to supply a set of *negative* examples. These negative examples are randomly selected from a list of all SWISS-PROT [3] proteins, which do not occur in the set of positive or uncertain examples.

**d) Induction.** The most natural solution to the multi-table problem is to use inductive logic programming (ILP) [21]. ILP is the form of machine learning that is based on first-order logic and is particularly suitable for problems where the data is structured, there is a large amount of background knowledge, and where the formation of comprehensible rules is desirable. This is a key advantage of using ILP. We used the ILP system Aleph [22] version 2.75 which is based on inverse entailment. Aleph (an the related program Progol) have been successfully applied to a variety of problems in computational biology, such as learning rules to obtain Structure-Activity Relationships (SARs) [14,15], and protein topology prediction [35]. Aleph searches for logic programs (rules) which are true for positive examples and not true for the negative examples. In HI the positive examples are the sequences known to be homologous by use of the SSS, and the negative examples are 1000 random sequences that are not homologous. We generated the set of negative examples from SWISS-PROT proteins not occuring in the list of possible homologues. As the problem of remote homology detection is a real world application, one cannot omit the possibility of errors in the data. To accommodate this possibility, Aleph was set to accept learning rules with up to a 15% noise. Furthermore, to avoid overfitting of the rules, a minimum of ten positive examples is required to allow to proceed to the induction step. Aleph is in general versatile, bringing together the power of first order logic and the possibility of using background knowledge. However, it is not very suitable for use directly on numerical values, as Aleph searches the lattice for each single value for one attribute; the search using numerical values can be inefficient, depending on the number of distinctively different values. Possible solutions are to introduce operators, such as *less than* and *greater than* or to use discretisation. We choose to discretise all numerical values into 10 levels.

**e) Application.** After the rules were learnt they were applied to the uncertain examples. If the rule was true for an uncertain example, this was considered evidence, along with the weak sequence similarity towards identifying the example as homologous. We therefore used the rules to identify proteins which have uncertain evidence for homology based only on sequence, but have sufficient evidence based on sequence and the other information from our annotated deductive database. Following the induction step, initial results collected from PSI-BLAST are re-arranged according to the rules found by Aleph. This is done by modifying the original E-value reported by PSI-BLAST. The results covered by the rules found, are assigned with an lower E-value, while proteins not covered persist with the same value as before. This is done by multiplying the original E-value, received by PSI-BLAST, with a constant evidence factor (EF; with EF $< 1$). This approach is based on the assumption that if protein covered by a rule then this gives further evidence of homology. Hence, it should be moved further up the list of close homologous sequences found by PSI-BLAST. We call the resulting value $E_{HI}$-value.

### 2.2 Experiment

To assess the accuracy of homology detection it is necessary to have a "gold standard" set of known homologies. To test HI we used the systematic approach of Park *et. al.* [27], which uses a subset of the Structural Classification of Protein (SCOP) database [23]. The SCOP database is a classification database of proteins of known function and structure. The subset used for testing includes all proteins in the SCOP database with equal or less than 40 per cent sequence similarity (PDB40D database). The evaluation of a SSSs is done by investigating each entry in the PDB40D database and accumulating the results. In theory, a perfect homology search algorithm should be able to detect all homologous relationships in PDB40D. However, in most cases, unrelated, non-homologous proteins can be found in the so called twilight zone (errors of commission); while at the same time evolutionary related proteins are omitted (errors of omission).

It is clear that for a high cut-off value non-homologous sequences will be considered to be homologous; while for a low cut-off value homologous sequences will be considered not to be homologous. Using a fixed cut-off value together with a simple error rate would therefore be a crude measure for comparison of homology searches. A further reason for not using error rates as a measure of comparison, is the inability to take into account different costs for different types of prediction errors. In most inference problems, the cost of predicting an example to be negative when it is actually positive (an error of *omission*), is not equal to the cost of predicting an example to be positive when it is actually negative (an error of *commission*). To counter the problem of different costs and cut-off values, Receiver Operating Characteristic (ROC) curves are used to compare prediction and classification problems and where first introduced in signal detection [36,8,33,4]. The value of a ROC curve is that: if one prediction method produces a curve to the left of another method, then the method to the left is superior. This conclusion is true regardless of the particular costs associated with errors of commission and omission (assuming linearity of costs). We use ROC curves as our main method for comparison between the standard method PSI-BLAST and HI.

**Two Different Test Set Ups.** To illustrate that the HI approach is robust and can work equally well with data generated from sequence alone, two different setting were used. The first setting made use of the full database described in the previous section, called $HI^{all}$. The second setting used purely sequence based information, called $HI^{seq}$. All entries from the database originating from SWISS-PROT, except *mol_weight* and *seq_length* as this information could be computed from sequence, were removed. This left 19 possible terms to be learnt from. These two settings correspond to the two most common uses for homology searching: setting one - searching for a homologous protein with known structure; setting two - annotating a newly sequenced gene.

## 3 Results

### 3.1 Rules

We performed the HI algorithm with the two different settings on the SCOP (PDB40D) database having 1,434 entries. 409 entries had less than 10 SWISS-

PROT hits, and no rules could be learnt. In these cases the original PSI-BLAST results were considered to be the HI output. This left 1025 examples to be filtered.

**HI$^{all}$ Setting.** For the HI$^{all}$ setting, Aleph could induce rules for 1,015 PDB40D examples. For 14 examples no rules could be learnt, and the PSI-BLAST results were taken as output. For the remaining 1,015 cases we collected the results and applied the induced rules to the uncertain examples of each PDB40D entry. For 701 PDB40D entries Aleph induced one single rule, for 133 entries rule sets consisting of two separate rules, while producing three or more separate rules for 177. Altogether, HI$^{all}$ produced 1851 rules for the 1,015 PDB40D entries, 1030 using only one predicate. The most commonly used predicate of the single predicate rules was database references to other databases (*db_ref*), utilised by 651 rules. These rules consisted mainly of references to Prosite (639) and some to the HSSP database (12). This can be expected as both databases cluster homologous families of proteins together.

**HI$^{seq}$ Setting.** For the HI$^{seq}$ setting, Aleph could only induce rules for 949 PDB40D entries, compared to 1,015 for HI$^{all}$. As before, the original PSI-BLAST output was taken in cases where no rules could be learnt. Although, this seems to be relatively similar to the number of rules learnt before, the distribution of the number of the rules in a rule set is very different. Only 371 examples could be explained with one single rule. A further 228 examples had 2 rules, and 137 examples had 3 rules. For 213 examples, a rule set with more than 3 rules was induced.

To give an example of how differently the two HI setting induced rules, we present the two results of the induction of Myoglobin with the PDB entry 1MBD.

### 3.2 ROC Analysis for HI$^{all}$, HI$^{seq}$, and PSI-BLAST

The first method we investigated to compare PSI-BLAST and HI was based on the concepts of precision, recall and accuracy from information retrieval[31]. This comparison is more elementary than that of ROC curves. Table 1 shows the precision and recall for PSI-BLAST, HI$^{all}$ and HI$^{seq}$ using a cut-off E-value of 10. The accuracy measure for all methods is very high, as the PDB40D database has 8022 true homology relationships, and 2,046,900 false ones. This makes the measure of accuracy inappropriate, as the number of negative relationships compared to the number of positive relations is very small. Although both HI accuracies are higher than PSI-BLAST, it is not clear at first sight if it is significantly higher. To test significance we performed a two-sample $\chi^2$ test to compare the actual frequency of a prediction with the estimated frequency of the prediction. For HI$^{all}$ the $\chi^2$ value is 45.35 and for HI$^{seq}$ is 47.85. Comparing these values with the critical $\chi^2$ values from a significance table [16], indicate that both methods are independent from each other. The critical value of $\chi^2$ for 1 degree of freedom

```
PDB 1MBD Myoglobin (Deoxy, pH 8.4)
SCOP 1.1.1.1.4 HI^all:
Rules found:
 1 homologous(A) :- db_ref(A,prosite,ps01033,B,C).
```

**Fig. 1.** The rule induced for the Myglogin 1MBD, considers all proteins to be homologous which possess a database reference connecting them to the Prosite sequence pattern database entry PS01033. The PS01033 pattern is the GLOBIN pattern. Globins are heme-containing proteins involved in binding and/or transporting oxygen and are a well studied group of proteins. Myoglobin are a type of globin responsible for storing oxygen in vertebrates. The only positive example not included in this rule is a leghemoglobin, fitting the Prosite pattern PS00208 for plant globins. Two out of four possible uncertain examples are covered by this rule, these are both hemoglobins. Hemoglobins belong to the same family as the query sequence and are homologous to myoglobins. The two uncertain examples *not* covered by this rule are a protein associated with microtubule, and a serine hydroxymethyltransferase protein, neither are homologous to myoglobins. In summary the HI rule uses the prosite information to improve on the standard PSI-BLAST method.

**Table 1.** Precision, recall and accuracy for all three methods.

| Method | Precision | Recall | Accruracy in per cent |
|---|---|---|---|
| PSI-BLAST | 0.34 | 0.717 | 99.68991 |
| $HI^{all}$ | 0.32 | 0.787 | 99.70072 |
| $HI^{seq}$ | 0.30 | 0.789 | 99.69449 |

and 99.995% confidence is 7.879, which indicates that $HI^{seq}$ and $HI^{all}$ are both significantly better than PSI-BLAST.

This test is based on one cut-off value (i.e. one set of costs). To test all linear costs we performed a ROC analysis. Both HI set-ups ($HI^{all}$ and $HI^{seq}$) were compared with PSI-BLAST.

With HI the results for the uncertain examples are re-organised according to their e-values. This is done by multiplying the original e-value, received by PSI-BLAST, with a factor. To optimise this factor, the area under ROC curve (AUROC) [4,29,30] was calculated for possible factor settings to maximise the area. This approach was taken instead of a full cross-validation, as cross-validation would be computationally prohibitive and the large size of the database makes the estimate robust.

A variety of different factors were used, starting with $9 \times 10^{-1}$, ending with $1 \times 10^{-100}$. The initial step for changing a factor is 0.1, resulting in the AUROCs calculated for the factors 0.9, 0.8, 0,7, ..., 0.1 . Then the factors were changed by an order of magnitude to 0.09, 0.08, 0.07, ... , 0.01. Figure 3 shows the different results from this analysis. For $HI^{all}$ the AUROC peaked at $2 \times 10^{-5}$, while for $HI^{seq}$ it peaked at only $8 \times 10^{-2}$. The maximum AUROC value for $HI^{a}ll$ is 0.7571, while the maximum AUROC for $HI^{s}eq$ is 0.7515. The AUROC for PSI-BLAST is 0.7508.

```
PDB 1MBD Myoglobin (Deoxy, pH 8.4)
SCOP 1.1.1.1.4 HI^seq:

Rules found: 7

1 homologous(A) :- amino_acid_ratio_rule(A,a,10),
                   amino_acid_pair_ratio_rule(A,l,s,10),
                   amino_acid_pair_ratio_rule(A,a,l,10).
2 homologous(A) :- mol_wt_rule(A,6),
                   sec_struc_coil_rule(A,5,8),
                   sec_struc_coil_rule(A,1,6).
3 homologous(A) :- sec_struc_rule(A,a,4,9),
                   sec_struc_rule(A,a,4,10).
4 homologous(A) :- sec_struc_alpha_rule(A,7,10),
                   sec_struc_alpha_rule(A,6,1).
5 homologous(A) :- sec_struc_distribution_rule(A,c,5),
                   sec_struc_distribution_rule(A,b,1),
                   sec_struc_conf_rule(A,10).
6 homologous(A) :- domain_rule(A,4,9,4,4).
7 homologous(A) :- signalip1_rule(A,9),
                   sec_struc_beta_rule(A,4,6).
```

**Fig. 2.** This complex set of rules consists out of seven separate rules. The first rule translates follows: *Consider every example to be homologous, if its amino acid sequence has a high Alanine content, very high frequencies of Leucine-Serine, and very high frequencies of Alanine-Leucine.* The second rule translates similarly to: *Consider every example to be homologous, if it has a molecular weight slightly above the median, a relatively long predicted secondary coil structure in the middle of the sequence, and a medium length predicted secondary coil structure at the beginning of the sequence.* Although HI produced an extensive amount of rules, none of the four uncertain examples are covered by the rule set.

The resulting ROC curves using the optimal re-sorting factor can be seen in figure 4, together with the ROC curve for PSI-BLAST. The dominating curve is the curve produced by $HI^{all}$, being to the left of the other two curves. Although the ROC curve of $HI^{seq}$ produced a higher AUROC than the curve produced by PSI-BLAST, it does not entirely dominate the PSI-BLAST ROC curve. For large sections of the false positive axis, the two curves have a similar true positive rate. Only in the false positive rate interval of 0.38 to 0.5 does the ROC curve produced by $HI^{seq}$ dominate the one produced by PSI-BLAST.

## 4 Web Server

The HI method is available for use in as web/mail server (http://www.aber.ac.uk/~phiwww/hi_V2/index.html). To the best of our knowledge this is the first internet server providing an ILP service. The server is a simple HTML form,

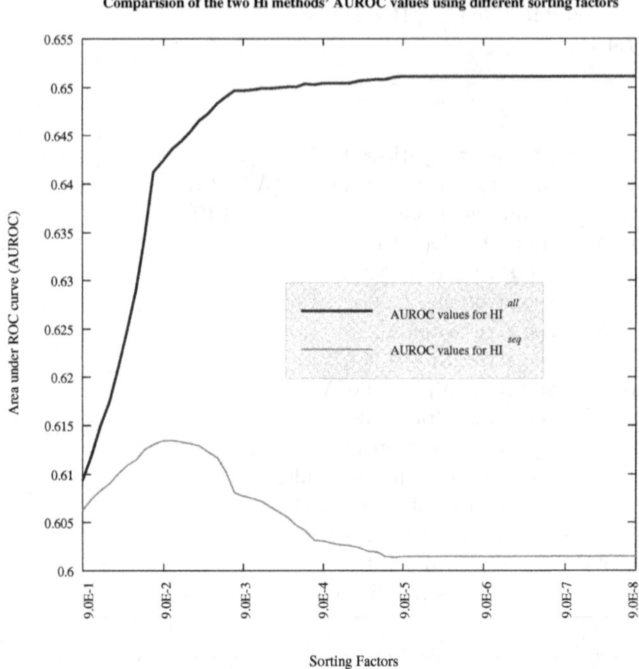


**Fig. 3.** This figure shows the calculated areas under ROC curve for both HI methods ($HI^{all}$ and $HI^{seq}$) for a variety of re-sorting factors. The two curves follow a very different pattern. The AUROC values for $HI^{all}$ increases steadily and reaches its maxim value at $6 \times 10^{-5}$ with a value of 0.651169; while the AUROC values for $HI^{seq}$ first increases and then decreases again with a peak at $8 \times 10^{-2}$ with an AUROC value of 0.613467. Comparing both methods with PSI-BLAST shows that $HI^{seq}$ has offers only a slight improvement over PSI-BLAST with an AUROC value of 0.606764. In contrast, $HI^{all}$ increases the AUROC value by approximately 7.4 per cent.

supplying the desired information to a CGI-Perl script. The user has the opportunity to select the parameters of the initial PSI-BLAST search, like inclusion e-value, maximum e-value to be reported, number of PSI-BLAST iterations, and if a low complexity sequence filter should be used. The user is also offered the possibility to select a different e-value to divide between positive examples and examples in the twilight zone. In the induction step, it is possible to select which datalog facts to be used in the induction, as well as Aleph specific options, like the minimum number of positive examples required and the percentage of noise allowed.

All this information, including the amino acid sequence in question, is passed to a CGI-Perl script checking for inconsistencies. In case the information is regarded as being consistent, the script sends an email to a daemon which distributes the job to a specified computer. At the moment it uses just one ma-

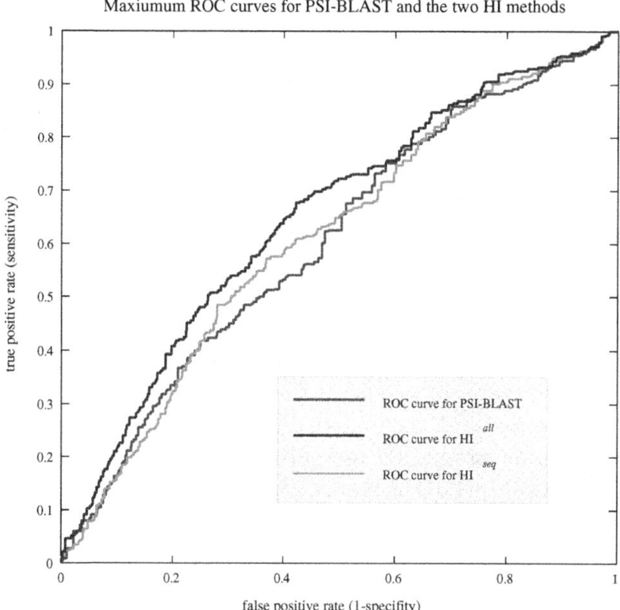


**Fig. 4.** The three ROC curves produced by PSI-BLAST, $\mathrm{HI}^{all}$, and $\mathrm{HI}^{seq}$ for predictions in the twilight zone. While the ROC curve for PSI-BLAST results from applying ROC analysis directly to the results produced, the ROC curves for both HI methods are maximised using an optimal value for re-sorting. The ROC curve for $\mathrm{HI}^{all}$ dominates over the other two curves at all times; while the curves for PSI-BLAST and $\mathrm{HI}^{seq}$ oscillate around each other. $\mathrm{HI}^{seq}$ dominates the PSI-BLAST curve between $\sim 0.38$ and $\sim 0.5$.

chine, however, it is possible to have multiple parallel jobs running on different machines running.

## 5 Discussion and Conclusion

HI is a first step in the application of ILP to aid in the inference of homology by exploiting bioinformatic data other than the basic sequence. We have shown that HI is more sensitive than the state-of-the-art sequence method PSI-BLAST, and that HI performs better for all error costs. Although this result only shows that HI is an improvement over PSI-BLAST, the basic approach of HI is applicable to all sequence-based homology search methods. We therefore expect a similar level of improvement over other methods such as Hidden Markov Models. Many improvements are possible to HI. Other sources of bioinformatic data and more biological background knowledge could be used. For example: comment lines from SWISS-PROT could be included (although this would require a more refined computational linguistic analysis); database links to Medline abstracts could be exploited, etc. Much of the data in the deductive database is still propositional in form, and this does not fully exploit the power of ILP. More background knowledge could be used to allow ILP to use: $\leq$ and $\geq$, numerical neighbourhoods, hierarchies of keywords, phylogenic trees, etc. Cross-validation could be used to get better estimates of the accuracy of rules. Data mining algorithms such as WARMR [6] could be used to pre-process the data to find frequent patterns which would make learning easier and more successful. Multiple theories could be learnt and combined, e.g. using boosting and bagging [10,5]. Also different algorithms could be used and their predictions combined together [34]. We expect that these improvements would greatly improve the sensitivity of homology detection over the level achieved by HI. There is a need for new approaches to inferring homology. One of the most interesting results of Park *et. al.* [26] was how relatively uncorrelated the errors were from the three different homology prediction methods examined. This means that better results could be obtained by combining prediction methods when inferring homology. This can be seen as another example of the statistical principle stated in the introduction: all available relevant information should be used. We believe that HI should be seen in this light. It is far from being the last word in inferring homology, but it is a valuable new approach.

## References


1. S. F. Altschul, W. Gish, W. Miller, Eugene W. Myers, and D. J. Lipman. Basic local alignment search tool. *J. Mol. Biol.*, 215:403–410, 1990.
2. S. F. Altschul, T L. Madden, A. A. Schäffer, J. Zhang, Z. Zhang, W. Miller, and D. J. Lipman. Gapped BLAST and PSI-BLAST: a new generation of protein database search programs. *Nucleic Acids Research*, 25(17):3389–3402, 1997.
3. A. Bairoch and R. Apweiler. The SWISS-PROT protein sequence data bank and its supplement TrEMBL in 2000. *Nucleic Acids Research*, 28:45–48, 2000.
4. A. P. Bradley. The use of area under ROC curve in the evaluation of learning algorithms. *Pattern Recognition*, 30(7):1145–1159, 1995.
5. L. Breiman. Bagging predictors. *Machine Learning*, 26(2):123–140, 1996.
6. L. Dehaspe. *Frequent Pattern Discovery in First-Order Logic.* PhD thesis, Department of Computer Science, Katholieke Universiteit Leuven, Belgium, 1998.
7. S. Dzeroski. Inductive logic programming and knowledge discovery. In U. M. Fayyad, G. Piatetsky-Sharpiro, P. Smyth, and R. Uthurusamy, editors, *Advances in Knowledge Discovery and Data Mining*, pages 117–152. AAAI/MIT Press, 1996.
8. J. P. Egan. *Signal Detection Theory and ROC Analysis.* Cognition and Perception. Academic Press, New York, 1975.
9. D. Eisenberg. Three-dimensional structure of membrane and surface proteins. *Ann. Rev. Biochem*, 53:595–623, 1984.
10. Y. Freud and R. E. Schapire. A decision-theoretic generalization of on-line learning and an application to boosting. *Journal of Computer and System Sciences*, 55(1):119–139, 1997.
11. U. Hobohm and C. Sander. A sequence property approach to searching protein database. *J. Mol. Biol.*, 251:390–399, 1995.

12. T. Jaakola, M. Diekhans, and D. Haussler. Using Fisher kernel method to detect remote protein homologies. In *Proceedings of the Seventh International Conference on Intelligent Systems for Molecular Biology*, pages 149–158. AAAI, AAAI Press, 1999.
13. K. Karplus, C. Barrett, and R. Hughey. Hidden markov models for detecting remote protein homologies. *Bioinformatics*, 14(10):846–856, 1998. SAM-T98 paper.
14. R. D. King, S. Muggleton, A. Srinivasan, and M. J. E. Sterberg. Structure-activity relationships derived by machine learning: The use of atoms and their bond connectivities to predict mutagenicity by inductive logic programming. *Proc. Natl. Acad. Sci. USA*, 93:438–442, 1996.
15. Ross D. King and Ashwin Srinivasan. The discovery of indicator variables for qsar unsing inductive logic programming. *Journal of Compter-Aided Molecular Design*, 11:571–580, 1997.
16. E. R. Kirk. *Statistics: An Introduction.* Hardcourt Brace College, USA, fourth edition, 1999.
17. N. Lavrac and S. Dzeroski. *Inductive Logic Programming: Techniques and Applications.* Ellis Horwood, 1994.
18. D. J. Lipman. Gapped BLAST and PSI-BLAST: A new generation of protein database search programs. *Nucleic Acids Research*, 25:3389–3402, 1997.
19. D. J. Lipman and W. R. Pearson. Rapid and sensitive protein similarity searches. *Science*, 277:1435–1441, March 1985.
20. R. M. MacCallum, L. A. Kelley, and M. J. E. Sternberg. SAWTED: Structure Assignment With TExt Description - enhanced detection of remote homologues with automated SWISS-PROT annotation comparision. *Bioinformatics*, 16(2):125–129, 2000.
21. Stephen Muggleton. Inductive logic programming. *New Generation Computing*, 8(4):295–318, 1990.
22. Stephen Muggleton. Inverse entailment and progol. *New Generation Computing Journal*, 13:245–286, 1995.
23. A. G. Murzin, S. E. Brenner, T. Hubbard, and C. Chothia. SCOP: a structural classification of proteins database for the investigation of sequences and structures. *J. Mol. Biol.*, 247:536–540, 1995.
24. S. B. Needleman and C. D. Wunsch. A general method applicable to the research for similarities in the amino acid sequencesof two proteins. *J. Mol. Biol.*, 48:443–453, 1970.
25. H. Nielsen, J. Engelbrecht, S. Brunack, and G. von Heijne. Identification of prokaryotic and eukariotic signal peptides and prediction of their cleavage sites. *Protein Engineering*, 10:1–6, 1997.
26. J. Park, K. Karplus, C. Barrett, R. Hughey, D. Haussler, T. Hubbard, and C. Chothia. Sequence comparisons using multiple sequences detect three times as many remote homologues as pairwise methods. *J. Mol. Biol.*, 284:1201–1210, 1998.
27. J. Park, S. A. Teichmann, T. Hubbard, and C. Chotia. Intermediate sequences increase the detection of homology between sequences. *J. Mol. Biol.*, 273:349–354, 1997.
28. W. R. Pearson and D. J. Lipman. Improved tools for biological sequence comparison. *Proc. Natl. Acad. Sci. USA*, pages 2444–2448, 1988.
29. F. Provost, T. Fawcett, and R. Kohavi. The case against accuracy estimation for comparing induction algorithms. In *Proc. 15th International Conf. on Machine Learning*, pages 445–453. Morgan Kaufmann, San Francisco, CA, 1998.

30. F. J. Provost and T. Fawcett. Robust classification systems for imprecise environments. In *AAAI/IAAI*, pages 706–713, 1998.
31. Vijay Raghavan, Peter Bollmann, and Gwang S. Jung. A critical investigation of recall and presicion as measuers of retrievel system performance. *ACM Transactions of Information Systems*, 7(3):205–229, 1989.
32. T. F. Smith and M. S. Waterman. Identification of common molecular subsequences. *J. Mol. Biol.*, 147:195–197, 1981. Smith, Waterman, dynamic, programming, local, alignment.
33. J. A. Swets and R. M. Pickett. *Evaluation of Diagnostic Systems: Methods from Signal Detection Theory.* Academic Press, New York, 1982.
34. G. Tecuci. *Building Intelligent Agents: An Apprenticeship Multistrategy Learning Theory, Methodology, Tool and Case Studies.* Academic Press, 1998.
35. M. Turcotte, Steven. H. Muggleton, and Micheal J. E. Sternberg. Application of inductive logic programming to discover rules governing the three-dimensional topology of protein structure. In C. D. Page, editor, *Proc. 8th International Conference on Inductive Logic Programming (ILP-98)*, pages 53–64. Spinger Verlag,Berlin, 1998.
36. H. L. Van Trees. *Detection, estimation, and modulation theory.* Wiley, New York, 1971.
37. W Wright, P. Scordis, and T. K. Attwood. BLAST PRINTS - alternative perspectives on sequence similarity. *Bioinformatics*, 15(6):523–524, 1999.
38. P. Young. PrePRINTS. http://www.bioinf.man.ac.uk/ConceptualBlast.html.

# Adaptive Bayesian Logic Programs

Kristian Kersting and Luc De Raedt

Institute for Computer Science, Machine Learning Lab
Albert-Ludwigs-University, Georges-Köhler-Allee, Gebäude 079,
D-79085 Freiburg i. Brg., Germany
{kersting,deraedt}@informatik.uni-freiburg.de

**Abstract.** First order probabilistic logics combine a first order logic with a probabilistic knowledge representation. In this context, we introduce *continuous* Bayesian logic programs, which extend the recently introduced Bayesian logic programs to deal with continuous random variables. Bayesian logic programs tightly integrate definite logic programs with Bayesian networks. The resulting framework nicely seperates the qualitative (i.e. logical) component from the quantitative (i.e. the probabilistic) one. We also show how the quantitative component can be learned using a gradient-based maximum likelihood method.

## 1 Introduction

In recent years, there has been an increasing interest in integrating probability theory with first order logic leading to different types of "first order probabilistic logics". One of the streams [22,20,11,15,12] concentrates on first order extensions of Bayesian networks [21], i.e. it aims at integrating two powerful and popular knowledge representation frameworks: Bayesian networks and first order logic. When investigating the state-of-the-art in this stream (cf. [20,11,15,12]), then there are two important shortcomings of the mentioned techniques. They either do not allow to model continuous[1] random variables or do not use (logical) languages that allow for functor symbols. Nevertheless, both of these features are highly desirable for true "first order probabilistic logics". Indeed, almost every real-world domain, including biology, medicine and finance involves continuous variables, and also, domains involving a potentially infinite number of random variables occur quite naturally in practice (e.g. temporal processes), which requires the use of functors to model the domain.

The first contribution of this paper is the introduction of *continuous* Bayesian logic programs, which allow to model infinite domains using functors as well as continuous random variables. The semantics of these Bayesian logic programs is given in the context of discrete-time stochastic processes. Because, as we have argued in [12], (*discrete*) Bayesian logic programs[2] can serve as a kind of common kernel of first order extensions of Bayesian networks such as probabilistic

[1] We understand in this paper a continuous variable as a variable having $\mathbb{R}$ or a compact interval in $\mathbb{R}$ as domain. A discrete random variable has a countable domain.

[2] Discrete Bayesian logic programs are Bayesian logic programs allowing only for discrete random variables, see [12].

C. Rouveirol and M. Sebag (Eds.): ILP 2001, LNAI 2157, pp. 104–117, 2001.

logic-programs[20], relational Bayesian networks [11] and probabilistic relational models [15], *continuous* Bayesian logic programs are novel. They generalize dynamic Bayesian networks, Kalman filters, hidden Markov models, etc.

The second contribution of this paper addresses the famous question: "*where do the numbers, the parameters of the quantitative aspects come from?*". So far, this issue has not yet attracted much attention in the context of first order extensions of Bayesian networks (with the exception of [16,7] ). In this context, we present for the first time how to calculate the *gradient* for a maximum likelihood estimation of the parameters of Bayesian logic programs. This gives one a rich class of optimization techniques such as conjugate gradient and the possibility to speed up techniques based on the EM algorithm, see [18].

We proceed as follows. After motivating continuous Bayesian logic programs with a simplified example from quantitative genetics in Section 3 we introduce continuous Bayesian logic programs in Section 4. In Section 5 we formulate the likelihood of the parameters of a Bayesian logic program given some data and, based on this, we present in Section 5 a gradient-based method to find that parameters which maximize the likelihood. After discussing related work in Section 7 and reporting experimental experiences in Section 8 we conclude. We assume some familiarity with logic programming (see e.g. [17]) as well as with Bayesian networks [21].

## 2 Quantitative Genetics

A natural domain where Bayesian logic programs should help is *genetics*. Here, the family relationship forms the basis for the dependencies between the random variables and the biological laws provide the probability distribution. Even if the genotype may best be modeled using discrete random variables, some phenotypes such as the height of a person are naturally represented using continuous variables. Moreover, in many situations phenotypes can be influenced by environmental (continuous) quantities such as the amount of nuclear radiation. The subfield of genetics which deals with continuous phenotype is called *quantitative genetics* (cf. [6]).

As an example consider a simplified model of the inheritance of the heights of persons. The height $h(X)$ of a specific person $X$ interpreted as a continuous random variable (having the $\mathrm{dom}(h) = \mathbb{R}$) depends on its genotype $g(X)$, a discrete random variable. The genotype $g(X)$ itself depends on the genotype of the mother $g(M)$ and father $g(F)$. Furthermore, we could assume that $h(X)$ is influenced by the heights of its mother $h(M)$ and father $h(F)$. Figure 1 shows a graph modelling the described dependencies. The graph can be seen as the dependency structure of a Bayesian network [21]. Thus, we are interested in representing the *joint probability density function* (jpdf) $p(g(X), g(M), g(F), h(X), h(M), h(F))$. Let $p$ denote a probability density and $P$ a probability distribution. The chain rule of probability states $p(x_1, \ldots, x_n) = \prod_{i=1}^{n} p(x_i \mid x_{i-1}, \ldots, x_1)$ for a set $\{x_1, \ldots, x_n\}$ of random variables. The known biological dependencies express conditional independency statements such as $g(X)$ is conditional independent

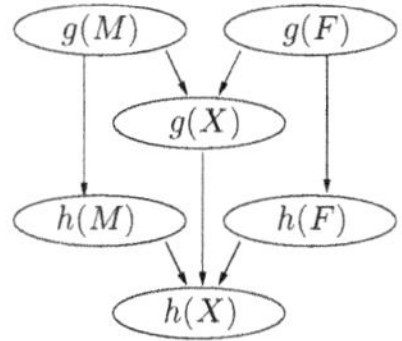


**Fig. 1.** The dependencies of the genetic domain. The height $h(X)$ of a person $X$ depends on the heights $h(M), h(F)$ of its mother $M$ and father $F$.

from $h(X)$ given a joint state of $g(M), g(F)$, i.e. $p(g(X), h(X) \mid g(M), g(F)) = p(g(X) \mid g(M), g(F))$. From the chain rule and the biological laws it follows that

$$\begin{aligned} p(g(X),&g(M), g(F), h(X), h(M), h(F)) = \\ &p(g(X) \mid g(M), g(F)) \cdot p(g(M)) \cdot p(g(F)) \cdot \\ &p(h(X) \mid h(M), h(F)) \cdot p(h(M)) \cdot p(h(F)). \end{aligned} \tag{1}$$

Thus, we must define an infinite set of densities for $h(X)$, one for every possible joint value $\mathbf{u}$ of its parents $\mathbf{Pa}(h(X)) = \{h(M), h(F)\}$ (the direct predecessors of a variable in the dependency graph) can take. Hence, for each $u \in \mathrm{dom}(h(X))$ we have a function $cpd(h(X) \mid \mathbf{Pa}(h(X)))(u \mid \mathbf{u})$ that denotes the conditional probability density $p(h(X) = u \mid \mathbf{Pa}(h(X)) = \mathbf{u})$. We will call such a function a probability density function (pdf). Note, that the used upper types for $X$, $F$ and $M$ do not indicate that they are variables in a logical sense. The representation so far is inherent propositional, i.e. the regularities cannot intensionally be represented. We have to describe it for each "family" $X, M, F$. The framework of *continuous* Bayesian logic programs aims at intensionally representing such regularities.

## 3 (Continuous) Bayesian Logic Programs

A Bayesian logic program $B$ consist of two components, firstly a *logical* one, a set of Bayesian clauses (cf. below) that encodes the assertions of conditional independence in Equation (1), and secondly a *quantitative* one, a set of conditional probability functions and combining rules (cf. below) corresponding to that logical structure. In particular, a *Bayesian (definite) clause* $c$ is an expression of the form

$$A \mid A_1, \ldots, A_n \tag{2}$$

where $n \geq 0$, the $A, A_1, \ldots, A_n$ are Bayesian atoms and all Bayesian atoms are (implicitly) universally quantified. We define $head(c) = A$ and $body(c) = \{A_1, \ldots, A_n\}$. The differences between a *Bayesian* and a *logical* clause are : (1) the atoms $p(t_1, ..., t_m)$ and predicates arising are Bayesian, i.e. they have an associated domain $\mathrm{dom}(p)$, and (2) we use " | " instead of ":-". Furthermore, most other *logical* notions carry over to Bayesian logic programs. So,

```
m(uta,john).
f(peter,john).
g(uta).
g(peter).
g(john)  | m(uta,john),g(uta),f(peter,john),g(peter).
h(uta)   | g(uta).
h(peter) | g(peter).
h(john)  | g(john), m(uta,john),h(uta),f(peter,john),h(peter).
```

**Fig. 2.** A Bayesian logic program which essentially encodes the Bayesian network in Figure 1. Here, Uta and Peter are the parents of John. The Bayesian logic program is the grounded version of the Bayesian logic program in Figure 3.

we will speak of Bayesian predicates, terms, constants, functors, substitutions, ground Bayesian clauses, etc. For instance, consider the Bayesian clause $c_1$ `h(X) | m(X,M), h(M)` where $\text{dom}(m) = \{true, false\}$ and $\text{dom}(h) = \mathbb{R}$. It says that the height of a person $X$ depends on the height of its mother $M$. Intuitively, a Bayesian predicate generically represents a set of random variables. More precisely, each Bayesian ground atom $p(t_1, \ldots, t_m)$ corresponds to a random variable with $\text{dom}(p(t_1, \ldots, t_m)) := \text{dom}(p)$. As long as no ambiguity occurs, we do not distinguish between a Bayesian predicate (atom) and its corresponding logical predicate (atom).

In order to represent a probabilistic model we associate to each Bayesian clause $c$ a probability density function $cpd(c)$ encoding $p(head(c) \mid body(c))$. It generically represents the conditional probability densities of all ground instances $c\theta$ of the clause $c$. In general, one may have many clauses, e.g. $c_1$ and the clause $c_2$ `h(X) | f(X,F),h(F)` and corresponding substitutions $\theta_i$, that ground the clauses $c_i$ such that $head(c_1\theta_1) = head(c_2\theta_2)$. They specify $cpd(c_1\theta_1)$ and $cpd(c_2\theta_2)$, but one needs $p(head(c_1\theta_1) \mid body(c_1) \cup body(c_2))$. The standard solution to obtain the densities required are so called *combining rules* (see e.g. [20]), functions which map finite sets $\{p(A \mid A_{i1}, \ldots, A_{in_i}) \mid i = 1, \ldots, m\}$ of conditional probability functions onto one *combined* conditional probability function $p(A \mid B_1, \ldots, B_k)$ with $\{B_1, \ldots, B_k\} \subset \bigcup_{i=1}^{m} \{A_{i1}, \ldots, A_{in_i}\}$. We assume that for each Bayesian predicate $p$ there is a corresponding combining rule $cr(p)$, such as noisy_or in the case of discrete random variables or a linear regression model in the case of Gaussian variables.

To summarize, a *Bayesian logic program* $B$ consists of a (finite) set of Bayesian clauses. To each Bayesian clause $c$ there is an associated conditional probability function $cpd(c)$, and for each Bayesian predicate $p$ there is exactly one associated combining rule $cr(p)$.

The declarative semantics of Bayesian logic programs is given by the annotated *dependency graph.* The *dependency graph* $DG(B)$ is that directed graph whose nodes correspond to the ground atoms in the least Herbrand model $\text{LH}(B)$ (cf. below). It encodes the *directly influenced by* relation over the random variables in $\text{LH}(B)$: there is an edge from a node $x$ to a node $y$ if and only if there exists a clause $c \in B$ and a substitution $\theta$, s.t. $y = head(c\theta)$, $x \in body(c\theta)$ and for all atoms $z$ appearing in $c\theta : z \in \mathrm{LH}(B)$. The least Herbrand model $\mathrm{LH}(B)$ consists of all *proper* random variables. It is defined as if $B$ would be a logical definite program (cf. [17]). It is the least fix point of the *immediate consequence* operator[3](cf. [17]) applied on the empty set. Now, to each node $x$ in $DG(B)$ the *combined* pdf is associated which is the result of the combining rule $cr(p)$ of the corresponding Bayesian predicate $p$ applied on the set of $cpd(c\theta)$'s where $head(c\theta) = x$ and $body(c\theta) \subset \mathrm{LH}(B)$. Thus, the dependency graph encodes similar to Bayesian networks the following independency assumption:

> *each node $x$ is independent of its non-descendants given a joint state of its parents* $\mathbf{Pa}(x)$ *in the dependency graph.*

E.g. the program in Figure 3 renders $h(john)$ independent from $g(uta)$ given a joint state of $g(john), h(uta), h(peter), m(uta, john), f(peter, john)$. Using this assumption the following proposition holds:

**Proposition 1.** *Let $B$ be a Bayesian logic program. If $B$ fulfills (1) that* $\mathrm{LH}(B) \neq \emptyset$, *(2) that $DG(B)$ is acyclic in the usual graph theoretical sense, and (3) that each node in $DG(B)$ is influenced by a finite set of random variables then it specifies a unique probability density over* $\mathrm{LH}(B)$.

*proof sketch (For a detailed proof see [13].).* The least Herbrand $\mathrm{LH}(B)$ always exists, is unique and countable. Thus, $DG(B)$ uniquely exists, and due to condition (3) the combined pdf for each node of $DG(B)$ is computable. Furthermore, because of condition (1) a total order $\pi$ of $DG(B)$ exists, so that one can see $B$ together with $\pi$ as a stochastic process over $\mathrm{LH}(B)$. An inductions "along" $\pi$ together with condition 2 shows that the family of finite-dimensional distribution of the process is projective (cf. see [1]), i.e the jpdf over each finite subset $s \subseteq \mathrm{LH}(B)$ is uniquely defined and $\int_y p(s, x = y)\, dy = p(s)$. With that, the preconditions of *Kolmogorov's theorem* [1, page 307] hold, and it follows that $B$ given $\pi$ specifies a probability density function $p$ over $\mathrm{LH}(B)$. This proves the proposition because the total order $\pi$ used for the induction does not refer to any specific total order of $DG(B)$.

A program fulfilling conditions 1, 2 and 3 is called *well-defined* and we will consider such programs for the rest of the paper. One can think of Bayesian networks as a simple example of well-defined programs. Their graphically represented dependencies are encoded as a finite propositional Bayesian logic program as shown in Figure 2. A program encoding the intensional regularities in our genetic domain is given in Figure 3. Some interesting properties follow from the proof sketch.

---

[3] We assume that all clauses in a Bayesian logic program are range-restricted: all variables appearing in the conclusion part of a clause also appear in the condition part. This is a common restriction in computational logic, because then all facts entailed by the program are ground (cf. [17]).

```
m(uta,peter).
f(john, peter).
g(uta).
g(peter).
g(X)       | m(M,X), g(M), f(F,X), g(F).
h(uta)     | g(uta).
h(peter)   | g(peter).
h(X)       | g(X), m(M,X), h(M), f(F,X), h(F).
```

**Fig. 3.** A Bayesian logic program encoding the example in our genetic domain.

- We interpreted a Bayesian logic program as a stochastic process. This places them in a wider context of what Cowell et. al. call *highly structured stochastic systems* (HSSS, cf. [3]) because Bayesian logic programs represent discrete-time stochastic processes in a more flexible manner. Well-known probabilistic frameworks such as dynamic Bayesian networks, first order hidden Markov models or Kalman filters are special cases of them.
- Together with the unique semantics for pure discrete programs [12] it is clear that hybrid programs, i.e. programs over discrete and continuous variables have a unique semantics.

Moreover, the proof in [13] indicates the important *support network* concept. Support networks are a graphical representation of the finite-dimensional distribution (cf. [1]) and are needed for the formulation of the likelihood function (see below) as well as for answering probabilistic queries in Bayesian logic programs. The *support network* $N$ of a variable $x \in \mathrm{LH}(B)$ is defined as the induced subnetwork of $S = \{x\} \cup \{y \mid y \in \mathrm{LH}(B)$ and $y$ is influencing $x\}$. The support network of a finite set $\{x_1, \ldots, x_k\} \subseteq \mathrm{LH}(B)$ is the union of the networks of each single $x_i$. Because we consider well-defined Bayesian logic programs, each $x \in \mathrm{LH}(B)$ is influenced by a finite subset of $\mathrm{LH}(B)$. So, it is provable that the support network $N$ of a finite set $\{x_1, \ldots, x_k\} \subseteq \mathrm{LH}(B)$ of random variables is always a finite Bayesian network and computable in finite time. Because the support network $N$ models the finite-dimensional distribution specified by $S$, any interesting probabilistic density value over subsets of $S$ is specified by $N$. For the proofs and an effective inference procedure (together with an implementation using Prolog) we refer to [13].

## 4 Maximum Likelihood Estimation

So far, we have assumed that there is an expert who designs a Bayesian logic program. This is not always the case. Often, there is no-one possessing necessary expertise or knowledge. However, we often have access to data. We focus here on the classical *maximum likelihood estimation* (MLE) method to learn the parameters of the associated probability density functions of a given Bayesian logic program.

Let $B$ be a Bayesian logic program consisting of the Bayesian clauses $c_1, \ldots, c_n$, and let $\mathbf{D} = \{D_1, \ldots, D_m\}$ be a set of data cases. A data case $D_i \in \mathbf{D}$ is a partially observed joint state of some variables in LH($B$). Examples of data cases are

$$\{m(peter, uta) = true, f(peter, john) = true, h(uta) = 165.98, h(peter) = 175.8\},$$
$$\{g(peter) = ?, h(uta) = 165.98, h(peter) = 174.4, h(john) = 170\},$$
$$\{h(uta) = 167.9, h(john) = ?\},$$

where '?' stands for an unobserved state. The parameters $\boldsymbol{\lambda}(c_i) = \{\lambda(c_i)_1, \ldots, \lambda(c_i)_{e_i}\}$, $e_i > 0$, affecting the associated pdfs *cpd*($c_i$) constitute the set $\boldsymbol{\lambda} = \bigcup_{i=1}^{n} \boldsymbol{\lambda}(c_i)$ and the version of $B$ where the parameters are set to $\boldsymbol{\lambda}$ is denoted by $B(\boldsymbol{\lambda})$[4]. Now, the likelihood $L(\mathbf{D}, \boldsymbol{\lambda})$ is the probability of the observed data $\mathbf{D}$ as a function of the unknown parameters $\boldsymbol{\lambda}$:

$$L(\mathbf{D}, \boldsymbol{\lambda}) := P_B(\mathbf{D} \mid \boldsymbol{\lambda}) = P_{B(\boldsymbol{\lambda})}(\mathbf{D}). \tag{3}$$

Thus, the search space $\mathcal{H}$ is spanned by the product space over the possible values of $\lambda(c_i)$ and we seek to find $\boldsymbol{\lambda}^* = \max_{\boldsymbol{\lambda} \in \mathcal{H}} P_{B(\boldsymbol{\lambda})}(\mathbf{D})$. Usually, $B$ specifies a density function over a (countably) infinite set of random variables and hence we cannot compute $P_{B(\boldsymbol{\lambda})}(\mathbf{D})$ by considering the whole dependency graph. But as we have argued at the end of the preceding section it is sufficient to consider the support network $N(\boldsymbol{\lambda})$ of the random variables occurring in $\mathbf{D}$ to compute $P_{B(\boldsymbol{\lambda})}(\mathbf{D})$. Thus, remembering that the logarithm is monotone we seek to find

$$\boldsymbol{\lambda}^* = \max_{\boldsymbol{\lambda} \in \mathcal{H}} \log P_{N(\boldsymbol{\lambda})}(\mathbf{D}). \tag{4}$$

In other words, we have expressed the original problem in terms of the parameter MLE problem of Bayesian networks. However, we need to be more careful. Some of the nodes in $N(\boldsymbol{\lambda})$ are hidden, that is, their values are not observed in $\mathbf{D}$[5]. Furthermore, it should be noted, that not only $L(\mathbf{D}, \boldsymbol{\lambda})$ but also $N(\boldsymbol{\lambda})$ itself depends on the data, i.e. the data cases determine the sufficient subnetwork of *DG*($B$) to calculate the likelihood. On the one hand, this may affect the generalization of the learned program, but on the other hand, this is a similar situation as for "unrolling" dynamic Bayesian networks [5] or recurrent neural networks [24].

Finally, our learning setting can be used for MLE of the parameters of intensional rules only. Assume that if we observe *h*(*john*) then *h*(*john*) = 172.06 holds. In this case, it is problematic to estimate the ML parameters of *h*(*john*). But, we can still estimate the ML parameters of `h(X) | g(X)` based on the support network of the data cases: the intensional rules together with the data

[4] As long as no ambiguities occur we will not distinguish between the parameters $\boldsymbol{\lambda}$ themselves and a particular instance of them.

[5] If all nodes are observed in each $D_i \in \mathbf{D}$, then simple counting is all that is needd for ML parameter estimation in Bayesian networks (see e.g. [9]).

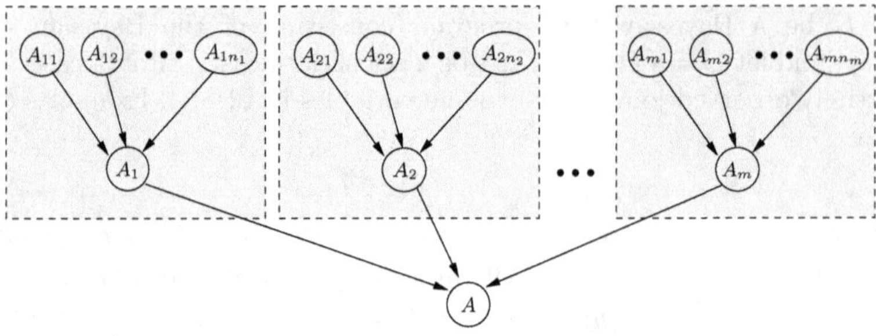


**Fig. 4.** The scheme of decomposable combining rules. Each rectangle corresponds to a ground instance of a Bayesian clause (cp. definition of a combining rule). The node $A$ is a deterministic node.

cases induce a Bayesian network over the variables of the data cases. This is not surprising if one sees our learning setting as a probabilistic extension of the ILP setting *learning from interpretation.* For a discussion on how this analogy can be used for learning intensional Bayesian clauses (not only the parameters of the associated densities) we refer to [14].

## 5 The Gradient

How can we maximize the likelihood? A classical method for finding a maximum of an evaluation function is *gradient ascent*, also known as *hill climbing.* Here, one computes the *gradient* vector $\nabla_{\boldsymbol{\lambda}}$ of partial derivatives with respect to the parameters of the pdfs at a given point $\boldsymbol{\lambda} \in \mathcal{H}$. Then it takes a small step in the direction of the gradient to the point $\boldsymbol{\lambda} + \alpha\nabla_{\boldsymbol{\lambda}}$ where $\alpha$ is the step-size parameter. The algorithm will converge to a local maximum for small enough $\alpha$. Thus, we have to compute the partial derivatives of $P_{N(\boldsymbol{\lambda})}(\mathbf{D})$ with respect to some particular parameter $\lambda(c)_t$ [6]. For the sake of simplicity we will assume *decomposable* combining rules[7]. Such rules can be expressed using a set of separate, deterministic nodes in the support network, as shown in Figure 4. Most combining rule commonly employed in Bayesian networks such as noisy_or or linear regression are decomposable (cp. [10]).

Decomposable combining rules imply that for each node $x \in N$ there exist at most one clause $c$ and a substitution $\theta$ s.t. *body*$(c\theta) \subset \mathrm{LH}(B)$ and *head*$(c\theta) = x$. Thus, while the same clause $c$ can induce more than one node in $N$, all of these nodes have identical local structure: the associated pdfs (and so the parameters)

[6] In the algorithm, this requires an additional step. We have to make sure that (1) each *cpd*$(c)$ maps into $[0,1]$, and (2) for each $u \in \mathrm{dom}(\mathit{head}(c))$ and for each $\mathbf{u} \in \mathrm{dom}(\mathit{body}(c))$ : $\int_{-\infty}^{+\infty} \mathit{cpd}(c)(u,\mathbf{u})du = 1$. This can be done by renormalizing $\nabla_{\boldsymbol{\lambda}}$ to the constrained surface before taking a step in the direction of $\nabla_{\boldsymbol{\lambda}}$.

[7] In the case of more general combining rules the partial derivatives of a inner function has to be computed. This may be difficult or even not possible (in a close form).

have to be identical, i.e. $\forall$ *subst.* $\theta$ : $cpd(c\theta) = cpd(c)$. As an example consider the clause defining `h(X)` and the nodes `h(uta)`, `h(peter)` and `h(john)`. This is the same situation as for dynamic Bayesian networks where the parameters that encode the stochastic model of state evolution appear many times in the network.

In the following we will adapt a solution based on the chain rule of differentiation given in [2] for dynamic Bayesian networks. For simplicity, we fix the current instantiation of the parameters $\boldsymbol{\lambda}$ and, hence, we write $B$ and $N(\mathbf{D})$. Applying the chain rule on (4) yields

$$\frac{\partial \log P_N(\mathbf{D})}{\partial \lambda(c)_t} = \sum_{\substack{\text{subst. } \theta \text{ with} \\ support(c\theta)}} \frac{\partial \log P_N(\mathbf{D})}{\partial \lambda(c\theta)_t} \tag{5}$$

where $\theta$ refers to grounding substitutions and $support(c\theta)$ is true iff $\{head(c\theta)\} \cup body(c_i\theta) \subset N$. Assuming that the data cases $D_l \in \mathbf{D}$ are independently sampled from the same distribution we can separate the contribution of the different data cases to the partial derivative of a single ground instance $c\theta$ resulting in[8]:

$$\frac{\partial \log P_N(\mathbf{D})}{\partial \lambda(c\theta)_t} = \sum_{l=1}^{m} \frac{\partial \log P_N(D_l)}{\partial \lambda(c\theta)_t} =$$
$$\sum_{l=1}^{m} \int_{-\infty}^{+\infty} \cdots \int_{-\infty}^{+\infty} \frac{p_N(head(c\theta) = u, body(c\theta) = \mathbf{u} \mid D_l)}{cpd(c\theta)(u, \mathbf{u})} \times \frac{\partial cpd(c\theta)(u, \mathbf{u})}{\partial \lambda(c\theta)_t} \, du d\mathbf{u} \tag{6}$$

where $u \in \mathrm{dom}(head(c\theta)$, $\mathbf{u} \in \mathrm{dom}(body(c\theta)$. The term $p_N(u, \mathbf{u} \mid D_l)$ cannot be exactly calculated for all kinds of distributions. If not, stochastic simulation techniques such as Markov chain Monte Carlo methods (see e.g. [3, Appendix B]) should help. Another often used solution is to restrict the types of the random variable. Most continuous Bayesian networks have used Gaussian distributions for the density functions (e.g. *conditional Gaussian* distributions [3]). This can be done with Bayesian logic programs, too, so that the solution of the integrand in Equation (6) has a closed form which can be adapted from [2], and an inference engine for Bayesian logic programs can be used to get an exact solution. But still in general, the integrals in Equation (6) are intractable. Here again, stochastic simulation algorithms may solve the problem. We finally would like to state the equations of the partial derivatives for pure discrete programs. Doing the same steps as before (Equations (5), (6)) and noting that the densities are now distributions parameterized by their entries yields:

$$\frac{\partial \log P_N(\mathbf{D})}{\partial cpd(c)_{jk}} = \sum_{\substack{\text{subst. } \theta \text{ with} \\ support(c\theta)}} \sum_{l=1}^{m} \frac{P_N(head(c\theta) = u_j, body(c\theta) = \mathbf{u}_k \mid D_l)}{\partial cpd(c\theta)_{jk}} \tag{7}$$

where $u_i \in \mathrm{dom}(head(c))$, $\mathbf{u}_j \in \mathrm{dom}(body(c))$ and $i, j$ refer to the corresponding entries in $cpd(c)$ and $cpd(c\theta)$. With this, it is not difficult to adapt the equations

[8] Due to space restrictions we leave the derivation of the equation out. It is basically the derivation of equation (10) in [2] adapted to our notation.

**Table 1.** A simplified skeleton of the algorithm for *adaptive Bayesian logic programs.*.

```
function BASIC-ABLP(B, D) returns a modified Bayesian logic program
    inputs: B, a Bayesian logic program; associated pdfs are parameterized by λ
            D, a finite set of data cases

λ ←INITIALPARAMETERS
N ←SUPPORTNETWORK(B, D)
repeat until Δλ ≈ 0
    Δλ ← 0
    set pdfs of N according to λ
    for each D_l ∈ D
        set the evidence in N from D_l
        for each clause c ∈ B
            for each ground instance cθ s.t. {head(cθ)} ∪ body(cθ) ⊂ N
                for each single parameter λ(cθ)_t
                    Δλ(c)_t ← Δλ(c)_t + (∂ log P_N(D_l)/∂λ(cθ)_t)
    Δλ ←PROJECTIONONTOCONSTRAINTSURFACE(Δλ)
    λ ← λ + α · Δλ
return B
```

for hybrid Bayesian logic programs. A simplified skeleton of a gradient-based algorithm is shown in Table 1.

## 6 Related Work

To some extent, Bayesian logic programs are related to the BUGS language [8] which aims at carrying out Bayesian inference using Gibbs sampling. It uses concepts of imperative programming languages such as for-loops to model regularities in probabilistic models. Therefore, the relation between Bayesian logic programs and BUGS is akin to the general relation between logical and imperative languages. This holds in particular for relational domains such as that used in this paper: family relationships. Without the notion of objects and relations among objects family trees are hard to represent. Furthermore, a single BUGS program specifies a probability density over a finite set of random variables, whereas a Bayesian logic program can represent a distribution over an infinite set of random variables.

There is work on parameter estimation within "first order probabilistic logics" which do not rely on Bayesian networks. Cussens [4] investigates EM methods to estimate the parameters of stochastic logic programs [19]. Sato et al. [23] have shown that there is an efficient method for EM learning of PRISM programs.

Learning within Bayesian networks is well-investigated in the Uncertainty in AI community, see e.g. [9]. Binder et. al. [2] whose approach we have adapted present results for a gradient-based method. But so far, there has not been much work on ML parameter estimation within first order extensions of Bayesian networks. Koller and Pfeffer [16] adapt the EM algorithm for probabilistic logic programs [20], a framework which in contrast to Bayesian logic programs sees ground atoms as states of random variables. Although the framework seems to theoretically allow for continuous random variables there exists no (practical) query-answering procedure for this case; to the best of our knowledge Ngo and Haddawy [20] give only a procedure for variables having finite domains. Furthermore, Koller and Pfeffer's approach utilizes support networks, too, but requires the intersection of the support networks of the data cases to be empty. This could be in our opinion in some cases too restrictive, e.g. in the case of dynamic Bayesian networks. However, if the data cases fulfill the property then inference is faster. Friedman et al. [7] concentrate on learning within probabilistic relational models, a framework that combines entity/relationship models with Bayesian networks. They adapt the EM algorithm to estimate the parameters and to learn the structure based on techniques known from Bayesian network learning. So, they consider a more general problem setting than we do, but on the other hand the entity/relationship model lacks the concept of functors. Thus, they are limited to finite sets of entities and relations. For a more detailed discussion of the relations of Bayesian logic programs to other first order extensions of Bayesian networks such as probabilistic logic programs [20], relational Bayesian networks [11] and probabilistic relational models [15] we refer to [12,13].

Therefore, the related work on first order extensions of Bayesian networks mainly differs in two points from ours: (1) The underlying (logical) frameworks lack important knowledge representational features which Bayesian logic programs have. (2) They adapt the EM algorithm which is particularly easy to implement. However, there are problematic issues both regarding speed of convergence as well as convergence towards a local (sub-optimal) maximum of the likelihood function. Different accelerations based on the gradient are discussed in [18]. Also, the EM algorithm is difficult to apply in the case of general probability density functions because it relies on computing the sufficient statistics (cf. [9]).

## 7 Experimental Prospects

The experimental results of [16] and [2] can be summarized as follows: (1) the support network is a good approximation of the entire likelihood, (2) equality constraints over parameters speed up learning, and (3) gradient-based methods are promising. Therefore, we prove the basic principle of our approach by testing the hill-climbing algorithm on a simple model of our genetic domain. We generated 100 data cases from a version of the program in Figure 3 where the genetical information expressed by $g$ is omitted. It describes the family tree of 12 person. The associated probability functions are $cpd(m(M,X))(true) = cpd(f(F,X))(true) = 1.0$, $cpd(h(X)) = \mathcal{N}(165,20)$ and the one in Table 2, where $\mathcal{N}(165,20)$ denotes a normal density with mean 165 and variance 20. The learning task was to estimate $a$ in the function of Table 2 and the mean $b$ of

| $m(M, X)$ | $f(F, X)$ | $cpd(c)(h(X) \mid h(M), h(F))$ |
|---|---|---|
| *true* | *true* | $\mathcal{N}(0.0 + 0.5 \cdot h(M) + 0.5 \cdot h(F), 20)$ |
| *true* | *false* | $\mathcal{N}(165, 20)$ |
| *false* | *true* | $\mathcal{N}(165, 20)$ |
| *false* | *false* | $\mathcal{N}(165, 20)$ |

**Table 2.** The probability density function used in our experiments. Only in the case *true*, *true* the heights of the parents a taken into account as weighted sum. The constant addend in the mean of the first normal densities is denoted as $a$. i.e. $a = 0.0$.

$cpd(h(X))$ starting with $a = 165.0$ and $b = 0.0$. After 13 iterations the estimated parameters were $a = -0.1856$ and $b = 164.7919$ using a step-size of 1.0. The implementation obviously suffers from the well-known dependency on the chosen initial parameters and fixed step-size. In the future we will investigate more advanced gradient-based methods like e.g. Conjugate-Gradient. We also conducted experiments with learning the weights of the sum in the function of Table 2, i.e. 0.5 and 0.5. Here, the algorithm converges to weights almost summing to 1.0 which are local minima w.r.t. our data generating model and the likelihood.

## 8 Conclusions

We made two contributions. First, we have introduced continuous Bayesian logic programs. We have argued that the basic query-answering procedure for discrete programs is still applicable: The ability to represent both intensional regularities between the variables as well as continuous random variables reduces the size of many modelled domains. Second, we have addressed the question "where do the numbers come from?" by showing how to compute the gradient of the likelihood based on ideas known for (dynamic) Bayesian networks. The intensional representation of Bayesian logic programs, i.e. their compact representation should speed up learning and provide good generalization.

In the future, we will perform a detailed comparison of our learning approach with the EM algorithm. Accelerations of the EM algorithm based on the gradient are interesting. Our ultimate goal is learning the structure. We are currently (see [14]) looking for combinations of techniques known from Inductive Logic Programming, such as refinement operators, with techniques like scoring functions of the Bayesian networks. Just like ML parameter estimation is a basic technique for structural learning of Bayesian networks, it seems to be a basic technique for structural learning of Bayesian logic programs.

### Acknowledgments

The authors would like to thank Stefan Kramer and Manfred Jaeger for helpful discussions on the ideas of the paper. Also, thanks to the anonymous reviewers for their helpful comments.

## References


1. Heinz Bauer. *Wahrtscheinlichkeitstheorie*. Walter de Gruyter, Berlin, New York, 4. edition, 1991.
2. J. Binder, D. Koller, S. Russell, and K. Kanazawa. Adaptive probabilistic networks with hidden variables. *Machine Learning*, pages 213–244, 1997.
3. R. G. Cowell, A. P. Dawid, S. L. Lauritzen, and D. J. Spiegelhalter. *Probabilistic networks and expert systems*. Springer-Verlag New York, Inc., 1999.
4. J. Cussens. Parameter estimation in stochastic logic programs. *Machine Learning*, 2001. to appear.
5. T. Dean and K. Kanazawa. Probabilistic temporal reasoning. In *Proceedings of the Seventh National Conference on Artificial Intelligence (AAAI-1988)*, 1988.
6. D. S. Falconer. *Introduction to quantitative genetics*. Longman Inc., New York, 2. edition, 1981.
7. N. Friedman, L. Getoor, D. Koller, and A. Pfeffer. Learning probabilistic relational models. In *Proceedings of the Sixteenth International Joint Conferences on Artificial Intelligence (IJCAI-1999)*, 1999.
8. W. R. Gilks, A. Thomas, and D. J. Spiegelhalter. A language and program for complex bayesian modelling. *The Statistician*, 43, 1994.
9. D. Heckerman. A Tutorial on Learning with Bayesian Networks. Technical Report MSR-TR-95-06, Microsoft Research,, 1995.
10. D. Heckerman and J. Breese. Causal Independence for Probability Assessment and Inference Using Bayesian Networks. Technical Report MSR-TR-94-08, Microsoft Research, 1994.
11. M. Jaeger. Relational Bayesian networks. In *Proceedings of the Thirteenth Annual Conference on Uncertainty in Artificial Intelligence (UAI-1997)*, 1997.
12. K. Kersting and L. De Raedt. Bayesian logic programs. In *Work-in-Progress Reports of the Tenth International Conference on Inductive Logic Programming (ILP -2000)*, 2000. `http://SunSITE.Informatik.RWTH-Aachen.DE/Publications/CEUR-WS/Vol-35/`.
13. K. Kersting and L. De Raedt. Bayesian logic programs. Technical Report 151, University of Freiburg, Institute for Computer Science, April 2001.
14. K. Kersting and L. De Raedt. Towards Combining Inductive Logic Programming and Bayesian Networks. In this volume, 2001.
15. D. Koller. Probabilistic relational models. In *Proceedings of Ninth International Workshop on Inductive Logic Programming (ILP-1999)*, 1999.
16. D. Koller and A. Pfeffer. Learning probabilities for noisy first-order rules. In *Proceedings of the Fifteenth Joint Conference on Artificial Intelligence (IJCAI-1997)*, 1997.
17. J. W. Lloyd. *Foundations of Logic Programming*. Springer, Berlin, 2. edition, 1989.
18. G. J. McKachlan and T. Krishnan. *The EM Algorithm and Extensions*. John Eiley & Sons, Inc., 1997.
19. S. Muggleton. Stochastic logic programs. In L. De Raedt, editor, *Advances in Inductive Logic Programming*. IOS Press, 1996.
20. L. Ngo and P. Haddawy. Answering queries form context-sensitive probabilistic knowledge bases. *Theoretical Computer Science*, 171:147–177, 1997.
21. J. Pearl. *Reasoning in Intelligent Systems: Networks of Plausible Inference*. Morgan Kaufmann, 2. edition, 1991.
22. D. Poole. Probabilistic Horn abduction and Bayesian networks. *Artificial Intelligence*, 64:81–129, 1993.

23. T. Sato and Y. Kameya. A viterbi-like algorithm and em learning for statistical abduction. In *Proceedings of UAI2000 Workshop on Fusion of Domain Knowledge with Data for Decision Support*, 2000.
24. R. J. Williams and D. Zipser. Gradient-Based Learning Algorithms for Recurrent Networks and Their Computatinal Complexity. In *Back-propagation:Theory, Architectures and Applications.* Hillsdale, NJ: Erlbaum, 1995.

# Towards Combining Inductive Logic Programming with Bayesian Networks

Kristian Kersting and Luc De Raedt

Institute for Computer Science, Machine Learning Lab
Albert-Ludwigs-University, Georges-Köhler-Allee, Gebäude 079,
D-79085 Freiburg i. Brg., Germany
{kersting,deraedt}@informatik.uni-freiburg.de

**Abstract.** Recently, new representation languages that integrate first order logic with Bayesian networks have been developed. Bayesian logic programs are one of these languages. In this paper, we present results on combining *Inductive Logic Programming* (ILP) with Bayesian networks to learn both the qualitative and the quantitative components of Bayesian logic programs. More precisely, we show how to combine the ILP setting *learning from interpretations* with score-based techniques for learning Bayesian networks. Thus, the paper positively answers Koller and Pfeffer's question, whether techniques from ILP could help to learn the logical component of first order probabilistic models.

## 1 Introduction

In recent years, there has been an increasing interest in integrating probability theory with first order logic. One of the research streams [24,22,11,6,14] aims at integrating two powerful and popular knowledge representation frameworks: Bayesian networks [23] and first order logic. In 1997, Koller and Pfeffer [16] address the question "*where do the numbers come from?*" for such frameworks. At the end of the same paper, they raise the question whether techniques from inductive logic programming (ILP) could help to learn the logical component of first order probabilistic models. In [15] we suggested that the ILP setting *learning from interpretations* [4,5,1] is a good candidate for investigating this question. With this paper we would like to make our suggestions more concrete. We present a novel scheme to learn intensional clauses within Bayesian logic programs [13,14]. It combines techniques from ILP with techniques for learning Bayesian networks. More exactly, we will show that the *learning from interpretations* setting for ILP can be integrated with score-based Bayesian network learning techniques for learning Bayesian logic programs. Thus, we positively answer Koller and Pfeffer's question.

We proceed as follows. After briefly reviewing the framework of Bayesian logic programs in Section 2, we dicuss our learning approach in Section 3. We define the learning problem, introduce the scheme of the algorithm, and discuss it applied on a special class of propositional Bayesian logic programs, well-known

C. Rouveirol and M. Sebag (Eds.): ILP 2001, LNAI 2157, pp. 118–131, 2001.

under the name Bayesian networks, and applied on general Bayesian logic programs. Before concluding the paper, we relate our approach to other work in Section 5. We assume some familiarity with logic programming or Prolog (see e.g. [26,18]) as well as with Bayesian networks (see e.g. [23,2]).

## 2 Bayesian Logic Programs

Throughout the paper we will use an example from genetics which is inspired by Friedman et al. [6]: "it is a genetic model of the inheritance of a single gene that determines a person's `X` blood type `bt(X)`. Each person `X` has two copies of the chromosome containing this gene, one, `mc(Y)`, inherited from her mother `m(Y,X)`, and one, `pc(Z)`, inherited from her father `f(Z,X)`." We will use $\mathbf{P}$ to denote a probability distribution, e.g. $\mathbf{P}(x)$, and the normal letter $P$ to denote a probability value, e.g. $P(x = v)$, where $v$ is a state of $x$.

The Bayesian logic program framework we will use in this paper is based on the Datalog subset of definite clausal logic, i.e. no functor symbols are allowed. The idea is that each Bayesian logic program specifies a Bayesian network, with one node for each (Bayesian) ground atom (see below). For a more expressive framework based on pure Prolog we refer to [14].

A Bayesian logic program $B$ consist of two components, firstly a *logical* one, a set of Bayesian clauses (cf. below), and secondly a *quantitative* one, a set of conditional probability distributions and combining rules (cf. below) corresponding to that logical structure. A *Bayesian (definite) clause* $c$ is an expression of the form

$$A \mid A_1, \ldots, A_n$$

where $n \geq 0$, the $A, A_1, \ldots, A_n$ are Bayesian atoms and all Bayesian atoms are (implicitly) universally quantified. We define $head(c) = A$ and $body(c) = \{A_1, \ldots, A_n\}$. So, the differences between a *Bayesian clause* and a *logical* one are : (1) the atoms $p(t_1, ..., t_n)$ and predicates $p$ arising are Bayesian, which means that they have an associated (finite) domain[1] dom($p$), and (2) we use " | " instead of ":-". For instance, consider the Bayesian clause $c$

```
bt(X) | mc(X), pc(X).
```

where dom($bt$) $= \{a, b, ab, 0\}$ and dom($mc$) $=$ dom($pc$) $= \{a, b, 0\}$. It says that the blood type of a person $X$ depends on the inherited genetical information of $X$. Note that the domain dom($p$) has nothing to do with the notion of a domain in the logical sense. The domain dom($p$) defines the states of random variables. Intuitively, a Bayesian predicate $p$ generically represents a set of (finite) random variables. More precisely, each Bayesian ground atom $g$ over $p$ represents a (finite) random variable over the states dom($g$) := dom($p$). E.g. $bt(ann)$ represents

[1] For the sake of simplicity we consider finite random variables, i.e. random variables having a finite set dom of states. However, the ideas generalize to discrete and continuous random variables.

the blood type of a person named Ann as a random variable over the states $\{a, b, ab, 0\}$. Apart from that, most other *logical* notions carry over to Bayesian logic programs. So, we will speak of Bayesian predicates, terms, constants, substitutions, ground Bayesian clauses, Bayesian Herbrand interpretations etc. We will assume that all Bayesian clauses are range-restricted. A clause is *range-restricted* iff all variables occurring in the head also occur in the body. Range restriction is often imposed in the database literature; it allows one to avoid derivation of non-ground true facts.

In order to represent a probabilistic model we associate with each Bayesian clause $c$ a conditional probability distribution *cpd*($c$) encoding $\mathbf{P}(\mathit{head}(c) \mid \mathit{body}(c))$. To keep the expositions simple, we will assume that *cpd*($c$) is represented as table, see Figure 1. More elaborate representations like decision trees or rules are also possible. The distribution *cpd*($c$) generically represents the conditional probability distributions of all ground instances $c\theta$ of the clause $c$. In general, one may have many clauses, e.g. clauses $c_1$ and the $c_2$

```
bt(X) | mc(X).
bt(X) | pc(X).
```

and corresponding substitutions $\theta_i$ that ground the clauses $c_i$ such that $\mathit{head}(c_1\theta_1) = \mathit{head}(c_2\theta_2)$. They specify $\mathit{cpd}(c_1\theta_1)$ and $\mathit{cpd}(c_2\theta_2)$, but not the distribution required: $\mathbf{P}(\mathit{head}(c_1\theta_1) \mid \mathit{body}(c_1) \cup \mathit{body}(c_2))$. The standard solution to obtain the distribution required are so called *combining rules*; functions which map finite sets of conditional probability distributions $\{\mathbf{P}(A \mid A_{i1}, \ldots, A_{in_i}) \mid i = 1, \ldots, m\}$ onto one (*combined*) conditional probability distribution $\mathbf{P}(A \mid B_1, \ldots, B_k)$ with $\{B_1, \ldots, B_k\} \subseteq \bigcup_{i=1}^{m} \{A_{i1}, \ldots, A_{in_i}\}$. We assume that for each Bayesian predicate $p$ there is a corresponding combining rule $cr$, such as noisy_or.

To summarize, a *Bayesian logic program* $B$ consists of a (finite) set of Bayesian clauses. To each Bayesian clause $c$ there is exactly one conditional probability distribution *cpd*($c$) associated, and for each Bayesian predicate $p$ there is exactly one associated combining rule *cr*($p$).

The declarative semantics of Bayesian logic programs is given by the annotated *dependency graph*. The *dependency graph* $DG(B)$ is that directed graph whose nodes correspond to the ground atoms in the least Herbrand model $\mathrm{LH}(B)$ (cf. below). It encodes the *directly influenced by* relation over the random variables in $\mathrm{LH}(B)$: there is an edge from a node $x$ to a node $y$ if and only if there exists a clause $c \in B$ and a substitution $\theta$, s.t. $y = \mathit{head}(c\theta)$, $x \in \mathit{body}(c\theta)$ and for all atoms $z$ appearing in $c\theta : z \in \mathrm{LH}(B)$. The direct predecessors of a graph node $x$ are denoted as its parents, $\mathbf{Pa}(x)$. The Herbrand base $\mathrm{HB}(B)$ is the set of all random variables we could talk about. It is defined as if $B$ were a logic program (cf. [18]). The least Herbrand model $\mathrm{LH}(B) \subseteq \mathrm{HB}(B)$ consists of all *relevant* random variables, the random variables over which a probability distribution is defined by $B$, as we will see. Again, $\mathrm{LH}(B)$ is defined as if $B$ were be a logic program (cf. [18]). It is the least fix point of the *immediate consequence operator* applied on the empty interpretation. Therefore, a ground atom which is true in the logical sense corresponds to a relevant random variables. Now,

```
m(ann,dorothy).
f(brian,dorothy).
pc(ann).
pc(brian).
mc(ann).
mc(brian).

mc(X)  | m(Y,X),mc(Y),pc(Y).
pc(X)  | f(Y,X),mc(Y),pc(Y).
bt(X)  | mc(X),pc(X).
```
(1)

| $mc(X)$ | $pc(X)$ | $\mathbf{P}(bt(X))$ |
|---|---|---|
| $a$ | $a$ | $(0.97, 0.01, 0.01, 0.01)$ |
| $b$ | $a$ | $(0.01, 0.01, 0.97, 0.01)$ |
| ... | ... | ... |
| 0 | 0 | $(0.01, 0.01, 0.01, 0.97)$ |

(2)

**Fig. 1.** (1) The Bayesian logic program *bloodtype* encoding our genetic domain. To each Bayesian predicate, the identity is associated as combining rule. (2) A conditional probability distribution associated to the Bayesian clause `bt(X) | mc(X), pc(X)` represented as a table.

to each node $x$ in $DG(B)$ the combined conditional probability distribution is associated which is the result of the combining rule $cr(p)$ of the corresponding Bayesian predicate $p$ applied on the set of $cpd(c\theta)$'s where $head(c\theta) = x$ and $\{x\} \cup body(c\theta) \subseteq \mathrm{LH}(B)$. Thus, if $DG(B)$ is acyclic and not empty then it would encode a Bayesian network, because Datalog programs have a finite least Herbrand model which always exists and is unique. Therefore, the following independency assumption holds: *each node $x$ is independent of its non-descendants given a joint state of its parents $\mathbf{Pa}(x)$ in the dependency graph.* E.g. the program in Figure 1 renders $bt(dorothy)$ independent from $pc(brian)$ given a joint state of $pc(dorothy), mc(dorothy)$. Using this assumption the following proposition is provable:

**Proposition 1.** *Let $B$ be a Bayesian logic program. If $B$ fulfills that*

1. $\mathrm{LH}(B) \neq \emptyset$ *and*
2. $DG(B)$ *is acyclic*

*then it specifies a unique probability distribution $\mathbf{P}_B$ over* $\mathrm{LH}(B)$.

To see this, remember that if the conditions are fulfilled then $DG(B)$ is a Bayesian network. Thus, given a total order $x_1 \ldots, x_n$ of the nodes in $DG(B)$ the distribution $P_B$ factorizes in the usual way: $\mathbf{P}_B(x_1 \ldots, x_n) = \prod_{i=1}^{n} \mathbf{P}(x_i \mid \mathbf{Pa}\, x_i)$, where $\mathbf{P}(x_i \mid \mathbf{Pa}\, x_i)$ is the combined conditional probability distribution associated to $x_i$. A program $B$ fulfilling the conditions is called *well-defined*, and we will consider such programs for the rest of the paper. The program *bloodtype* in Figure 1 encodes the regularities in our genetic example. Its grounded version, which is a Bayesian network, is given in Figure 2. This illustrates that Bayesian networks [23] are well-defined propositional Bayesian logic programs. Each node-parents pair uniquely specifies a propositional Bayesian clause; we associate the identity as combining rule to each predicate; the conditional probability distributions are the ones of the Bayesian network.

```
m(ann,dorothy).
f(brian,dorothy).
pc(ann).
pc(brian).
mc(ann).
mc(brian).
mc(dorothy) | m(ann, dorothy),mc(ann),pc(ann).
pc(dorothy) | f(brian, dorothy),mc(brian),pc(brian).
bt(ann)     | mc(ann), pc(ann).
bt(brian)   | mc(brian), pc(brian).
bt(dorothy) | mc(dorothy),pc(dorothy).
```

**Fig. 2.** The grounded version of the Bayesian logic program of Figure 1. It (directly) encodes a Bayesian network.

## 3 Structural Learning of Bayesian Logic Programs

Let us now focus on the logical structure of Bayesian logic programs. When designing Bayesian logic programs, the expert has to determine this (logical) structure of the Bayesian logic program by specifying the extensional and intensional predicates, and by providing definitions for each of the intensional predicates. Given this logical structure, the Bayesian logic program induces (the structure of) a Bayesian network whose nodes are the *relevant*[2] random variables. It is well-known that determining the structure of a Bayesian network, and therefore also of a Bayesian logic program, can be difficult and expensive. On the other hand, it is often easier to obtain a set $D = \{D_1, \ldots, D_m\}$ of data cases. A data case $D_i \in D$ has two parts, a logical and a probabilistic part.

The logical part of a data case $D_i \in D$, denoted as $Var(D_i)$, is a Herbrand interpretation. Consider e.g. the least Herbrand model $LH(bloodtype)$ (cf. Figure 2) and the logical atoms $LH(bloodtype')$ in the following case:

$$\{m(cecily, fred), f(henry, fred), pc(cecily), pc(henry), pc(fred),$$
$$mc(cecily), mc(henry), mc(fred), bt(cecily), bt(henry), bt(fred)\}$$

These (logical) interpretations can be seen as the least Herbrand models of unknown Bayesian logic programs. They specify different sets of *relevant* random variables, depending on the given "extensional context". If we accept that the genetic laws are the same for both families then a learning algorithm should transform such extensionally defined predicates into intensionally defined ones, thus compressing the interpretations. This is precisely what ILP techniques are doing. The key assumption underlying any inductive technique is that the rules that are valid in one interpretation are likely to hold for any interpretation.

[2] In a sense, *relevant* random variables are those variables, which Cowell et al. [2, p. 25] mean when they say that the first phase in developing a Bayesian network involves to "*specify the set of 'relevant' random variables*".

It thus seems clear that techniques for *learning from interpretations* can be adapted for learning the logical structure of Bayesian logic programs. *Learning from interpretations* is an instance of the non-monotonic learning setting of ILP (cf. [19]), which uses only only positive examples (i.e. models).

So far, we have specified the logical part of the learning problem: we are looking for a set $H$ of Bayesian clauses given a set $D$ of data cases s.t. $\forall D_i \in D : \mathrm{LH}(H \cup \mathit{Var}(D_i)) = \mathit{Var}(D_i)$, i.e. the Herbrand interpretation $\mathit{Var}(D_i)$ is a model for $H$. The hypotheses $H$ in the space $\mathcal{H}$ of hypotheses are sets of Bayesian clauses. However, we have to be more careful. A candidate set $H \in \mathcal{H}$ has to be acyclic on the data that means that for each $D_i \in D$ the induced Bayesian network over $\mathrm{LH}(H \cup \mathit{Var}(D_i))$ has to be acyclic. Let us now focus on the quantitative components. The quantitative component of a Bayesian logic program is given by the associated conditional probability distributions and combining rules. We assume that the combining rules are fixed. Each data case $D_i \in D$ has a probabilistic part which is a partial assignment of states to the random variables in $\mathit{Var}(D_i)$. We say that $D_i$ is a *partially observed joint state* of $\mathit{Var}(D_i)$. As an example consider the following two data cases:

$$\{m(cecily, fred) = true, f(henry, fred) = ?, pc(cecily) = a, pc(henry) = b, pc(fred) = ?,$$
$$mc(cecily) = b, mc(henry) = b, mc(fred) = ?, bt(cecily) = ab, bt(henry) = b, bt(fred) = ?\}$$

$$\{m(ann, dorothy) = true, f(brian, dorothy) = true, pc(ann) = b,$$
$$mc(ann) = ?, mc(brian) = a, mc(dorothy) = a, pc(dorothy) = a,$$
$$pc(brian) = ?, bt(ann) = ab, bt(brian) = ?, bt(dorothy) = a\},$$

where ? denotes an unknown state of a random variable. The partial assignments induce a joint distribution over the random variables of the logical parts. A candidate $H \in \mathcal{H}$ should reflect this distribution. In Bayesian networks the conditional probability distributions are typically learned using gradient descent or EM for a fixed structure of the Bayesian network. A scoring mechanism that evaluates how well a given structure $H \in \mathcal{H}$ matches the data is maximized. Therefore, we will assume a function $\mathit{score}_D : \mathcal{H} \mapsto \mathbb{R}$.

To summarize, the learning problem can be formulated as follows:

**Given** a set $D = \{D_1, \ldots, D_m\}$ of data cases, a set $\mathcal{H}$ of Bayesian logic programs and a scoring function $\mathit{score}_D : \mathcal{H} \mapsto \mathbb{R}$.

**Find** a candidate $H^* \in \mathcal{H}$ which is acyclic on the data such that for all $D_i \in D$ : $\mathrm{LH}(H^* \cup \mathit{Var}(D_i)) = \mathit{Var}(D_i)$, and $H^*$ matches the data $D$ best according to $\mathit{score}_D$.

The best match in this context refers to those parameters of the associated conditional probability distributions which maximize the scoring function. For a discussion on how the best match can be computed see [12] or [16]. The chosen scoring function is a crucial aspect of the algorithm. Normally, we can only hope to find a sub-optimal candidate. A heuristic learning algorithm solving this problem is given in Algorithm 1.

| $\mathbf{P}(A \mid A_1, \ldots, A_n)$ | | | | | |
|---|---|---|---|---|---|
| *true* | *false* | $A_1$ | $A_2$ | $\ldots$ | $A_n$ |
| 1.0 | 0.0 | *true* | *true* | | *true* |
| 0.0 | 1.0 | *false* | *true* | | *true* |
| $\vdots$ | $\vdots$ | $\vdots$ | $\vdots$ | | $\vdots$ |
| 0.0 | 1.0 | *false* | *false* | | *false* |

**Table 1.** The conditional probability distribution associated to a Bayesian clause $\mathtt{A} \mid \mathtt{A_1}, \ldots, \mathtt{A_n}$ encoding a logical one.

Background knowledge can be incorporated in our approach in the following way. The background knowledge can be expressed as a fixed Bayesian logic program $B$. Then we search for a candidate $H^*$ which is together with $B$ acyclic on the data such that for all $D_i \in D : \mathrm{LH}(B \cup H^* \cup \mathit{Var}(D_i)) = \mathit{Var}(D_i)$, and $B \cup H^*$ matches the data $D$ best according to $\mathit{score}_D$. In [14], we show how pure Prolog programs can be repesented as Bayesian logic prorgams w.r.t. the conditions 1 and 2 of Proposition 1. The basic idea is as follows. Assume that a logical clause $\mathtt{A} :- \mathtt{A_1}, \ldots, \mathtt{A_n}$ is given. We encode the clause by the Bayesian clause $\mathtt{A} :- \mathtt{A_1}, \ldots, \mathtt{A_n}$ where $A, A_1, \ldots, A_n$ are now Bayesian atoms over $\{\mathit{true}, \mathit{false}\}$. We associate to the Bayesian clause the conditional probability distribution of Figure 1, and set the combining rule of $A$'s predicate to *max*:

$$\max\{\mathbf{P}(A \mid A_{i1}, \ldots, A_{in_i}) \mid i = 1, \ldots, n\} = \mathbf{P}(A \mid \cup_{i=1}^{n}\{A_{i1}, \ldots, A_{in_i}\}) := \max_{i=1}^{n}\{\mathbf{P}(A \mid A_{i1}, \ldots, A_{in_i})\}. \tag{1}$$

We will now explain Algorithm 1 and its underlying ideas in more details. The next section illustrates the algorithm for a special class of Bayesian logic programs: Bayesian networks. For Bayesian networks, the algorithm coincides with score-based methods for learning within Bayesian networks which are proven to be useful by the UAI community (see e.g. [9]). Therefore, an extension to the first order case seems reasonable. It will turn out that the algorithm works for first order Bayesian logic programs, too.

### 3.1 A Propositional Case: Bayesian Networks

Here we will show that Algorithm 1 is a generalization of score-based techniques for structural learning within Bayesian networks. To do so we briefly review these score-based techniques. Let $x = \{x_1, \ldots, x_n\}$ be a fixed set of random variables. The set $x$ corresponds to a least Herbrand model of an unknown propositional Bayesian logic program representing a Bayesian network. The probabilistic dependencies among the relevant random variables are not known, i.e. the propositional Bayesian clauses are unknown. Therefore, we have to select such a propositional Bayesian logic program as a *candidate* and estimate its parameters. The data cases of the data $D = \{D_1, \ldots, D_m\}$ look like

```
Let H be an initial (valid) hypothesis;
S(H) := score_D(H);
repeat
   H' := H;
   S(H') := S(H);
   foreach H'' ∈ ρ_g(H') ∪ ρ_s(H') do
      if H'' is (logically) valid on D then
         if the Bayesian networks induced by H'' on the data are acyclic
         then
            if score_D(H'') > S(H) then
               H := H'';
               S(H) := S(H'');
            end
         end
      end
   end
until S(H') = S(H);
Return H;
```

**Algorithm 1.**
A greedy algorithm for searching the structure of Bayesian logic programs.

$$\{m(ann, dorothy) = true, f(brian, dorothy) = true, pc(ann) = a,$$
$$mc(ann) = ?, mc(brian) = ?, mc(dorothy) = a, mc(dorothy) = a,$$
$$pc(brian) = b, bt(ann) = a, bt(brian) = ?, bt(dorothy) = a\}$$

which is a data case for the Bayesian network in Figure 2. Note, that the atoms have to be interpreted as propositions. The set of candidate Bayesian logic programs spans the hypothesis space $\mathcal{H}$. Each $H \in \mathcal{H}$ is a Bayesian logic program consisting of $n$ propositional clauses: for each $x_i \in x$ a single clause $c$ with $head(c) = x_i$ and $body(c) \subseteq x \setminus \{x_i\}$. To traverse $\mathcal{H}$ we (1) specify two *refinement* operators $\rho_g : \mathcal{H} \mapsto 2^{\mathcal{H}}$ and $\rho_s : \mathcal{H} \mapsto 2^{\mathcal{H}}$, that take a candidate and modify it to produce a set of candidates. The search algorithm performs informed search in $\mathcal{H}$ based on $score_D$. In the case of Bayesian networks the operator $\rho_g(H)$ deletes a Bayesian proposition from the body of a Bayesian clause $c_i \in H$, and the operator $\rho_s(H)$ adds a Bayesian proposition to the body of $c_i \in H$ . Usually, instances of scores are e.g. the *minimum description length* score [17] or the Bayesian scores [10].

As a simple illustration we consider a greedy hill-climbing algorithm incorporating $score_D(H) := LL(D, H)$, the log-likelihood of the data $D$ given a candidate structure $H$ with the best parameters. We pick an initial candidate $S \in \mathcal{H}$ as starting point (e.g. the set of all propositions) and compute the likelihood $LL(D, S)$ with the best parameters. Then, we use $\rho(S)$ to compute the legal "neighbours" (candidates being acyclic) of $S$ in $\mathcal{H}$ and score them. All neighbours

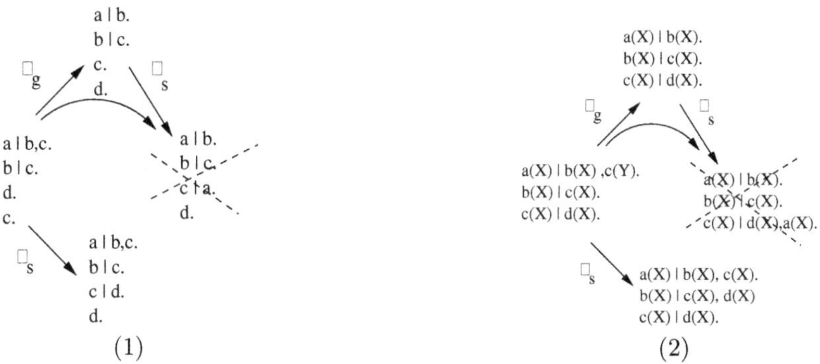


**Fig. 3.** (1) The use of refinement operators during structural search for Bayesian networks. We can add ($\rho_s$) a proposition to the body of a clause or delete ($\rho_g$) it from the body. (2) The use of refinement operators during structural search within the framework of Bayesian logic programs. We can add ($\rho_s$) a constant-free atom to the body of a clause or delete ($\rho_g$) it from the body. Candidates crossed out in (1) and (2) are illegal because they are cyclic.

are valid (see below for a definition of validity). E.g. replacing `pc(dorothy)` with `pc(dorothy) | pc(brian)` gives such a "neighbour". We take that $S' \in \rho(S)$ with the best improvements in the score. The process is continued until no improvements in score are obtained. The use of the two refinement operators is illustrated in Figure 3.

### 3.2 The First Order Case

Here, we will explain the ideas underlying our algorithm in the first order case. On the logical level it is similar to the ILP setting *learning from interpretation* which e.g. is used in the CLAUDIEN system ([4,5,1]): (1) all data cases are interpretations, and (2) a hypothesis should reflect what is in the data. The first point is carried over by enforcing each data case $D_i \in \{D_1, \ldots, D_m\}$ to be a partially observed joint state of a Herbrand interpretation of an unknown Bayesian logic program. This also implies that all data cases are probabilistically independent[3]. The second point is enforced by requiring all hypotheses to be (logically) true in all data cases, i.e. the logical structure of the hypothesis is certain. Thus, the logical rules valid on the data cases are constraints on the space of hypotheses. The main difference to the pure logical setting is that we have to take the probabilistic parts of the data case into account.

**Definition 1 (Characteristic induction from interpretations).** *(adapted w.r.t. our purposes from [5]) Let $D$ be a set of data cases and $\mathcal{C}$ the set of all clauses that can be part of a hypothesis. $H \subseteq \mathcal{C}$ is a logical solution iff $H$ is a logically maximally general valid hypothesis. A hypothesis $H \subseteq \mathcal{C}$ is (logically)*

[3] An assumption which one has to verify if using our method. In the case of families the assumption seems reasonable.

*valid iff for all $D_i \in D$: $H$ is (logically) true in $D_i$. A hypothesis $H \subseteq \mathcal{C}$ is a probabilistic solution iff $H$ is a valid hypothesis and the Bayesian network induced by $H$ on $D$ is acyclic.*

It is common to impose syntactic restrictions on the space $\mathcal{H} = 2^{\mathcal{C}}$ of hypotheses through the language $\mathcal{L}$, which determines the set $\mathcal{C}$ of clauses that can be part of a hypothesis. The language $\mathcal{L}$ is an important parameter of the induction task.

**Language Assumption.** *In this paper, we assume that the alphabet of $\mathcal{L}$ only contains constant and predicate symbols that occur in one of the data cases, and we restrict $\mathcal{C}$ to range-restricted, constant-free clauses containing maximum $k = 3$ atoms in the body. Furthermore, we assume that the combining rules associated to the Bayesian predicates are given.*

Let us discuss some properties of our setting. (1) Using partially observed joint states of interpretations as data cases is the first order equivalent of what is done in Bayesian network learning. There each data case is described by means of a partially observed joint state of a fixed, finite set of random variables. Furthermore, it implicitly corresponds to assuming that all relevant ground atoms of each data case are known: all random variables not stated in the data case are regarded to be *not relevant* (false in the logical sense). (2) Hypotheses have to be valid. Intuitively, validity means that the hypothesis holds (logically) on the data, i.e. that the induced hypothesis postulates true regularities present in the data cases. Validity is a monotone property at the level of clauses, i.e. if $H_1$ and $H_2$ are valid with respect to a set of data cases $D$, then $H_1 \cup H_2$ is valid. This means that all well-formed clauses in $\mathcal{L}$ can (logically) be considered completely independent of each other. Both arguments (1) and (2) together guarantee that no possible dependence among the random variables is lost. (3) The condition of maximal generality appears in the definition because the most interesting hypotheses in the logical case are the most informative and hence the most general. Therefore, we will use a logical solution as initial hypotheses. But the best scored hypothesis has not to be maximally general, as the initial hypothesis in the next example shows. Here, our approach differs from the pure logical setting. We consider probabilistic solutions instead of logical solutions. The idea is to incorporate a scoring function known from learning of Bayesian networks to evaluate how well the given probabilistic solution matches the data.

The key to our proposed algorithm is the well-known definition of logical entailment (cf. [18]). It induces a partial order on the set of hypotheses. To compute our initial (valid) hypotheses we use the CLAUDIEN algorithm. Roughly speaking, CLAUDIEN works as follows (for a detailed discussion we refer to [5]). It keeps track of a list of candidate clauses $Q$, which is initialized to the maximally general clause (in $\mathcal{L}$). It repeatedly deletes a clause $c$ from $Q$, and tests whether $c$ is valid on the data. If it is, $c$ is added to the final hypothesis, otherwise, all maximally general specializations of $c$ (in $\mathcal{L}$) are computed (using a so-called refinement operator $\rho$, see below) and added back to $Q$. This process continues until $Q$ is empty and all relevant parts of the search-space have been considered. We now have to define operators to traverse $\mathcal{H}$. A logical specialization (or generalization) of a set $H$ of Bayesian clauses could be achieved by specializing (or generalizing) single clauses $c \in H$. In our approach we use the two refinement operators $\rho_s : 2^{\mathcal{H}} \mapsto \mathcal{H}$ and $\rho_g : 2^{\mathcal{H}} \mapsto \mathcal{H}$. The operator $\rho_s(H)$ adds constant-free atoms to the body of a single clause $c \in H$, and $\rho_g(H)$ deletes constant-free atoms from the body of a single clause $c \in H$. Figure 3 shows the different refinement operators for the general first order case and the propositional case for learning Bayesian networks. Instead of adding (deleting) propositions to (from) the body of a clause, they add (delete) according to our language assumption constant-free atoms. Furthermore, Figure 3 shows that using the refinement operators each probabilistic solution could be reached.

As a simple instantiation of Algorithm 1 we consider a greedy hill-climbing algorithm incorporating $score_D(H) := LL(D, H)$. It picks up a (logical) solution $S \in \mathcal{H}$ as starting point and computes $LL(D, S)$ with the best parameters. For a discussion of how these parameters can be found we refer to [12,16]. E.g. having data cases over *LH*(*bloodtype*) and *LH*(*bloodtype*′), we choose as initial candidate

```
mc(X)   | m(Y, X).
pc(X)   | f(Y, X).
bt(X)   | mc(X).
```

It is likely that the initial candidate is not a probabilistic solution, although it is a logical solution. E.g. the blood type does not depend on the fatherly genetical information. Then, we use $\rho_s(S)$ and $\rho_g(S)$ to compute the legal "neighbours" of $S$ in $\mathcal{H}$ and score them. E.g. one such a "neighbour" is given by replacing `bt(X) | mc(X)` with `bt(X) | mc(X), pc(X)`. Let $S'$ be that valid and acyclic neighbour which is scored best. If $LL(D, S) < LL(D, S')$, then we take $S'$ as new hypothesis. The process is continued until no improvements in score are obtained. During the search we have to take care to prune away every hypothesis $H$ which is invalid or leads to cyclic dependency graphs (on the data cases). This could be tested in time $O(s \cdot r^3)$ where $r$ is the number of random variables of the largest data case in $D$ and $s$ is the number of clauses in $H$. To do so, we build the Bayesian networks induced by $H$ over each $Var(D_i)$ by computing the ground instances for each clause $c \in H$ where the ground atoms are members of $Var(D_i)$. This takes $O(s \cdot r_i^3)$. Then, we test in $O(r_i)$ for a topological order of the nodes in the induced Bayesian network.

## 4 Preliminary Experiments

We have implemented the algorithm in Sicstus Prolog 3.8.1. The implementation has an interface to Matlab to score hypotheses using the BNT toolbox [21]. We considered two totally independent families using the predicates given by *bloodtype* having 12 respectively 15 family members. For each least Herbrand model 1000 samples from the induced Bayesian network were gathered.

The general question was whether we could learn the intensional rules of *bloodtype*. Therefore, we first had a look at the (logical) hypotheses space. The space could be seen as the first order equivalent of the space for learning the structure of Bayesian networks (see Figure 3). In a further experiment the goal was to learn a definition for the predicate *bt*. We had fixed the definitions for the other predicates in two ways: (1) to the definitions the CLAUDIEN system had computed, and (2) to the definitions from the *bloodtype* Bayesian logic program. In both cases, the algorithm scored `bt(X) | mc(X), pc(X)` best, i.e. the algorithm has re-discovered the intensional definition which was originally used to build the data cases. Furthermore, the result shows that the best scored solution was independent of the fixed definitions. This could indicate that ideas about decomposable scoring functions can or should be lifted to the first order case. Although, these experiments are preliminary, they suggest that ILP techniques can be adapted for structural learning within first order probabilistic frameworks.

## 5 Related Work

To the best of our knowledge, there has not been much work on learning within first order extensions of Bayesian networks. Koller and Pfeffer [16] show how to estimate the maximum likelihood parameters for Ngo and Haddawys's framework of probabilistic logic programs [22] by adapting the EM algorithm. Kersting and De Raedt [12] discuss a gradient-based method to solve the same problem for Bayesian logic programs. Friedman et al. [6,7] tackle the problem of learning the logical structure of first order probabilistic models. They used Structural-EM for learning probabilistic relational models. This algorithm is similar to the standard EM method except that during iterations of this algorithm the structure is improved. As far as we know this approach, it does not consider logical constraints on the space of hypotheses in the way our approach does. Therefore, we suggest that both ideas can be combined. There exist also methods for learning within first order probabilistic frameworks which do not build on Bayesian networks. Sato et al. [25] give a method for EM learning of PRISM programs. They do not incorporate ILP techniques. Cussens [3] investigates EM like methods for estimating the parameters of stochastic logic programs. Within the same framework, Muggleton [20] uses ILP techniques to learn the logical structure. The used ILP setting is different to *learning from interpretations* and seems not to be based on learning of Bayesian networks.

Finally, Bayesian logic programs are somewhat related to the BUGS language [8]. The BUGS language is based on imperative programming. It uses concepts such as for-loops to model regularities in probabilistics models. So, the differences between Bayesian logic programs and BUGS are akin to the diferences between declarative programming languages (such as Prolog) and imperative ones. Therefore, adapting techniques from Inductive Logic Programming to learn the structure of BUGS programs seems not to be that easy.

## 6 Conclusions

A new link between ILP and learning within Bayesian networks is presented. We have proposed a scheme for learning the structure of Bayesian logic programs.

It builds on the ILP setting *learning from interpretations*. We have argued that by adapting this setting score-based methods for structural learning of Bayesian networks could be updated to the first order case. The ILP setting is used to define and traverse the space of (logical) hypotheses. Instead of score-based greedy algorithm other UAI methods such as Structural-EM may be used. The experiments we have are promising. They show that our approach works. But the link established between ILP and Bayesian networks seems to be bi-directional. Can ideas developed in the UAI community be carried over to ILP?

The research within the UAI community has shown that score-based methods are useful. In order to see whether this still holds for the first-order case we will perform more detailed experiments. Experiments on real-world scale problems will be conducted. We will look for more elaborated scoring functions like e.g. scores based on the *minimum description length* principle. We will investigate more difficult tasks like learning multiple clauses definitions. The use of refinement operators adding or deleting non constant-free atoms should be explored. Furthermore, it would be interesting to weaken the assumption that a data case corresponds to a complete interpretation. Not assuming all relevant random variables are known would be interesting for learning intensional rules like `nat(s(X)) | nat(X)`. Lifting the idea of decomposable scoring function to the first order case should result in a speeding up of the algorithm. In this sense, we believe that the proposed approach is a good point of departure for further research.

**Acknowledgments**

The authors would like to thank Stefan Kramer and Manfred Jaeger for helpful discussions on the proposed approach. Also, many thanks to the anonymous reviewers for their helpful comments on the initial draft of this paper.

## References

1. H. Blockeel and L. De Raedt. ISIDD: An Interactive System for Inductive Databse Design. *Applied Artificial Intelligence*, 12(5):385, 421 1998.
2. R. G. Cowell, A. P. Dawid, S. L. Lauritzen, and D. J. Spiegelhalter. *Probabilistic networks and expert systems*. Springer-Verlag New York, Inc., 1999.
3. J. Cussens. Parameter estimation in stochastic logic programs. *Machine Learning*, 2001. to appear.
4. L. De Raedt and M. Bruynooghe. A theory of clausal discovery. In *Proceedings of the Thirteenth International Joint Conference on Artificial Intelligence (IJCAI-1993)*, pages 1058–1063, 1993.
5. L. De Raedt and L. Dehaspe. Clausal discovery. *Machine Learning*, (26):99–146, 1997.
6. N. Friedman, L. Getoor, D. Koller, and A. Pfeffer. Learning probabilistic relational models. In *Proceedings of Sixteenth International Joint Conference on Artificial Intelligence (IJCAI-1999)*, Stockholm, Sweden, 1999.

7. L. Getoor, D. Koller, B. Taskar, and N. Friedman. Learning probabilistic relational models with structural uncertainty. In *Proceedings of the AAAI-2000 Workshop on Learning Statistical Models from Relational Data*, 2000.
8. W. R. Gilks, A. Thomas, and D. J. Spiegelhalter. A language and program for complex bayesian modelling. *The Statistician*, 43, 1994.
9. D. Heckerman. A tutorial on learning with Bayesian networks. Technical Report MSR-TR-95-06, Microsoft Research, Advanced Technology Division, Microsoft Corporation, One Microsoft Way, Redmond, WA 98052, March 1995.
10. D. Heckerman, D. Geiger, and D. M. Chickering. Learning Bayesian networks: The combination of knowledge and statistical data. Technical Report MSR-TR-94-09, Microsoft Research, 1994.
11. M. Jaeger. Relational Bayesian networks. In *Proceedings of UAI-1997*, 1997.
12. K. Kersting and L. De Raedt. Adaptive Bayesian Logic Programs. In this volume.
13. K. Kersting and L. De Raedt. Bayesian logic programs. In *Work-in-Progress Reports of the Tenth International Conference on Inductive Logic Programming (ILP -2000)*, 2000. `http://SunSITE.Informatik.RWTH-Aachen.DE/Publications/CEUR-WS/Vol-35/`.
14. K. Kersting and L. De Raedt. Bayesian logic programs. Technical Report 151, University of Freiburg, Institute for Computer Science, April 2001.
15. K. Kersting, L. De Raedt, and S. Kramer. Interpreting Bayesian Logic Programs. In *Working Notes of the AAAI-2000 Workshop on Learning Statistical Models from Relational Data*, 2000.
16. D. Koller and A. Pfeffer. Learning probabilities for noisy first-order rules. In *Proceedings of the Fifteenth International Joint Conference on Artificial Intelligence (IJCAI-1997)*, pages 1316–1321, Nagoya, Japan, August 23-29 1997.
17. W. Lam and F. Bacchus. Learning Bayesian belief networks: An approach based on the MDL principle. *Computational Intelligence*, 10(4), 1994.
18. J. W. Lloyd. *Foundations of Logic Programming.* Springer, Berlin, 2. edition, 1989.
19. S. Muggleton and L. De Raedt. Inductive logic programming: Theory and methods. *Journal of Logic Programming*, 19(20):629–679, 1994.
20. S. H. Muggleton. Learning stochastic logic programs. In L. Getoor and D. Jensen, editors, *Proceedings of the AAAI-2000 Workshop on Learning Statistical Models from Relational Data*, 2000.
21. K. P. Murphy. *Bayes Net Toolbox for Matlab.* U. C. Berkeley. `http://www.cs.berkeley.edu/~murphyk/Bayes/bnt.html`.
22. L. Ngo and P. Haddawy. Answering queries form context-sensitive probabilistic knowledge bases. *Theoretical Computer Science*, 171:147–177, 1997.
23. J. Pearl. *Reasoning in Intelligent Systems: Networks of Plausible Inference.* Morgan Kaufmann, 2. edition, 1991.
24. D. Poole. Probabilistic Horn abduction and Bayesian networks. *Artificial Intelligence*, 64:81–129, 1993.
25. T. Sato and Y. Kameya. A viterbi-like algorithm and EM learning for statistical abduction. In *Proceedings of UAI2000 Workshop on Fusion of Domain Knowledge with Data for Decision Support*, 2000.
26. L. Sterling and E. Shapiro. *The Art of Prolog: Advanced Programming Techniques.* The MIT Press, 1986.

# Demand-Driven Construction of Structural Features in ILP

Stefan Kramer

Institute for Computer Science, Machine Learning Lab
Albert-Ludwigs-University, Georges-Köhler-Allee, Gebäude 079,
D-79110 Freiburg i. Brg., Germany
skramer@informatik.uni-freiburg.de

**Abstract.** This paper tackles the problem that methods for propositionalization and feature construction in first-order logic to date construct features in a rather unspecific way. That is, they do not construct features "on demand", but rather in advance and without detecting the need for a representation change. Even if structural features are required, current methods do not construct these features in a goal-directed fashion.
In previous work, we presented a method that creates structural features in a class-sensitive manner: We queried the molecular feature miner (MolFea) for features (linear molecular fragments) with a minimum frequency in the positive examples and a maximum frequency in the negative examples, such that they are, statistically significant, over-represented in the positives and under-represented in the negatives. In the present paper, we go one step further. We construct structural features in order to discriminate between those examples from different classes that are particularly problematic to classify. In order to avoid overfitting, this is done in a boosting framework. We are alternating AdaBoost re-weighting episodes and feature construction episodes in order to construct structural features "on demand". In a feature construction episode, we are querying for features with a minimum cumulative weight in the positives and a maximum cumulative weight in the negatives, where the weights stem from the previous AdaBoost iteration. In summary, we propose to construct structural features "on demand" by a combination of AdaBoost and an extension of MolFea to handle weighted learning instances.

## 1 Introduction

In the past few years, both machine learning and inductive logic programming have devoted a lot of attention to feature construction [21,13,4,3,15] . Features are constructed either in a class-blind [4] or in a class sensitive manner [21]. However, current methods still construct features in a rather unspecific way. That is, they do not construct features "on demand", but rather in advance and without detecting the need for a representation change. Even if structural features are required, current methods usually do not construct these features in

C. Rouveirol and M. Sebag (Eds.): ILP 2001, LNAI 2157, pp. 132–141, 2001.

a goal-directed fashion. In this paper, we investigate the possibility of a "demand-driven" construction of structural features.

Changing the representation on demand in ILP is not new. The system MODELER [23] formed new concepts if the number of exceptions to a rule became unplausibly large. De Raedt [5] proposed to shift the bias to a more expressive representation language if the current language is not sufficient to express the concept. The present work is also related to other approaches that shift the bias to increasingly expressive representation languages, but do not focus on the demand-driven aspect [2,1]. The work described in this paper differs in several respects. Firstly, the expressiveness of the representation language is not changed. Secondly, the learning setting is the one of inductive concept learning, where we assume noise in the data. Thirdly, we deal with the demand-driven construction of structural features.

The idea of demand-driven feature construction in ILP is also related to the idea of using ILP methods only where propositional learning fails, or, more precisely, of using an ILP algorithm in order to correct the mistakes made by a propositional learning algorithm. One submission by Srinivasan and co-workers to the PTE-2 challenge [22] based on this idea turned out to be optimal under certain cost functions and/or class distributions according to ROC analysis.

In previous work, we introduced the *Molecular Feature Miner* (MolFea) [7,16,17], a domain specific inductive database that is capable of searching for linear molecular fragments (corresponding to features) of interest in large databases of chemical compounds. For instance, one can query the system for features (linear molecular fragments) with a minimum frequency in the positive examples and a maximum frequency in the negative examples, such that they are, statistically significant, over-represented in the positives and under-represented in the negatives. Recent evidence with MolFea [16] showed, that such a class-sensitive feature construction can be beneficial in conjunction with classical Machine Learning systems. In the present paper, we go one step further. We construct structural features in order to discriminate between those examples from different classes that are particularly problematic to classify. In order to avoid overfitting, this is done in a boosting framework. In a feature construction episode, we are querying for features with a minimum cumulative weight in the positives and a maximum cumulative weight in the negatives. This requires an extension of MolFea to handle not only frequencies of instances, but also weights.

This paper is organized as follows. Sections 2 and 3 introduce the molecular feature miner and its extension for handling weighted instances. In Section 4, we present our approach to the demand-driven construction of structural features. After the section on experimental results, we conclude the paper.

## 2 The Molecular Feature Miner MolFea

In this section, we briefly review the Molecular Feature Miner (MolFea). MolFea is a domain specific inductive database which aims at mining molecu-

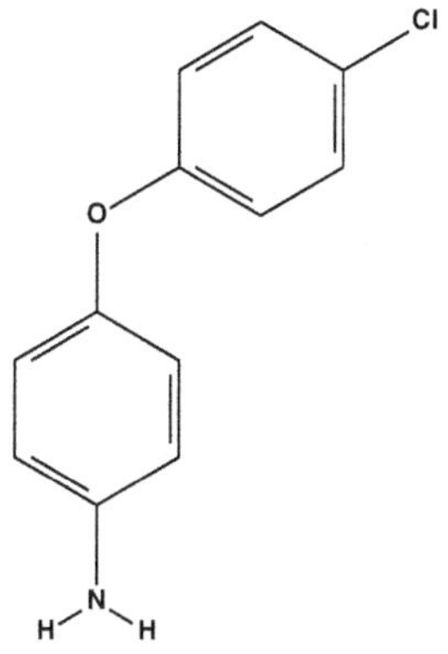

**Fig. 1.** Example compound in a 2-D representation. '$cl - c \sim c \sim c \sim c - o$' is an example fragment occurring in the molecule.

lar fragments (features) of interest in chemical data. The level-wise version space algorithm (cf. [18]) forms its basis. More information can be found in [7,16,17]. Inductive databases follow Mannila and Toivonen's [18] formulation of the general pattern discovery task. Given a database $r$, a language $\mathcal{L}$ for expressing patterns, and a constraint $q$, find the theory of $r$ with respect to $\mathcal{L}$ and $q$, i.e. $Th(\mathcal{L}, r, q) = \{\phi \in \mathcal{L} \mid q(r, \phi) \text{ } is \text{ } true\}$. Viewed in this way $Th(\mathcal{L}, r, q)$ contains all sentences within the pattern language considered that make the constraint $q$ true.

## 2.1 Molecular Fragments

A *molecular fragment* is defined as a sequence of linearly connected atoms. For instance, '$o - s - c$' is a fragment meaning: "an oxygen atom with a single bond to a sulfur atom with a single bond to a carbon atom". In such expressions '$c$', '$n$', '$cl$', etc. denote elements, and '$-$' denotes a single bond, '$=$' a double bond, '#' a triple bond, and '$\sim$' an aromatic bond. As common in the literature, we only consider "heavy" (i.e., non-hydrogen) atoms in this paper.

We assume that the system is given a database of example compounds and that each of the example compounds in the database is described using a 2-D representation. The information given there consists of the elements of the atoms of a molecule and the bond orders (single, double, triple, aromatic). An example compound in such a representation is shown in Fig. 1.

A molecular fragment $f$ *covers* an example compound $e$ if and only if $f$ considered as a graph is a subgraph of example $e$. For instance, fragment '$cl - c \sim c \sim c \sim c - o$' covers the example compound in Fig. 1.

There are a number of interesting properties of the language of molecular fragments $\mathcal{M}$:

- fragments in $\mathcal{M}$ are partially ordered by the *is more general than* relation; when fragment $g$ is more general than fragment $s$ we will write $g \leq s$;

- within this partial order, two syntactically different fragments are equivalent only when they are a reversal of one another; e.g. '$c - o - s$' and '$s - o - c$' denote the same substructure;
- $g \leq s$ if and only if $g$ is a subsequence of $s$ or $g$ is a subsequence of the reversal of $s$; e.g. '$c - o$' $\leq$ '$c - o - s$'.

Note that the representation of molecular fragments is relatively restricted compared to some other representations employed in data mining, such as first-order queries [4] or subgraphs [12]. Although fragments are a relatively restricted representation of chemical structure, it is easy for trained chemists to recognize the functional group(s) that a given fragment occurs in. Thus, the interpretation of a fragment reveals more than meets the eye.

### 2.2 Constraints on Fragments

The features that will be constructed can be declaratively specified using a conjunction of primitive constraints $c_1 \wedge ... \wedge c_n$. The primitive constraints $c_i$ that can be imposed on the unknown target fragments $f$ are :

- $f \leq p$, $p \leq f$, $\neg(f \leq p)$ and $\neg(p \leq f)$: where $f$ is the unknown target fragment and $p$ is a specific pattern; this type of primitive constraint denotes that $f$ should (not) be more specific (general) than the specified fragment $p$; e.g. the constraint '$c - o$' $\leq f$ specifies that $f$ should be more specific than '$c - o$', i.e. that $f$ should contain '$c - o$' as a subsequence;
- $freq(f, D)$ denotes the relative frequency of a fragment $f$ on a set of molecules $D$; the relative frequency of a fragment $f$ w.r.t. a dataset $D$ is defined as the percentage of molecules in $D$ that $f$ covers;
- $freq(f, D_1) \leq t$, $freq(f, D_2) \geq t$ where $t$ is a positive real number and $D_1$ and $D_2$ are sets of molecules; this constraint denotes that the relative frequency of $f$ on the dataset $D_i$ should be larger than (resp. smaller than) or equal to $t$; e.g. the constraint $freq(f, Pos) \geq 0.95$ denotes that the target fragments $f$ should have a minimum relative frequency of 95 % on the set of molecules $Pos$.

If weights are associated with instances, we can generalize frequency-related constraints to weight-related constraints:

- $sum\_weights(f, D)$ denotes the sum of the weights of the instances in $D$ covered by a fragment $f$;
- $sum\_weights(f, D_1) \leq t$, $sum\_weights(f, D_2) \geq t$ where $t$ is a positive real number and $D_1$ and $D_2$ are sets of molecules; these constraints denote that the sum of the weights of those examples in $D_1$ (resp. $D_2$) covered by $f$ should be smaller than (resp. larger than) or equal to $t$.

These primitive constraints can now conjunctively be combined in order to declaratively specify the target fragments of interest. Note that the conjunction may specify constraints w.r.t. any number of datasets, e.g. imposing a minimum frequency on a set of active molecules, and a maximum one on a set of inactive ones. E.g. the following constraint:

$$('c-o' \leq f) \wedge \neg(f \leq 'c-o-s-c-o-s') \wedge$$

$$(freq(f, Act) \geq 0.95) \wedge freq(f, Inact) \leq 0.05)$$

queries for all fragments that include the sequence '$c-o$', are not a subsequence of '$c-o-s-c-o-s$', have a frequency on *Act* that is larger than 95 percent and a frequency on *Inact* that is smaller than 5 percent.

## 3 Solving Constraints

In this section, we show that the solution space $sol(c_1 \wedge ... \wedge c_n)$ in $\mathcal{M}$ for a conjunctive constraint $c_1 \wedge ... \wedge c_n$ is a version space and can therefore be represented by its borders.

Due to the fact that the primitive constraints $c_i$ are independent of one another, it follows that

$$sol(c_1 \wedge ... \wedge c_n) = sol(c_1) \cap ... \cap sol(c_n)$$

So, we can find the overall solutions by taking the intersection of the primitive ones.

Secondly, each of the primitive constraints $c$ is monotonic or anti-monotonic w.r.t. generality (cf. [18]). A constraint $c$ is *monotonic* (resp. anti-monotonic) w.r.t. generality whenever

$$\forall s, g \in \mathcal{M} : (g \leq s) \wedge (g \in sol(c)) \rightarrow (s \in sol(c))$$

(resp. $(s \in sol(c)) \rightarrow (g \in sol(c))$). The basic anti-monotonic constraints in our framework are: $(f \leq p), (freq(f, D) \geq m), (sum\_weights(f, D) \geq m)$, the basic monotonic ones are $(p \leq f), (freq(f, D) \leq m), (sum\_weights(f, D) \leq m)$. Furthermore the negation of a monotonic constraint is anti-monotonic and vice versa.

Monotonic and anti-monotonic constraints are important because their solution space is bounded by a border. This fact is well-known in both the data mining literature (cf. [18]), where the borders are often denoted by $BD^+$, as well as the machine learning literature (cf. [19]), where the symbols $S$ and $G$ are typically used.

To define borders, we need the notions of minimal and maximal elements of a set w.r.t. generality. Let $F$ be a set of fragments, then define

$$min(F) = \{f \in F \mid \neg\exists q \in F : f \leq q\}$$
$$max(F) = \{f \in F \mid \neg\exists q \in F : q \leq f\}^1$$

[1] Note that *min* gives the minimally general elements, and *max* the maximally general ones. In contrast, $g \leq s$ means that $g$ is more general than $s$.

We can now define the borders $S(c)$ and $G(c)$[2] of a primitive constraint $c$ as

$$G(c) = max(sol(c)) \text{ and } S(c) = min(sol(c))$$

Anti-monotonic constraints $c$ will have $G(c) = \{\top\}$ and for proper constraints $S(c) \neq \{\bot\}$; proper monotonic constraints have $S(c) = \{\bot\}$ and $G(c) \neq \{\top\}$. Furthermore, as in Mitchell's version space framework we have that

$$sol(c) = \{f \in \mathcal{M} \mid \exists s \in S(c), \exists g \in G(c) : g \leq f \leq s\}$$

This last property implies that $S(c)$ (resp. $G(c)$) are proper borders for anti-monotone (resp. monotone) constraints.

So, we have that the set of solutions $sol(c_i)$ to each primitive constraint is a simple version space completely characterized by $S(c_i)$ and $G(c_i)$. Therefore, the set of solutions $sol(c_1 \wedge ... \wedge c_n)$ to a conjunctive constraint $c_1 \wedge ... \wedge c_n$ will also be completely characterized by the corresponding $S(c_1 \wedge ... \wedge c_n)$ and $G(c_1 \wedge ... \wedge c_n)$.

Elsewhere [7,6], we have presented algorithms for computing the $S$ and $G$ sets corresponding to the constraints. The algorithm basically integrates the levelwise algorithm by Mannila and Toivonen [18] with Mellish's description identification algorithm. In principle, one might also employ Hirsh's version space merging algorithm [11].

## 4 Constructing Structural Features on Demand

In the previous section, we summarized the basic ideas underlying our domain specific inductive database MolFea. Using MolFea, we can declaratively specify the features of interest by a set of constraints. The space of all fragments (and corresponding to the fragments, the features) satisfying the constraints takes the form of a version space.

In order to construct structural features on demand, we performed two preliminary experiments: in the first one, we performed iterations of feature construction, where we queried for features that discriminate two individual, misclassified examples from different classes. In the second, we queried for features that discriminate between the false positives (resp. false negatives) and the positives (resp. negatives), either in one or in several iterations. In all of these cases, there were indications of overfitting. Thus, we devised a novel approach in the framework of boosting.

In the novel approach, we interleave AdaBoost [10] re-weighting episodes and feature construction episodes. Another view on the approach would be that we are boosting a weak learner that consists of weight-sensitive feature construction and some propositional learning algorithm.

In Table 1, the pseudo-code of our novel approach is shown. As the pseudo-code indicates, we perform regular AdaBoost iterations. In the first iteration,

[2] At this point, we will follow Mitchell's terminology, because he works with two dual borders (a set of maximally general solutions $G$ and a set of maximally specific ones $S$). In data mining, one typically only works with the $S$-set.

**Table 1.** Pseudo-code of AdaBoost, as instantiated in the presented approach. The basic AdaBoost procedure repeatedly queries MolFea for features (fragments) that are over-represented in the positive examples $E_+$ and under-represented in the negative examples $E_-$. These features are used in a propositional learner. For simplicity of presentation, we included two exit statements in the pseudocode.

```
procedure AdaBoost(E+, E-, PropFeatures, MaxIt)

All training examples in E+ ∪ E- are weighted by w_i = 1/N
j := 1;
repeat
   if   j = 1
   then Fs_j := PropFeatures
   else Fs_j := MolFea(E+, E-);
   if Fs_j = ∅ then exit
   H_j := PropLearner(Fs_j, E+, E-);
   ε_j := weighted error rate of H_j on E+ ∪ E-
   if ε_j = 0 or ε_j > 1/2 then exit
   β_j := log(ε_j / (1 − ε_j))
   for each e_i ∈ E+ ∪ E- do
      if    misclassifies(H_j, e_i)
      then  w_i := w_i (1 − ε_j) / ε_j
   renormalize all weights w_i to sum up to 1
until j = MaxIt
return hypotheses H_j weighted by β_j
```

we use the initial propositional features *PropFeatures* that are given as an input argument. In further iterations, MolFea attempts to construct structural features with a high cumulative weight in the positive examples and a low cumulative weight in the negatives. Thus, the feature construction algorithm (like the propositional learner applied subsequently) focuses attention on those examples that are difficult to classify.

The parameters for calling MolFea are determined as follows: We are seeking features (fragments) that are over-represented in the positive examples $E_+$ and under-represented in the negative examples $E_-$. If we had a dataset with a weight of one for each instance, we could do the following: We are interested in fragments with a minimum frequency of, say, 6, 10, 15, 20, respectively, and apply the $\chi^2$-Test to a $2 \times 2$ contingency table with the class as one variable and the occurrence of the fragment as the other one to determine the maximum allowable frequency in the negative examples. If we multiply the AdaBoost weights of the examples by $N$, the number of training examples, then we can proceed in

**Table 2.** Results of the new approach in standard ILP benchmark domains. *It.* denotes the number of iterations, *Acc.* denotes the predictive accuracy of ten-fold cross-validation if the maximum number of iterations was set to the resp. value; *# H.'s* denotes the number of hypotheses from ten-fold cross-validation that are constructed in the resp. iteration (note that the process can stop due to a number of reasons); *Av. C.* denotes the average number of conditions in PART hypotheses of the resp. iteration (also note that PART might just return the empty default theory).

| | PTE | | | Mutag. | | | Biodeg. | | |
|---|---|---|---|---|---|---|---|---|---|
| *It.* | *Acc.* | *# H.'s* | *Av. C.* | *Acc.* | *# H.'s* | *Av. C.* | *Acc.* | *# H.'s* | *Av. C.* |
| 1 | 62.9 | 10 | 1.0 | 81.4 | 10 | 6.3 | 59.5 | 10 | 2.1 |
| 2 | 62.9 | 10 | 7.9 | 79.8 | 10 | 14.8 | 67.7 | 10 | 9.0 |
| 3 | 63.8 | 10 | 2.6 | 88.8 | 10 | 25.6 | 72.9 | 10 | 7.9 |
| 4 | 63.8 | 3 | 0.3 | 85.6 | 10 | 22.9 | 73.8 | 9 | 4.9 |
| 5 | 63.8 | 1 | 0.0 | 86.7 | 10 | 14.8 | 74.7 | 5 | 4.6 |
| 6 | – | – | – | 88.3 | 10 | 9.9 | 74.7 | 3 | 0.3 |
| 7 | – | – | – | 88.3 | 8 | 2.1 | 74.7 | 1 | 0.0 |
| 8 | – | – | – | 88.8 | 5 | 3.6 | – | – | – |
| 9 | – | – | – | 87.8 | 5 | 3.0 | – | – | – |
| 10 | – | – | – | 88.3 | 3 | 1.0 | – | – | – |

analogy to the above case in order to determine the values of the minimum and maximum cumulative weights in the queries posed to MolFea.[3]

## 5 Experimental Results

The goal of the experimentation (as described in this section) was to show

- that it is possible to improve upon the initial propositional representation by the construction of new structural features, and
- that the approach is not prone to overfitting.

We performed experiments in three real-world domains: carcinogenicity prediction [22] (the PTE-2 dataset), mutagenicity prediction [20] and biodegradability prediction [8]. For biodegradation prediction, we used a two-class version (degradable or not) with a half-life time (HLT) threshold of 4 weeks.

The initial propositional features were: the result of the Ames test for the PTE data, the LUMO and logP values for mutagenicity, and the molecular weight and the logP for biodegradability. The maximum number of iterations was set to 10. PART [9], one of the best rule learning systems available today, was chosen as the propositional learner in the AdaBoost iterations. The settings for feature construction were as described above: the minimum cumulative weight (multiplied by $N$) was set to 6, 10, 15 and 20, respectively. The maximum cumulative weight was set dependent on the class distribution (that is actually modified during AdaBoost iterations).

[3] Note that the sum of weights of the training examples is always one in AdaBoostM1.

Table 2 summarizes the results from 10-fold cross- validation: In all three domains, it shows that the approach is able to improve upon the initial representation. As the number of iterations increase, the generalization performance increases as well, and peaks after a few iterations. Thus, we may conclude that the approach indeed improves over the initial propositional representation and that it shows no sign of overfitting. Interestingly, the algorithm stops quite early in several cases, since MOLFEA cannot find any more statistically significant structural features in the data.

Note that we did not make any attempts to tune the parameters: we just used AdaBoostM1 in conjunction with PART *as is* (the default settings). Besides, as mentioned above, our goal was to show that the overall approach improves upon the initial representation and that it does not overfit the training data.

## 6 Conclusion

In this paper we tackled the problem of a demand-driven construction of structural features by a combination of weight-related queries posed to the molecular feature miner MOLFEA and the AdaBoost framework. Although the approach was presented in the context of molecular fragments, it is possible to adapt it to other pattern domains, such as, e.g., first-order Datalog queries. We believe that many extensions of this work are conceivable. Different pattern domains, different machine learning systems and different variants of boosting could be investigated in the future.

## References


1. I. Bournaud, M. Courtine, J.-D. Zucker. Abstractions for knowledge organization of relational descriptions. in: *Proceedings of the 4th International Symposium on Abstraction, Reformulation, and Approximation (SARA-00)*, 87–106, Springer, 2000.
2. C. Carpineto. Shift of bias without operators. in: *Proceedings of the 10th European Conference on Artificial Intelligence*, 471–473, IOS Press, 1992.
3. E. Alphonse, C. Rouveirol. Lazy propositionalization for relational learning. in: *Proceedings of the 14th European Conference on Artificial Intelligence*, IOS Press, 2000.
4. L. Dehaspe, H. Toivonen. Discovery of frequent datalog patterns, *Data Mining and Knowledge Discovery*, 3(1):7–36, 1999.
5. L. De Raedt. *Interactive Concept Learning.* PhD thesis, Katholieke Universiteit Leuven, Leuven, Belgium, 1991.
6. L. De Raedt. A logical database mining query language. in: *Proceedings of the 10th Inductive Logic Programming Conference*, 78–92, Lecture Notes in Artificial Intelligence, Vol. 1866, Springer, 2000.
7. L. De Raedt, S. Kramer. The levelwise version space algorithm and its application to molecular fragment finding. in: *Proceedings of the Seventeenth International Joint Conference on Artificial Intelligence (IJCAI-01)*, 2001.

8. S. Džeroski, H. Blockeel, B. Kompare, S. Kramer, B. Pfahringer, W. Van Laer. Experiments in predicting biodegradability. in: *Proceedings of the 9th International Workshop on Inductive Logic Programming (ILP-99)*, 80–91, Springer, 1999.
9. E. Frank, I.H. Witten. Generating Accurate Rule Sets Without Global Optimization. in: *Proceedings of the Fifteenth International Conference on Machine Learning (ICML-98)*, Morgan Kaufmann Publishers, San Francisco, CA, 1998.
10. Y. Freund, R.E. Schapire. A decision theoretic generalization of on-line learning and an application to boosting. *Journal of Computer and System Sciences*, 55:119–139, 1997.
11. H. Hirsh. Generalizing version spaces. *Machine Learning*, 17(1): 5–46, 1994.
12. A. Inokuchi, T. Washio, H. Motoda. An Apriori-based algorithm for mining frequent substructures from graph data. in: D. Zighed, J. Komorowski, J. Zyktow (eds.), *Proceedings of the European Conference on Principles and Practice of Knowledge Discovery in Databases 2000*, Lecture Notes in Artificial Intelligence, Vol. 1910, Springer, 2000.
13. S. Kramer. *Relational Learning vs. Propositionalization: Investigations in Inductive Logic Programming and Propositional Machine Learning*, PhD thesis, Vienna University of Technology, Vienna, Austria, 1999. `http://www.informatik.uni-freiburg.de/~skramer/phd.ps.gz`
14. S. Kramer, E. Frank. Bottom-Up Propositionalization. In the *Proceedings of the Work-in-Progress Track at the 10th International Conference on Inductive Logic Programming*, 156–162, 2000.
15. S. Kramer, N. Lavrač, P. Flach. Propositionalization Approaches to Relational Data Mining. in: S. Džeroski, N. Lavrač (eds.), *Relational Data Mining*, Springer, 2001.
16. S. Kramer, L. De Raedt. Feature construction with version spaces for biochemical applications. in: *Proceedings of the Eighteenth International Conference on Machine Learning (ICML-01)*, 2001.
17. S. Kramer, L. De Raedt, C. Helma. Molecular Feature Mining in HIV Data. in: *Proceedings of the Seventh ACM SIGKDD International Conference on Knowledge Discovery and Data Mining (KDD-01)*, 2001.
18. H. Mannila, H. Toivonen. Levelwise search and borders of theories in knowledge discovery. *Data Mining and Knowledge Discovery*, 1(3):241–258, 1997.
19. T. Mitchell. Generalization as search. *Artificial Intelligence*, 18(2), 1982.
20. A. Srinivasan, S. Muggleton, R. D. King, M. Sternberg. Theories for mutagenicity: a study of first-order and feature based induction. *Artificial Intelligence*, 85(1-2):277–299, 1996.
21. A. Srinivasan, R. King. Feature construction with inductive logic programming: a study of quantitative predictions of biological activity aided by structural attributes. *Data Mining and Knowledge Discovery*, 3(1):37–57, 1999.
22. A. Srinivasan, R. D. King, D. W. Bristol. An assessment of submissions made to the predictive toxicology evaluation challenge. in: *Proceedings of the International Joint Conference on Artificial Intelligence 1999*, 270–275, 1999.
23. S. Wrobel. Demand-driven concept formation. in: K. Morik (ed.), *Knowledge Representation and Organization in Machine Learning*, 289–319, Springer, 1989.

# Transformation-Based Learning Using Multirelational Aggregation

Mark-A. Krogel and Stefan Wrobel

Otto-von-Guericke-Universität, Magdeburg, Germany
{krogel,wrobel}@iws.cs.uni-magdeburg.de

**Abstract.** Given the very widespread use of multirelational databases, ILP systems are increasingly being used on data originating from such warehouses. Unfortunately, even though not complex in structure, such business data often contain highly non-determinate components, making them difficult for ILP learners geared towards structurally complex tasks. In this paper, we build on popular transformation-based approaches to ILP and describe how they can naturally be extended with relational aggregation. We experimentall y show that this results in a multirelational learner that outperforms a structurally-oriented ILP system both in speed and accuracy on this class of problems.

## 1 Introduction

Relational databases and data warehouses are arguably the most widespread and commonly used technology for storing information in business, industry, and administration. The increasing popularity of data warehouses in particular has highlighted the fact that there is a large reservoir of application problems in the business area which would benefit from multirelational analysis techniques. Business databases, however, present somewhat different challenges than those found in the classical show case areas of ILP, such as molecular biology or language learning. Whereas the latter often involve highly complex structural elements, perhaps requiring deep nesting and recursion, business databases are usually structurally simple and restricted to a function-free representation. Their challenges are in two other directions. Firstly, it is quite normal that such databases are highly non-determinate — consider the case of a bank where a separate table stores thousands of transactions of a particular customer. Secondly, even though the number of involved relations may not be huge, the total size of these relations often will be, and scalability to perhaps millions of tuples is important.

Given these differing characteristics, an interesting question is whether it would not be beneficial to construct ILP learning systems that are optimised for these kinds of applications, just as many of today's state-of-the-art ILP systems are geared more towards structurally complex applications. In this paper, we show that indeed it is possible to construct a learning system that is well suited to such domains by building on approaches from the fields of ILP and the field of databases.

C. Rouveirol and M. Sebag (Eds.): ILP 2001, LNAI 2157, pp. 142–155, 2001.

In particular, to ensure scalability, we have adopted a *transformation-based approach* where an ILP-problem is first transformed into a propositional problem, and then handled by a fast propositional learner. Whereas existing ILP learners based on transformation either handle only constrained or determinate clauses [12], such as LINUS [7] or DINUS [8], or use heuristically or bias-selected clauses as simple binary features [6,9], in our approach we fully treat non-determinate clauses by emploing the idea of *aggregation* from the area of databases, thus allowing non-determinate relationships to be represented in summary features of the propositional representation.

In an experimental evaluation on different learning problems arising from the multirelational data supplied by the ECML-1998 and the PKDD-1999/PKDD-2000 challenges, respectively, we show that indeed this approach outperforms both more restricted transformation-based learners, as well as a state-of-the-art ILP learning system geared more towards structurally complex domains. We compare the use of decision trees and support vector machines as propositional learners, and conclude that our approach reaches a good performance and fast runtimes with both of these.

The paper is organised as follows. In Section 2, we give an introduction to transformation-based approaches to ILP. In Section 3, we provide details of our own feature construction method, discuss its declarative bias language which is based on *foreign links*, and show how it incorporates the aggregation operator. In Section 4, we give a detailed experimental evaluation of our method, comparing it both to simpler transformation-based learners and to a state-of-the-art non-transformation-based ILP system. Section 5 provides references to related work, and Section 6 concludes and gives pointers to future work.

## 2 Transformation-Based Approaches

As usual in ILP, in this paper we assume that we are given a set of positive examples $E^+$, a set of negative examples $E^-$, and background knowledge $B$. Since we are dealing with data originating in relational databases, we will assume that $E^+$ is a set of ground $p$-atoms, i.e., atoms the predicate of which is the target predicate $p$ (of arity $a$). Similarly, $E^-$ is a set of ground negated $p$-atoms, and $B$ is a set of ground atoms using different background knowledge predicates. The learning task can then be defined as follows.

- **Given:** $E^+$, $E^-$, $B$ as described above, such that $E^+ \cup E^- \cup B \not\models \Box$ and $B \not\models E^+$
- **Find:** A hypothesis $h$ from a set of allowed hypotheses $H$ such that the error of $h$ on future instances is minimised.

In ILP, $h$ is usually a set of first-order clauses, and a new instance is classified as positive if and only if it is covered by this set of clauses. In a *transformation-based* approach to ILP, on the other hand, we assume we are given a transformation function $\tau$ which transforms the given $E^+$, $E^-$, and $B$ into a single propositional table. One then uses a propositional learner on this table, producing a propositional hypothesis $h$ which can then be used to classify future instances (which of course first need to be transformed by $\tau$ as well)[1].

In principle, designers of transformation-based ILP systems are not restricted to any particular form of $\tau$ functions. In practice, it is commonplace to base the transformation on an implicit first-order hypothesis space $H$, and use the literals and variable bindings of the clauses in $H$ to define the transformation. For example, in the pioneering work on LINUS [7], a space of constrained clauses was used, whereas in its successor system DINUS [8], a space of determinate clauses [12] was used instead. As an alternative, if selected arbitrary clauses are used, one can apply existential transformations and use the clauses as binary features [6,9]. In order to better understand this framework, and to allow for an easier description of our own work, we will now describe this process of defining transformation functions in more detail.

### 2.1 Transformation Functions Based on Clauses

We will start by assuming that we are given a set $\mathcal{C}$ of clauses upon which feature generation is to be based. Note that $\mathcal{C}$ can be a systematically defined entire hypothesis space, but could also consist of a few selected clauses, so the following formalisation also covers the case of using individual clauses (perhaps learned by a non-transformation-based ILP learner) for feature generation as it is suggested in [9]. As a piece of notation, for a target predicate $p$ of arity $a$, let

$$\top := p(X_1, ..., X_a) \tag{1}$$

denote the most general $p$-atom. Since we are considering a single predicate learning task, we can assume without loss of generality that all $C \in \mathcal{C}$ have $\top$ as head.

Let $bvars(C)$ denote the ordered set of body variables of $C$. For a clause $C$ with

$$bvars(C) = \{Y_1, ..., Y_m\} \tag{2}$$

and a ground $p$-atom $e$, let

$$val(C, e) := \{(Y_1\sigma, ..., Y_m\sigma) \mid C\sigma \subseteq B \cup \{e\}\} \tag{3}$$

denote the different value combinations assumed by the body variables of $C$ when matching the clause head against the example and the clause body against the background knowledge[2]. Note that for determinate clauses [12], $val(C, e)$ contains exactly one tuple.

[1] Depending on the transformation and the propositional learner that are used, in certain cases it is even possible to transform the propositional learning results back into an equivalent clausal theory [7,8].

[2] To simplify our notation, we are treating $B$ as constant and do not mention it explicitly in our definitions.

We can now define a propositionalisation function $\varphi$ as follows:

$$\varphi : C, e, T \mapsto (v_1, ..., v_{n_{\varphi,C}}) \ , \tag{4}$$

where $C \in \mathcal{C}$, $e$ is a ground $p$-atom, and $T$ is a set of tuples of width $\mid bvars(C) \mid$. In other words, $\varphi$ produces the tuple of desired feature values for an example $e$ with respect to the literals and variable bindings of the clause $C$. Sometimes, it will be useful to also have a function which generates not the individual feature *values*, but the list of *names* (and types) of the features that are the result of propositionalising based on $C$:

$$\Phi : C \mapsto Att_1, ..., Att_{n_{\varphi,C}} \ . \tag{5}$$

Note that since in a propositional table, all examples must have the same attributes, $\Phi$ and the width of $\varphi$ must not depend on $e$. Also note that for both $\varphi$ and $\Phi$, we implicitly assume that the variables of each clause are typed, so $\varphi$ and $\Phi$ can make use of this information when performing the propositionalisation.

Here are two simple examples of using clauses in their entirety as features. The first is the transformation used in [6,9] on selected (parts of) clauses to transform them into binary features.

*Example 1 (Existential Features).* This transformation simply records whether $C$ is present in $e$:

$$\varphi_{\exists}(C, e, T) := \begin{cases} (1) & \text{if } \mid T \mid > 0 \ , \\ (0) & \text{otherwise.} \end{cases} \tag{6}$$

*Example 2 (Counting Features).* As a slight generalisation of the previous example, this function counts how often $C$ can be matched against the example $e$ and background knowledge $B$:

$$\varphi_{\#}(C, e, T) := (\mid T \mid) \ . \tag{7}$$

In order to define the complete row of features corresponding to a particular example, we simply concatenate the features generated with respect to each clause in $\mathcal{C}$ with the values of the variables in $\top$. For a $p$-atom $e = \top\sigma$, the propositionalisation with respect to $\mathcal{C}$ is defined as follows:

$$prop(\mathcal{C}, e) := (X_1\sigma, ..., X_a\sigma) \bigoplus_{C \in \mathcal{C}} \varphi(C, e, val(C, e)) \ , \tag{8}$$

where $\bigoplus$ denotes tuple concatenation.

Finally, the propositionalised table of examples is defined as the union of all example propositionalisations, adding in the class attribute[3]:

$$\tau(\mathcal{C}, E^+, E^-) := \{prop(\mathcal{C}, e) \oplus (1) \mid e \in E^+\} \cup \{prop(\mathcal{C}, e) \oplus (0) \mid \neg e \in E^-\} \ . \tag{9}$$

[3] Note that this definition can easily be adapted to the case where one of the arguments of $\top$ is the attribute to be predicted.

## 2.2 Local Functions and Redundancy

An important class of propositionalisation functions is the class of *local* propositionalisation functions which compute propositional features taking into account only one of the body variables at a time.

$\varphi$ is *local* iff there is a function $\varphi'$ such that

$$\varphi(C,e,T) = \bigoplus_{i=1..width(T)} \varphi'(\pi_{(i)}(T)) \ , \tag{10}$$

where $\pi_{(i)}$ denotes projection on the i-th column.

This class of propositionalisation functions is important because it easily allows the removal of redundant features whenever there are *functional dependencies* between a single predicate (or set of predicates) and another predicate.

If $D$ is a set of atoms, $L$ an atom, then $D \rhd L$ is a *functional dependency* iff for any $\sigma$ such that

$$D\sigma \subseteq E \cup B \ , \tag{11}$$

there is *exactly* one $\theta$ such that

$$L\sigma\theta \in E \cup B \ . \tag{12}$$

Note that functional dependencies are closely related to the idea of *determinate literals* [12], except that for determinate literals, one often allows *at most* one substitution given the preceding literals, whereas a functional dependency requires that there be *exactly* one such substitution.

For local propositionalisation functions, we can drop all the features generated based on one clause if there is another clause which differs from it only in that it contains an additional functionally dependent literal. The reason for this is expressed in the following lemma.

**Lemma 1.** *Let $C$ and $C'$ two clauses from $\mathcal{C}$ such that*

$$C' = C \cup \{L\} \ . \tag{13}$$

*If there is a functional dependency $D \rhd L$ such that*

$$D \succeq C \tag{14}$$

*($D$ $\theta$-subsumes $C$), then for any* local *$\varphi$, and any p-atom $e$,*

$$\varphi(C',e,val(C',e)) = \varphi(C,e,val(C,e)) \bigoplus_{z \in V_L} \varphi'(\pi_{(z)}(val(C',e)) \ , \tag{15}$$

*where we assume that $V_L$ are the variables of $L$ not occurring in $C$.*

*Proof.* Clearly, due to the functional dependency, for any variable binding tuple in $val(C,e)$ there will be exactly one completion resulting in a matching tuple in $val(C',e)$. This means that $val(C,e)$ and $val(C',e)$ are different, but since the transformation function is local, the extra columns in $val(C',e)$ do not influence the computation of the feature values on variables contained in both $C$ and $C'$, so the feature values computed for these variables with respect to $C$ and $C'$ will be identical.

This means, it suffices to consider $C'$ when constructing $prop(C, e)$ since the features constructed based on $C$ will be redundant.

Note that this lemma can be generalised to cases where there is more than one additional functionally dependent literal, and to cases where $\varphi$ also produces existential or counting features.

In our approach to be described in the next section, we assume that the functional dependencies to be used for redundancy removal are explicitly given by the user. However, it will of course also be possible to use one of the existing algorithms for functional dependency discovery to automate this step.

## 3 Propositionalisation by Automatic Aggregation

As pointed out in the introduction, the primary challenge in propositionalising ILP data is due to the non-determinacy of most applications. In the terminology introduced in the preceding section, this means that $val(C, e)$ can become quite a large set. This is especially true in business applications, where it is quite possible for example that a company maintains hundreds of transactions on record for a single customer. Previous approaches to propositionalisation in ILP that were restricted to determinate clauses thus cannot adequately handle such datasets.

*Transformation function.* In order to design our approach to transformation-based ILP learning, we have therefore borrowed the idea of *aggregation* that is commonplace in the database area [2] and often used in preprocessing for propositional learners. Aggregation is an operation that replaces a set of values by a suitable single value that summarises properties of the set. For numerical values, simple statistical descriptors such as average, maximum, and minimum can be used, for nominal values, we can use the mode (the most frequent value) or count the number of occurences of the different possible values.

More precisely, in the framework of the preceding section, we define a local propositionalisation function $\varphi'$ as follows. Let $C$ be a clause with $bvars(C) = \{Y_1, \ldots, Y_m\}$. For a numeric variable $Y_i \in bvars(C)$, let $T_i := \pi_{(i)} val(C, e)$. Then define

$$\varphi'(T_i) := (avg(T_i), max(T_i), min(T_i), sum(T_i)) \ , \tag{16}$$

where $avg(T_i)$, $max(T_i)$, $min(T_i)$, and $sum(T_i)$ compute the average, maximum, minimum, and sum of the values in $T_i$, respectively. For a nominal variable $Y_i \in bvars(C)$, let $T_i$ as above. Then define

$$\varphi'(T_i) := \bigoplus_{v \in domain(Y_i)} (count(v, T_i)) \ , \tag{17}$$

where $domain(Y_i)$ is the ordered set of possible values for $Y_i$, and $count(v, T_i)$ is a function that provides the number of occurences of value $v$ in $T_i$ (again, $\bigoplus$ denotes tuple concatenation). In addition, we use the total size of the set $T := val(C, e)$ as a feature, resulting in the transformation function

$$\varphi(C, e, T) := (|\, T\, |) \bigoplus_{i=1..m} \varphi'(T_i) \ . \tag{18}$$

A function $\Phi$ was chosen to produce attribute names for the tuples resulting from propositionalisation. This function ensures unique attribute names by including the following information about the items used in the computation of the attribute values: a short name of the aggregate function applied, the name of the predicate from $E$ or $B$ concerned, the position/name of the argument, if applicable, and an identification of $C \in \mathcal{C}$.

*Clause set.* In order to decide which clause set $\mathcal{C}$ to use as the basis of our transformation, consider again the nature of business databases. Typically, they will exploit foreign key relationships to structure their data. We have therefore chosen to generate the set $\mathcal{C}$ on the basis of the *foreign link* bias language which was first introduced in MIDOS [14,15] and allows to easily model the structure of such databases. This bias is an ordered set of links $\mathcal{L}$, where each $l \in \mathcal{L}$ provides information about the argument positions of literals of two predicates where variables may be shared. As an additional level of control, our declarative bias language allows the specification of an upper limit on the number of literals with which a given literal may share variables. This limit effectively controls the branching factor in the tree of literals generated by the foreign links.

*Redundancy removal.* In order to exploit the potential offered by Lemma 1 for removing redundant features, we also allow the user to specify a set of functional dependencies $\mathcal{F}$.

The components discussed above result in an algorithm which is given in Table 1. Step 2 of the algorithm implements the clause construction process based on foreign links, removing redundant clauses (and thus the redundant features they would otherwise give rise to) in step 2b. Steps 3 to 5 implement the actual construction of the propositional table based on the transformation function $\varphi$ defined above. Step 6 finally is a normalisation step which maps the value range of each numeric attribute to the interval $[-1, 1]$; this is used for propositional learners which benefit from normalised value ranges.

*Example 3.* The following examples are based on the financial dataset of the PKDD-1999/PKDD-2000 challenge that is utilised in the first half of the experiments. For illustrative purposes, the number of relations and examples is reduced here, and all but the key attributes (with primary keys always in the first argument positions) are invented.

Let the sets of positive and negative examples be
$E^+ = \{e\}$ with $e =$ `loan(1,1)`, $E^- = \emptyset$ .

Let the set of background knowledge atoms be
$B = \{$ `account(1)`,
`disposition(1,1,1,10,a)`, `disposition(2,1,2,20,b)`,
`client(1,1000)`, `client(2,2000)`,
`card(1,1,100)`, `card(2,2,200)`, `card(3,2,300)`$\}$ .

Let the ordered set of foreign links (obeying the pattern:
`link(<rel1>:<pos1>, <rel2>:<pos2>`, with "rel" for relation, "pos" for argument position) be

**Table 1.** RELAGGS algorithm

1. **Accept** as input: $E$, $B$ ($n$ predicates), $\mathcal{L}$, $\mathcal{F}$
2. **Construct** $\mathcal{C}$:
   (a) **Generate** all clauses $C$ as ordered sets of literals $L$ subject to following restrictions:
      i. $\mid C \mid \leq n+1$
      ii. For $L, L' \in C : predicate(L) \neq predicate(L')$
      iii. First $L \in C : predicate(L) =$ target predicate
      iv. $L \in C$: most general, i.e. variables in argument positions
      v. $L, L' \in C$, $L$ non-first, $\exists L'$ before $L$ in $C$: $l \in \mathcal{L}$ such that $L$ shares variable with $L'$
   (b) **Eliminate** $C$ if there is $C'$ such that $C = C_1 L_1$, $C' = C L_2 C_2$, with $f \in \mathcal{F}$ specifying functional dependency between $L_1$ and $L_2$
3. **Generate** new line for $TABLE$
4. **For** all $C \in \mathcal{C}$
   (a) **Determine** $\Phi(C)$
   (b) **For** all $Att_i \in \Phi(C)$, append $Att_i$ to $TABLE$
5. **For** all $e \in E$
   (a) **Generate** new line for $TABLE$
   (b) **For** all $C \in \mathcal{C}$
      i. Determine $T = val(C, e)$
      ii. Determine $\varphi(C, e, T)$
      iii. For all $v \in \varphi(C, e, T)$ append $v$ to $TABLE$
   (c) **Append** class value of $e$ to $TABLE$
6. **Normalise** feature values of $TABLE$ to $[-1, 1]$ and append those to $TABLEnorm$
7. **Output** $TABLE$ and $TABLEnorm$

$\mathcal{L} = \{$ `link(loan:2,account:1),`
`link(account:1,disposition:2),`
`link(disposition:3,client:1),`
`link(disposition:1,card:2)`$\}$ .

Now consider
$C_1 =$ `loan(A,B) :- account(B), disposition(C,B,D,X1,X2).`
In a first step, $val(C_1, e, T)$ is determined, which is depicted in Table 2. Here, each line corresponds to a tuple of values of $val(C_1, e, T)$. In a second step, $\varphi$ and $\tau$ are applied and result in Table 3, which shows the propositionalised table of $E$ and $B$ with $\mathcal{C} = C_1$.

**Table 2.** The value set $val(C_1, e)$

| $A\sigma$ | $B\sigma$ | $C\sigma$ | $D\sigma$ | $X1\sigma$ | $X2\sigma$ |
|---|---|---|---|---|---|
| 1 | 1 | 1 | 1 | 10 | a |
| 1 | 1 | 2 | 2 | 20 | b |

**Table 3.** The propositionalised table based on $C_1$ ($\tau(C_1, E^+, E^-)$)

| count | avg(X1) | max(X1) | min(X1) | sum(X1) | count(X2=a) | count(X2=b) | class |
|---|---|---|---|---|---|---|---|
| 2 | 15 | 20 | 10 | 30 | 1 | 1 | 1 |

Let $C_1$ as above, $C_2$ =
`loan(A,B) :- account(B), disposition(C,B,D,X1,X2), client(D,Y).`
Let us assume, the set of functional dependencies $\mathcal{F}$ contains a description of such a dependency between `disposition` and `client`, i.e.

$$\{\texttt{disposition(\_,\_,D,\_,\_)}\} \triangleright \texttt{client(D,\_)}.$$

Then, $val(C_2, e)$ produces tuples as depicted in Table 4 on the left. The result of $val(C_2, e)$ differs from $val(C_1, e)$ only in the additional column for `Y`. Especially, the columns for `X1` and `X2` are the same in both tables such that any local aggregate function applied here would not yield different results for $val(C_1, e)$ and $val(C_2, e)$. Hence, we can decide to not consider $C_1$.

**Table 4.** The value sets $val(C_2, e)$ and $val(C_3, e)$

| $A\sigma$ | $B\sigma$ | $C\sigma$ | $D\sigma$ | $X1\sigma$ | $X2\sigma$ | $Y\sigma$ |
|---|---|---|---|---|---|---|
| 1 | 1 | 1 | 1 | 10 | a | 1,000 |
| 1 | 1 | 2 | 2 | 20 | b | 2,000 |

| $A\sigma$ | $B\sigma$ | $C\sigma$ | $D\sigma$ | $X1\sigma$ | $X2\sigma$ | $E\sigma$ | $Z\sigma$ |
|---|---|---|---|---|---|---|---|
| 1 | 1 | 1 | 1 | 10 | a | 1 | 100 |
| 1 | 1 | 2 | 2 | 20 | b | 2 | 200 |
| 1 | 1 | 2 | 2 | 20 | b | 2 | 200 |

Let now $C_2$ as above, $C_3$ =
`loan(A,B) :- account(B), disposition(C,B,D,X1,X2), card(E,Z).`
For this clause, the functional dependency given above does not apply. Table 4 shows $val(C_3, e)$, on the right. Here, there are differences with respect to the columns for `X1` and `X2` of $val(C_2, e)$ and $val(C_3, e)$. This way, there can be different aggregates as well. For example, the average of `X1` for $val(C_2, e)$ is 15, while it is 16.6 for $val(C_3, e)$. This can be viewed as weighting the property `X1` of a disposition in the light of the number of credit cards issued for this disposition. This illustrates why our algorithm will consider both $C_2$ and $C_3$ for the computation of the final propositionalised table.

## 4 Experimental Evaluation

The goal of our experiments was to see whether indeed the business databases that we are focusing on possess properties that distinguish them from other ILP learning problems in such a way that they lead to markedly different behaviour of state-of-the-art ILP learners (which are not optimised for such problems) compared to our own approach which we will call RELAGGS. As the basis of our experiments, we have therefore used eight learning problems originating from business domains, in particular from the discovery challenges that took place in conjunction with PKDD-1999/PKDD-2000 and ECML-1998, respectively.

The first discovery challenge problem from PKDD that we used involves learning to classify bank loans into good and bad loans [1]. The data set comprises of 8 relations and contains for each loan, customer information such as personal data, credit card ownership data, and socio-demographic data, moreover, account information is provided including permanent orders and up to several hundreds of transactions per account. This problem is thus typical of the non-determinacy that was discussed in the introduction.

The application gives rise to four different learning problems. The first two problems feature 234 examples which consist of all loans that are finished, i.e., either paid back in full or defaulted. Since certain learning systems exhibited marked differences in learning result depending on whether the good or the bad loans were used as target concept, we chose to split this task into two problems: learning using the good loans as target concept (Loan234A), and learning using the bad loans as target concept (Loan234B). Similarly, there are two further problems based on a data set of 682 examples which also contain loans that are still "in progress", but for which a classification of current loan rating (good or bad) is available (Loan682AC uses the good loans, Loan682BD the bad loans as target concept).

The other learning problems are taken from the customer data warehouse of a large Swiss insurance company (cf. [5]), where 10 tables were extracted for the ECML challenge mentioned above. Again, information is included about the customers (called partners), plus information about their contracts, their roles in the contracts, their households etc. In this application, two unspecified learning tasks were provided with challenge data; they involve learning (different) classifications of 17,267 customers (Part1 and Part2 in the table) and 12,934 households (Hhold1 and Hhold2).

In order to evaluate the hypotheses, we chose to compare our approach RELAGGS to two other systems. First, we compared with DINUS-C, a learner based on transformations in the style of DINUS [8], i.e. using only the features that are determinate, and using C4.5rules [13] as propositional learner. Second, we compared to PROGOL [11], a very powerful state-of-the-art ILP learner capable of learning in structurally very complex domains. For PROGOL, we used standard parameter settings. We also experimented with other parameter settings, however, this did not yield better results.

The aggregates produced by RELAGGS comprise of 938 attributes for the Loan tasks, while those for the Part and Hhold tasks consist of 1,688 and 2,232 columns, respectively. In order to examine whether the success of our transformation-based approach depends on the propositional learner that is used, we used two variants of RELAGGS: RELAGGS-C uses C4.5rules [13], whereas RELAGGS-S uses SVM$^{light}$ [3], a fast support vector machine implementation. For C4.5rules, we used standard parameter settings, while for SVM$^{light}$, we used normalised data and parameter settings as applied in experiments reported in [4].

All experimental evaluations were carried out as ten-fold cross-validations. Table 5 shows, for each of the participating learners, the average error across the ten folds and the standard deviation; the best result on each problem is marked in **bold**. In addition, we provide the order of magnitude of the time taken for each learning run[4].

**Table 5.** Error rate averages and standard deviations from 10-fold cross-validation, and runtime order of magnitude for single training runs (C – C4.5rules, S – SVM$^{light}$)

| Task | Measurand | DINUS-C | RELAGGS-C | RELAGGS-S | PROGOL |
|---|---|---|---|---|---|
| Loan234A | Error rate | 14.9 ± 10.3 | 12.0 ± 6.5 | **12.0 ± 5.3** | 54.3 ± 10.5 |
| | Runtime | **sec** | min | min | h |
| Loan234B | Error rate | 14.9 ± 10.3 | 12.0 ± 6.5 | **12.0 ± 5.3** | 13.3 ± 7.1 |
| | Runtime | **sec** | min | min | min |
| Loan682AC | Error rate | 11.1 ± 3.6 | **5.9 ± 3.2** | 9.2 ± 3.2 | n.a. |
| | Runtime | **sec** | min | min | d |
| Loan682BD | Error rate | 11.1 ± 3.6 | **5.9 ± 3.2** | 9.2 ± 3.2 | 11.3 ± 3.6 |
| | Runtime | **sec** | min | min | h |
| Part1 | Error rate | 18.1 ± 0.6 | **8.3 ± 0.7** | 9.9 ± 0.4 | n.a. |
| | Runtime | **min** | h | h | d |
| Part2 | Error rate | 18.1 ± 0.6 | **8.3 ± 0.7** | 9.9 ± 0.4 | n.a. |
| | Runtime | **min** | h | h | d |
| Hhold1 | Error rate | 39.6 ± 1.6 | **6.0 ± 0.9** | 14.3 ± 1.5 | n.a. |
| | Runtime | **min** | h | h | d |
| Hhold2 | Error rate | 39.6 ± 1.6 | **6.0 ± 0.9** | 14.3 ± 1.5 | n.a. |
| | Runtime | **min** | h | h | d |

As can be seen from the table, the business databases used here indeed seem to possess properties that make it appear useful to use an aggregating learner like RELAGGS. On all eight problems, it is one of the RELAGGS variants which shows the lowest error. In addition, it is remarkable that RELAGGS strikes a reasonable balance in runtime between the use of determinate features only and the use of a non-transformation based learner like PROGOL. Interestingly, the complex search performed by PROGOL does not lead to good accuracies here, indicating that such business domains present quite different challenges from the problems on which PROGOL excels.

The differences between the learners are in fact statistically significant. Table 6 shows the win-loss-tie statistics, where a comparison was counted as a win if the difference was significant according to a paired t-test at level $\alpha = 0.05$. As can be seen there, the RELAGGS variant using C4.5rules significantly outperforms both RELAGGS with SVM as well as the other two learners.

[4] Five PROGOL runs were aborted after running more than two days; the corresponding fields are marked n.a.

**Table 6.** Win-loss-tie for rows vs. columns: differences statistically significant according to paired t-test at level $\alpha = 0.05$ (C – C4.5rules, S – SVM$^{light}$)

| | DINUS-C | PROGOL | RELAGGS-S |
|---|---|---|---|
| RELAGGS-C | 6-0-2 | 2-0-1 | 6-0-2 |
| RELAGGS-S | 4-0-4 | 1-0-2 | |

## 5 Related Work

Our approach is based on the general idea to transform multirelational representations of data into representations amenable for efficient propositional learners, as instantiated by LINUS [7], DINUS [8], and others systems [9,6].

LINUS [7] and DINUS [8] both use a restricted class of expressions (constrained and determinate literals), whereas our approach handles arbitrary general classes. In terms of the general transformation framework introduced in this paper, systems such as LINUS and DINUS can be seen as using a suitably restricted set of classes $\mathcal{C}^*$ in order to ensure that $\{val(C,e) \mid (C \in \mathcal{C}, e \in E)\}$ is a singleton set, thus allowing the values of this single tuple to be used as features without further transformations.

Our approach is also related to [9] and [6] where general classes are allowed, but where the subsequent transformation mainly consists of checking whether such a class has instances or not (the $\varphi_\exists$ function defined above). In contrast, our approach uses a more general class of transformation functions including aggregation and counting, thus using the information in $val(C,e)$ in a more sophisticated way.

Finally, our approach of generating the clause set $\mathcal{C}$ is closely related to the declarative bias language of MIDOS [14]. Here, we supplement the set of foreign links $\mathcal{L}$ by information about functional dependencies $\mathcal{F}$ between predicates of examples $E$ and background knowledge $B$. This supplement ensures efficiency by avoiding redundant features during the propositionalisation process for larger multirelational databases.

Note that our approach is open towards using different ways of generating $\mathcal{C}$, e.g. by stochastic search as suggested in [6], or based on different biases as in [9].

## 6 Conclusion

In this paper, we have presented RELAGGS, a transformation based ILP learner specifically geared to the challenges presented by business databases, which are often structurally quite simple, but large in size with massive amounts of non-determinacy. We have presented a general framework for such transformation-based learners which encompasses also the simpler transformations of [8,6,9], and have described how aggregation operations can naturally be used to define the transformation functions for our learner. In addition, we have shown how functional dependencies can be used to eliminate redundant features as long as the transformation function is local.

Our experimental evaluation on eight learning problems from two business domains shows that indeed such applications have special properties that make them difficult both for determinate literal based transformation learners as well as for non-transformation based learners that are geared more towards structurally complex domains. While RELAGGS beats these learners in a statistically significant way, our experiments did not show that much of a difference between variants of RELAGGS using C4.5rules and SVMs as propositional learners, with slight advantages for RELAGGS with C4.5rules.

In future work, we will evaluate RELAGGS on further domains, in particular problems with an even larger number of tuples and relations. It will be interesting to see, if the parity between C4.5rules and SVMs holds up when the number of relations and thus the number of features, is further increased. We will then also investigate whether some of the results of selecting or filtering features heuristically during propositionalisation could be of use (cf. [6,10]). Finally, we will work on the transformation function of RELAGGS, incorporating further aggregate descriptors.

**Acknowledgements**

This work was partially supported by the DFG (German Science Foundation), project FOR345/1-1TP6.

## References

1. Petr Berka. Guide to the Financial Data Set. In A. Siebes and P. Berka, editors, *PKDD2000 Discovery Challenge*, 2000.
2. Luce Cabibbo and Riccardo Torlone. A Framework for the Investigation of Aggregate Functions in Database Queries. In C. Beeri and P. Bruneman, editors, *Proceedings of the Seventh International Conference on Database Theory (ICDT)*. Springer-Verlag, 1999.
3. Thorsten Joachims. Making Large-Scale SVM Learning Practical. In B. Schölkopf, C. Burges, and A. Smola, editors, *Advances in Kernel Methods - Support Vector Learning*. MIT Press, 1999.
4. Thorsten Joachims. Estimating the Generalization Performance of an SVM Efficiently. In P. Langley, editor, *Proceedings of the Seventeenth International Conference on Machine Learning (ICML)*. Morgan Kaufmann, 2000.
5. Jörg-Uwe Kietz, Regina Zücker, and Anca Vaduva. MINING MART: Combining Case-Based Reasoning and Multistrategy Learning into a Framework for Reusing KDD-Applications. In R. S. Michalski and P. Brazdil, editors, *Proceedings of the Fifth International Workshop on Multistrategy Learning (MSL)*, 2000.
6. Stefan Kramer, Bernhard Pfahringer, and Christoph Helma. Stochastic Propositionalization of Non-Determinate Background Knowledge. In D. Page, editor, *Proceedings of the Eighth International Conference on Inductive Logic Programming (ILP)*. Springer-Verlag, 1998.

7. Nada Lavrač. *Principles of knowledge acquisition in expert systems.* PhD thesis, University of Maribor, Ljubljana, Slovenia, 1990.
8. Nada Lavrač and Sašo Džeroski. *Inductive Logic Programming: Techniques and Applications.* Ellis Horwood, 1993.
9. Nada Lavrač and Peter Flach. An extended transformation approach to Inductive Logic Programming. Technical Report CSTR-00-002, Department of Computer Science, University of Bristol, March 2000.
10. Nada Lavrač, Dragan Gamberger, and Peter Turney. A relevancy filter for constructive induction. *IEEE Intelligent Systems*, 13(2):50–56, 1998.
11. Stephen Muggleton. Inverse entailment and Progol. *New Generation Computing, Special issue on Inductive Logic Programming*, 13(3-4):245–286, 1995.
12. Stephen Muggleton and Cao Feng. Efficient Induction of Logic Programs. In S. Arikawa, S. Goto, S. Ohsuga, and T. Yokomori, editors, *Proceedings of the First International Workshop on Algorithmic Learning Theory (ALT).* Springer-Verlag/Ohmsha Publishers, 1990.
13. Ross Quinlan. *C4.5: Programs for Machine Learning.* Morgan Kaufmann, 1993.
14. Stefan Wrobel. An algorithm for multi-relational discovery of subgroups. In J. Komorowski and J. Zytkow, editors, *Proceedings of the First European Symposium on Principles of Data Mining and Knowledge Discovery (PKDD).* Springer-Verlag, 1997.
15. Stefan Wrobel. Inductive Logic Progamming for Knowledge Discovery in Databases. In N. Lavrač and S. Džeroski, editors, *Relational Data Mining.* Springer-Verlag, Berlin, New York, 2000.

# Discovering Associations between Spatial Objects: An ILP Application

Donato Malerba and Francesca A. Lisi

Dipartimento di Informatica, Università degli Studi di Bari,
Via Orabona 4, 70126 Bari, Italy
{malerba, lisi}@di.uniba.it

**Abstract.** In recent times, there is a growing interest in both the extension of data mining methods and techniques to spatial databases and the application of inductive logic programming (ILP) to knowledge discovery in databases (KDD). In this paper, an ILP application to association rule mining in spatial databases is presented. The discovery method has been implemented into the ILP system SPADA, which benefits from the available prior knowledge on the spatial domain, systematically explores the hierarchical structure of task-relevant geographic layers and deals with numerical aspatial properties of spatial objects. It operates on a deductive relational database set up by selecting and transforming data stored in the underlying spatial database. Preliminary experimental results have been obtained by running SPADA on geo-referenced census data of Manchester Stockport, UK.

## 1 Introduction

One of the great challenges for the near future is knowledge discovery in ever growing spatial sets [4]. Nevertheless, most work in the KDD community up to now has been almost exclusively focused on pattern discovery in relational and transaction databases. Only in recent times, data mining methods and techniques have been proposed for *the extraction of implicit knowledge, spatial relations, or other patterns not explicitly stored in spatial databases* [8]. Peculiarity of the spatial domain is that the attributes of the neighbors of some spatial object of interest may have an influence on it and therefore have to be considered as well [6]. Thus, spatial data mining algorithms cannot neglect the implicit relations of spatial neighborhood (e.g. topological relations) that are defined by the explicit location and extension of spatial objects.

As the interest in KDD is generally increasing, many recent applications of ILP methods and techniques to KDD have also emerged [3]. We claim that spatial data mining is a promising ILP application domain for two main reasons. First, ILP relies on the theory of computational logic which supplies representation and reasoning means appropriate for the spatial domain where relations among objects play a key role and are often inferred by qualitative reasoning. Second, ILP offers an elegant solution to multi-relational mining whereas traditional approaches to spatial data mining usually solve the problem by collapsing multiple relations into the universal

C. Rouveirol and M. Sebag (Eds.): ILP 2001, LNAI 2157, pp. 156–163, 2001.

relation [9]. To the best of our knowledge, very few contributions from ILP to knowledge discovery in spatial databases have been reported in the literature. GwiM [14] is a general-purpose ILP system that can solve several spatial data mining tasks, though no insight in the algorithmic issues has been provided. INGENS [11] is an inductive GIS with learning capabilities that currently support the classification task.

In this paper, we focus our attention on the task of mining *spatial* association rules, namely the detection of associations between spatial objects, and propose to accomplish the task by means of a novel special-purpose ILP system, called SPADA (Spatial PAttern Discovery Algorithm) [12]. It benefits from the available prior knowledge on the spatial domain, systematically explores the hierarchical structure of task-relevant geographic layers and deals with numerical aspatial properties of spatial objects. Furthermore, it operates on a *deductive relational database* (DDB) set up by selecting and transforming data stored in the underlying spatial database. The analysis of geo-referenced census data have been chosen as an application domain. Indeed, the advances in the practice of geo-referencing socioeconomic phenomena allow census data to be conceptualized as spatial objects with numerical aspatial properties.

The paper is organized as follows. Section 2 introduces the spatial data mining problem solved by SPADA. Experimental results on geo-referenced census data of Stockport, one of the ten Metropolitan Districts of Greater Manchester, UK, are reported in Section 3. Conclusions are given in Section 4.

## 2 Mining Spatial Association Rules with SPADA

The discovery of spatial association rules is a descriptive mining task aiming at the detection of associations between *reference objects* and *task-relevant objects*, the former being the main subject of the description while the latter being spatial objects that are relevant for the task at hand and spatially related to the former. For instance, we may be interested in describing a given area by finding associations among large towns (reference objects) and spatial objects in the road network, hydrography and administration layers (task-relevant objects). Some kind of taxonomic knowledge on task-relevant geographic layers may also be taken into account to get descriptions at different concept levels (*multiple-level association rules*). As usual in association rule mining, we search for associations with large support and high confidence (*strong rules*). Formally, SPADA can solve the following spatial data mining problem:

*Given*

- a spatial database (SDB),
- a set of reference objects $S$,
- some task-relevant geographic layers $R_k$, $1 \le k \le m$, together with spatial hierarchies defined on them,
- two thresholds for each level $l$ in the spatial hierarchies, *minsup*[$l$] and *minconf*[$l$]

*Find* strong multiple-level spatial association rules.

To solve the problem Koperski and Han propose a top-down, progressive refinement method which exploits taxonomies both on topological relations and spatial objects [9]. The method has been implemented in the module Geo-associator of the spatial data mining system GeoMiner [7]. We propose an upgrade of Geo-Associator to first-order logic representation of data and patterns. The approach is inspired to the work on multi-relational data mining reported in [2] and operates on a DDB set up by a preliminary feature extraction step from SDB and denoted *D*(*S*). In particular, we resort to Datalog [1], whose expressive power allows us to specify also prior knowledge (BK) such as spatial hierarchies, spatial constraints and rules for spatial qualitative reasoning. Given a set of Datalog atoms *A*, a *spatial association rule* in *D*(*S*) is an implication of the form *P*□ *Q* (*s%*, *c%*), where *P*□*A*, *Q*□*A*, *P*□ *Q*=□ , and at least one atom in *P*□ *Q* represents a spatial relationship. The percentages *s* and *c* are called the support and the confidence of the rule respectively. An example of spatial association rule in our framework is:

is_a(A, large_town), intersects(A,B), intersects(A,C), is_a(C, regional_road), intersects(D,C), D\=A, C\=B □ is_a(B, main_trunk_road), is_a(D, large_town) (54%, 86%)

"GIVEN THAT *54% of large towns intersect both a main trunk road and a regional road the latter intersecting a large town distinct from the previous one,* IF *a large town A intersects two spatial objects the former being an unknown B while the latter being a regional road which in turn intersects some spatial object D distinct from A* THEN WITH CONFIDENCE 86% *B is a main trunk road and D is a large town*".

The choice of an ILP algorithm to accomplish the mining task at hand heavily affects the whole KDD process. Indeed, *D*(*S*) is obtained by selecting and transforming the portion of *SDB* that concerns the set of reference objects *S* and adding it to the *BK*. Data selection encompasses the retrieval of spatial objects eventually together with their spatial and aspatial properties and the extraction of spatial relationships between reference objects and task-relevant objects. In particular, SPADA can extract topological relations whose semantics has been defined according to the 9-intersection model [5]. It is noteworthy that finding the right compromise between on-line computation (time-consuming solution) and materialization (space-consuming solution) of spatial relations is a hot topic in spatial data mining. More sophisticated computational solutions are reported in [6, 9]. Once selected, this data needs to be transformed in a suitable format. For instance, numerical properties of spatial objects with a large domain must be discretized in order to be handled by logic-based data mining methods. SPADA currently implements an adaptation of the relative unsupervised discretization algorithm RUDE [10] to the first-order case.

The spatial data mining step requires the solution to two sub-tasks: 1) Find large (or frequent) spatial patterns; 2) Generate strong spatial association rules. The reason for this decomposition is that frequent patterns are commonly not considered useful for presentation to the user as such. They can be efficiently post-processed into association rules that exceed given threshold values of support and confidence. It is noteworthy that SPADA, analogously to Geo-Associator but differently from WARMR [2], exploits is-a taxonomies for extracting multiple-level patterns and association rules. Thus, *largeness* and *strength* depend on the level currently explored in the hierarchical structure of task-relevant geographic layers. To be more precise, a pattern *P* is *large* (or frequent) at level *l* if □(*P*)□*minsup*[*l*] and all ancestors of *P* with respect to the spatial hierarchies are large at their corresponding levels. A spatial association rule *P*□ *Q* is *strong* at level *l* if the pattern *P*□ *Q* is large and the confidence is high at level *l*, namely □(*Q*|*P*)□*minconf*[*l*]. In SPADA, the counting procedures for support and confidence are based on the coverage test of spatial observations, being it the ILP counterpart of counting the number of reference objects that satisfy a certain spatial pattern. Indeed, the *spatial observations* are portions of *D*(*S*), each of which concerns one and only one reference object. Thus, the two percentages associated to *P*□ *Q* mean that *s*% of spatial observations in *D*(*S*) are covered by *P*□ *Q* and *c*% of spatial observations in *D*(*S*) that are covered by *P* are also covered by *P*□ *Q* respectively.

Further details about representation and algorithmic issues can be found in [12].

## 3 An Application to Stockport Census Data

In some works on spatial representation from the social scientist's perspective, socio-economic phenomena have been conceptualized as *spatial objects* in the sense of entities having both spatial location and spatially independent attribute characteristics [13]. Population data are among the potentially spatial socioeconomic data. They are usually geo-referenced with respect to areal spatial objects such as census zones, electoral constituencies, local government areas, or regular grid squares. In the UK, for instance, the geo-referencing areal units are ED (enumeration district), Ward, District, and County. They form a hierarchy based on the *inside* relationship among locations. Thus the ED is the smallest unit for which census data are published nowadays. Furthermore, the digital ED boundaries produced for the 1991 UK census enable the spatial representation of census data in the computer databases. Generally speaking, population censuses of the 1990s provided an added impetus to the application of GIS to socioeconomic uses. One of the most interesting topic areas for identifying potential users of such GIS applications is the public debate over Unitary Development Plans (UDP) in the UK. The district chosen for investigation is Stockport, one of the ten Metropolitan Districts of Greater Manchester, UK. It is divided into twenty-two wards for a total of 589 EDs. The case study is expected to show the potential benefit of data mining methods and techniques to one or more potential users. In particular, census data are extremely important for policy analysis and, once geo-referenced and conceptualized as spatial objects with numerical aspatial properties, supply a good test-bed to SPADA. Thus census data (89 tables, each with 120 attributes in average) and digital ED boundaries have been loaded into an Oracle-Spatial database, i.e. a relational DBMS extended with spatial data handling facilities. The ED code allows the joining of the two kinds of data and the generation of test data.

We have focused our attention on transportation planning, which is one of key issues in the UDP. Let us suppose that some decision-making process about the motorway M63 is ongoing. Describing the area of Stockport served by M63 (i.e. the wards of Brinnington, Cheadle, Edgeley, Heaton Mersey, South Reddish) may be of support to the planners. In this paper we report the preliminary results obtained by applying SPADA to the task of discovering multiple-level spatial association rules relating EDs intersected by the motorway M63 (*S*) and all EDs in the area served by M63 (*R*) to be characterized with respect to data about commuting.

This spatial data mining query raises several application issues for SPADA. First, census data are available at the ED level. Thus, an is-a hierarchy for the Stockport ED layer has been obtained by grouping EDs on the basis of the ward they belong to (see Figure 1) and expressed as Datalog facts in BK. Indeed, the current version of SPADA deals only with *is-a* hierarchies where the is-a relationship is overloaded, i.e. it may stand for *kind-of* as well as for *instance_of* depending on the context. Further is-a hierarchies could be derived by resorting to clustering algorithms.

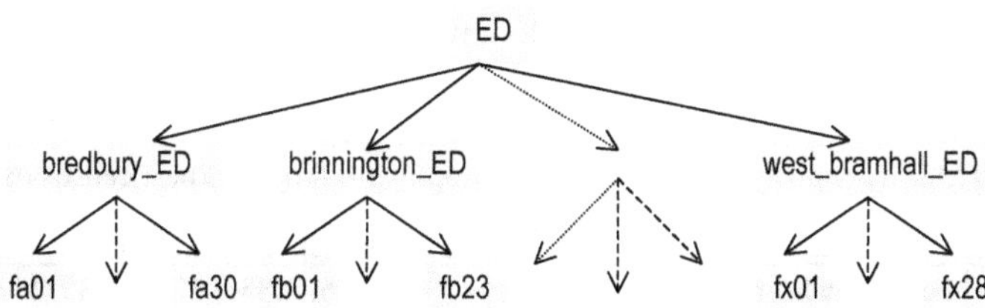


**Fig. 1.** An is-a hierarchy for the Stockport ED layer

Second, census data are all numeric (more precisely, integer values). The attributes that we have selected for this experiment (see Table 1) refer to residents aged 16 and over, thus they have been normalized with respect to the total number of residents aged 16 and over (s820001). Each couple of consecutive cut points *a* and *b* has generated an interval of the kind [a..b].

Last, some spatial computation is necessary. In particular, the relations of intersection (EDs-motorways) and adjacency (EDs-EDs) have been extracted as concerns the area of interest and transformed into Datalog facts of *D*(*S*). It is noteworthy that the relations of accessibility and closeness have been defined by means of spatial qualitative reasoning:

```
linked_to(X, Y) :- intersect(X, m63), intersect(Y, m63), Y\=X.
close_to(X, Y) :- adjacent_to(X, Z), adjacent_to(Z, Y), Y\=X.
```

These rules have been added to BK together with the aforementioned spatial hierarchies and also the spatial constraint:

```
ed_on_M63(X) :- intersect(X, m63).
```

which defines the instances of *S*.

SPADA has been run on the obtained *D*(*S*) with thresholds *min_sup*[1]=0.7 and *min_conf*[1]=0.9 at the first level, and *min_sup*[2]=0.5 and *min_conf*[2]=0.8 at the second level. The whole discovery process has taken 490.21 sec on a PC Pentium III with 128 Mb RAM (37.84 sec for level 1, and 452.31 sec for level 2). It has returned 744 frequent patterns out of 17619 candidate patterns and 24964 strong rules out of 40465 generated rules. Some interesting patterns have been discovered. For instance, at level *l*=2 in the spatial hierarchies, the following candidate *P*:

```
ed_on_M63(A), close_to(A,B), is_a(B, south_reddish_ED), linked_to(A,C), C\=B,
s820161(C, [52.632..54.167]), is_a(C, cheadle_ED)
```

has been generated after *k*=6 refinement steps and has been evaluated with respect to *D*(*S*). Since six of ten spatial observations (|*S* |=10) are covered and all the ancestor patterns are large at their level (*l*□2), the pattern is a large one at level *l*=2 with 60% support. For the sake of clarity, the following pattern

ed_on_M63(A), close_to(A,B), is_a(B, ed_in_M63_area), linked_to(A,C), C\=B, s820161(C, [52.632..54.167]), is_a(C, ed_in_M63_area)

is one of the large ancestors for the pattern *P*. It has been generated after *k*=6 refinement steps at level *l*=1 and is supported by 90% EDs intersected by M63. Such way of taking the taxonomies into account during the pattern discovery process implements what we refer to as the systematic exploration of the hierarchical structure of task-relevant geographic layers. Furthermore, the use of both variables and atoms of the kind \= allow SPADA to distinguish between multiple instances of the same class of spatial objects (e.g. the class ed_in_M63_area).

**Table 1.** Numerical attributes in the application to Stockport census data.

| **Attribute** | **Description** | **Cut points in the attribute domain** |
|---|---|---|
| s820161 | Persons who work out of the district of usual residence and drive to work | 0.0, 6.25, 8.333, 12.973, 17.241, 19.048, 20.943, 23.529, 25.0, 25.926, 27.586, 29.032, 29.865, 31.25, 33.333, 34.375, 36.182, 38.235, 40.0, 42.105, 45.455, 46.667, 48.194, 50.0, 51.515, 52.632, 54.167, 56.0, 57.143, 58.333, 58.824, 60.0, 60.714, 61.538, 63.889, 65.217, 66.667, 67.742, 69.565, 71.429, 72.902, 100.0 |
| s820213 | Employees and self-employed who reside in households with 3 or more cars and drive to work | 0.0, 2.222, 15.385, 28.0, 29.521, 31.034, 33.333, 35.068, 37.5, 38.095, 38.889, 41.043, 42.857, 48.387, 72.727 |
| s820221 | Employees and self-employed who reside in households with 3 or more cars and work out of the district of usual residence | 0.0, 2.222, 4.762, 9.091, 10.345, 13.636, 18.182, 19.355, 21.131, 23.529, 25.0, 28.571 |

One of the strong rules that have been derived from the frequent pattern *P* is:

ed_on_M63(A), close_to(A,B), is_a(B,south_reddish_ED)
□ linked_to(A,C), is_a(C,cheadle_ED), B\=C, s820161(C,[52.632..54.167]) (60%, 100%)

"GIVEN THAT *60% of EDs intersected by M63 are close to a South Reddish ED and are linked via M63 to a Cheadle ED where 52-54% residents aged 16 and over work out of the district of usual residence and drive to work,* IF *an ED intersected by M63 is close to a South Reddish ED* THEN WITH CONFIDENCE 100% *it is linked via M63 to a Cheadle ED where ...* ".

Other examples of strong rule at the second level are:

ed_on_M63(A), close_to(A,B), s820221(B,[10.345..13.636])
□ linked_to(A,C), is_a(C,brinnington_ED), B\=C (60%, 86%)

"GIVEN THAT *60% of EDs intersected by M63 are close to an ED - where 10-13% residents aged 16 and over are employees and self-employed who reside in households with 3 or more cars and work out of the district of usual residence - and are linked via M63 to a Brinnington ED distinct from the previous one,* IF *an ED intersected by M63 is close to an ED where ...* THEN WITH CONFIDENCE 86% *it is linked via M63 to a Brinnington ED distinct from the previous one* ".

ed_on_M63(A), close_to(A,B), s820221(B,[19.355..21.131])
 □ is_a(B,heaton_mersey_ED) (70%, 100%)

"GIVEN THAT *70% of EDs intersected by M63 are close to a Heaton Mersey ED where 19-21% residents aged 16 and over are employees and self-employed who reside in households with 3 or more cars and work out of the district of usual residence* IF *an ED intersected by M63 is close to an ED where ...* THEN WITH CONFIDENCE 100% *the latter ED belongs to the ward of Heaton Mersey".*

One may wonder whether these frequent patterns and strong rules convey novel knowledge and, in positive case, what kind of knowledge. The evaluation of data mining results is beyond the scope of this paper. Nevertheless a naive interpretation of results in our application might lead us to state that the motorway M63 intersects an area of Stockport which is characterized by a high percentage of commuters by car who may benefit from some improvement of the road network.

## 4 Conclusions and Future Work

The work presented in this paper reports an ILP application to spatial association rule mining. Experimental results obtained by applying the novel special-purpose ILP system SPADA to geo-referenced census data of Manchester Stockport show that the expressive power of first-order logic enables us to tackle applications that cannot be handled by the traditional approach to spatial data mining. Furthermore, DDBs offer effective representation means for domain knowledge, constraints and qualitative reasoning. In particular, we can embed rules for the inference of implicit spatial relationships that are too numerous to be either stored in the spatial database or computed by computational geometry algorithms.

For the near future, we plan to face the issues of efficiency and scalability in SPADA. Particular attention will be also drawn on the issue of robustness. Indeed, data pre-processing in spatial data mining is remarkably error-prone. For instance, the generation of the predicate close_to is based on the user-defined semantics of the closeness relation, which should necessarily be approximated. Further work on the data selection and transformation is expected to give some hints on noise handling in this application domain. As for the test on real-world spatial data sets, much work has still to be done. In particular, we are interested in experiments with mixed census-topographic data because they show that the interpretation of spatial relations can change as spatial objects are added.

**Acknowledgements**

This work is supported by the IST project SPIN! (http://www.ccg.leeds.ac.uk/spin/). We would like to thank Jim Petch, Keith Cole and Mohammed Islam (MIMAS, University of Manchester, England) and Chrissie Gibson (Department of Environmental and Geographical Sciences, Manchester Metropolitan University, England) for providing census data and digital ED boundaries of Manchester Stockport.

## References

1. Ceri, S., Gottlob, G., Tanca, L.: What you Always Wanted to Know About Datalog (And Never Dared to Ask). IEEE Transactions on Knowledge and Data Engineering 1(1) (1989) 146-166.
2. Dehaspe, L., Toivonen, H.: Discovery of frequent Datalog patterns. Data Mining and Knowledge Discovery 3(1) (1999) 7-36.
3. Dzeroski, S.: Inductive Logic Programming and Knowledge Discovery in Databases. In: Fayyad, U.M., Piatetsky-Shapiro, G., Smyth, P., Uthurusamy, R. (eds): Advances in Knowledge Discovery and Data Mining. AAAI Press/The MIT Press (1996) 117-152.
4. Egenhofer, M.J., Glasgow, J., Günther, O., Herring, J.R., Peuquet, D.J.: Progress in Computational Methods for Representing Geographic Concepts. Int. J. Geographical Information Science 13(8) (1999) 775-796.
5. Egenhofer, M.J., Herring, J.R.: Categorizing Binary Topological Relations Between Regions, Lines, and Points in Geographic Databases. In Egenhofer, M.J., Mark, D.M., Herring, J.R. (eds): The 9-Intersection: Formalism and its Use for Natural-language Spatial Predicates. Technical Report 94-1, U.S. NCGIA (1994.).
6. Ester, M., Kriegel, H.P., Sander, J.: Spatial Data Mining: A Database Approach. In: Scholl, M., Voisard, A. (Eds.): Advances in Spatial Databases. LNCS 1262, Springer-Verlag, Berlin (1997) 47-66.
7. Han, J., Koperski, K., Stefanovic, N.: GeoMiner: A System Prototype for Spatial Data Mining. In: Peckham, J. (Ed.): SIGMOD 1997, Proceedings of the ACM-SIGMOD Int. Conf. on Management of Data. SIGMOD Record 26(2) (1997) 553-556.
8. Koperski, K., Adhikary, J., Han, J.: Spatial Data Mining: Progress and Challenges. In: Proc. Workshop on Research Issues on Data Mining and Knowledge Discovery, Montreal, Canada (1996).
9. Koperski, K., Han, J.: Discovery of Spatial Association Rules in Geographic Information Databases. In: Egenhofer, M.J., Herring, J.R. (Eds.): Advances in Spatial Databases. LNCS 951, Springer-Verlag, Berlin (1995) 47-66.
10. Ludl, M.-C., Widmer, G.: Relative Unsupervised Discretization for Association Rule Mining. In D.A. Zighed, H.J. Komorowski, J.M. Zytkow (Eds.): Principles of Data Mining and Knowledge Discovery. LNCS 1910, Springer-Verlag, Berlin (2000) 148-158.
11. Malerba, D., Esposito, F., Lanza, A., Lisi, F.A.: Discovering geographic knowledge: The INGENS system. In: Ras, Z.W., Ohsuga, S. (Eds.): Foundations of Intelligent Systems, LNAI 1932, Springer-Verlag , Berlin (2000) 40-48.
12. Malerba, D., Esposito, F., Lisi, F.A.: A Logical Framework for Frequent Pattern Discovery in Spatial Data. In: Russell, I., Kolen, J. (Eds.): Proc. 14th Int. FLAIRS Conference. AAAI, Menlo Park:CA (2001) 557-561.
13. Martin, D.J.: Spatial representation: the social scientist's perspective. In: Longley, P.A., Goodchild, M.F., Maguire, D.J., Rhind, D.W. (eds): Geographical Information Systems, vol.1, Principles and Technical Issues, 2nd edition. John Wiley & Sons (1999) 71-80.
14. Popelinsky, L.: Knowledge Discovery in Spatial Data by means of ILP. In: Zytkow, J.M., Quafalou, M. (Eds.): Principles of Data Mining and Knowledge Discovery. LNAI 1510, Springer-Verlag, Berlin (1998) 185-193.

# $\theta$-Subsumption in a Constraint Satisfaction Perspective

Jérôme Maloberti[1] and Michèle Sebag[2,1]

(1) LRI, Bat 490, Université Paris-Sud, F-91405 Orsay
(2) LMS, Ecole Polytechnique, F-91128 Palaiseau
Jerome.Maloberti@lri.fr, Michele.Sebag@polytechnique.fr

**Abstract.** The covering test intensively used in Inductive Logic Programming, i.e. $\theta$-subsumption, is formally equivalent to a Constraint Satisfaction problem (CSP). This paper presents a general reformulation of $\theta$-subsumption into a binary CSP, and a new $\theta$-subsumption algorithm, termed *Django*, which combines some main trend CSP heuristics and other heuristics specifically designed for $\theta$-subsumption.
*Django* is evaluated after the CSP standards, shifting from a worst-case complexity perspective to a statistical framework, centered on the notion of *Phase Transition* (PT). In the PT region lie the hardest on average CSP instances; and this region has been shown of utmost relevance to ILP [4]. Experiments on artificial $\theta$-subsumption problems designed to illustrate the phase transition phenomenon, show that *Django* is faster by several orders of magnitude than previous $\theta$-subsumption algorithms, within and outside the PT region.

## 1 Introduction

Supervised learning intensively relies on the generality operator, or covering test, calculating whether a given hypothesis covers a given example. As the evaluation of a candidate hypothesis depends on its coverage, the covering test must imperatively be efficient.

The complexity of the covering test is one main concern facing Inductive Logic Programming (ILP) [10, 12]. The covering test commonly used in ILP, i.e. $\theta$-subsumption [13], is exponentially complex in the size of the candidate hypothesis. How to manage this complexity has motivated numerous studies on learning biases, restricting the size and/or the number of hypotheses explored through syntactic or search biases [11]. In parallel, new algorithms for achieving efficient $\theta$-subsumption [8, 18] and ILP learners based on a correct approximation of $\theta$-subsumption [19], have been proposed.

In this paper, is presented a new correct and complete $\theta$-subsumption algorithm termed *Django*, based on a Constraint Satisfaction Problem (CSP) approach.

Although it is long known that $\theta$-subsumption is equivalent to a Constraint Satisfaction problem (CSP), ILP problems have only recently been put in a CSP

C. Rouveirol and M. Sebag (Eds.): ILP 2001, LNAI 2157, pp. 164–178, 2001.

perspective [3, 4]. The focus is thereby shifted from a worst-case complexity analysis, to a statistical approach [7].

The covering test complexity is handled as a random variable, measuring the computational cost of $\theta$-subsumption for some order parameters (e.g. the number of variables & predicates in the hypothesis, the number of literals & constants in the example). Surprisingly, the computational cost is almost zero for most problems, referred to as trivial. For instance, assuming that all predicates in the hypotheses also appear in the examples, a short hypothesis will cover almost surely all examples; inversely, a long hypothesis will almost surely cover no example at all. In both cases, the $\theta$-subsumption cost remains low as the $\theta$-subsumption problem corresponds to an under or over-constrained satisfaction problem. But in a narrow region, termed *phase transition* (PT), where the probability for a hypothesis to cover an example is close to 50%, the covering test reaches its maximum complexity on average [3].

The PT phenomenon is of utmost importance for ILP, for two reasons. First, there is ample evidence of phase transition in artificial problems statistically modeled from ILP real-world problems [3]. Second, intensive experimentations on artificial problems have shown that this region behaves as an attractor on existing ILP learners[1] [4].

This paper is concerned with designing a $\theta$-subsumption algorithm with good average performances on the most relevant and critical instances of $\theta$-subsumption problems, i.e. lying within the PT. To this aim, is first presented a general transformation of a $\theta$-subsumption problem referred to as *primal problem*, into another constraint satisfaction problem, termed *dual problem.* Along the transformation, each literal (involved in the hypothesis, primal CSP) becomes a constrained variable in the dual CSP; conversely, a variable in the primal CSP derives a set of dual constraints; furthermore, specific constraints encoding the $\theta$-subsumption structure are automatically generated. On the dual CSP is applied a combination of well-known CSP algorithms, forming the *Django* system. The approach is validated on artificial $\theta$-subsumption problems designed after [4] to sample the Phase Transition region. Intensive experiments show that *Django* improves by several orders of magnitude on average on all problems within and outside the PT in the considered range, compared to previous $\theta$-subsumption algorithms [8, 18].

The paper is organized as follows. Next section briefly introduces $\theta$-subsumption and reviews existing $\theta$-subsumption algorithms [8, 18]. Section 3 presents the Constraint Satisfaction framework and the main heuristics used to solve CSPs. Section 4 describes the transformation of a $\theta$-subsumption problem into a dual binary CSP, and presents the combinations of CSP heuristics involved in the *Django* system. Experimental setting and results are reported and discussed in section 5, and the paper ends with some perspectives for further research.

[1] E.g. for almost all target concepts, FOIL [15] selects its final hypotheses in the PT region.

## 2 $\theta$-Subsumption, Definition and Algorithms

Let hypothesis $\mathcal{C}$ denote a conjunction of literals with no function symbols, and $arg(\mathcal{C})$ denote the set of variables in $\mathcal{C}$. Example $Ex$ likewise is a conjunction of literals with no function symbols, $arg(Ex)$ being the set of variables and constants in $Ex$.

By definition, $\mathcal{C}$ $\theta$-subsumes $Ex$ according to $\theta$, iff $\theta$ is a mapping from $arg(\mathcal{C})$ onto $arg(Ex)$, mapping variables in $\mathcal{C}$ onto variables and constants in $Ex$ such that $\mathcal{C}\theta$ be included in $Ex$. Instead of mapping variables in $\mathcal{C}$ onto variables and constants in $Ex$, it is often more computationally efficient to map literals in $\mathcal{C}$ onto those literals in $Ex$ built on the same predicate symbol. Through a literal mapping, each variable in $\mathcal{C}$ is associated to a set of variables and constants in $Ex$; the literal mapping is termed *consistent* if it maps each variable in $\mathcal{C}$ onto a single variable or constant in $Ex$.

The main stream algorithm for $\theta$-subsumption is based on Prolog SLD resolution [16]. It performs a depth first exploration of literal mappings (associating to the first literal in $\mathcal{C}$ the first literal built on the same symbol in $Ex$, and so on), and it backtracks if an inconsistency occurs (e.g. one variable in $\mathcal{C}$ is associated to two constants in $Ex$). Literals in $\mathcal{C}$ and $E$ are explored in their order of apparition, which has a significant impact on the SLD efficiency, as known by all Prolog programmers.

A first improvement has been proposed by [8], based on the notion of determinate matching. It consists of reordering the literals in $\mathcal{C} = p_1..p_K$ in such a way that, if possible, there is a single candidate literal $p' = \theta(p_i)$ in $Ex$ for $p_i$ in $\mathcal{C}$, which is consistent with the previous assignments (such that $\{p_1/\theta(p_1), ..p_i/\theta(p_i)\}$ is consistent). After all determinate literals in $\mathcal{C}$ have been mapped onto literals in $Ex$, and if necessary, the search resumes using SLD resolution.

The scope of determinate matching is extended by [18], using a *graph context* to prune the candidate literals. To each literal $p$ in $\mathcal{C}$ (resp. in $Ex$) is associated its neighborhood; the 1-neighbors of $p$ are all literals sharing at least one variable (resp. one variable or one constant) with $p$; the $i$-th neighbors are recursively constructed, as 1-neighbors of $i-1$-neighbors. It is shown, that, unless all predicate symbols occurring in $p$ $i$-th neighbors also occur among $p'$ $i$-neighbors, $p$ cannot be mapped onto $p'$, and the latter can be removed from the candidate literals for $p$. [18] further define a *substitution graph*, connecting two pairs of literals $(p, p')$ and $(q, q')$ iff mapping $(p/p', q/q')$ is consistent. The SLD search is replaced by a maximal clique search in the substitution graph. The worst-case complexity remains exponential, but the advantage is to perform the consistency check only once.

Another heuristics used by [8] proceeds by decomposing the substitution graph into mutually independent components (*k-locality*). Such a decomposition significantly reduces the complexity of the problem..

## 3 Constraint Satisfaction Problem

This section briefly introduces CSPs together with the main stream heuristics; the reader is referred to [21] for a comprehensive presentation.

A CSP involves i) a set of variables $X_1, .., X_n$, with $dom(X_i)$ being the value domain for $X_i$, and ii) a set of constraints, specifying the simultaneously admissible values of the variables. A constraint can conveniently be thought of as a predicate $r(X_{i_1}, ..X_{i_M})$, while the admissible values are described as a set of literals $r(a_{1,i_1}, ..a_{1,i_M}), \ldots, r(a_{l,i_1}, ..a_{l,i_M})$, $a_{j,i_k} \in dom(X_{i_k})$. The constraint scope, noted $arg(r)$ is the set of variables $X_{i_1}, ..X_{i_k}$. The constraint domain, noted $dom(r)$, is the set of literals built on[2] $r$.

A CSP solution assigns to each variable $X_i$ a value $a_i$ in $dom(X_i)$ such that all constraints are satisfied; it can be viewed as a mapping $\theta = \{X_i/a_i\}$ such that for each constraint $r(X_{i_1}, ..X_{i_k})$, $r\theta = r(a_{i_1}, ..a_{i_k})$ belongs to $dom(r)$. In other words, the CSP defined by constraints $r_1, ..r_K$ is satisfiable iff $r_1, ..r_K$ $\theta$-subsumes the conjunction $dom(r_1), ..dom(r_K)$. Likewise, the CSP complexity is exponential in the number $n$ of variables, and linear in the number $m$ of constraints: if $|a|$ is the number of possible values for a variable, the complexity is $\mathcal{O}(|a|^n \times m)$. (A first way of decreasing the complexity is by decomposing the CSP into fewly related subproblems – hierarchizing the set of variables [6] or the set of constraints [2] – in the same spirit as $k$-locality [8]).

Two CSPs are *equivalent* iff they are defined on same variables and admit same solutions. As any CSP can be embedded into a binary CSP, i.e. with binary constraints only, most CSP algorithms only consider binary and unary constraints. Further, with no loss of generality, one assumes that there exists at most one constraint on each variable pair.

CSP algorithms are made up of two kinds of heuristics. Reduction heuristics are meant to transform a CSP into an equivalent CSP of lesser complexity, through reducing the variable domains. Search heuristics are concerned with the search strategy.

### 3.1 Reduction

Reduction proceeds by pruning the candidate values for each variable $X$. Value $a$ in $dom(X)$ is locally *consistent* if, for all variables $Y$ such that there exists a constraint $r(X, Y)$, there exists some candidate value $b$ in $dom(Y)$ such that $r(a, b)$ holds (belongs to $dom(r)$). Clearly, if $a$ is not locally consistent, $X$ cannot be mapped onto $a$, which can thus soundly be removed from $dom(X)$.

Local consistency is extended as follows; $a$ is $k$-consistent with $X$ if for each set of constraints $r_1(X, Y_1), r_2(Y_1, Y_2), ..r_k(Y_{k-1}, Y_k)$, there exists a $k-1$-tuple $(b_1, .., b_k)$ such that $r_1(a, b_1), r_2(b_1, b_2), ..r_k(b_{k-1}, b_k)$, holds.

[2] In all generality, the constraint domain can be infinite (e.g. a numerical constraint on real-valued variables). Only finite domains are considered in the rest of the paper.

A CSP is $k$-consistent iff each value domain $dom(X_i)$ includes $k$-consistent values only – and is not empty[3]. Checking $k$-consistency is exponentially complex with respect to $k$; therefore, only 2-consistency, or *arc consistency* is used in practice. The best complexity of reduction algorithms is $\mathcal{O}(m|a|^2)$, with $m$ being the number of constraints and $|a|$ the value domain size.

### 3.2 Search

CSP algorithms incrementally construct a solution $\{X_i/a_i\}$ through a depth first exploration of the substitution tree; a node corresponds to a variable $X_i$, to which is assigned some candidate value $a_i$. On each assignation, consistency is checked; on failure, another candidate value for the current node is considered; if no other value is available, the search backtracks.

Several approaches have been proposed in order to improve: (i) the backtracking procedure (*look-back* heuristics); (ii) the choice of the next variable and candidate value to consider (*look-ahead* heuristics).

Look-back heuristics aim at preventing the repeated exploration of a same substitution subtree on backtracking (*thrashing*). For instance, Conflict Based Jumping (CBJ) [14] registers all variable conflicts occurred during the exploration, which allows for backtracking directly to the appropriate tree level. On the other hand, it may happen that the overhead due to maintaining the conflict registers offsets the look-back advantages for some particular CSP instances.

Look-ahead heuristics aim at minimizing the number of assignments considered. The best known look-ahead heuristics is constraint propagation; in each step, the candidate values which are inconsistent with the current assignment, are pruned. This way, inconsistencies are detected earlier and less nodes are visited; in counterpart, the assignment operation becomes more expensive as it involves the constraint propagation step.

Forward checking (FC) employs a limited propagation, only pruning the candidate values for the next variable (partial arc-consistency). Maintaining arc consistency (MAC) checks the arc-consistency on each variable assignment. Again, the overhead due to constraint propagation might offset its advantages on medium-size weakly constrained CSPs. Currently, the most generally efficient algorithms combine FC and CBJ.

In addition, the variable order can be optimized, either statically (once for all), or dynamically (the yet unassigned variables are reordered on each assignment). Dynamic variable ordering is generally more efficient than static variable ordering. One criterion for reordering the variables is based on the First Fail Principle [1], preferring the variable with the smallest domain. This way, failures will occur sooner rather than later.

Last, the candidate values can be ordered too; the value with less conflicts with the other variable domains is commonly preferred.

---

[3] The use of graph contexts to prune the candidate literals [18] can be viewed as a $k$-consistency check (more on this in section 4.2).

## 4 CSP Heuristics for $\theta$-Subsumption

This section formalizes $\theta$-subsumption as a binary CSP problem, and presents a new combination of CSP heuristics for $\theta$-subsumption, *Django*.

### 4.1 Representation

It has been shown (section 2) that a CSP problem is equivalent to a $\theta$-subsumption problem. However, $\theta$-subsumption generally considers n-ary predicates. An ad hoc representation is thus necessary to enable the use of standard CS heuristics.

$$\begin{array}{ll} \mathcal{C}: & tc(X_0), p(X_0,X_1), p(X_1,X_2), p(X_2,X_3), q(X_0,X_2,X_3) \\ Ex: & tc(a_0), p(a_0,a_1), p(a_1,a_2), p(a_2,a_3), p(a_3,a_4), p(a_0,a_3), q(a_0,a_2,a_3), q(a_0,a_1,a_3) \end{array}$$

We choose to consider the dual constraint satisfaction problem defined as follows. Each dual variable $Y_{p.i}$ corresponds to a literal in $\mathcal{C}$, namely the $i$-th literal built on predicate symbol $p$ (subscript $.i$ will be omitted for readability when there is a single literal built on the predicate symbol); its domain $dom(Y_{p.i})$ is the set of all literals in $Ex$ built on the same predicate symbol $p$, e.g. $dom(Y_{p.1}) = \{p(a_0,a_1), p(a_1,a_2), p(a_2,a_3), p(a_3,a_4), p(a_0,a_3)\}$.
A dual constraint $r(Y_{p.i}, Y_{q.j})$ is set on a variable pair $(Y_{p.i}, Y_{q.j})$ iff the corresponding literals in $\mathcal{C}$ share a (primal) variable; for instance, as $tc(X_0)$ and $p(X_0,X_1)$ share variable $X_0$, there is a dual constraint linking $Y_{tc}$ and $Y_{p.1}$. This constraint specifies that, for each literal $p'$ in $dom(Y_{p.i})$, there must be a literal $q'$ in $dom(Y_{q.j})$ such that the literal mapping $\{p.i/p', q.j/q'\}$ is consistent with respect to $\theta$-subsumption. In our toy example, dual constraint $r(Y_{tc}, Y_{p.1})$ is only satisfied for the dual value pair $(tc(a_0), p(a_0,a_1))$.
The difference between such dual constraints and the substitution graph in [18] is that the substitution graph specifies whether a given literal assignment $\{p/p'\}$ is consistent with another one $\{q/q'\}$. In contrast, dual constraints require that, for each pair of literals $p, q$ in $\mathcal{C}$ sharing one variable, there exists a pair $p', q'$ of literals in $Ex$, such that $\{p/p', q/q'\}$ is consistent.

The dual CSP is enriched by associating to each dual variable (literal in $\mathcal{C}$) and candidate value (literal in $Ex$) a *signature*, encoding the literal links (shared variables) with all others literals. For instance, the signature associated to $p(X_0,X_1)$ states that the first variable appear in a literal built on symbol $tc$, position 1, and a literal built on $p$, position 1; and the second variable appear in a literal built on symbol $p$, positions 1 and 2. Signatures allow one to prune the candidate literals through arc-consistency, in a similar way to graph contexts [18]; the signature of the literal in $\mathcal{C}$ must be included in the signature of the candidate literal in $Ex$. The difference is that signatures are deliberately limited to depth 1 (only 1-neighborhoods are considered), which allows for an optimized implementation.

Last, the case of literals sharing several variables is considered; signatures associated to pairs of such literals, termed 2-signatures, are designed and used to prune candidate literals too.

## 4.2 Resolution

As mentioned earlier, there is no such thing as a universally efficient CSP heuristics; it is thus desirable to evaluate carefully how relevant a given CSP heuristics is wrt $\theta$-subsumption problems. Several combinations of heuristics have been experimented in *Django* (summarized in Table 1).

The baseline version **V1** combines arc-consistency checking [9] and forward checking (the propagation of the current assignment is restricted to the next variable domain).

**Table 1.** *Django*, Versions **V1** to **V8**.

| | **Base line** |
|---|---|
| **V1** | Arc consistency + simple Forward Checking (propagation of the current assignment wrt the next variable) |
| | **Dynamic Variable Ordering** |
| **V2** | V1 + DVO based on minimal domain (random choice in case of tie) |
| **V3** | V1 + DVO based on maximal connectivity (random choice in case of tie) |
| **V4** | V1 + DVO based on min. domain + max. connectivity (minimal domain, then maximal connectivity) |
| **V5** | V1 + DVO based on max. connectivity + min. domain (maximal connectivity then minimal domain) |
| | **Forward Checking** |
| **V6** | **V4** + improved Forward Checking propagation of forced assignments (singleton candidate value) |
| | **Arc Consistency** |
| **V7** | **V6** + AC based on signatures |
| **V8** | **V7** + AC based on signatures and 2-signatures |

We first investigate the influence of variable ordering on the search efficiency. Versions **V2** to **V5** implement several dynamic variable orderings, all based on the First Fail Principle. In **V2**, variables with minimal domain are ranked first[4]. In **V3**, variables subject to a maximal number of dual constraints are ranked first (prefer the literals in $C$ which are most connected to others literals). Both criteria are combined in versions **V4** and **V5**, with different priorities.

Secondly, we investigate the influence of Forward Checking. In Version **V6**, besides the 1-step propagation of the current assignment, forced assignments (singleton candidate value for any variable) are propagated.

Last, we investigate the influence of arc consistency, using signatures and 2-signatures. Version **V7** differs from Version **V6** as it considers the literal signatures; version **V8** considers both signatures and 2-signatures.

[4] Note that the determinate matching heuristics in the primal $\theta$-subsumption problem [8] corresponds to a particular case of the minimal domain heuristics with regard to the dual CSP.

# 5 Experimental Validation

## 5.1 Experimental Setting

As mentioned earlier, CSP algorithms are mainly tested in the PT region, which concentrates the hardest on average problems.

Following [3], artificial data were constructed to examine the algorithm behavior within and outside the PT region. Artificial $\theta$-subsumption problems (pairs (hypothesis $\mathcal{C}$, example $Ex$)), are constructed from four order parameters: the number $n$ of variables in $\mathcal{C}$; the number $m$ of literals in $\mathcal{C}$, all built on distinct predicate symbols; the number $N$ of literals built on each predicate symbol in $Ex$; the number $L$ of constants in $Ex$.

In order to keep the total computational cost beyond reasonable limits, $n$ is set to 10, $N$ is set to 100, $m$ varies in $[10, 50]$ and $L$ varies in $[10, 50]$. For each pair $(m, L)$, 1,000 pairs (hypothesis $\mathcal{C}$, example $Ex$) are constructed with random uniform distribution [3], and $cost(m, L)$ is reported as the average $\theta$-subsumption cost over all 1,000 trials, measured in seconds (*Django* is implemented in $C^{++}$ and runs on a PC Pentium2). All *Django* versions are experimented and compared with three $\theta$-subsumption reference algorithms, respectively SLD Prolog, determinate matching [8] and graph contexts [18]; in the latter cases, we used the algorithm implementation kindly given by T. Scheffer.

## 5.2 Results and Discussion

As might have been expected, Prolog SLD does not keep up when hypothesis $\mathcal{C}$ involves more than a few literals, and it had to be stopped for $m > 5$ (being reminded that example $Ex$ involves $100 \times m$ literals). Determinate matching [8] does significantly better than SLD for small size hypotheses; however, it runs out of resources for $m > 10$; in retrospect, this heuristics is poorly suited to the random structure of the examples.

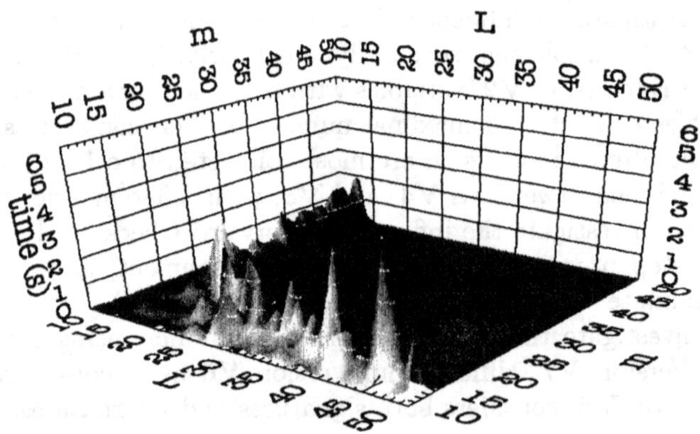


**Fig. 1.** $\theta$-subsumption cost$(m, L)$ for *Django*.**V1**, averaged on 1,000 pairs $(\mathcal{C}, Ex)$ with $m$ : nb predicates in $\mathcal{C}$ in[10,50], $L$ nb constants in $Ex$ in[10,50]

Graph contexts also turned out to be hardly applicable, mostly for efficiency reasons (see below); finally only the maximal clique search (MCS) [18] was experimented in the same range as *Django*.

The behavior of each algorithm is conveniently pictured as the surface $cost(m, L)$. Fig. 1 displays the cost landscape obtained for the baseline version of *Django*.

In a CPS perspective [7], three complexity regions are distinguished. The PT region appears as a mountain chain of hyperbolic shape in the $(m, L)$ plane; it concentrates the hardest on average $\theta$-subsumption problems.
The *YES* region, besides the PT (for low values of $m$ or $L$), contains trivial (hypothesis,example) pairs, where the hypothesis almost surely subsumes the example; in this region typically lie overly general, complete and incorrect hypotheses wrt the dataset.
The *NO* region, beyond the PT, contains trivial (hypothesis,example) pairs, where the hypothesis almost never subsumes the example; in this region lie the hypotheses covering no training examples, which are thus found to be correct.

The cost landscape obtained for MCS [18] is depicted in Fig. 2 (higher costs by factor 6 compared to Fig. 1). Interestingly, the phase transition region is larger than for *Django*.**V1**. Note that the complexity is not negligible in the *NO* region. This suggests that MCS does not early detect the inconsistencies, achieving unnecessary exploration of the substitution graph in the *NO* region.

On the other hand, MCS [18] first step concerns the construction of the whole substitution graph, which is exploited in the second step along a maximal clique search. This first step is computationally heavy; it represents a significant amount of the total cost, unless the problem size is large. For large-size prob-

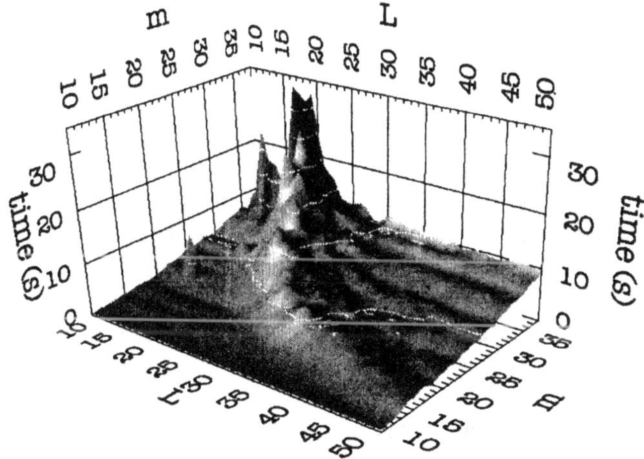


**Fig. 2.** $\theta$-subsumption cost$(m, L)$ for MCS, averaged on 1,000 pairs $(C, Ex)$ $m$ : nb predicates in $C$ in[10,38], $L$ nb constants in $Ex$ in[10,50] (scale factor × 6 compared to Fig. 1)

lems, the graph construction effort is negligible compared to the maximal clique search, and worthwhile as it significantly speeds up the maximal clique search. Unfortunately, the memory resources needed to store the substitution graph for large problems, are hardly tractable; no 2-graph contexts could be used with MCS for $m > 10$.

In contrast, *Django* interleaves the search and the constraint propagation; this way, the construction of the whole graph is avoided whenever a solution might be found along the search.

The $\theta$-subsumption costs (with multiplicative factor 100) are summarized in Table 2, averaged over all three regions.

**Table 2.** Average $\theta$-subsumption cost (×100) in the *YES*, *NO* and PT regions.

| | YES region | | Phase Transition | | NO region | |
|---|---|---|---|---|---|---|
| | cost | ± | cost | ± | cost | ± |
| MCS | 344.69 | 589.93 | 841.53 | 1325.83 | 800.74 | 908.22 |
| *Django*.**V1** | 20.25 | 32.80 | 116.83 | 142.01 | 6.67 | 17.25 |
| **V2** | 4.18 | 5.97 | 4.99 | 6.92 | 2.19 | 2.71 |
| **V3** | 4.80 | 6.70 | 8.79 | 11.84 | 2.44 | 3.33 |
| **V4** | 4.25 | 6.09 | 4.56 | 6.45 | 2.22 | 2.75 |
| **V5** | 4.51 | 6.44 | 6.70 | 9.77 | 2.33 | 3.09 |
| **V6** | 4.24 | 5.86 | 4.79 | 6.32 | 1.98 | 2.45 |
| **V7** | 2.20 | 3.15 | 3.53 | 4.55 | 1.58 | 1.93 |
| **V8** | 2.48 | 3.78 | 3.15 | 4.40 | 0.95 | 1.41 |

Cost $(m, L)$ is counted in the *YES*, PT or *NO* region, depending on the fraction $f$ of clauses $C$ subsuming examples $Ex$, over all pairs $(C, Ex)$ generated to estimate $cost(m, L)$ (with *YES* region $=_d$ $[f > 90\,\%]$; PT region $=_d$ $[f \in [10\,\%,\ 90\,\%]]$; *NO* region $=_d$ $[f < 10\,\%]$).

Some care must be exercised when interpreting the results, due to the high variability of the measures; this variability was hardly reduced by increasing the number of experiments for a given pair $(m, L)$ from 100 to 1,000 trials.

This variability is explained as only "simple" Forward Checking and Arc-Consistency heuristics were considered. Though these heuristics are very efficient on average, they do not manage well with "pathological" cases, which considerably increases the average resolution cost. Further experiments will consider the use of Maintained Arc Consistency heuristics, and see whether the gain achieved on hard $\theta$-subsumption problems (as MAC is optimal with regard to worst-case complexity) compensates for the loss on easier problem instances.

The phase transition phenomenon is most marked for *Django*.**V1** (Fig. 1), the cost in the PT region being 10 times the cost in the *YES* region and 20 times the cost in the *NO* region. Note that the performance gain of *Django*.**V1** over MCS is not uniform; the gain factor is about 30 in the *YES* region, 7 in the PT, and 200 in the *NO* region.

The addition of dynamic variable ordering heuristics visibly improves the performances, especially in the PT region, smoothening the complexity peak. Other heuristics, especially signature-based heuristics, also seem to contribute to the global efficiency[5]. The best gain factor compared to MCS is about 100 in the *YES* region, 200 in the PT region, and 700 in the *NO region* (Fig. 3).

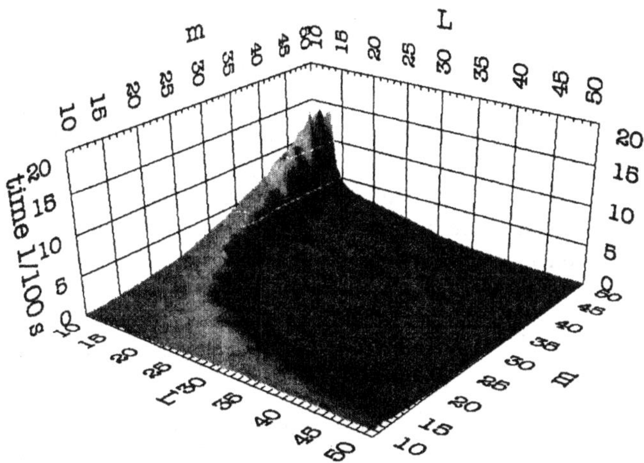


**Fig. 3.** $\theta$-subsumption cost$(m, L)$ for *Django*.**V8**, averaged on 1,000 pairs $(C, Ex)$ (scale factor $\div$ 25 compared to Fig. 1)

Similar gain factors have been obtained for experiments (not shown for space limitations) on the $N$-queen problem, for $N = 10..30$.

Last, artificial problems derived from the real-world Mutagenesis problem [20] have been used to compare *Django* and MCS. Each hypothesis $C$ considered involves $m$ literals and $n$ variables, where $m$ and $n$ respectively range in 1..10 and 2..10; $C$ is tested against all 229 examples in the training set. For a given $m$ and $n$, $C$ is randomly generated from $m$ *bond* literals $bond(X_i, X_j)$, where $X_i$ and $X_j$ are each selected among $n$ variables in such a way that $X_i \neq X_j$ and $C$ is connected.

Results obtained with *Django* show the presence of phase transition when the number of literals and variables in the hypothesis are around 4 and 5 respectively, though this change in the covering probability is not coupled with a complexity peak. The worst effective complexity is observed for hypotheses with $n$ literals and $n + 1$ variables (chains of atoms).

MCS obtains good results on the "artificial mutagenesis" $\theta$-subsumption problems. Since a single predicate symbol is actually considered, the substi-

[5] This contrasts with the inefficiency observed for graph contexts [18], though formally equivalent to signatures. However, this seems to be mostly due to implementation matters: for the sake of generality, 1-neighborhoods are implemented as lists of lists, whereas signatures are coded as boolean vectors.

tution graph is not relevant, and the maximal clique search efficiently solves the search. On this problem, *Django* outperforms MCS by a gain factor between 50 and 700.

### 5.3 Scope and Relevance of the Experimental Study

Artificial problems considered in the paper differ from real-world $\theta$-subsumption problems encountered in ILP in three respects.

In the general case, a major issue is to decompose the problem at hand into fewly or not related subproblems [6, 2] (e.g. decomposing the hypothesis into $k$-local components [5, 8]), as successful decomposition entails exponential savings in the resolution cost.
In this study, artificial problems are designed in such a way that they are *not* decomposable into two or more disjoint CSPs [3]. The $\theta$-subsumption average cost reported for a given $m$-literal clause and $L$-constant example thus corresponds to a pessimistic (non-decomposable case) estimate.

A second issue regards the uniform distribution of the $\theta$-subsumption problems considered. Each predicate symbol occurs once in the hypothesis, and $N = 100$ times in the example.
In real-world problems, some predicate symbols occur more frequently than others in the examples. Wrt the dual CSP, this means that constrained variables have domains with diverse sizes. Such a diversity makes CSP heuristics, e.g. constraint propagation or dynamic variable ordering, more effective. In this respect, considering predicate symbols with same number of literals built on them leads to a pessimistic estimate of the average $\theta$-subsumption cost.

The third issue concerns the arity of the predicate symbols, which is restricted to 2 in our artificial setting. With respect to worst-case complexity, the predicate arity does not affect the dual CSP; the dual CSP size is $\mathcal{O}(N^m)$, the size of dual domains exponentiated by the number of dual constraints, which does not depend on the arity. But the predicate arity dictates the number of dual constraints. Assume that a (primal) variable in hypothesis $C$ occurs in $o$ distinct literals in $C$; this is accounted for in the dual CSP by $\frac{o\times(o-1)}{2}$ dual constraints[6].

Assuming that all predicates are $k$-ary, their $m \times k$ arguments are selected among $n$ primal variables. Assuming this selection is uniform (which is not as one has to ensure the clause connectivity), each variable intervenes on average in $\frac{m\times k}{n}$ literals in $C$, and thus the total number of dual constraints is $\mathcal{O}\left(\frac{m^2\times k^2}{n}\right)$. According to this preliminary analysis, increasing the predicate arity by a factor $\sqrt{t}$ can be likened to decreasing the number of variables by factor $t$. Experimentally, decreasing the number of variables causes the phase transition to move toward shorter hypotheses everything else being equal (left region in Fig. 1), with exponential decrease of the complexity peak [3].

[6] Note that if a primal variable occurs twice in a single literal $p$ in $C$, this amounts to a dual unary constraint on the dual constrained variable $Y_p$, directly accounted for by reducing the associated dual domain.

In summary, the artificial $\theta$-subsumption problems considered were meant to study the worst *average* case with respect to decomposability and distributional diversity.

## 6 Conclusion and Perspectives

This paper presents a new $\theta$-subsumption algorithm, *Django*, operating on a constraint satisfaction-like representation of $\theta$-subsumption. *Django* combines well-known CS heuristics (arc consistency, forward checking and dynamic variable ordering) with $\theta$-subsumption-specific heuristics (signatures). Intensive experimental validation on artificial worst average instances show that *Django* outperforms previous $\theta$-subsumption algoritms [8, 18] by several orders of magnitude in computational cost.

This computational gain might be a good news as ILP systems routinely perform thousands of subsumption tests.

Even more interesting is the fact that the $\theta$-subsumption complexity gives indications regarding the current situation of the ILP search, as located in the *YES*, PT or *NO* regions after the CSP framework [7].

This might open several perspectives to ILP.

On one hand, the relevance of the *YES*, *NO* and PT regions might be questioned in regard to real-world examples, whose distribution model could be arbitrarily different from the uniform model used in the artificial problems. How to characterize and exploit a generative model in order to refine and simplify the representation of an ILP problem, is investigated in the field of reformulation and abstraction (see [17] among others).

On the other hand, it appears reasonable that, unless the target concept belongs to the *YES* region, relevant hypotheses lie in the PT region. This is due to the fact that most ILP learners prefer most general hypotheses provided that they are sufficiently correct (Occam's Razor); therefore, no learner will engage in the *NO* region. In this perspective, new refinement operators directly searching the PT region would be most appreciated.

Further research is first concerned with improving *Django*, checking whether other CS heuristics such as path-consistency are appropriate to $\theta$-subsumption. In the same spirit, the CSP translation proposed for $\theta$-subsumption will be extended to $\theta$-reduction. The idea is that matching a clause with itself might give some information about the redundant literals.

Another perspective is to use *Django* to compare alternative representations for an ILP problem, and select the representation with minimal $\theta$-subsumption cost for randomly generated hypotheses.

Last, an interesting question is whether and how the partial results of *Django* (values or variable links leading to most failures) can be used to navigate in the PT region, by repairing a clause into a clause with same complexity.

**Acknowledgments**

We gratefully acknowledge Lorenza Saitta, Attilio Giordana and Marco Botta, for many lively discussions about Phase transitions and its consequences on ILP. Thanks also to Tobias Scheffer, who kindly gave us his implementation of graph contexts and determinate matching.

## References

1. C. Bessière and J.-C. R/'egin. Mac and combined heuristics: Two reasons to forsake FC (and CBJ ?) on hard problems. In *2nd Int. Conf. on Principles and Practice of Constraint Programming*, pages 61–75, 1996.
2. R. Dechter and J. Pearl. Tree clustering for constraint networks. *Artificial Intelligence*, 38:353–366, 1989.
3. A. Giordana and L. Saitta. Phase transitions in relational learning. *Machine Learning*, 2:217–251, 2000.
4. A. Giordana, L. Saitta, M. Sebag, and M. Botta. Analyzing relational learning in the phase transition framework. In P. Langley, editor, *17th Int. Conf. on Machine Learning*, pages 311–318. Morgan Kaufmann, 2000.
5. G. Gottlob and A. Leitsch. On the efficiency of subsumption algorithms. *Journal of the Association for Computing Machinery*, 32(2):280–295, 1985.
6. M. Gyssens, P. G. Jeavons, and D. A. Cohen. Decomposing constraint satisfaction problems using database techniques. *Artificial Intelligence*, 66:57–89, 1994.
7. T. Hogg, B. Huberman, and C. Williams. Phase transitions and the search problem. *Artificial Intelligence*, 81:1–15, 1996.
8. J.-U. Kietz and M. Lübbe. An efficient subsumption algorithm for inductive logic programming. In W. Cohen and H. Hirsh, editors, *11th Int. Conf. on Machine Leaning.* Morgan Kaufmann, 1994.
9. A. K. Mackworth. Consistency in networks of relations. *Artificial Intelligence*, 8:99–118, 1977.
10. S. Muggleton and L. De Raedt. Inductive logic programming: Theory and methods. *Journal of Logic Programming*, 19:629–679, 1994.
11. C. Nédellec, C. Rouveirol, H. Adé, F. Bergadano, and B. Tausend. Declarative bias in ILP. In L. de Raedt, editor, *Advances in ILP*, pages 82–103. IOS Press, 1996.
12. S. Nienhuys-Cheng and R. de Wolf. *Foundations of Inductive Logic Programming.* Springer Verlag, 1997.
13. G. D. Plotkin. A note on inductive generalization. In B. Meltzer and D. Michie, editors, *Machine Intelligence*, volume 5, pages 153–163, 1970.
14. P. Prosser. Hybrid algorithms for the constraint satisfaction problem. *Computational Intelligence*, 9:268–299, 1993.
15. J.R. Quinlan. Learning logical definitions from relations. *Machine Learning*, 5(3):239–266, 1990.
16. J. Robinson. A machine-oriented logic based on the resolution principle. *Journal of the ACM*, 12(1):23–41, 1965.
17. L. Saitta and J.-D. Zucker. Semantic abstraction for concept representation and learning. In AAAI, editor, *Symposium on Abstraction, Reformulation and Approximation (SARA98)*, 1998.

18. T. Scheffer, R. Herbrich, and F. Wysotzki. Efficient $\theta$-subsumption based on graph algorithms. In S. Muggleton, editor, *Proceedings Int. Workshop on Inductive Logic Programming*. Springer-Verlag, 1997.
19. M. Sebag and C. Rouveirol. Resource-bounded relational reasoning: Induction and deduction through stochastic matching. *Machine Learning*, 38:41–62, 2000.
20. A. Srinivasan, S.H. Muggleton, M.J.E. Sternberg, and R.D. King. Theories for mutagenicity: a study in first order and feature-based induction. *Artificial Intelligence*, 85:277–299, 1996.
21. E. Tsang. *Foundations of Constraint Satisfaction*. Academic Press, 1993.

# Learning to Parse from a Treebank: Combining TBL and ILP*

Miloslav Nepil

NLP Laboratory, Faculty of Informatics, Masaryk University
Botanická 68a, CZ-602 00 Brno, Czech Republic
nepil@fi.muni.cz

**Abstract.** Considering the difficulties inherent in the manual construction of natural language parsers, we have designed and implemented our system GRIND which is capable of learning a sequence of context-dependent parsing actions from an arbitrary corpus containing labelled parse trees. To achieve this, GRIND combines two established methods of machine learning: transformation-based learning (TBL) and inductive logic programming (ILP). Being trained and tested on corpus SUSANNE, GRIND reaches the accuracy of 96 % and the recall of 68 %.

**Keywords:** grammar induction, corpus-based parser construction, transformation-based learning, inductive logic programming

## 1 Introduction

Automated natural language understanding seems to be a very tempting issue, which has become an important area of research in recent decades. One of the means needed for its solution is to have a machine system – called *parser* – capable of translating natural language inputs into an internal representation suitable for subsequent computer manipulation. Although this translation is being performed mainly on the level of syntax, practical experience reveals that the manual construction of natural language grammar (and consequently the manual development of parser as well) is a very time-consuming and error-prone task. To cover the complexity of natural language syntax with its enormous amount of irregularities, the appropriate grammar is usually being amended with new rules 'ad hoc'.

As a result of that practice, it is very difficult – even for educated computational linguists – to preserve consistency and adequacy of the grammar in the course of development and maintenance. Really significant improvements of the grammar, especially those involving conceptual changes, are preferably postponed due to their toughness and uncertain impact on the grammar's performance. Shortly, there is a need for a system which would involve some level of automation during the process of natural language grammar (and parser) construction.

* This research has been partially supported by the Czech Ministry of Education under the grant JD MSM 143300003.

C. Rouveirol and M. Sebag (Eds.): ILP 2001, LNAI 2157, pp. 179–192, 2001.

The empirical alternative replaces hand-generated grammar rules with models obtained automatically by training over language corpora. Corpus-based methods for natural language syntax acquisition are generally referred to as *grammar induction*. Basically, there has been presented a variety of approaches to grammar induction which vary primarily in (1) the form of required inputs and in (2) the form of expected outputs.

1. **required inputs:** This criterion concerns the level of annotation present in training corpora. Although some systems have used raw (completely unannotated) text for grammar induction, those employing some kind of annotation (morphological or even syntactical) have produced more accurate parsers.
2. **expected outputs:** This criterion concerns the level of analysis which the target system is expected to carry out. It also matters whether the outcome of the learning process should be a generative grammar (a system able to generate new sentences) or only a parser (a system designed just to analyse given sentences).

In this contribution, we present a method for fully automated parser construction from a treebank. It means that our system's *required input* is a *treebank* (a corpus of syntactically annotated sentences) and its *expected output* is a *parser* (a tool for analysing constituent structure of given sentences).

The paper is organised as follows: Section 2 provides a brief outline of our system GRIND, Sections 3 and 4 detail the used learning techniques, in Section 5 the experiments and their comparison with relevant works are presented, and, finally, Section 6 summarises our results, highlights the main advantages of our approach and mentions some intended improvements.

## 2 Outline of the System GRIND

Our approach to the task of automated parser construction has resulted in the design and implementation of the system GRIND (**Gr**ammar **Ind**uction) which is capable of learning a sequence of context-dependent parsing actions from a given corpus containing labelled parse trees. To achieve this, GRIND combines two established methods of machine learning: transformation-based learning (TBL) and inductive logic programming (ILP).

During the TBL phase, a sequence of *deepening operators* (as we call them) is induced. The *deepening operator* is a pair $\langle Sub, sym\rangle$ consisting of a string of symbols *Sub* and a symbol *sym*. Each deepening operator is designed to recognise a particular constituent (e.g. a phrase, a clause, etc.) within a given sentence. It needs to be mentioned that the deepening operators themselves work regardless of the context. It means that if $\langle Sub, sym\rangle$ is the current deepening operator being applied and if there is the substring *Sub* in the current state of analysis, then *Sub* is considered as a new constituent which is consequently labelled with the symbol *sym*. Since *Sub* need not actually represent a constituent in every context, or *Sub* might sometimes represent a constituent with a different label, the uncontrolled application of deepening operators is very likely to produce inadequate analyses.

Provided the training corpus contains a complete syntactic analysis for each sentence, GRIND is able to generate and distinguish automatically the parsing configurations in which a substring *Sub* should, or should not, be recognised as a constituent and labelled with a symbol *sym*.

Thus, the ILP learning phase can exploit these positive and negative examples of the correct and incorrect application of various deepening operators to induce a set of *forbidding predicates* (as we call them). The *forbidding predicate* has got four arguments describing a particular parsing configuration (a left context, a questioned substring, a right context, and a suggested label) and makes a decision whether, in the given context, the questioned substring really represents a constituent with the suggested label. So, in effect, the forbidding predicates make the deepening operators context-dependent. For the task of inducing the forbidding predicates, we have tried two ILP systems: ALEPH[1] and TILDE[2].

In the operating mode, when parsing a fresh text, GRIND takes tag sequences rather than string of words as the input. It means that the text needs to be provided with unambiguous part-of-speech tagging before it is submitted to GRIND.

# 3 TBL Phase

## 3.1 Application of Deepening Operators

The transformation-based learning phase takes a set of training sentences accompanied by their correct parse trees as the input. At each learning step, every training sentence is associated with an actual list of parse trees (we call it a *treelist*, but an alternative term would be an *ordered forest*). In the beginning, each treelist consists of elementary trees only. The elementary trees have got just one leaf (represented by a particular word) and a root labelled with a part-of-speech tag for this word. Thus, initially, each treelist represents an unambiguously morphologically tagged sentence. Then, the deepening operators gradually transform all treelists in such a manner as to make those structures more conformable with the correct parse trees present in the training set. Finally, each treelist consists of just one parse tree which is identical with the corresponding correct parse tree. As the output the TBL phase produces a sequence of those deepening operators which were used for transforming all the initial treelists into the final ones.

To make this idea clear, we show a demonstration run of the TBL phase. Our toy training set contains just one sentence with a parse tree taken from the corpus SUSANNE [8]. The parse tree $T$ is displayed in Figure 1.

Figure 2 shows the initial treelist $T_0$ associated with the training sentence as well as the gradually transformed treelists $T_1$, $T_2$ and $T_3$. In the treelist $T_i$, the overbraces indicate all currently applicable deepening operators.[3] What we obtain after their application is the treelist $T_{i+1}$ ($T_4$ is not shown here, but it corresponds to $T$).

[1] `http://web.comlab.ox.ac.uk/oucl/research/areas/machlearn/Aleph`

[2] `http://www.cs.kuleuven.ac.be/~hendrik/Tilde/tilde.html`

[3] Applicable deepening operators are always determined by innermost parentheses.

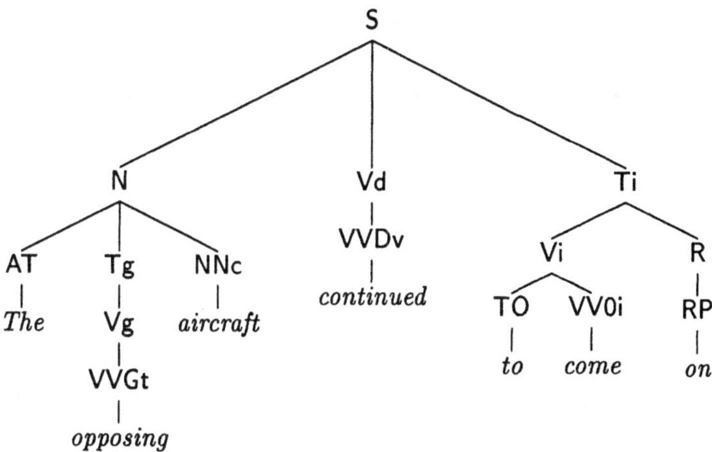


**Fig. 1.** The correct parse tree $T$ for the sentence *"The opposing aircraft continued to come on."*

The resulting sequence of deepening operators attained during our demonstration TBL phase is shown in Figure 3. The sequence comprises all applied operators in the order of their application.

When parsing an unseen sentence in the operating mode, each member of the learned sequence is taken just once[4] and applied to the actual treelist, wherever it is possible. For example, the deepening operator ⟨'AT Tg NNc', N⟩ would take effect on all occurences of the substring of roots 'AT Tg NNc'. Perhaps we should emphasise that our TBL setting is rather special since all transformations performed by deepening operators are irreversible. Therefore, this is not the case that new transformation rules (i.e. deepening operators) added to the sequence can correct errors left by the previous ones. On this account, application of deepening operators must be controlled by forbidding predicates (see Section 4).

Evidently, GRIND employs bottom-up parsing scheme and its deepening operators resemble context-free grammar rules. However, their operational semantics is different from shift-reduce parsing: deepening operators work on treelists instead of a stack and there is just one applicable operator at each parsing configuration,[5] thus no backtracking is needed.

Although the set of deepening operators is simply given by the training data, we need to determine their appropriate order so as to maximise the accuracy of resulting analyses.

---

[4] It means that some deepening operators can possibly have multiple occurences in the sequence.

[5] Note that we mean the operational mode in which the sequence of operators is already learned.

Vg Vd Vi R
((AT ((VVGt )) NNc ) (VVDv ) ((TO VVOi ) (RP )))
*The opposing aircraft continued to come on*

Tg Ti
((AT (Vg ) NNc ) Vd ( Vi R ))
*The* VVGt *aircraft* VVDv TO VVOi RP
*opposing continued to come on*

Treelist $T_0$. Treelist $T_1$.

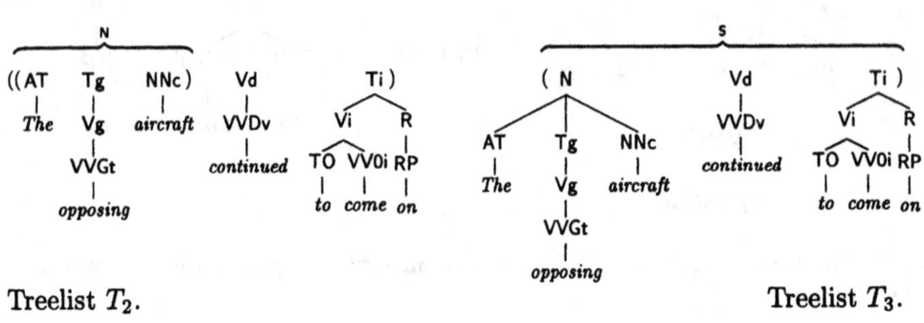


Treelist $T_2$. Treelist $T_3$.

**Fig. 2.** Gradual transformation of the initial treelist conducted by application of deepening operators.

$$T_0 \longrightarrow \begin{bmatrix} \langle\text{`VVGt', Vg}\rangle \\ \langle\text{`VVDv', Vd}\rangle \\ \langle\text{`TO VVOi', Vi}\rangle \\ \langle\text{`RP', R}\rangle \end{bmatrix} \longrightarrow T_1$$

$$T_1 \longrightarrow \begin{bmatrix} \langle\text{`Vg', Tg}\rangle \\ \langle\text{`Vi R', Ti}\rangle \end{bmatrix} \longrightarrow T_2$$

$$T_2 \longrightarrow \langle\text{`AT Tg NNc', N}\rangle \longrightarrow T_3$$

$$T_3 \longrightarrow \langle\text{`N Vd Ti', S}\rangle \longrightarrow T_4$$

**Fig. 3.** The resulting sequence of deepening operators. For the sake of clarity, they are grouped with respect to the transitions between particular treelists.

### 3.2 Evaluation Function

At each learning step there is generally a lot of applicable deepening operators. Therefore, GRIND makes use of an *evaluation function* to decide which operator performs best in transforming treelists into the ones which are closer to the corresponding correct parse tree. Then the best scoring operator is selected – in accordance with the *hill-climbing search strategy* – and, at the same time, it becomes the next deepening operator in the sequence of operators being learned. This procedure is carried out repeatedly until all treelists are transformed into their final state (which corresponds to the correct parse tree).

In order to define the evaluation function, we assign one of four possible categories (1 = *exact match*, 2 = *partial match*, 3 = *redundant node*, or 4 = *crossing brackets*) to each node from the current treelist $T_1$ and similarly we assign one of two possible categories (5 = *recognised node* or 6 = *unrecognised node*) to each node from the correct parse tree $T_2$.

A node $n_e \in T_1$ represents an *exact match* if there is a corresponding node $n'_e \in T_2$ which has got exactly the same set of leaves in its subtree and also its label is the same. A node $n_p \in T_1$ represents a *partial match* if there is a corresponding node $n'_p \in T_2$ with the same set of leaves, but the labels of nodes $n_p$ and $n'_p$ differ. A node $n_r \in T_1$ is called *redundant* if it does not violate the phrase nesting, but there is no corresponding node $n'_r \in T_2$ spanning the same portion of given sentence. All the remaining nodes $n_c \in T_1$ which cannot be classified by previous categories give rise to *crossing brackets*. On the other hand, a node $m_r \in T_2$ was *recognised* if there is a node $m'_r \in T_1$ anchoring a subtree with the same set of leaves. (Node labels do not matter in this case.) If the node $m_u \in T_2$ was not recognised, then we add it into the category *unrecognised*. Every occurence of an exact match or a recognised node is favourable whereas the other categories decrease accuracy of the obtained parse tree.

The value of the deepening operator $Oper = \langle Sub, sym \rangle$ is determined as follows. For each treelist containing the substring of roots *Sub*, the count of nodes in each category would increase (possibly by zero) if the operator *Oper* were applied there.[6] GRIND computes the difference in the count of nodes for each category and adds up these numbers over all treelists. Thus, let $D_i$ be the total difference for the category $i$. Further, each category has got its own weight (a real number). If a weight $W_i$ is assigned to the category $i$, then the value $\mathcal{V}(Oper)$ of the operator *Oper* can be expressed by the formula $\mathcal{V}(Oper) = \sum_{i=1}^{6} D_i W_i$.

In the current implementation, the weights are a priori preset to fixed values due to relevance of the corresponding category. The favourable categories have got positive weights whereas the others have got negative ones.

# 4 ILP Phase

## 4.1 Meaning of Forbidding Predicates

Each positive (negative) example generated during the previous TBL phase describes an instance of an incorrect (a correct)[7] application of a particular deepening operator. Both positive and negative examples have got the form `forbid(Tag, Lctx, Phrase, Rctx)` where `Tag` is a suggested label for the new node which is to be constructed, `Phrase` is a treelist whose elements (subtrees) would be attached to the new node so as to form a new subtree and `Lctx` and `Rctx` are treelists representing the left and the right contexts, respectively. The head of every learned rule has got the same form as the learning examples.

[6] The counts of recognised and unrecognised nodes can even decrease.

[7] Indeed, the positive examples represent *inappropriate* configurations for the given operator (and vice versa) because the forbidding predicate is intended to succeed in the case when the particular application should be discarded.

As mentioned above in Section 3, forbidding predicates are used to control application of deepening operators in operating mode. For example, if the deepening operator ⟨'NN1c P', Ns⟩ is to be applied on a particular treelist, then the substring of roots 'NN1c P' can have multiple occurrences there. Every such occurrence represents a ground instantiation of the goal

```
?- forbid('N', Lctx, [tree('NN1c',LN1), tree('P',LN2)], Rctx).
```

where the variables LN1 and LN2 are bound to lists of subtrees whose roots have the ancestors NN1c and P, respectively.

If this ground goal succeeds – which depends on the learned theory –, the corresponding deepening operator is discarded in the given context.

### 4.2 Background Knowledge

Our background knowledge consists of predicates which are designed to explore the structure of given treelists. Hereafter, we will obey the notation used in ALEPH: input variables are preceded by the sign '+' and constants (ground terms) are marked by the sign '#'. Assuming that the mode and type declaration of the target predicate is

```
forbid(+tag,+treelist,+treelist,+treelist),
```

we use the following background predicates:

- `tag(+tag,#tag)` simply checks the suggested *tag* of proposed node.
- `roots(+treelist,#scope,#pattern)` succeeds, if in the given *treelist* there is a sublist of roots which matches the *pattern* of symbols. The *pattern* may include wildcards. Moreover, the search within *pattern* is narrowed by the term *scope*.
- `leaves(+treelist,#scope,#pattern)` acts similarly to the previous predicate, but it tries to match the given *pattern* against a sublist of leaves (rather than roots) from the given *treelist*. The term *scope* has an analogical meaning here.
- `path(+treelist,#scope,#pattern)` succeeds, if there is a path evolving from some root in the given *treelist* and the symbols from this path match the *pattern*.
- `node_succ(+treelist,#scope,#tag,#pattern)` looks for a node (somewhere in the given *treelist*) which is labelled with the *tag* and the list of its successors contains a sublist matching the *pattern*.
- `empty_ctx(+treelist)` succeeds only when the given *treelist* is empty.

To make the idea of our background knowledge more transparent, we present a small demonstration. For example, the induced rule in Figure 4 succeeds if all the three following conditions hold: the first tree on the left has got the leaf AT, somewhere within the sublist `Phrase` there is a tree with the root P, and the right context is empty. As demonstrated on the treelist in Figure 4,

```
forbid(Tag, Lctx, Phrase, Rctx) :-
    leaves(Lctx, first(1), ['AT']),
    roots(Phrase, somewhere, ['P']),
    empty_ctx(Rctx).
```

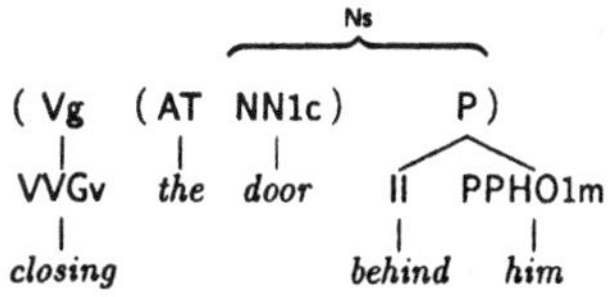

**Fig. 4.** An example of a forbidding rule and a configuration in which this rule succeeds, thus discarding the application of deepening operator ⟨'NN1c P', Ns⟩.

```
   Tag  =  'Ns'
  Lctx  =  [tree('AT',[]),
            tree('Vg',[tree('VVGv',[])])]
Phrase  =  [tree('NN1c',[]),
            tree('P',[tree('II',[]),tree('PPHO1m',[])])]
  Rctx  =  []
```

**Fig. 5.** A full instantiation of the goal `forbid(Tag, Lctx, Phrase, Rctx)` in the configuration displayed above. Note that the treelist `Lctx` is reversed and the forbidding rule considers pre-terminals, instead of word forms, as leaves.

in this case the forbidding rule discards the application of deepening operator ⟨'NN1c P', Ns⟩. Figure 5 explicitly shows the corresponding instantiation of the goal `forbid(Tag, Lctx, Phrase, Rctx)`.

From the viewpoint of ILP, the main asset of TBL phase follows from the fact that the parser construction problem was reduced to a classification task. Intuitively, a direct induction of deepening operators by means of ILP alone would imply higher computational requirements.

Two ILP systems were tested for the task of inducing the forbidding predicates: ALEPH and TILDE. ALEPH is an ILP system that supersedes P-PROGOL and its inductive algorithm is based on a technique called mode-directed inverse entailment [7]. ALEPH employs top-down search and covering strategy to propose hypotheses (sets of clauses) from examples. TILDE is an ILP system that learns hypotheses in the form of first-order logical decision trees [1]. The decision trees, induced in top-down manner from a set of pre-classified examples, can be used to classify unseen examples. Unlike ALEPH, TILDE follows divide-and-conquer strategy.

The reason for having chosen these two particular systems was that we had not to develop two completely different implementations of background knowledge predicates. The necessary modifications were mainly of syntactic nature. Moreover, both the systems can introduce constants into the body of a clause, which is an especially useful feature for our purpose.

## 5 Experiments and Results

### 5.1 Training and Testing Data

The SUSANNE [8] corpus comprises a subset of the Brown Corpus of American English annotated in accordance with the SUSANNE scheme. We randomly chose 500 training and 500 testing trees from this corpus. The training set and the test set were disjoint. Sentences from the test set were from 2 to 20 words long and the average length was 11.8. The words within sentences were replaced with their corresponding tags.

### 5.2 Evaluation Criteria

In order to measure the performance of our system, we have used evaluation criteria according to Grammar Evaluation Interest Group scheme [4]: *overall accuracy* and *recall*. If $C$ (*Correct*) is the number of those nodes in the obtained parse tree which do not give rise to crossing brackets and $T_o$ (*Total Obtained*) is the total number of nodes in this tree, then the overall accuracy is an average fraction $C/T_o$ of the non-crossing nodes per test sentence. On the other hand, if $R$ (*Recognised*) is the number if recognised nodes in the correct parse tree and $T_c$ (*Total Correct*) is the total number of nodes in this tree, then the recall is an average fraction $R/T_c$ of the recognised nodes per test sentence.

### 5.3 Accuracy and Recall

At first, we measured overall accuracy and recall of GRIND in relation to the cardinality of the training set. To achieve this, we were selecting gradually larger subsets from the original training set, starting with 50 trees and adding next 50 trees step by step. It means that a smaller training set was always included in a larger one. Performance parameters were measured on the same test set in each case. Figures 6 and 7 show learning curves for overall accuracy and recall, respectively. As for this part of evaluation, we present only the results achieved with ALEPH since the performance of TILDE was very similar. In both figures, the solid line with crosses represents performance of the system without ILP learning phase employed. In other words, the solid line describes results with no forbidding predicates used. On the other hand, the dashdot line with circles represents performance parameters achieved when application of deepening operators was guarded by forbidding predicates.

Another important criterion regarding accuracy is the ratio of sentences from the test set which were analysed with no crossing brackets or with, at most, a small number of them. As for the recall, we observed the ratio of sentences which were analysed with all constituents recognised or with, at most, a small number of them missing. Tables 1 and 2 show these performance parameters obtained on the training set with 500 trees.

Finally, we carried out an experiment which regards the richness of used tagset. As mentioned above, GRIND parses tag sequences. It means that given

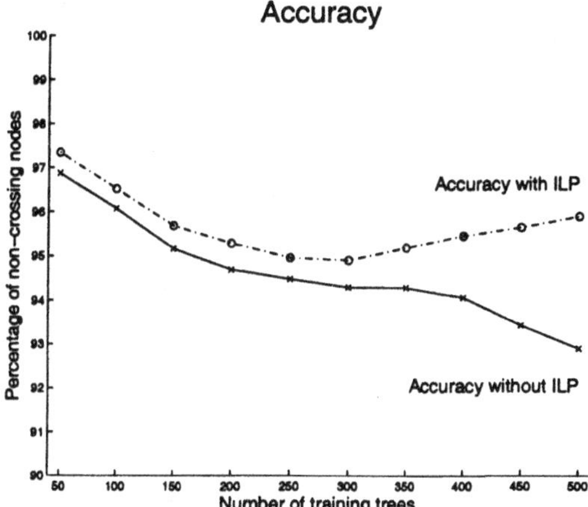


**Fig. 6.** Learning curves for overall accuracy. At first, the accuracy decreases due to the increase of recall: more nodes are recognised, thus more of them give rise to crossing brackets. However, from the count of 300 training trees and more, the accuracy with ILP (ALEPH) rises up to 95.9 %, while the curve for accuracy without ILP still falls.

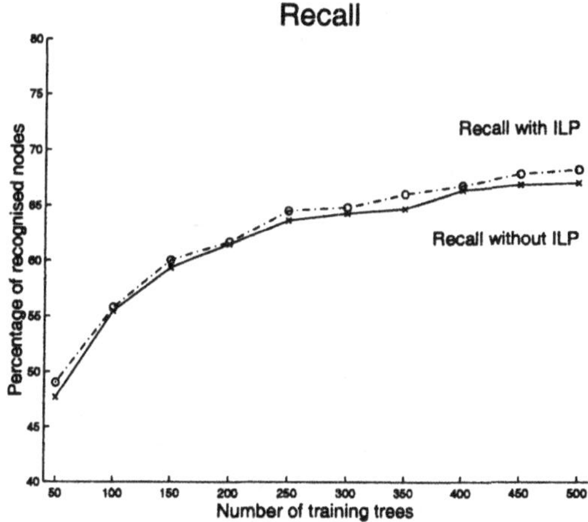


**Fig. 7.** Learning curves for recall. Initially, with the small number of training trees the recall grows rapidly, but then its growth slowly diminishes. We can see that application of ILP (ALEPH) always slightly increases the recall, so that the curve for recall with ILP continually rises up to 68.2 %.

an input sentence, some preliminary work outside the GRIND must be done to assign a part-of-speech tag to each individual word. The more ambiguities need to be solved, the more demanding this preliminary work could possibly be. So the ideal situation would be if there were just one possible tag for each word. On the other hand, a richer tagging, if disambiguated, would convey more of syntactic information useful for the parsing task. Bearing this fact in mind, we

**Table 1.** Accuracy in terms of percentage of those trees which had only a small number of crossing brackets. The training set contained 500 trees.

| Accuracy | | |
|---|---|---|
| Number of crossing brackets | Percentage of corresponding sentences | |
| | ALEPH | TILDE |
| $= 0$ | 73.8 % | 70.8 % |
| $\leq 1$ | 81.8 % | 85.5 % |
| $\leq 2$ | 94.5 % | 94.4 % |
| $\leq 3$ | 97.2 % | 98.3 % |
| $\leq 4$ | 99.3 % | 99.3 % |
| $\leq 5$ | 99.8 % | 99.9 % |

**Table 2.** Recall in terms of percentage of those trees which had only a small number of missing nodes. The training set contained 500 trees.

| Recall | | |
|---|---|---|
| Number of missing nodes | Percentage of corresponding sentences | |
| | ALEPH | TILDE |
| $= 0$ | 16.2 % | 16.2 % |
| $\leq 1$ | 30.5 % | 30.9 % |
| $\leq 2$ | 46.5 % | 47.8 % |
| $\leq 3$ | 62.2 % | 64.5 % |
| $\leq 4$ | 75.5 % | 78.2 % |
| $\leq 5$ | 85.7 % | 87.7 % |

tried to prune the original SUSANNE tagset to see how GRIND would perform if it were provided with less information due to a smaller tagset with a lower number of possible tags per word.

Initially, the training trees together with the test sentences contained 477 distinct tags. Table 3 shows complete results which we have achieved on 500 training trees when using this original tagset. To prune it, all tags were gradually truncated in two steps. For the first time, the maximum length of tag was set to three characters and all exceeding tags were shortened to this length. In this way, we obtained a tagset which had only 316 distinct tags (for corresponding results see Table 4). For the second time, all tags were further shortened to the maximum length of two characters. Then, the tagset shrunk to 130 distinct tags (resulting performance parameters are in Table 5).

Tables 3, 4 and 5 should demonstrate that the application of ILP systems managed to compensate the partial loss of information in training data. Without ILP, the important parameters (namely the overall accuracy) got noticeably worse, whereas after the employment of ILP the performance stayed at reasonable level. Tables 3, 4 and 5 present also the ratio of exact matches, partial matches and redundant nodes. Using the pruned tagset, GRIND starts to make

**Table 3.** Comparison of the results achieved on 500 training trees, using the original tagset which contained 477 distinct tags.

| Original tagset – 477 distinct tags | | | |
|---|---|---|---|
| | without ILP | with ALEPH | with TILDE |
| Overall Accuracy | 92.9 % | 95.9 % | 94.5 % |
| Recall | 67.0 % | 68.2 % | 69.1 % |
| Exact Match | 55.2 % | 69.4 % | 68.2 % |
| Partial Match | 1.3 % | 1.2 % | 1.1 % |
| Redundant Nodes | 36.4 % | 25.3 % | 25.2 % |
| Crossing Brackets | 7.1 % | 4.1 % | 5.5 % |

**Table 4.** The results achieved on 500 training trees, using a tagset whose tags were truncated to 3 characters – it yielded 316 distinct tags.

| All tags truncated to 3 characters – 316 distinct tags | | | |
|---|---|---|---|
| | without ILP | with ALEPH | with TILDE |
| Overall Accuracy | 91.1 % | 94.6 % | 94.4 % |
| Recall | 66.5 % | 68.7 % | 67.6 % |
| Exact Match | 52.0 % | 64.6 % | 66.1 % |
| Partial Match | 5.0 % | 6.2 % | 6.0 % |
| Redundant Nodes | 34.1 % | 23.8 % | 22.1 % |
| Crossing Brackets | 8.9 % | 5.4 % | 5.6 % |

**Table 5.** The results achieved on 500 training trees, using a tagset whose tags were truncated to 2 characters – it yielded 130 distinct tags.

| All tags truncated to 2 characters – 130 distinct tags | | | |
|---|---|---|---|
| | without ILP | with ALEPH | with TILDE |
| Overall Accuracy | 88.6 % | 93.1 % | 92.6 % |
| Recall | 69.8 % | 69.0 % | 68.1 % |
| Exact Match | 36.4 % | 48.4 % | 49.0 % |
| Partial Match | 16.7 % | 22.8 % | 21.8 % |
| Redundant Nodes | 35.5 % | 21.9 % | 21.8 % |
| Crossing Brackets | 11.4 % | 6.9 % | 7.4 % |

more errors in determining the correct label for nodes (the *exact match* goes down in contrast to the *partial match*). Nevertheless, the frequency of the most serious error (the *crossing brackets*) does not rise too much.

From the tables and figures mentioned above we can see that forbidding predicates induced by ILP improve essentially the parsing accuracy of GRIND, whereas the increase of recall after their application is not very high. Both ALEPH and TILDE performance parameters seem to be surprisingly similar. This is probably due to the fact that both systems used the same background knowledge.

### 5.4 Comparison with Relevant Works

Zelle and Mooney [9] tested their system CHILL [6] on a portion of ATIS corpus. One of their reported experiments had a very similar setting to ours since CHILL was adjusted to parse tag sequences. The authors also used similar performance criteria, but the terminology slightly differs: their *consistent brackets accuracy* refers to our overall accuracy and their *zero crossing brackets accuracy* refers to our percentage of sentences with no crossing brackets. After training on 525 sentences, CHILL constructed a parser which achieved 90 % of consistent brackets (GRIND 95.9 %) and 64 % of zero crossing brackets (GRIND 73.8 %). However, these figures should be handled with care, since the parser constructed by CHILL was designed to produce binary-branching trees[8] while GRIND normally generates $n$-ary structures. It is easy to see that a tree containing a single, flat constituent covering the entire sentence always yields a perfect crossing score.

Therefore we tried to compare the two systems also in terms of recall. Zelle and Mooney used a *partial match accuracy* which does not agree with our definition of partial match, but its basic idea is related to our notion of node pairing. In [9], two constituents are said to match if they span exactly the same words in the sentence. If constituents match and have got the same label, then they are identical. The overlap between the obtained tree and the correct tree is computed by trying to match each constituent of the obtained tree with a constituent in the correct tree. If an identical constituent is found, the score is 1.0. A matching constituent with an incorrect label scores 0.5. The sum of the scores for all constituents is the overlap score $O$. The partial match accuracy for a sentence is consequently computed as $\left(\frac{O}{F} + \frac{O}{C}\right)/2$ where $F$ and $C$ are the numbers of constituents in the obtained tree and in the correct tree, respectively. We have found out that the partial match accuracy of GRIND is 81.3 %, which is fairly comparable with Zelle and Mooney's test (they report 84 %).

The performance of GRIND can also be compared with the system of Brill [2, 3]. He ran experiments on the Wall Street Journal corpus. After training on 500 sentences with the average sentence length 10.8, his transformation-based parser achieved a *bracketing accuracy* (which coincides with our overall accuracy) of 89.3 % (GRIND 95.9 %). As reported in [2], the percentages of sentences in the test set which had no crossing constituents, or one at most, or two at most, were 53.7 %, 72.3 %, and 84.6 %, respectively. Corresponding GRIND's results are 73.8 %, 81.8 %, and 94.5 %. However, it should be noted that Brill's parser always produces a binary-branching tree.

Unfortunately, we cannot confront our results with the system GRIDS of Langley [5], although his work was a primary inspiration for us. The reason is that he ran experiments on unrealistic, toy data only. Furthermore, he does not care about descriptive adequacy of the induced grammar and reports only results concerning the probability of accepting a legal sentence and the probability of generating a legal sentence while our system is not designed to work as an acceptor or a generator.

---

[8] But if the parser runs into a dead-end while parsing a test sentence, then the returned tree needn't be binary.

## 6 Conclusions and Future Work

We have presented a new approach to automated parser construction which is based on combination of two techniques already used: transformation-based learning and inductive logic programming. Our system GRIND achieved relatively better accuracy rate in comparison with related systems, despite the slightly lower recall. In this respect, GRIND follows the voice of many linguists which claim that NLP systems should preferably "do less than make errors". Moreover, our parsing scheme is easy to understand and therefore it represents a suitable starting point for further development of a system which would involve a human-machine co-operation during the process of natural language parser construction.

In the future, we intend to improve GRIND in these points: to replace the *hill-climbing strategy* in TBL phase with the *beam search*, to invent a technique for automatic adjustment of the values for weights rather than set them fixed, and to make the system towards human-machine co-operation.

**Acknowledgement**

I thank Luboš Popelínský for helpful discussions and continual encouragement.

## References

1. Blockeel, H. and de Raedt, L.: Top-down induction of logical decision trees. KU Leuven, Department of Computer Science. Technical report CW 247 (1997)
2. Brill, E.: Automatic grammar induction and parsing free text: A transformation--based approach. In *Proceedings of 31st Annual Meeting of the Association for Computational Linguistics*, Somerset, NJ (1993) 259–265
3. Brill, E.: Transformation-based error-driven parsing. In Bunt, H. and Tomita, M. (eds.), *Recent Advances in Parsing Technology*. Kluwer Academic Publishers (1996)
4. Harrison P., Abney S., Black E., Flickinger D., Gdaniec C., Grishman R., Hindle D., Ingria R., Marcus M., Santorini B. and Strzalkowski T.: Evaluating Syntax Performance of Parser/Grammars of English. *Language Processing Systems Evaluation Workshop*, Technical Report RL-TR-91-36, Rome Laboratory, Air Force Systems, Command, Griffis Air Force Base, NY 13441-5700 (1991)
5. Langley, P.: Learning context-free grammars with a simplicity bias. In de Mantaras, R. L. and Plaza, E. (eds.), *Proceedings of the 11th European Conference on Machine Learning*, LNAI **1810**, Berlin, Springer Verlag (2000) 220–228
6. Mooney, R. J.: Inductive logic programming for natural language processing. In Muggleton, S. (ed.), *Inductive Logic Programming: Selected Papers from the 6th International Workshop*, Berlin, Springer Verlag (1997) 3–22
7. Muggleton, S.: Inverse entailment and Progol. In *New Generation Computing*, special issue on inductive logic programming **13** (1995) 245–286
8. Sampson, G.: *English for the Computer.* Clarendon Press, Oxford, 1st edition (1995)
9. Zelle, J. M. and Mooney, R. J.: An inductive logic programming method for corpus--based parser construction. University of Texas, Austin. Unpublished technical note (1997)

# Induction of Stable Models

Ramón P. Otero

AI Lab. - Dept. of Computer Science
University of Corunna
15071 Corunna, Galicia, SPAIN
otero@dc.fi.udc.es

**Abstract.** In the line of previous work by S. Muggleton and C. Sakama, we extend the logical characterization of inductive logic programming, to normal logic programs under the stable models semantics. A logic program in this non-monotonic semantics can be contradictory or can have one or several models. We provide a complete characterization on the hypotheses solution to induction of this kind of programs.

## 1 Introduction

Consider the following motivating example.

*Example 1.* Given normal logic program $B$

$$p \leftarrow not\ q$$
$$q \leftarrow not\ p$$

assume we want an extension of this program, $B \cup H$, for the atoms of the set $E = \{p\}$ to be consequence of the extension, $B \cup H \models E$. Note that $B$ has two stable models $\{p\}$ and $\{q\}$. Thus there are not literals consequence of $B$. □

Consider the following solutions:

$$H_1 = \{p \leftarrow\},\ H_2 = \{p \leftarrow q\},\ H_3 = \{p \leftarrow not\ p\},\ H_4 = \{p \leftarrow not\ p, q\}.$$

Solution $H_1$ is directly a fact about the wanted atom and it can be induced by current ILP methods. Solutions $H_3$ and $H_4$ contain rules with negation as failure, thus only non-monotonic ILP could induce them.

But in fact $H_3$ and $H_4$ are not inducible using current NM-ILP methods for the following reasons.

• The program $B$ has several stable models, and, in particular, no atomic consequences. Thus the *enlarged bottom set* of E-IE [5], and the *expansion set* $M^+$ of NM-IE [8] are empty. Then there is no set from which to get possible candidates for body literals of the hypothesis $H$.

• The literal $p$ appears both in the body and in the head of $H$, that is not allowed in these methods, furthermore this makes $H_3$ alone inconsistent.

The most interesting case is solution $H_2$ because it is a positive rule, thus current ILP methods could be able to induce it. But it is not the case because

C. Rouveirol and M. Sebag (Eds.): ILP 2001, LNAI 2157, pp. 193–205, 2001.

IE is only defined for Horn logic programs and this is not the case of $B$ in the example. In other words, $q$ is not entailed by $B$ so it cannot be in the body of $H$. This last fact is also the reason why $H_2$ is not discovered by NM-IE (despite NM-IE is defined for non-Horn programs).

*Example 2.* Consider another normal logic program $B$

$$q \leftarrow not\, p$$
$$q \leftarrow not\, q$$

we want to learn $E = \{p\}$. Program $B$ has only one stable model, $\{q\}$. Thus the literals consequence of $B$ are $\{q, not\, p\}$. □

Consider the following tentative solutions:

$$H_1 = \{p \leftarrow\},\ H_2 = \{p \leftarrow q\},\ H_3 = \{p \leftarrow not\, p\},\ H_4 = \{p \leftarrow not\, p, q\}.$$

Hypothesis $H_1$ is not a solution, it makes the program $B \cup H_1$ contradictory, i.e. there is no stable model. In fact none of the four tentative hypotheses is a solution, because for any of them $B \cup H_i$ is contradictory.

These are all the hypotheses built from the literals consequence of $B$. Thus is there no solution? No, actually there are solutions. Consider $H_5 = \{p \leftarrow,\ q \leftarrow p\}$. The program $B \cup H_5 \models E$ and it is not contradictory, the unique stable model is $\{p, q\}$.

Inverse Entailment (IE) [4] and Enlarged Inverse Entailment (E-IE) by Muggleton [5], and Non-monotonic IE by Sakama [8], rely on the set of literals consequence of $B$ to define the hypothesis $H$ solution to induction.

When extending induction to nonmonotonic LP, the background knowledge $B$—containing negative literals in the rules—is no longer representable by the set of literals consequence of it. In Example 2, an alternative $B = \{q \leftarrow not\, p\}$, with the same set of consequences, $\{q, not\, p\}$, would accept $H_1$ as solution.

There is another extension made to the basic setting of ILP in these examples, namely, the predicate of the examples can be already present in the rules of $B$.

When this extension of $B$ is considered, the contribution of the background knowledge to the learning task is not only to provide facts about other predicates on which the induced rules can rely. But also to act as a constraint background knowledge that can forbid some solutions.

This fact is also present in basic ILP, e.g. the (extended) background knowledge can already entail one negative example, making induction impossible.

Part of this study is centered in the identification of the constraint effect of the background.

Finally there is another effect when $B$ is a normal program: some consequences of $B$ may not be preserved after induction. Consider $p \leftarrow not\, q$ the consequences are $\{p\}$, we want to learn $\{q\}$ then $H = \{q \leftarrow\}$ is a solution, but now the consequences of $B \cup H$ are $\{q\}$, i.e. $p$ is no longer a consequence. These are 'nonmonotonic' consequences of $B$, i.e. consequences that relied on default assumptions about an atom being false.

In the next section we recall the definition of stable models. Then induction of stable models is characterized. We conclude discussing the results and commenting on related work.

## 2 Normal Logic Programs and Stable Models

A (ground) normal logic program is a set of rules of the form

$$A_0 \leftarrow A_1, \ldots, A_m, not\ A_{m+1}, \ldots, not\ A_n \tag{1}$$

where $n \geq m \geq 0$, and each $A_i$ is a ground atom. If a rule or a program does not contain the *not* operator it is called *positive.*

The stable model semantics of a normal logic program [2] is defined in two steps. First let $B$ be a positive program, then the *stable models* are the minimal sets of atoms $M$ that satisfy the condition: For each rule

$$A_0 \leftarrow A_1, \ldots, A_m$$

from $B$, if $A_i \in M$, for all $i : 1, \ldots, m$, then $A_0 \in M$.

Now let $B$ be a general ground program. For any set $M$ of atoms, let $B^M$ be the program obtained from $B$ by deleting

1. each rule that has a formula *not* $A$ in its body with $A \in M$, and
2. all formulas of the form *not* $A$ in the bodies of the remaining rules.

The program $B^M$ is positive; if $M$ is the stable model of this program then $M$ is a stable model of $B$.

Note that, by the definition, for positive programs the stable model is unique and coincides with the least Herbrand model of the program. This result also holds for Horn programs, as shown in [5], when the program is not contradictory; otherwise there is no least Herbrand model, nor stable model. Even for normal programs, when the least Herbrand model exists, the stable model coincides with it (and is unique), e.g. *stratified* normal programs. The difference is for the other normal programs, for which there can be no stable model, one or several stable models, e.g. $\{p \leftarrow not p, not q\}$ does not have stable model; $\{p \leftarrow not q,\ q \leftarrow not p\}$ has two stable models, $\{p\}$ and $\{q\}$.

A program is not contradictory iff it has one or more stable models. When there are several stable models, the atoms consequence of the program are the atoms common to all the stable models.

Stable models (and least Herbrand models) are minimal models; to further differentiate a stable model from (just) a model, i.e. not necessary minimal, we will call the latter a monotonic model of the program.

A set of atoms is a *monotonic model* of a rule (1) iff whenever $M$ satisfies the body, $A_i \in M$, for all $i : 1, \ldots, m$, and $A_j \notin M$, for each $j : m+1, \ldots, n$, then $M$ satisfies the head, $A_0 \in M$.

A set of atoms $M$ is a monotonic model of a program iff it is a monotonic model of each rule of the program.

It is easy to verify that every stable model is a monotonic model of the program.

## 3 Characterization of Induction in Stable Models

In this section we propose necessary and sufficient conditions for the existence of solution to induction of normal logic programs under stable models semantics. We do the characterization in three steps. First for induction from a complete set of examples, then induction in the usual ILP setting for which the set of examples is not complete. Finally induction from several sets of examples—a new ILP setting that is relevant in stable models programming.

### 3.1 Induction from Complete Sets

Consider the particular ILP setting in which the set of examples is complete, i.e. for every ground literal of the program there is either a positive example on it or a negative example. In this case, the set of examples corresponds to one model of the program.

In this setting, the task of finding an extension of $B$ that entails the set of examples is an application of the representation theorem for LP. Instead of finding a program that has a particular set of facts as consequence, it is to find an extension of a given program $B$ that has the particular set as consequence. (Without $B$ there is a simple solution, viz., a set of fact rules, one for each positive example.) But with $B$—as mentioned before—there can be no solution, e.g. when $B$ already entails one of the negative examples.

When $B$ is a normal program its behavior as a constraint on the solutions is stronger. As show in Example 2 in the introduction, even a program $B$ that does not entail negative examples, does not accept the simple solution of a set of facts on the positive examples.

**Theorem 1. (Existence of solution, necessary condition)** *Given a normal logic program $B$, and a possible model $M$, there is no extension $H$ of $B$, such that $M$ is a stable model of $B \cup H$ if $M$ is not a monotonic model of $B$.*

*Proof.* Every stable model of a program is a monotonic model of it. The addition of more formulas $H$ to a given program $B$ only deletes monotonic models of $B$ (they have to satisfy $H$ also.) Thus if $M$ is not a monotonic model of $B$ the effect of adding more rules will not recover $M$ as monotonic model. □

Note that if we change monotonic model by stable model in the previous proof, the facts do not hold, we would be in a nonmonotonic formalism.

Given a complete set of examples $E = \{a_1, \ldots, a_n, not\, b_1, \ldots, not\, b_m\}$, it directly corresponds to one possible model $M$ denoted $\{a_1, \ldots, a_n\}$ of the program $B$. Thus if there is a solution $H$, $B \cup H \models E$, then the set $E$ considered as model, $M$, is a monotonic model of $B$.

Next we will show that the converse of Theorem 1 also holds, providing a complete characterization on the existence of solution to induction problems for a complete set of examples, under the stable model semantics.

**Theorem 2. (Existence of solution, sufficient condition)** *Given a normal logic program $B$, and a possible model $M$, there is an extension $H$ of $B$, such that $M$ is an stable model of $B \cup H$ if $M$ is a monotonic model of $B$.*

*Proof.* We will construct an $H$ that is solution. Consider $H = \{a_i \leftarrow | a_i \in M\}$ a set of fact rules corresponding to each of the positive atoms $a_i \in M$. Note that, by construction, $M$ is a monotonic model of $H$. (Each of the rules $a_i \leftarrow$ constructed from $M$ is satisfied by it.) As $M$ is a monotonic model of $B$, then it is a monotonic model of $B \cup H$.

Then we will verify that it is stable. Consider the reduct $(B \cup H)^M = B^M \cup H^M = B^M \cup H$ because $H$ is a positive program. $M$ is a stable model iff it is the minimal model of the positive program $B^M \cup H$. As $M$ is a monotonic model of $B$ it is a monotonic model of $B^M$ (the reduct $B^M$ has a subset of the rules of $B$, and for the remaining rules the negative literals deleted are satisfied by $M$). Assume $M$ is not minimal, then there is another (monotonic) model $M'$ of $B^M \cup H$ such that $M' \subset M$, then there is one atom, assume it is $a_k$, $a_k \in M$, $a_k \notin M'$. By construction of $H$ there is one fact rule $a_k \leftarrow$. Then $M'$ is not a monotonic model of this fact rule, thus it is not a monotonic model of $B^M \cup H$. □

In fact, there are other $H$ solutions when $M$ is a monotonic model of $B$. But the $H$ formed with facts is always a solution.

*Example 2 (cont.)* Theorem 2 may seem surprising if we recall Example 2 in the introduction. In that example it is shown that the simple $H$ formed with facts is not a solution, and, nevertheless, there are other solutions. The key observation is that $\{p\}$ in Example 2 is not a monotonic model of $B$. Thus this model, that entails the example set $E = \{p\}$ is not valid. The solution shown corresponds to the model $\{p, q\}$; and this do is a monotonic model of $B$.

There is a solution in Example 2 because $E$ is not considered a complete set (in the sense that *not* $q$ is not in the set). (If the case were that the example set $\{p\}$ is complete, i.e. $\{p, not\ q\}$, then by the previous result we would conclude that there is no solution.) □

The previous characterization of the existence of solution for induction of stable models, needs to detect whether a model is a monotonic model of a program or not.

Theoretically a model is a monotonic model of a program iff the model satisfies the program. Thus the model corresponding to the complete set of examples can be tested for satisfiability, constituting an implementation of induction in stable models.

Alternatively, the following result can be used to verify that a set is a monotonic model. We will use the same name to denote a set of atoms $M = \{a_1, \ldots, a_n\}$, and a set of fact rules on the atoms of the set, $M = \{a_1 \leftarrow, \ldots, a_n \leftarrow\}$.

**Proposition 1.** *Given a normal logic program $B$, $M$ is monotonic model of $B$ iff $M$ is a stable model of $B \cup M$.*

*Proof.* Consider the program $B \cup M$. If $M$ is a stable model of it then it is a monotonic model of $B \cup M$. Thus it has to be a monotonic model of both $B$ and $M$.

Proof in the other direction is similar to that of Theorem 2. □

Proposition 1 identifies monotonic models $M$ with those that verify they are stable models of $B \cup M$. In fact, in the conditions of Proposition 1, $M$ is the unique stable model of $B \cup M$. (Any other stable model $M'$ of $B \cup M$, will satisfy $M$, thus $M \subset M'$ and then $M'$ is not stable.)

System *smodels* by Niemela et al. [6] is a sound and complete implementation to find the stable models of a normal program.

The system smodels can be used to induce normal programs under the stable models semantics for the setting of complete sets of examples. Just consider the example set $E$ as a possible model $M$, try program $B \cup M$, if $M$ is a stable model of it, then there is a solution to induction, e.g. $H = M$ is a solution. If $M$ is not a stable model of it, then there is no solution.

*Example 1 and 2 (cont.)* Recall Example 1 in the introduction. Consider $B \cup E = \{p \leftarrow not\ q,\ q \leftarrow not\ p,\ p \leftarrow\}$ the stable model is $\{p\}$. Then $H = \{p \leftarrow\}$ is a solution.

For Example 2 consider $B \cup E = \{q \leftarrow not\ q,\ q \leftarrow not\ p,\ p \leftarrow\}$, there is no stable model. Then there is no solution.

Instead consider the examples set $E' = \{p, q\}$, $B \cup E'$ has $E'$ as stable model, then $H = \{p \leftarrow,\ q \leftarrow\}$ is a solution. □

### 3.2 Induction from Non-complete Sets

Consider that the set of examples is not complete—the usual ILP setting. The definition of solution to an induction problem is as follows.

Given the two parts of the set of examples $E = E^+ \cup E^-$, i.e. the positive examples $E^+$ and the negative examples $E^-$, there is a solution $H$, in the presence of background knowledge $B$, iff $B \cup H \models E^+$, $B \cup H \not\models E^-$, and $B \cup H \not\models \bot$.

**Definition 1 (Complete extension)** *Given a set of examples $E = E^+ \cup E^-$, an interpretation $M$ (of $B \cup E$) is a complete extension of $E$ iff $E^+ \subset M$ and $M \cap E^- = \emptyset$.* □

The following result identifies the existence of solution using the results for the case of complete set of examples.

**Theorem 3. (Existence of solution)** *Given a normal logic program $B$, and a set of examples $E = E^+ \cup E^-$ there is a solution $H$ to induction iff there is (at least) one complete extension $M$ of $E$ that is a monotonic model of $B$.*

*Proof.* If there is a solution then the stable model $M$ of $B \cup H$ exists (because $B \cup H \not\models \bot$), thus it is a monotonic model of $B$. Furthermore, $M$ is a complete extension of $E$, because $B \cup H \models E^+$ thus $M \models E^+$ ($E^+ \subset M$), and $B \cup H \not\models E^-$, thus $M \not\models E^-$ ($M \cap E^- = \emptyset$). (Note that the last relation means that $M \not\models e_j^-$ for every $e_j^- \in E^-$.)

If there is a monotonic model $M$ of $B$ that is a complete extension of $E$, then by Theorem 2 there is an extension $H = M$ such that $M$ is stable model of $B \cup H$. Then $B \cup H \not\models \bot$. As $M$ is a complete extension of $E$, $M \models E^+$ and $M \not\models E^-$. Thus $B \cup H \models E^+$ and $B \cup H \not\models E^-$. (Recall that, in fact, $M$ is the unique stable model of $B \cup M$.) □

For an alternative characterization as we did for the complete set case, we can recall also those results here. Then from the previous theorem and Proposition 1, we get the following.

**Corollary 1.** *Given a normal logic program $B$, and a set of examples $E = E^+ \cup E^-$ there is a solution $H$ to induction iff there is (at least) one complete extension $M$ of $E$ that is a stable model of $B \cup M$.* □

¿From an implementation point of view now it is needed to search the extensions of the set of examples for a complete set that is stable of itself added to $B$.

The direct implementation is to call several times the system smodels with $B$ and one of the complete extensions until one of them has itself as stable model. (If none of them are its own stable model then there is no solution.)

Note that in this setting we have a choice on the possible solutions. Several extensions of the set of examples can have solution. This is the usual choice in induction from the most specific solution to the most general solution.

In this setting, the search can be reduced using the following result.

**Proposition 2.** *Given a normal logic program $B$, $M'$ is monotonic model of $B$ if $M'$ is a stable model of $B \cup M$ and $M \subseteq M'$.*

*Proof.* Consider we add some atoms of $M'$, $M \subset M'$ to $B$, and $M'$ is a stable model of $B \cup M$. Then $M'$ is a monotonic model of $B \cup M$, thus it is also a monotonic model of $B$. □

Consider a set of examples $E = E^+ \cup E^-$. We extract from $E$ the subset of positive examples $M = E^+$. Sometimes $B \cup M$ does not have $M$ as stable model but some superset $M'$ as stable model. Then if $M'$ is a complete extension of $E$, there is solution to induction.

Even when $B \cup M$ does not have stable model at all, there can be a solution to induction. The situation in nonmonotonic induction is that $B \cup E^+$ can be contradictory and still an extension of $E^+$ provide a consistent extension for $B$. Thus we have to search for a consistent extension of $B$, and among all these extensions we can choose following particular generalization criteria.

Note that these results not only characterize the existence of solution to induction, but every $H$ solution to induction. There is a particular $H$ solution iff the model of $B \cup H$ is a monotonic model of $B$ and a complete extension of $E$.

In summary, there are three kinds of solutions in this setting of normal logic programs.

- *Minimally extended.* The $H$ that are facts on the positive examples *minimally extended* to avoid contradiction with $B$.
- *Generalizations.* The $H$ that are *generalizations* of the minimal ones, thus implying more atoms. These solutions can be constructed by just adding more fact rules to the minimal ones, or—as usual in ILP—by first-order generalization. But not every extension is solution, these extended $H$ have to verify the conditions of the characterization, in particular, the monotonic model condition (appart from the usual condition on complete extension).
- *Nonmonotonic.* There is a new kind of $H$ solution in this setting (also present in NM-IE [8]), viz., $H$ that use negation as failure, let us call them *nonmonotonic* hypotheses.

The nonmonotonic hypotheses do not really constitute solutions more specific than the minimally extended ones.

Furthermore, these nonmonotonic solutions have a property that is usually non-intended: the examples learned are not necessarily preserved after further induction (induction in several steps, or multiple predicate learning). The nonmonotonic behavior of $B \cup H$ is stronger than the one with minimally extended or generalized hypotheses, because part of the examples entailed by $B \cup H$ might rely on default assumptions.

Consider that we want to further extend $B \cup H$ with $H'$ to cover additional examples. If the task is performed by considering $B' = B \cup H$ and applying the basic procedure to arrive to $B' \cup H'$, then some of the previous examples covered by $H$ can become uncovered after the addition of $H'$. (The coverage of the previous examples has been done nonmonotonically, thus they are not necessarily entailed after any addition of more rules to the program.) On the other hand, any $H$ composed of fact rules, entails the examples monotonically, thus this situation cannot arise. (What can happen is the alternative situation, that some of the negative examples are covered after the addition of $H'$, but this is a well known fact already in ILP for Horn theories.)

**Induction from Non-complete Sets under Background Horn Theories.** So far we have shown that solutions composed of a collection of fact rules characterize the existence of solution in ILP for normal logic programs.

The extension made here only points out that precisely the set of facts from the positive examples does not need to be such a solution. Nevertheless, there is a restriction that precisely characterizes the existence of solution with the set of facts from the positive examples.

Consider that the background knowledge is a Horn theory, i.e. definite clauses and goal clauses (constraints), thus no clause contains the *not* operator.

Then the following result holds.

**Theorem 4. (Existence of solution)** *Given a Horn logic program $B$, and a (consistent) set of examples $E = E^+ \cup E^-$ there is a solution $H$ to induction iff $H = E^+$ is a solution.*

*Proof.* We only need to prove one direction. Obviously if $H = E^+$ is a solution, there is solution.

Assume there is a solution $H'$. Then we will verify that $H = E^+$ is also a solution. We will use the monotonic properties of Horn logic programs.

Consider that the stable model of $B \cup E^+$ exists, thus $B \cup E^+ \not\models \bot$. (Furthermore it is unique ( [5], Lemma 1) and coincides with the Least Herbrand model.) Now recall that Horn programs verify monotonic properties, thus $B \cup E^+ \models E^+$, simply because $E^+ \models E^+$. Finally $B \cup E^+ \not\models E^-$ because there is a solution $H'$ such that $B \cup H' \not\models E^-$ and $B \cup H' \models E^+$, thus we can add the consequences $B \cup H' \cup E^+ \not\models E^-$, and remove the hypothesis $B \cup E^+ \not\models E^-$.

Consider that there is no stable model of $B \cup E^+$. But if there is another solution, $B \cup H' \models E^+$ and $B \cup H' \not\models \bot$. Applying the monotonic properties of Horn programs, $B \cup H' \cup E^+ \models E^+$, thus $B \cup E^+ \not\models \bot$. Then there is a stable model of $B \cup E^+$ if there is any solution $H'$. □

### 3.3 Induction from Several Sets of Examples

Under stable models semantics, normal logic programs constitute a new declarative programming paradigm. The idea relies on the fact that logic programs can have no stable model, one or several stable models.

Each stable model is associated with one (alternative) solution to the problem described by the program. Thus when there are several stable models, the problem has several solutions; and when there is no stable model, the problem does not have a solution.

Typical problems of this kind are combinatorial problems, e.g. finding the different ways the nodes of a graph can be colored verifying that no adjacent nodes have the same color. Other typical examples are planning problems, i.e. finding the sequence of actions that lead to a given goal state from a given initial state of the domain.

For these kind of applications of stable models programming, induction would be welcomed. To this end the usual setting of ILP has to be extended. The direct extension is to consider several sets of examples. Each one corresponding to an intended solution to the problem.

**Definition 2 (Induction of (several) stable models)** *Given a logic program $B$, and several sets of examples $E_1, \ldots, E_n$ (each one composed of two parts, $E_i = E_i^+ \cup E_i^-$) there is a solution program $H$ to induction iff for each set $E_i$, $i : 1, \ldots, n$ there is a stable model, $M_i$ of $B \cup H$, such that $M_i \models E_i^+$ and $M_i \not\models E_i^-$ ($M_i \cap E_i^- = \emptyset$).* □

Note that the usual definition of induction in ILP is the particular case for a unique set of examples.

The previous results still worth to characterize induction of several stable models. Before we will need the concept of antichain and a result about it (similar to one by V. Marek and M. Truszczynski in [3]).

A collection of sets of atoms, $M_1, \ldots, M_n$ form an *antichain* iff whenever $M_i \subseteq M_j$ then $M_i = M_j$, for every $i, j : 1, \ldots, n$. Thus no set is subset of another set in the collection.

**Proposition 3.** *Given a normal logic program $B$, and a collection of monotonic models $\{M_i, i : 1, \ldots, n\}$ of $B$ that form an antichain, then there is an extension $H$ such that $B \cup H$ has the models $M_i, i : 1, \ldots, n$ as stable models (simultaneously).*

*Proof.* We have to propose a set of rules $H$ that when added to $B$ make all the $M_i, i : 1, \ldots, n$ stable.

One possibility is to add an $H_i$ to make each $M_i$ stable. But each of these $H_i$ has to be carefully chosen not to forbid the other intended stable $M_j$. This will be achieved if $H_i$ is able to make $M_i$ stable, while keeping all the monotonic models of $B$ (unless subsets of $M_i$). Then we have to add to $B$ rules that are not satisfied only by subsets of $M_i$ but any other set (not subset of $M_i$) will satisfy the rules in $H_i$.

Consider $H_i = \{a_l \leftarrow NB \mid a_l \in M_i\}$ where $NB = not\, b_1, \ldots, not\, b_m$ for all $b_j \notin M_i$. Each $H_i$ is a set of rules, one for each positive atom in $M_i$ as head, and the same body for all of them, the conjunction of the negative literals for the atoms not in $M_i$. Then every subset of $M_i$ does not have any $b_j$ and also does not have some $a_k$ positive in $M_i$. Thus it does not verify the rule in $H_i$ corresponding to $a_k$.

For any other model that is not a subset of $M_i$ then there is an $a_r$ that is not in $M_i$ thus the model does not verify *not* $a_r$ that is in every body of the rules of $H_i$, thus the model satisfies all the rules of $H_i$. Then $H_i$ does not delete any other model—unless subsets of $M_i$.

We show that $H_i$ makes $M_i$ stable. Consider the reduct $(B \cup H_i)^{M_i}$. It is equal to $B^{M_i} \cup M_i$, because $H_i^{M_i} = M_i$ (all the $b_j$ are not in $M_i$ thus all those literals are deleted in the reduct $H_i^{M_i}$, but the rules are kept as fact rules.) (From this point the proof of Theorem 2 can be directly followed.) As $M_i$ is a monotonic model of $B$, it is a monotonic model of $B^{M_i}$. By Proposition 1 it is a stable model of $B^{M_i} \cup M_i$. Thus $M_i$ is stable of $B \cup H_i$.

Finally the addition of the other $H_j$ to $B$ (for the other stable) do not interfere with each other if the $\{M_i, i : 1, \ldots, n\}$ collection form an antichain.

Recall—as mentioned above—that any other model $M_j$ that is not a subset of a given $M_i$, satisfy the rules in $H_i$ because there is one $a_r \in M_j$ that is present in the body of the rules of $H_i$ as *not* $a_r$. Thus $H_i^{M_j} = \emptyset$ for every $i, j : 1, \ldots, n$. Then the reduct $(B \cup H)^{M_i} = B^{M_i} \cup H_1^{M_i} \cup \ldots \cup H_n^{M_i} = B^{M_i} \cup H_i^{M_i}$. Thus every $M_i$ is a stable model of $B \cup H$. □

**Theorem 5. (Existence of solution)** *Given a normal logic program $B$, and several sets of examples $E_1, \ldots, E_n$ there is a solution $H$ to induction iff*

*i) for each set $E_i$ there is (at least) one complete extension $M_i$ of $E_i$ that is a monotonic model of $B$, and*

*ii) the set of complete extensions $\{M_i, i : 1, \ldots, n\}$ form an antichain.*

*Proof.* The antichain condition is needed because the collection of stable models of a program always form an antichain. (Recall that if a model is stable, no subset of it is (simultaneously) stable.)

The proof the this theorem follows that of Theorem 3.

If there is a solution $H$ then $B \cup H$ has a collection of stable models $\{M_i, i : 1, \ldots, n\}$, thus they form an antichain. Furthermore each $M_i$ is a monotonic model of $B$. Finally, for each $E_i$ there is an $M_i$ that is a complete extension of it, because $M_i \models E_i^+$ ($E_i^+ \subset M_i$), and $M_i \not\models E_i^-$ ($M_i \cap E_i^- = \emptyset$).

If there is a collection of monotonic models $\{M_i, i : 1, \ldots, n\}$ of $B$ that form an antichain, then by Proposition 3 there is an extension $H$ such that $B \cup H$ has the models $\{M_i, i : 1, \ldots, n\}$ as stable models (simultaneously).

As each $E_i$ has one $M_i$ that is a complete extension of it, $M_i \models E_i^+$ and $M_i \not\models E_i^-$. □

Note that the solution $H$ with only facts is not, in general, a solution for several sets of examples, as it was in the other settings.

This result shows that nonmonotonic hypotheses (i.e. with negation as failure in the body) are only truly needed when there are several sets of examples.

As in the other settings, the existence of solution does not mean that $H$ has to be just in the form we used for the proofs. Other solutions can exists, as we showed before, but recall that only when we are in the conditions of the result presented. In this sense, the collection of $\{H_i, i : 1, \ldots, n\}$ proposed can be thought of the *most specific* solution to the problem, and also the *most conservative* solution (in the sense that it keeps as many monotonic models of the extended program as possible).

For an implementation point of view, we can use the results on the other settings. Notice that induction from several sets can be made separately for each set, thus as a case of induction from a non-complete set. The only difference is that instead of using $H = M$ a set of facts, we have to test with the $H_i$ rules, $H_i = \{a_l \leftarrow not\, b_1, \ldots, not\, b_m \mid a_l \in M_i\}$, where $b_1, \ldots, b_m$ are all the $b_j \notin M_i$.

*Example 3.* Given normal logic program $B$

$$p \leftarrow not\, q$$

Assume we want an extension of this program, $B \cup H$, for the atoms of the sets $E_1 = \{p\}$ and $E_2 = \{q\}$ to be consequence of corresponding stable models of the extension. Note that $B$ has one stable model $\{p\}$.

Consider the complete extensions $M_1 = E_1^+$ and $M_2 = E_2^+$. They form an antichain collection. They are monotonic models of $B$. Thus there is solution. Build $H_1 = \{p \leftarrow not\, q\}$ and $H_2 = \{q \leftarrow not\, p\}$. Then $B \cup H_1 \cup H_2 = \{p \leftarrow not\, q,\ q \leftarrow not\, p\}$ indeed has $M_1$ and $M_2$ as stable models. □

*Example 4.* Consider a simple graph with two nodes $n(1)$, $n(2)$, connected by an arc $a(1, 2)$. We want to find the different ways the nodes of a graph can be colored with two colors, we will represent $w(X)$ as white, being black all the other nodes for which $w(X)$ is false.

Background knowledge $B$ is the graph, and the undirected condition of the graph

$$n(1) \leftarrow$$
$$n(2) \leftarrow$$
$$a(1,2) \leftarrow$$
$$a(X,Y) \leftarrow a(Y,X), n(X), n(Y)$$

The sets of examples inform on possible solutions, $E_1 = \{w(1), not\, w(2)\}$ and $E_2 = \{w(2)\}$. Notice that the union $E_1 \cup E_2$ is contradictory. And also that $B$ has a unique stable model $M_B = \{n(1), n(2), a(1,2), a(2,1)\}$.

Consider the complete extensions $M_1 = E_1^+ = \{w(1)\}$ and $M_2 = E_2^+ = \{w(2)\}$. They form an antichain collection. But they are not monotonic models of $B$. Consider the complete extensions $M_1 = E_1^+ \cup M_B = \{w(1), n(1), n(2), a(1,2), a(2,1)\}$ and $M_2 = E_2^+ \cup M_B = \{w(2), n(1), n(2), a(1,2), a(2,1)\}$. They form an antichain collection and they are monotonic models of $B$. Thus there is solution.

Build $H_1 = \{w(1) \leftarrow \textit{not}\ w(2)\}$ and $H_2 = \{w(2) \leftarrow \textit{not}\ w(1)\}$. (We are considering here only the $H$ with head the predicate of the examples, the other can also be added to $B$.) Then $B \cup H_1 \cup H_2$ indeed has $M_1$ and $M_2$ as stable models.

There are other solutions. Consider for instance $H_1' = \{w(1) \leftarrow \textit{not}\ w(2), a(1,2)\}$ and $H_2' = \{w(2) \leftarrow \textit{not}\ w(1), a(2,1)\}$. (Both can be generalized to $H'' = \{w(X) \leftarrow \textit{not}\ w(Y), a(X,Y)\}$.) They correspond to the same monotonic models as $H_1$ and $H_2$. We just added one of the monotonic consequences of $B$ to the body of the hypotheses, an addition that can always be made without affecting the stable models of a program. □

## 4 Discussion and Related Work

The results shown do actually apply to other ILP settings, as far as they use LP semantics for which stable models is a conservative extension.

This characterization can be understood as a basis on which alternative techniques for induction can be defined. For example, it would be interesting to find more efficient characterizations, in the line E-IE [5] or NM-IE [8] work on other settings, to reduce the search for solutions. Besides most of the work on ILP to identify the most general solution, or other criteria for preferred solution, will be worth in this new domain.

This characterization extends the proposal of NM-IE [8], characterizing induction, in general, for normal logic programs, including, e.g. from contradictory background knowledge, contradictory hypothesis. It also clarifies some of the results in [7] and [1].

Furthermore we identify necessary and sufficient conditions for the existence of solution to induction in normal programs. Recall for instance that the conditions of NM-IE hold on Example 2, $B$ has a unique stable, $H$ has a unique stable, including the $H$ solution. But there is no $H$ by the theoretical method (neither by the algorithm) in NM-IE because all of them lead to contradictory $B \cup H$. (Consider $B \cup \{not\ L\} = B \cup \{not\ p \leftarrow\}$ there is only one stable (the same as for $B$), $\{q\}$. The rules this stable is counter-model are the four tentative solutions in that example.)

Finally, induction from several sets of examples is defined and characterized.

### Acknowledgements

This research is partially supported by Government of Spain grant PB97-0228.

## References

1. M. Bain and S. Muggleton. Nonmonotonic learning. In S. Muggleton, editor, *Inductive Logic Programming*, pages 145–161. Academic Press, 1992.
2. Michael Gelfond and Vladimir Lifschitz. The stable model semantics for logic programming. In R. Kowalski and K. Bowen, editors, *Logic Programming: Proc. of the Fifth Int'l Conf. and Symp.*, pages 1070–1080, 1988.
3. W. Marek and M. Truszczynski. *Nonmonotonic Logic – Context-Dependent Reasoning.* Series Artificial Intelligence, Springer-Verlag, 1993.
4. S. Muggleton. Inverse entailment and Progol. *New Generation Computing*, 13:245–286, 1995.
5. S. Muggleton. Completing inverse entailment. In *Proc. of the 8th International Workshop on Inductive Logic Programming, ILP 98, LNAI 1446*, pages 245–249, 1998.
6. Ilkka Niemelä and Patrick Simons. Smodels - an implementation of the stable model and well-founded semantics for normal logic programs. In *Proc. of the 4th International Conference on Logic Programming and Nonmonotonic Reasoning, LPNMR 97, LNAI 1265*, pages 420–429, 1997.
7. C. Sakama. Some properties of inverse resolution in normal logic programs. In *Proc. of the 9th International Workshop on Inductive Logic Programming, ILP 99, LNAI 1634*, pages 279–290, 1999.
8. C. Sakama. Inverse entailment in nonmonotonic logic programs. In *Proc. of the 10th International Conference on Inductive Logic Programming, ILP 00, LNAI 1866*, pages 209–224, 2000.

# Application of Pruning Techniques for Propositional Learning to Progol

Tomonobu Ozaki[1] and Koichi Furukawa[2]

[1] Keio Research Institute at SFC.
[2] Graduate School of Media and Governance, Keio University.
5322 Endo, Fujisawa, Kanagawa, 252-8520, Japan
{tozaki,furukawa}@sfc.keio.ac.jp
http://bruch.sfc.keio.ac.jp/

**Abstract.** Since learning with Inductive Logic Programming (ILP) can be regarded as the search problem through the hypotheses space, it is essential to reduce the search space in order to improve the efficiency. In the propositional learning framework, an efficient admissible search algorithm called OPUS (Optimized Pruning for Unordered Search) has been developed. OPUS employed the effective pruning techniques for unordered search and succeeded in improving the efficiency. In this paper, we propose an application of OPUS to an ILP system Progol. However, because of the difference of representation language, it is not applicable to ILP directly. We make the conditions clear under which the pruning techniques in OPUS can be applied in the framework of Progol. In addition, we propose a new pruning criterion, which can be regarded as inclusive pruning. Experiments are conducted to assess the effectiveness of the proposed algorithms. The results show that the proposed algorithms reduce the number of candidate hypotheses to be evaluated as well as the computational time for a certain class of problems.

## 1 Introduction

Inductive Logic Programming (ILP)[17,6,20] employs predicate logic as its representation language, so that it can handle structural data and use background knowledge, whereas other propositional learner cannot or hardly do. For these reasons, ILP has been recognized as one of the most advanced technologies in the area of Data Mining and Knowledge Discovery in Databases recently[14,8].

However, ILP usually needs enormous computational time to obtain the results from a huge amount of data appearing in such problems as Data Mining. In order to resolve this drawback and to make ILP more practical, we need more efficient algorithms. Several kinds of techniques have been developed to overcome this problem. These include: pre and post pruning[10,11,12], application of Genetic Algorithm[26], probabilistic search[31], best-bound search in branch and bound method[24], introducing sampling techniques[30,28], integration with database management systems[1,4,23], efficient hypotheses evaluation[2,3,25,22], parallel implementation[21,15,9], and so on.

C. Rouveirol and M. Sebag (Eds.): ILP 2001, LNAI 2157, pp. 206–219, 2001.

Since learning with ILP can be regarded as the search problem, reduction of the search space as well as efficient hypotheses evaluation is essential in order to improve the efficiency. Inverse Entailment[18,36] is one of the most effective methods to reduce the search space. It computes the most specific hypothesis (MSH) that bounds the search space before search begins.

In the propositional learning framework, an efficient search algorithm called OPUS (Optimized Pruning for Unordered Search)[33,34] has been developed and succeeded in improving the efficiency. Note that both OPUS and Progol[18] are designed for the exhaustive and admissible search.

In this paper, we propose an application of OPUS to Progol. We consider the applicability of pruning criteria in OPUS. Since it is not possible to apply them directly because of the difference of representation languages, we give the condition under which these criteria can be applied to Progol. Furthermore, we propose a new pruning criterion called negative cover neutral inclusion, which can be regarded as a kind of inclusive pruning.

This paper is organized as follows. In section 2, we give a brief summary of OPUS and consider the relationship between OPUS and Progol. In section 3, we show the conditions under which the pruning techniques in OPUS can be applied to Progol. In addition, we propose a new pruning criterion. Experimental results are shown in section 4, and we conclude our paper and discuss future work in section 5.

## 2 Hypothesis Search in OPUS and Progol

In this section, we first give a brief summary of OPUS and then consider the similarity and difference of search in OPUS and that in Progol.

### 2.1 Brief Introduction of OPUS

OPUS (Optimized Pruning for Unordered Search)[33] is a best-bound search algorithm in branch and bound method, which enables efficient admissible search through the search space for unordered search. Unordered search means that the search problem for which the order of application of search operators, *i.e.* refinement operator[27] in case of ILP, is not significant. OPUS has succeeded in improving the efficiency in the propositional classification framework[34], and recently it has been applied to association rule mining under some restricted conditions[35].

There are two versions of OPUS, OPUS$^O$ and OPUS$^S$. OPUS$^O$ is designed for finding the best hypothesis through the search space. On the other hand, OPUS$^S$ is designed for obtaining all hypotheses which satisfy with some evaluation criteria. In this paper, we focus on OPUS$^O$ only. Henceforth we denote OPUS$^O$ as OPUS for the sake of simplicity.

We show the simplified version of OPUS algorithm in Fig. 1. While the original algorithm[34] contains five kinds of pruning techniques, this simplified algorithm mentions only three which we apply to Progol in this paper.

1. Put the start node $s$ on a list $OPEN$ of unexpanded nodes. Set $s.active$ to the set of all operators, $o_1, o_2, \ldots o_n$. Set $BEST$, the best node examined so far, to $s$.
2. If $OPEN$ is empty, return $BEST$.
3. Remove from $OPEN$ the node $n$, that maximized $Optimistic(n)$.
4. Initialize to $n.active$ a set containing those operators that are still under consideration, called $CUR$.
5. Initialize to $\{\}$ a set of nodes, called $NEW$, that will contain the descendants of $n$ that are not pruned.
6. For every operator $o$ in $n.active$
   (a) Generate $n'$ by application of $o$ to $n$. Set $n'.op$ to $o$.
   (b) If $value(n') > value(BEST)$
      Set $Best$ to $n'$. Remove from $OPEN$ all nodes $x$ such that $optimistic(x) \leq value(BEST)$. (application of optimistic pruning)
   (c) If $optimistic(n') > value(BEST)$ and $neg(n') \subset neg(n)$
      Add $n'$ to $NEW$.
   else
      Remove $n'.op$ from $CUR$. (application of optimistic pruning and negative cover neutral pruning)
7. For every node $n'$ in $NEW$
   (a) If there is another node $x$ in $NEW$ such that $neg(x) \subseteq neg(n')$ and $pos(x) \supseteq neg(n')$
      Remove $n'$ from $NEW$. Remove $n'.op$ from $CUR$. (application of relative cover pruning).
8. For every node $n'$ in $NEW$, selecting each time the node that minimizes $optimistic(n')$,
   (a) Remove $n'.op$ from $CUR$
   (b) If $optimistic(n') > value(BEST)$,
      Set $n'.active$ to $CUR$. Add $n'$ to $OPEN$.
9. Go to step 2.

$value(n)$ denotes the evaluation value of $n$, $optimistic(n)$ denotes the optimistic value of $n$, $neg(n)$ and $pos(n)$ denote the set of negative and positive examples covered by $n$, respectively.

**Fig. 1.** Simplified Version of OPUS Algorithm

The search efficiency of OPUS is achieved by several effective pruning techniques as well as the utilization of the operators to be applied to the current hypothesis. All of the pruning rules in OPUS, which include not only exclusive pruning but also inclusive pruning, are admissible for unordered search under some evaluation function [34]. Exclusive pruning prunes hypotheses which have some search operator, whereas inclusive one prunes those which do not have any search operator. OPUS gathers all of the possible search operators before search. During search, each hypothesis $n$ maintains a set of operators $n.active$ that can be applied for further specialization in the search space below $n$. By utilizing the operators in $n.active$, OPUS realizes the unordered search while avoiding the duplicated generation of the same hypotheses. Furthermore, OPUS uses these operators to reconstruct search space. Hypotheses which have less optimistic value have higher probability to be pruned, where *optimistic value* is the upper bound of the evaluation value of the descendants of the hypothesis. OPUS puts more operators for those hypotheses having less optimistic value to accelerate the pruning (step 8 in Fig. 1).

## 2.2 Comparison between OPUS and Progol

Both of the search in OPUS and $A^*$-like search in Progol are exhaustive and admissible searches based on branch and bound method. While OPUS gathers all possible search operators before search, Progol constructs MSH. This similarity suggests the applicability of OPUS to Progol.

Other than representation languages, the main difference between OPUS and Progol is how to traverse the search space. While OPUS employs unordered search, Progol employs fixed-order search in which the order of literals to be added are predefined. In Progol, the order of literals in MSH are fixed before the search and each candidate hypothesis has an indicate variable $k$. Progol adds $k$th literal in MSH to the hypothesis having $k$ as indicate variable if possible. The parent hypothesis replaces its indicate variable by $k + 1$, and the newly generated hypotheses also have $k + 1$ as their indicate variable. In this way, all combination of literals in MSH are considered.

We show an example of the search tree in Progol in Fig. 2. In this example, a hypothesis "p(A):- a(A),b(A,B)." will be generated by adding b(A,B) to p(A):-a(A). If the order of literals in MSH are different, the same hypothesis will be generated by different manner. For example, if MSH was p(A):-b(A,B),a(A),c(A),d(B)., then a(A) would be added to p(A):-b(A,B). This observation shows that there are some parts in search space of Progol in which the order of literals to be added is not significant, and thus to which we can apply the OPUS's unordered search. In order to introduce unordered search to Progol, as OPUS does, we associate each candidate hypothesis with a set of literals in MSH to be added for further refinement, instead of the indicate variable. In this paper, we regard MSH as the set of literals and do not consider variable-splitting in order to make the discussion simple. But the introduction of variable-splitting is straight forward.

We now consider the difference of pruning effects between unordered and fixed-order search. Suppose that a hypothesis "p(A):- a(A)." is pruned by optimistic pruning in Fig. 2. The optimistic pruning prunes the hypotheses whose optimistic value is less than or equal to the evaluation value of the best hypothesis. In this case, Progol prunes all hypotheses which is more specific than p(A):-a(A). Now, suppose that a hypothesis "p(A):-c(A)." is pruned. In this case, no hypothesis except p(A):-c(A) itself is pruned even if there are some hypotheses which are more specific than p(A):-c(A). This difference depends on the order of literals in MSH, thus the order is important for effective pruning in Progol. However, it is difficult to know which literal is useful for pruning a priori.

OPUS realizes the pruning by simply removing an operator from the operators of hypotheses, so that the effects of pruning are basically independent of the order of application of search operators. By introducing unordered search to

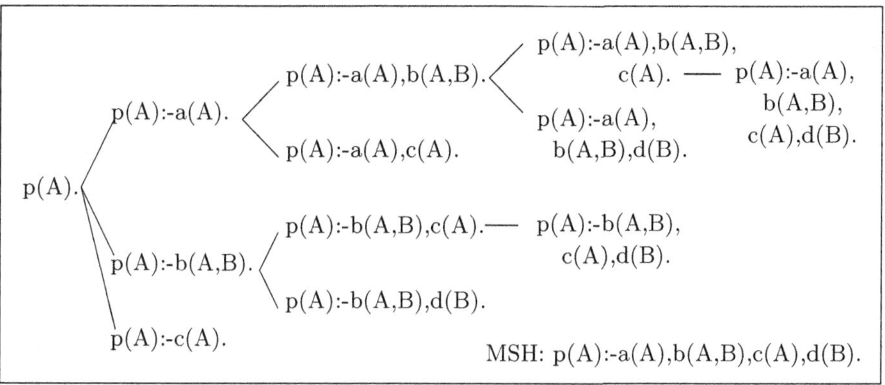


**Fig. 2.** An example of search tree of Progol

Progol, we can incorporate the effective pruning mechanism into Progol, which is basically independent of the order of literals in MSH.

## 3 Application of OPUS's Pruning to Progol

In this section, we first introduce some terminology used later in this section. Then we show the conditions under which the two pruning criteria in OPUS, *Negative Cover Neutral Pruning* and *Relative Cover Pruning*, can be applied to Progol. A new pruning criterion is also discussed.

Given a hypothesis $H$, $pos(H)$ and $neg(H)$ denote the set of positive and negative examples covered by $H$, respectively. $|H|$ denotes the number of literals in the body of $H$. $f(H)$ is the evaluation value of $H$. $H.active$ denotes the set of literals which $H$ maintains for further refinement. $V(\alpha)$ denotes the set of all variables appearing in a set of literals $\alpha$. We treat a clause as a set of literals. Given a clause $C$ and a literal $L \notin C$, $V^-(L, C)$ denotes $V(\{L\}) \setminus V(C)$, *i.e.* local variables to $L$. $Link(L, H)$ denotes the set of all variables in $H$ which appear in the variable chains from the head of $H$ to $L$. For example, $Link(s(D, E), p(A) :- q(A, B, C), r(B, D).) = \{A, B, D\}$.

In this paper, we assume that the evaluation function satisfies the *restricted monotonicity*[24].

**Definition 1.** ([24]) Let $H_1$ and $H_2$ be candidate hypotheses, $p_i$,$n_i$ be the number of positive and negative examples covered by $H_i$, respectively. Let $c_i$ be the number of literals in the body of $H_i$. Then it is said that the evaluation function $f$ satisfies the *restricted monotonicity* if the following condition holds.

If $p_2 \leq p_1$, $n_1 \leq n_2$, and $c_1 \leq c_2$ then $f(H_1) \geq f(H_2)$.

### 3.1 Application of Negative Cover Neutral Pruning

The negative cover neutral pruning rule in OPUS is given as follows.

**Negative cover neutral pruning in OPUS[34]:** For any node (*i.e.* candidate hypothesis in case of ILP) $n$, and an operator (*i.e.* literal) $o \in n.active$, if $neg(n) = neg(n \wedge o)$ then prune all potential solutions (*i.e.* candidate hypotheses) reached via application of $o$ from the search tree below $n$.

In propositional learning framework, if $neg(n) = neg(n \wedge o)$, then $neg(n \wedge \alpha) = neg(n \wedge o \wedge \alpha)$ holds, where $\alpha$ is some subset of $n.active \setminus \{o\}$. Furthermore, $pos(n \wedge o \wedge \alpha) \subseteq pos(n \wedge \alpha)$ holds because $n \wedge \alpha$ is more general than or equal to $n \wedge o \wedge \alpha$. Consequently, $f(n \wedge \alpha) \geq f(n \wedge o \wedge \alpha)$ holds.

In case of ILP, $neg(n \wedge \alpha) = neg(n \wedge o \wedge \alpha)$ does not hold in general, even if $neg(n) = neg(n \wedge o)$. Therefore, in order to apply this pruning rule to Progol, we need some conditions under which the above relation holds. The condition under which negative cover neutral pruning can be applied to ILP is proposed in [24]. Our condition can be regarded as a variant of that in [24].

**Negative cover neutral pruning in Progol:** Let $H$ be a candidate hypothesis, $L \in H.active$ be a literal, $H'$ be a candidate hypothesis generated by adding $L$ to $H$, $H'.active$ be $H.active \setminus \{L\}$, and $\alpha$ be a subset of $H'.active$. If the evaluation function satisfies the restricted monotonicity, and $H$ and $L$ satisfy the following conditions, then $f(H \wedge \alpha) \geq f(H' \wedge \alpha)$ holds. Thus we can prune all descendants of $H$ which has $L$.

1. $neg(H) = neg(H')$
2. any negative example covered by $H$ is derived with a unique substitution for variables in $Link(L, H) \cap V(H'.active)$
3. $V^-(L, H) \cap V(H'.active) = \emptyset$

*Proof.* From the first and second condition, a negative example derived from $H$ with a substitution for variables in $Link(L, H) \cap V(H'.active)$ has also to be derived from $H'$ with only the same substitution for these variables. From the third condition, $V(H) \cap V(\alpha) = V(H') \cap V(\alpha)$ holds. Therefore, a negative example derived from $H' \wedge \alpha$ with a substitution is also derived from $H \wedge \alpha$ with only the same substitution. Consequently, the equation $neg(H \wedge \alpha) = neg(H' \wedge \alpha)$ holds. Furthermore the equations, $pos(H \wedge \alpha) \supseteq pos(H' \wedge \alpha)$ and $|H \wedge \alpha| < |H' \wedge \alpha|$, hold. Thus $f(H \wedge \alpha) \geq f(H' \wedge \alpha)$ holds from the definition of the restricted monotonicity. □

Note that we consider only the substitution for the variables which connect to $L$ and also appear in $H'.active$, because other variables have no effect on the difference of the derivations of a negative example by $H \wedge \alpha$ and $H' \wedge \alpha$. From the same reason, we allow any local variables in $L$ if they do not appear in $H'.active$.

### 3.2 Application of Relative Cover Pruning

We give the relative cover pruning rule in OPUS as follows.

**Relative cover pruning in OPUS[34]:** For any node $n$ and an operator $o \in n.active$, if there exists another operator $a \in n.active$ such that $neg(n \wedge a) \subseteq neg(n \wedge o)$ and $pos(n \wedge o) \subseteq pos(n \wedge a)$ then prune all potential solutions reached via application of $o$ from the search tree below $n$.

In the propositional framework, if $neg(n \wedge a) \subseteq neg(n \wedge o)$ holds, the following two equations hold: (1) $neg(n \wedge a \wedge \alpha) \subseteq neg(n \wedge o \wedge \alpha)$ where $\alpha$ is a subset of $n.active \setminus \{n, o\}$, and (2) $neg(n \wedge a) = neg(n \wedge a \wedge o)$. The same equations also hold in case of positive examples. Here we divide all descendants of $n$ into two kinds. The formers do not have $a$ and the latters have. From the first equation, by replacing $o$ by $a$, we can build another hypothesis $n \wedge a \wedge \alpha$ which covers more positive and less negative examples than $n \wedge o \wedge \alpha$ does. Then, because $f(n \wedge a \wedge \alpha) \geq f(n \wedge o \wedge \alpha)$ holds, we can prune $n \wedge o \wedge \alpha$. From the second equation, we can prune $n \wedge a \wedge o$ by applying negative cover neutral pruning. Consequently, we can prune all descendants of $n$ which has $o$.

However, in case of ILP, the above equations do not hold in general. In addition, we have to consider the variable chain when replacing $o$ by $a$.

**Relative cover pruning in Progol:** Let $H$ be a candidate hypothesis, $L_1 \in H.active$ and $L_2 \in H.active \setminus \{L_1\}$ be literals, $H_1$ and $H_2$ be candidate hypotheses generated by adding $L_1$ and $L_2$ to $H$, respectively. Let $H_1.active$ be $H.active \setminus \{L_1\}$, $H_2.active$ be $H.active \setminus \{L_2\}$, $\alpha \subseteq H.active \setminus \{L_1, L_2\}$ be a set of literals. If the evaluation function satisfies the restricted monotonicity, and the following conditions are satisfied, then the equations $f(H_1 \wedge \alpha) \geq f(H_2 \wedge \alpha)$ and $f(H_1 \wedge \alpha) \geq f(H_1 \wedge L_2 \wedge \alpha)$ hold. Thus we can prune all descendants of $H$ which has $L_2$.

1. $neg(H_1) \subseteq neg(H_2)$ and $pos(H_2) \subseteq pos(H_1)$
2. any example covered by $H$ is derived with a unique substitution for variables in $Link(L_1, H) \cup Link(L_2, H)$
3. $V^-(L_1, H) \cap V(H1.active) = \emptyset$ and $V^-(L_2, H) \cap V(H2.active) = \emptyset$

*Proof.* From the second and third condition, any example covered by both of $H_1$ and $H_2$ has to be covered either by both of $H_1 \wedge \alpha$ and $H_2 \wedge \alpha$ or by none of them. Note that $V(H_1) \cap V(\alpha) = V(H_2) \cap V(\alpha)$ holds from the third condition. Also, from the first condition, $neg(H_1 \wedge \alpha) \subseteq neg(H_2 \wedge \alpha)$ and $pos(H_2 \wedge \alpha) \subseteq pos(H_1 \wedge \alpha)$ hold. Furthermore, the variable chains in $H_2 \wedge \alpha$ do not break even if we replace $L_2$ by $L_1$ from the third condition. Therefore, the equation $f(H_1 \wedge \alpha) \geq f(H_2 \wedge \alpha)$ holds from the definition of restricted monotonicity.

Besides, any negative example covered by both of $H_1$ and $H_2$ is also covered by $H_1 \wedge L_2$ from the second and third condition. Consequently, we can apply negative cover neutral pruning because the following three conditions hold: $neg(H_1) = neg(H_1 \wedge L_2)$; any negative example covered by $H_1$ is derived with a unique substitution for variables in $Link(L_2, H_1)$ ($\supseteq Link(L_2, H1) \cap V(H_1.active \setminus \{L_2\})$); and $V^-(L_2, H_1) \cap V(H_1.active \setminus \{L_2\}) = \emptyset$. Therefore, $f(H_1 \wedge \alpha) \geq f(H_1 \wedge L_2 \wedge \alpha)$ holds. □

### 3.3 Negative Cover Neutral Inclusion

Negative cover neutral pruning requires that local variables in literal $L$ which is added to a hypothesis $H$ do not appear in $H.active \setminus \{L\}$, the set of literals to be added for further refinement. If $L$ has some local variables which appear in $H.active \setminus \{L\}$, we can divide the subsets of $H.active \setminus \{L\}$, referred to as $\alpha$, into two kinds: those which do not have any literal including local variables in $L$, and those which have such a literal. If $H$ and $L$ satisfy the conditions of negative cover neutral pruning except the last condition, we can prune all descendants of $H \wedge L$ which are generated by using the former kind of $\alpha$ because $neg(H \wedge \alpha) = neg(H \wedge L \wedge \alpha)$ holds. We call this pruning negative cover neutral inclusion.

We summarize this pruning formally as follows.

**Negative cover neutral inclusion in Progol:** Let $H$ be a candidate hypothesis, $L \in H.active$ be a literal, $H'$ be a candidate hypothesis generated by adding $L$ to $H$, $H'.active$ be $H.active \setminus \{L\}$, and $\alpha$ be a subset of $H'.active$ such that $V^-(L, H) \cap V(\alpha) = \emptyset$. If the evaluation function satisfies the restricted monotonicity, and $H$ and $L$ satisfy the following conditions, then $f(H \wedge \alpha) \geq f(H' \wedge \alpha)$ holds. Thus we can prune all descendants of $H$ which has $L$ and $\alpha$

1. $neg(H) = neg(H')$
2. any negative example covered by $H$ is derived with a unique substitution for variables in $Link(L, H) \cap V(H'.active)$

*Proof.* The proof is directly derived from the proof of negative cover neutral pruning. □

## 4 Experiments

We implemented the proposed algorithms and developed the prototype system based on Progol's framework in SICStus Prolog. Current implementation can only take the determinate background knowledge, and can not handle variable-splitting. As the evaluation function, we adopt that of Progol which satisfies the restricted monotonicity.

We used four data sets to examine the effectiveness of the proposed algorithms: (1)Illegal positions in the KRK endgame (referred to as *KRKI*)[16], (2)Email classification (*Email*)[29], (3)Respiration during musical performance (*Respiration*)[13], and (4)Finite element mesh design (*Mesh*)[7]. All of these data sets have only determinate background knowledge (we used the determinate version of background knowledge for *Mesh*). *Email*, *Respiration* and *Mesh* have multiple classes. For *Email* and *Respiration*, one class was given as positive examples and remaining classes were given as negative examples. For *Mesh*, we learned each class by using the corresponding data set provided in the original data.

In the experiments, we compared the number of generated candidate hypotheses and search time. We show the experimental results in Table. 1–Table.

4. In each table, *hyp* and *time* denote the number of generated candidate hypotheses and search time (sec.), respectively. *Fixed*, *Unordered*, *Negative*, *Relative*, *Inclusion*, *All* denote fixed-order search, unordered search, negative cover neutral pruning, relative cover pruning, negative cover neutral inclusion and all pruning, respectively. While *Email* has 84 classes, because of the space limitation, we show the results of only those 20 classes which took more computational time in fixed-order search. *KRKI* and *Email* have no output variable, so that negative cover neutral inclusion was not applied. All of these except for *Fixed* adopt unordered search and we use the original pruning criteria in Progol, *i.e.* optimistic pruning, in every case. Each number in the parentheses of *Unordered* column is the ratio to *Fixed* and the others are the ratio to *Unordered*.

**Table 1.** Experimental results of *KRKI* Data

| | *Fixed* | *Unordered* | *Negative* | *Relative* | *All* | *All/Fixed* |
|---|---|---|---|---|---|---|
| *hyp* | 1092 | 851 (0.78) | 210 (0.25) | 210 (0.25) | 210 (0.25) | 0.19 |
| *time* | 95.3 | 72.9 (0.77) | 13.2 (0.18) | 13.2 (0.18) | 13.2 (0.18) | 0.14 |

**Table 2.** Experimental results of *Respiration* Data

| | *Fixed* | *Unordered* | *Negative* | *Relative* | *Inclusion* | *All* | *All/Fixed* |
|---|---|---|---|---|---|---|---|
| | expiration | | | | | | |
| *hyp* | 3022 | 2601 (0.86) | 2546 (0.98) | 2421 (0.93) | 2158 (0.83) | 1958 (0.75) | 0.65 |
| *time* | 19.8 | 17.6 (0.89) | 17.7 (1.01) | 16.3 (0.93) | 14.9 (0.85) | 14.0 (0.80) | 0.71 |
| | inspiration | | | | | | |
| *hyp* | 4771 | 4136 (0.87) | 3923 (0.95) | 3790 (0.92) | 3322 (0.80) | 3003 (0.73) | 0.63 |
| *time* | 32.2 | 28.2 (0.87) | 27.7 (0.98) | 26.0 (0.92) | 23.2 (0.82) | 21.9 (0.78) | 0.68 |
| | no | | | | | | |
| *hyp* | 2769 | 2297 (0.83) | 2188 (0.95) | 2097 (0.91) | 1940 (0.84) | 1759 (0.77) | 0.64 |
| *time* | 18.6 | 16.0 (0.86) | 15.5 (0.97) | 14.5 (0.91) | 13.9 (0.87) | 12.9 (0.81) | 0.69 |

As a whole, unordered search reduces the number of generated candidate hypotheses and the search time. For *KRKI* data, both of negative cover neutral and relative cover pruning work very effectively. We believe that the results of negative cover neutral and relative cover pruning became the same by accident. Negative cover neutral inclusion works well in *Respiration* data. Negative cover neutral and relative cover pruning also improve the efficiency in most classes for *Email* data. The results of *Mesh* data show the effectiveness of the combination of pruning.

There are some cases where *Unordered* took more time than *Fixed*, *e.g.* class4 in *Mesh*, and *Negative* and *Relative* took more time than *Unordered*, *e.g.* class4 and class5 in *Mesh*, respectively. We think the reason is the overheads for checking the conditions for pruning, as well as the garbage collection. And, we think the difference in speed-ups for different domains and different classes in the same domain comes from the characteristics of the data sets.

**Table 3.** Experimental results of *Email* Data

| class | | *Fixed* | *Unordered* | *Negative* | *Relative* | *All* | *All/Fixed* |
|---|---|---|---|---|---|---|---|
| c16 | *hyp* | 8682 | 5605 (0.65) | 1408 (0.25) | 414 (0.07) | 386 (0.07) | 0.04 |
| | *time* | 1604.5 | 1055.7 (0.66) | 247.1 (0.23) | 69.0 (0.07) | 64.0 (0.06) | 0.04 |
| c56 | *hyp* | 1737 | 990 (0.57) | 377 (0.38) | 193 (0.19) | 187 (0.19) | 0.11 |
| | *time* | 312.9 | 180.5 (0.58) | 64.9 (0.36) | 31.9 (0.18) | 30.8 (0.17) | 0.10 |
| c09 | *hyp* | 1611 | 1101 (0.68) | 475 (0.43) | 198 (0.18) | 191 (0.17) | 0.12 |
| | *time* | 293.7 | 204.5 (0.70) | 84.5 (0.41) | 33.4 (0.16) | 32.1 (0.16) | 0.11 |
| c28 | *hyp* | 1557 | 657 (0.42) | 466 (0.71) | 299 (0.46) | 299 (0.46) | 0.19 |
| | *time* | 274.4 | 113.9 (0.41) | 79.3 (0.70) | 50.0 (0.44) | 50.1 (0.44) | 0.18 |
| c17 | *hyp* | 1421 | 659 (0.46) | 425 (0.64) | 317 (0.48) | 317 (0.48) | 0.22 |
| | *time* | 247.3 | 114.4 (0.46) | 72.2 (0.63) | 53.2 (0.46) | 53.2 (0.46) | 0.22 |
| c12 | *hyp* | 1188 | 458 (0.39) | 327 (0.71) | 169 (0.37) | 162 (0.35) | 0.14 |
| | *time* | 212.7 | 79.8 (0.38) | 54.6 (0.68) | 27.2 (0.34) | 26.9 (0.34) | 0.13 |
| c53 | *hyp* | 1162 | 301 (0.26) | 235 (0.78) | 170 (0.56) | 170 (0.56) | 0.15 |
| | *time* | 208.9 | 53.3 (0.26) | 40.9 (0.77) | 29.2 (0.55) | 29.2 (0.55) | 0.14 |
| c57 | *hyp* | 1119 | 420 (0.38) | 316 (0.75) | 113 (0.27) | 113 (0.27) | 0.10 |
| | *time* | 199.7 | 73.8 (0.37) | 54.4 (0.74) | 18.3 (0.25) | 18.3 (0.25) | 0.09 |
| c05 | *hyp* | 652 | 169 (0.26) | 106 (0.63) | 62 (0.37) | 61 (0.36) | 0.09 |
| | *time* | 125.7 | 30.0 (0.24) | 18.0 (0.60) | 10.1 (0.34) | 9.9 (0.33) | 0.08 |
| c22 | *hyp* | 612 | 347 (0.57) | 281 (0.81) | 176 (0.51) | 175 (0.50) | 0.29 |
| | *time* | 108.5 | 60.3 (0.56) | 47.9 (0.79) | 29.5 (0.49) | 29.4 (0.49) | 0.27 |
| c04 | *hyp* | 595 | 198 (0.33) | 167 (0.84) | 71 (0.36) | 71 (0.36) | 0.12 |
| | *time* | 107.8 | 34.3 (0.32) | 28.6 (0.83) | 11.6 (0.34) | 11.6 (0.34) | 0.11 |
| c52 | *hyp* | 591 | 248 (0.42) | 214 (0.86) | 132 (0.53) | 131 (0.53) | 0.22 |
| | *time* | 102.2 | 42.1 (0.41) | 35.3 (0.84) | 21.1 (0.50) | 20.9 (0.50) | 0.20 |
| c36 | *hyp* | 583 | 204 (0.35) | 181 (0.89) | 109 (0.53) | 109 (0.53) | 0.19 |
| | *time* | 101.4 | 34.4 (0.34) | 30.2 (0.88) | 17.6 (0.51) | 17.6 (0.51) | 0.17 |
| c59 | *hyp* | 539 | 102 (0.19) | 101 (0.99) | 75 (0.74) | 75 (0.74) | 0.14 |
| | *time* | 96.1 | 17.3 (0.18) | 17.1 (0.99) | 12.6 (0.73) | 12.5 (0.72) | 0.13 |
| c06 | *hyp* | 513 | 651 (1.27) | 620 (0.95) | 111 (0.17) | 111 (0.17) | 0.22 |
| | *time* | 91.7 | 117.1 (1.28) | 110.9 (0.95) | 19.0 (0.16) | 19.0 (0.16) | 0.21 |
| c20 | *hyp* | 513 | 149 (0.29) | 149 (1.00) | 149 (1.00) | 149 (1.00) | 0.29 |
| | *time* | 88.4 | 27.8 (0.31) | 24.3 (0.87) | 24.3 (0.88) | 24.3 (0.88) | 0.28 |
| c85 | *hyp* | 460 | 172 (0.37) | 157 (0.91) | 102 (0.59) | 102 (0.59) | 0.22 |
| | *time* | 80.4 | 29.2 (0.36) | 26.4 (0.90) | 16.7 (0.57) | 16.6 (0.57) | 0.21 |
| c10 | *hyp* | 446 | 238 (0.53) | 224 (0.94) | 112 (0.47) | 112 (0.47) | 0.25 |
| | *time* | 78.5 | 41.3 (0.53) | 38.6 (0.94) | 18.8 (0.46) | 18.8 (0.46) | 0.24 |
| c43 | *hyp* | 444 | 342 (0.77) | 214 (0.63) | 122 (0.36) | 119 (0.35) | 0.27 |
| | *time* | 76.3 | 59.3 (0.78) | 35.6 (0.60) | 19.7 (0.33) | 18.9 (0.32) | 0.25 |
| c02 | *hyp* | 412 | 115 (0.28) | 101 (0.88) | 69 (0.60) | 69 (0.60) | 0.17 |
| | *time* | 73.0 | 19.4 (0.27) | 16.9 (0.87) | 11.2 (0.58) | 11.3 (0.58) | 0.15 |

**Table 4.** Experimental results of *Mesh* Data

| | *Fixed* | *Unordered* | *Negative* | *Relative* | *Inclusion* | *All* | All/ Fixed |
|---|---|---|---|---|---|---|---|
| class 1 | | | | | | | |
| *hyp* | 222039 | 199751 (0.90) | 188166 (0.94) | 199501 (1.00) | 177136 (0.89) | 160944 (0.81) | 0.72 |
| *time* | 34254 | 31280 (0.91) | 29020 (0.93) | 32003 (1.02) | 26145 (0.84) | 22616 (0.72) | 0.66 |
| class 2 | | | | | | | |
| *hyp* | 480007 | 475217 (0.99) | 458922 (0.97) | 474409 (1.00) | 448665 (0.94) | 405955 (0.85) | 0.85 |
| *time* | 79056 | 79885 (1.01) | 76388 (0.96) | 80483 (1.01) | 69041 (0.86) | 61087 (0.76) | 0.77 |
| class 3 | | | | | | | |
| *hyp* | 314054 | 303754 (0.97) | 295625 (0.97) | 301913 (0.99) | 279749 (0.92) | 262783 (0.87) | 0.84 |
| *time* | 47823 | 47473 (0.99) | 46514 (0.98) | 48285 (1.02) | 41329 (0.87) | 38686 (0.81) | 0.81 |
| class 4 | | | | | | | |
| *hyp* | 209686 | 208282 (0.99) | 206628 (0.99) | 208012 (1.00) | 193901 (0.93) | 190247 (0.91) | 0.91 |
| *time* | 35271 | 36003 (1.02) | 36401 (1.01) | 35790 (0.99) | 31437 (0.87) | 29551 (0.82) | 0.84 |
| class 5 | | | | | | | |
| *hyp* | 110948 | 91929 (0.83) | 90125 (0.98) | 90242 (0.98) | 87224 (0.95) | 85180 (0.93) | 0.77 |
| *time* | 16393 | 14809 (0.90) | 14723 (0.99) | 15160 (1.02) | 13048 (0.88) | 12435 (0.84) | 0.76 |
| class 6 | | | | | | | |
| *hyp* | 129172 | 122743 (0.95) | 120453 (0.98) | 122312 (1.00) | 113786 (0.93) | 111368 (0.91) | 0.86 |
| *time* | 21748 | 20724 (0.95) | 20556 (0.99) | 21238 (1.02) | 18668 (0.90) | 17859 (0.86) | 0.82 |
| class 7 | | | | | | | |
| *hyp* | 95406 | 82003 (0.86) | 75317 (0.92) | 74795 (0.91) | 59830 (0.73) | 48556 (0.59) | 0.51 |
| *time* | 13932 | 10763 (0.77) | 10208 (0.95) | 10160 (0.94) | 7350 (0.68) | 6249 (0.58) | 0.45 |
| class 8 | | | | | | | |
| *hyp* | 63624 | 51093 (0.80) | 48774 (0.95) | 48669 (0.95) | 42877 (0.84) | 37673 (0.74) | 0.59 |
| *time* | 10651 | 8558 (0.80) | 8237 (0.96) | 8133 (0.95) | 6562 (0.77) | 5749 (0.67) | 0.54 |
| class 9 | | | | | | | |
| *hyp* | 69989 | 57928 (0.83) | 55173 (0.95) | 57322 (0.99) | 52004 (0.90) | 47348 (0.82) | 0.68 |
| *time* | 12506 | 10414 (0.83) | 9843 (0.95) | 10286 (0.99) | 8534 (0.82) | 7768 (0.75) | 0.62 |
| class 10 | | | | | | | |
| *hyp* | 38806 | 27577 (0.71) | 26640 (0.97) | 27511 (1.00) | 19868 (0.72) | 17362 (0.63) | 0.45 |
| *time* | 6556 | 4176 (0.64) | 4041 (0.97) | 4200 (1.01) | 2614 (0.63) | 2351 (0.56) | 0.36 |
| class 11 | | | | | | | |
| *hyp* | 56819 | 50539 (0.89) | 50421 (1.00) | 49587 (0.98) | 45242 (0.90) | 38606 (0.76) | 0.68 |
| *time* | 8015 | 7130 (0.89) | 6962 (0.98) | 7160 (1.00) | 5863 (0.82) | 5037 (0.71) | 0.63 |
| class 12 | | | | | | | |
| *hyp* | 60527 | 49069 (0.81) | 45788 (0.93) | 48569 (0.99) | 41313 (0.84) | 33769 (0.69) | 0.56 |
| *time* | 8689 | 6905 (0.79) | 6217 (0.90) | 6903 (1.00) | 5290 (0.77) | 4335 (0.63) | 0.50 |

However, as a whole, these experimental results show the usefulness of the proposed algorithms.

## 5 Conclusion and Future Work

In this paper, we proposed an application of OPUS to Progol. We pointed out the applicability of the unordered search and showed the conditions under which the pruning techniques in OPUS can be applied in the framework of Progol.

In addition, we proposed a new pruning criterion called negative cover neutral inclusion. Note that the pre-computed MSH acts a crucial role in defining these conditions and pruning criteria.

Our future work includes the implementation of the system which can deal with variable-splitting and non determinate background knowledge. We think the encoding techniques of hypothesis proposed in [26] is useful for handling variable-splitting. In this encording, each candidate hypothesis is represented by an adjacency matrix. When we use this representation for the remaining operators to be applied to the candidate hypothesis, we can handle variable-splitting more directly. It would be expected that, in order to handle non determinate background knowledge, an additional cost is required for checking the uniqueness of substitution for the derivations of examples. However, we believe that this cost could be reduced by using techniques in deductive database[32], such as bottom-up computation, OLDT, relational calculus and so on. We are going to examine the effectiveness of the proposed algorithms by many kinds of data sets including non determinate background knowledge on the new implementation.

Beside, we are planning to apply the proposed algorithms to descriptive ILP systems such as WARMR[5], since OPUS has been applied to association rule mining recently[35].

## References


1. Blockeel, H. and De Raedt, L.: Relational Knowledge Discovery in Databases, *Proc.* of the Sixth International Workshop on Inductive Logic Programming, pp.199-211, 1996.
2. Blockeel, H., Dehaspe, L., Demoen, B., Janssens, G., Ramon, J. and Vandecasteele, H.: Executing query packs in ILP, *Proc.* of the Tenth International Conference on Inductive Logic Programming, pp.60-77, 2000.
3. Blockeel, H., Demoen, B., Janssens, G., Vandecasteele, H. and Van Laer, W.: Two Advanced Transformations for Improving the Efficiency of an ILP System, Cussens,J. and Frisch,A. editors, Tenth International Conference on Inductive Logic Programming, Work-in-Progress Reports, pp.43-59, 2000.
4. Brockhausen, P. and Morik, K.: Direct Access of an ILP Algorithm to a Database Management System, MLnet Sponsored Famiiarization Workshop, Data Mining with Inductive Logic Programming, 1996.
5. Dehaspe, L. and Toivonen, H.: Discovery of frequent datalog patterns, *Data Mining and Knowledge Discovery*, Vol.3, No.1, pp.7-36, 1999.
6. De Raedt, L.: *Advances in Inductive Logic Programming*, IOS Press, Ohmsha, 1996.
7. Dolsak, B. and Muggleton, S.: The application of Inductive Logic Programming to finite element mesh design, In S. Muggleton (ed.), *Inductive Logic Programming*, Academic Press, London, 1992.
8. Džeroski, S.: *Inductive Logic Programming and Knowledge Discovery in Databases*, in U.M.Fayyad, G.Piatetsky-Shapiro, P.Smyth and R.Uthurusamy (eds.), *Advanced in Knowledge Discovery and Data Mining, Chapter 5*, pp.117-152, AAAI Press/ The MIT Press, 1996.

9. Fujita, H., Yagi, N., Furukawa, K. and Ozaki, T.: A New Design and Implementation of Progol by Bottom-up Computation, *Proc.* of the Sixth International Workshop on Inductive Logic Programming, pp.163-174, 1996.
10. Fürnkranz, J.: Pruning Methods for Rule Learning Algorithms, S.Wrobel (ed.) *Proc.* of the Fourth International Workshop on Inductive Logic Programming, pp.321-336, GMD-Studien, Nr.237, 1994.
11. Fürnkranz, J.: Top-down pruning in relational learning. In A.G. Cohn (ed.), *Proc.* of the Eleventh European Conference on Artificial Intelligence (ECAI-94), pp. 453-457, Amsterdam, The Netherlands, John Wiley & Sons, 1994.
12. Fürnkranz, J.: A Tight Integration of Pruning and Learning (Extended Abstract). In N. Lavrac and S. Wrobel (eds.), *Proc.* of the Eighth European Conference on Machine Learning (ECML-95), pp. 291-294, Crete, Greece, 1995.
13. Igarashi, S., Ozaki, T., Ueno, K. and Furukawa, K.: Analysis of respiration during musical performance by ILP, Eleventh International Conference on Inductive Logic Programming, Work-in-Progress Report, 2001.
14. Lavrač, N., Džeroski, S. and Numao, M.: Inductive Logic Programming for Relational Knowledge Discovery, *New Generation Computing*, Vol.17, No.1, pp.3-23, 1999.
15. Matsui, T., Inuzuka, N., Seki, H. and Itoh, H.: Comparison of Three Parallel Implementations of an Induction Algorithm, *Proc.* of the Eighth International Paralle Computing Workshop, pp.181-188, 1998.
16. Muggleton, S. H., Bain, M. E., Hayes-Michie, J. and Michie, D.: An experimental comparison of human and machine learning formalisms, *Proc.* of the Sixth International Workshop on Machine Learning, 1989.
17. Muggleton, S.: Inductive Logic Programming, *New Generation Computing*, Vol.8, No.4, pp.295-317, 1991.
18. Muggleton, S.: Inverse Entailment and Progol, *New Generation Computing*, Vol.13, pp.245-286, 1995.
19. Muggleton, S.H.: Learning stochastic logic programs, *Proc.* of the AAAI 2000 workshop on Learning Statistical Models from Relational Data, AAAI, 2000.
20. Nienhuys-Cheng, S.-H. and De Wolf, R.: *Foundations of Inductive Logic Programming*, Springer, 1997.
21. Ohwada, H., Nishiyama, H. and Mizoguchi, F.: Concurrent Execution of Optimal Hypothesis Search for Inverse Entailment, *Proc.* of the Tenth International Conference on Inductive Logic Programming, pp.165-173, 2000.
22. Ozaki, T., Furukawa, K., Murakami, T., and Ueno, K.: Realizing Progol by Forward Reasoning, *Proc.* of the Seventh International Workshop on Inductive Logic Programming, pp.227-234, 1997.
23. Ozaki, T. and Furukawa, K.: Improving Search Algorithm in Progol integrated with Relational Databases, SIG-FAI/KBS-902, pp.83-88, 1999. (in Japanese)
24. Ohara, K., Babaguchi, N. and Kitahashi, T.: An Efficient Hypothesis Search Algorithm based on Best-Bound Strategy, J. Cussens and A. Frisch (Eds.), Tenth International Conference on Inductive Logic Programming, Work-in-Progress Reports, pp.212-225, 2000.
25. Santos Costa, V., Srinivasan, A. and Camacho, R.: A note on two simple transformations for improving the efficiency of an ILP system, *Proc.* of the Tenth International Workshop on Inductive Logic Programming, pp225-242, 2000.
26. Tamaddoni-Hezhad, A. and Muggleton, S. H.: Searching the subsumption lattice by a genetic algorithm, J. Cussens and A. Frisch (Eds.), *Proc.* of the Tenth International Conference on Inductive Logic Programming, LNAI 1866, pp.243-252, Springer, 2000.

27. Shapiro, E. Y.: Inductive Inference of Theories from Facts, Research Report 192, Department of Computer Science, Yale University, 1981.
28. Sebag, M. and Rouveirol, C.: Tractable induction and classification in FOL, *Proc.* of the Fifteenth International Joint Conference on Artificial Intelligence, pp.888-893, 1997.
29. Shimazu, K. and Furukawa, K.: KDD System, DB-Amp –Design, Implementation and Its Application to an Expert System–, *Journal* of Japanese Society for Artificial Intelligence, Vol.15, No.4, pp.629-637, 2000. (in Japanese)
30. Srinivasan, A.: A study of two sampling methods for analysing large datasets with ILP, Data Mining and Knowledge Discovery, Vol.3, No.1, pp.95-123, 1999.
31. Srinivasan, A.: A study of two probabilistic methods for searching large spaces with ILP, Data Mining and Knowledge Discovery (under review), (http://web.comlab.ox.ac.uk/oucl/work/ashwin.srinivasan/ pubs.html), 2000.
32. Ullman, J. D.: *Principles of Database and Knowledge-base Systems*. Computer Science Press, 1988.
33. Webb, G. I.: OPUS: An Efficient Admissible Algorithm for Unordered Search, *Journal of Artificial Intelligence Research*, Vol.3, pp.431-465, 1995.
34. Webb, G. I.: Inclusive Pruning: A New Class of Pruning Axiom for Unordered Search and its Application to Classification Learning, *Proc.* of the Nineteenth Australian Computer Science Confrence, pp.1-10, Melbourne, January, 1996.
35. Webb, G. I.: Efficient search for association rules, *Proc.* of *KDD-2000*, Bonston, MA, August, 2000.
36. Yamamoto, A.: Which Hypotheses Can Be Found with Inverse Entailment?, *Proc.* of the Seventh International Workshop on Inductive Logic Programming, pp.296-308, 1997.

# Application of ILP to Cardiac Arrhythmia Characterization for Chronicle Recognition

René Quiniou[1], Marie-Odile Cordier[1], Guy Carrault[2], and Feng Wang[2]

[1] IRISA, Campus de Beaulieu, 35042 Rennes Cedex FRANCE,
{Quiniou, Cordier}@irisa.fr
[2] LTSI, Campus de Beaulieu, 35042 Rennes Cedex FRANCE,
{Carrault, Wang}@ltsi3.univ-rennes1.fr

**Abstract.** We propose to use ILP techniques to learn sets of temporally constrained events called chronicles that a monitoring tool will use to detect pathological situations. ICL, a system providing a declarative bias language, was used for the experiments on learning cardiac arrhythmias. We show how to obtain properties, such as compactness, robustness or readability, by varying the learning bias.

## 1 Introduction

In medical domains such as cardiology, intensive care units make use of more and more sophisticated monitoring tools. These tools have improved the surveillance and care of patients suffering from strong disorders. However, many false alarms are still generated and, from our point of view, these tools rely too much on signal processing algorithms. There exists a gap between the understanding level of clinicians and the information displayed by monitoring tools. To be more informative and explicative we think, as Lavrăc et al. [8], that monitoring tools must manipulate more abstract knowledge such as temporal relations between interesting events reflecting the patient's state. We have proposed in [2] to associate signal processing techniques with high-level temporal reasoning for patient monitoring. The first module processes input signals and outputs symbolic attributed events that feed a chronicle recognizer which attempts to detect specific patterns among these events. Chronicles are event patterns which impose temporal constraints among a set of events.

As devising chronicles is not, in general, an easy task, we propose to use machine learning techniques in order to obtain accurate and interesting characterizations of pathological situations from examples of input signals related to disorders that may affect some patient. In the domain of coronary care units, the signals are multi-channel electrocardiograms (ECGs) and the situations to recognize are cardiac arrhythmias. As temporal relations among events are crucial as well as a specification language which can lead to informative explanations, we have chosen to use inductive logic programming (ILP). This is a major difference between Kardio [1] and our own approach. Kardio uses feature-based induction, thus, it can only learn predefined propositional structural relations. Target concepts are represented as first-order formulas in ILP. This makes the rules more

C. Rouveirol and M. Sebag (Eds.): ILP 2001, LNAI 2157, pp. 220–227, 2001.

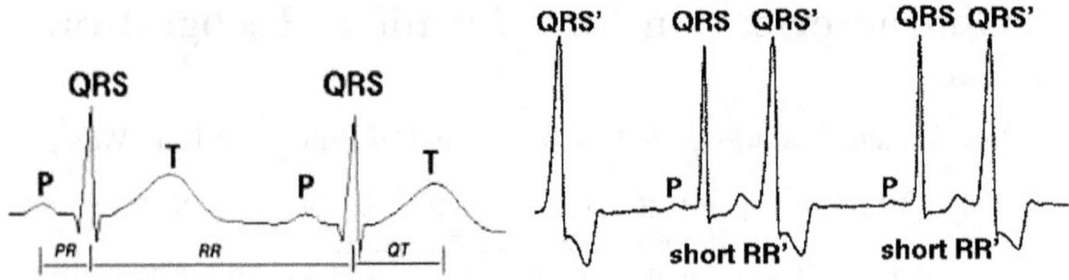


**Fig. 1.** A normal ECG (on the left) and a bigeminy ECG (on the right).

abstract and easier to understand and that is an essential point in our context as tools have to explain their results to users. Kókai et al. [6] proposed to learn attributed grammars for arrhythmia recognition in ECG from elementary curve segments. Their approach relies on grammar refinement which, they say, is not well suited to learning constraints in rules. Also, the learnt grammars specify only one cardiac cycle which is too short to describe recurrent phenomena as cardiac arrhythmias.

In this paper, our goal is to demonstrate that ILP is a powerful and smart technique that makes it relatively easy to learn knowledge adapted to the problem at hand. Precisely, we show how to play with bias specifications in order to learn concept definitions enjoying such different properties as robustness, readability or recognition efficiency. DLAB, the declarative bias language of ICL [12], has reveal quite useful and flexible to achieve this goal. The first section gives some basic knowledge about cardiac arrhythmias. The next section presents the data and learning materials. Next, we describe the results obtained on learning five arrhythmias. Finally, we conclude and give some perspectives to this work.

## 2 Electrocardiograms

The electrocardiogram provides very important cues for cardiac analysis and diagnosis. First of all, they can be recorded easily with non invasive leads that are put at particular locations of the body surface. Second, ECGs can be inspected visually by physicians in order to analyze the ordering and the shape of particular waves which can be related directly to the patient's heart activity. The most important waves are the P wave and the QRS complex which are related respectively to the depolarization of the atria and the depolarization of the ventricles. The ECG presents series of such waves which are organized in cardiac cycles representing a complete heart contraction and an electrical potential recovery. The normal cycle is a succession of: P wave - QRS complex - T wave. The temporal intervals between these waves are commonly used for diagnosis and noted PR, QT and RR (see figure 1, left part).

Cardiac arrhythmias are disorders of rates, rhythms and conduction originating in heart areas with dysfunctions. Arrhythmias can be recognized by specific arrangements of ECG waves satisfying temporal constraints. For example, figure 1 presents on the left a normal ECG where all heart elements (seem to) work fine. The ECG on the right is related to an arrhythmia called bigeminy, where one can note the presence of extra ventricular beats due to an ectopic focus which acts as an extra pacemaker . Bigeminy is classically defined by the wave sequence P - QRS - QRS' - P - QRS - QRS', where QRS' denotes a QRS having an abnormal shape together with the temporal constraints normal PR, short RR' and long R'R, where R' denotes the abnormal QRS. This is the kind of temporal patterns that chronicle recognition algorithms [4,3] are able to detect.

Clearly, the definition of bigeminy above is best represented by a first-order formula as it contains true relations between events. In fact, the following Prolog clause gives a straightforward specification of this definition:

$$\texttt{bigeminy} \leftarrow \texttt{qrs(R0,normal,P0,\_),qrs(R1,abnormal,P1,R0),rr1(R0,R1,short)}. \quad (1)$$

It states that, in bigeminy, the temporal interval between a normal and an abnormal QRS is short. To learn specifications like formula (1) we need methods that can induce temporal constraints such as simple or delayed precedence between events. Inductive logic programming (ILP) aims at inducing first-order representations of target concepts and is quite adapted to this task [10].

## 3 Learning Algorithms and Materials

In this section, we first recall some principles of ILP. Then we describe the learning data that were used to learn cardiac arrhythmias. Finally, we show how to formulate a bias in order to improve the learning efficiency.

**ICL: an Inductive Logic Programming system**

The aim of ICL is to find a first-order theory $H \subset L_H$ that is complete (it covers all the given positive examples) and is consistent (it covers no negative examples). $L_H$ is the hypothesis language and is generally a subset of first-order logic. An interesting feature of ILP systems is to provide the users with declarative tools which provide means to specify $L_H$. ICL [12] proposes a high-level concept specification language called DLAB in which the hypothesis language syntax can be defined. DLAB grammars are preprocessed in order to generate candidate hypotheses from the most general to the specific ones (under $\theta$-subsumption).

ICL enables also multi-class learning [7]. The idea beyond multi-class learning is simple: when learning one particular class consider as positive only those examples belonging to this class and as negative all the examples belonging to the remaining classes. This is an attractive option in our case as we want to discover definitions which discriminate among several ($> 2$) arrhythmias.

**Data**

In order to assess the versatility of ICL and DLAB, we have selected a subset of arrhythmias related to different cardiac disorders involving various parts of the heart: the atria-ventricular (AV) node for the Mobitz type II arrhythmia (class mobitz2), the left bundle branch for the left bundle branch block (class lbbb) and the ventricle for bigeminy. ECGs related to a normal heart activity were also added (class normal). These 4 classes are not so difficult to separate. To augment the difficulty, we have added one class: the premature ventricular

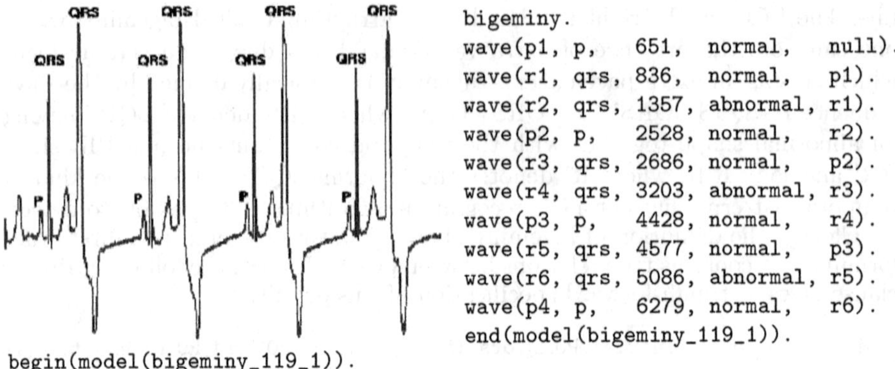


**Fig. 2.** A bigeminy arrhythmia ECG and its related specification as an ICL example

contraction arrhythmia (PVC) is characterized by sparse extra contractions due to an ectopic focus. The presence of ectopic beats makes this class close to bigeminy. The fact that ectopic beats are sparse makes this class close to the normal class as large portions of PVC ECGs are normal.

Real recorded ECG examples taken from the MIT BIH database [9] were used. 20 ECGs lasting 10s each were associated to each class. Every ECG is preprocessed by a signal processing algorithm and transformed into a symbolic representation based on P and QRS events [5]. This is the same module that is used on-line to produce symbolic events that will be processed by the chronicle recognizer. It aims: *i)* at detecting and at identifying the markers of the cardiac activity, P waves, QRS complexes, *ii)* at characterizing each wave by feature vector, and *iii)* at classifying waves in normal or abnormal classes. This module is not further detailed here (see [2]) but it is of major importance as the performance of the "symbolic part" of the system relies on good input data.

**Symbolic electrocardiograms**

Figure 2 presents an ECG example coded as a set of prolog clauses. To each event is associated its type, its occurrence time in the ECG and a qualification (normal or abnormal) of the related wave shape. This information is coded by the predicate `wave(Event, Type, Time, Qual, Pre_event)` which states that `Event` is related to a wave of type `Type` (`p` or `qrs`), which occurred at time `Time`, the shape of which is `Qual` (`normal` or `abnormal`) and `Pre_event` just precedes `Event` on the ECG. We chose to code the structural information (order of events) as a 5th argument of the predicate `wave`. We could have used an additional relational predicate as well.

**Background knowledge**

The aims of background knowledge is to ease learning by bringing knowledge of the domain from which the data come from as well as search knowledge which will be used to prune the clause space. In [11], the concept of declarative learning bias is studied and its importance and properties are clearly demonstrated.

```
1    1-1:[
2      len-len:[p_wave(P1, 1-1:[normal, abnormal], R0),
3          qrs(R1, 1-1:[normal, abnormal], P1),
4          0-len:[rr1(R0, R1, 1-1:[short, normal, long]),
5            pr1(P1, R1, 1-1:[short, normal, long])]],
6      len-len:[p_wave(P1, 1-1:[normal, abnormal], R0),
7          pp1(P0, P1, 1-1:[short, normal, long])],
8      len-len:[qrs(R1, 1-1:[normal, abnormal], R0),
9          0-1:[rr1(R0, R1, 1-1:[short, normal, long])]]
10         ],
```

**Fig. 3.** Syntactic specification of a cardiac cycle in DLAB

ICL [12] comes with DLAB, a declarative language for bias specification. A DLAB grammar consists in rule templates that fixes the syntactic form of clauses defining the target concept. These templates have the form `Head <- Body` where Head and Body are DLAB terms. A term is either an atomic formula or a set specification having the form `l-h:[el1,el2,...,eln]`. Such an expression means: choose from `l` to `h` elements from the set `[el1,el2,...,eln]`. The special symbol `len` can be used to specify the total length of the list. These expressions are used as combinatorial generators that can produce all the possible instances satisfying the templates. For example, the DLAB term `p(2-len:[el1,el2,el3])` generates the following expressions:
`p(el1,el2)`, `p(el1,el3)`, `p(el2,el3)`, `p(el1,el2,el3)`.

Figure 3 shows how the specification of a cardiac cycle may be formulated in DLAB. It says that a cardiac cycle is composed of exactly one (range `1-1` line 1) of the following configurations:

- a P-wave followed by a QRS complex followed by optional (range `0-len`) temporal constraints ( `pr1` and `rr1` in lines 2-5). For instance, the following expression satisfies this DLAB specification:
  `p_wave(P1, normal, R0), qrs(R1, abnormal, P1), pr1(P1, R1, long)`,
- a P-wave alone, in this case the temporal constraint between this wave and the preceding one is mandatory (lines 6 and 7),
- a QRS complex alone, in this case the temporal constraint between this wave and the preceding one is optional (lines 8 and 9).

Finally, a rule body is a sequence of such DLAB expressions telling ICL that an arrhythmia is defined by one or several cardiac cycles. Such a specification may appear quite sophisticated and restrictive. We have tried more permissive biases but either they led to prohibitive learning times or the quality of induced rules was very poor. Our objective has been to induce clauses that could be tailored in order to take into account such notions as readability, efficiency or robustness. Basing the induction on the notion of cardiac cycle enables readability since this is a concept that is commonly used by specialists for arrhythmia description or for diagnosis.

```
class(bigeminy) :-      %[13, 0, 0, 0, 0], [5, 19, 18, 18, 17]
   qrs(R0, abnormal, _), p_wave(P1, normal, R0), qrs(R1, normal, P1),
   qrs(R2, abnormal, R1), rr1(R1, R2, short).
class(bigeminy) :-      %[5, 0, 0, 0, 0], [13, 19, 18, 18, 17]
   qrs(R0, normal, _), p_wave(P1, normal, R0), qrs(R1, abnormal, P1).
class(lbbb) :-          %[0, 19, 0, 0, 0], [18, 0, 18, 18, 17]
   qrs(R0, abnormal, _), p_wave(P1, normal, R0), qrs(R1, abnormal, P1).
class(mobitz2) :-       %[0, 0, 16, 0, 0], [18, 19, 2, 18, 17]
   p_wave(P0, normal, _), equal(P0, R0),
   p_wave(P1, normal, R0), qrs(R1, normal, P1).
class(mobitz2) :-       %[0, 0, 2, 0, 0], [18, 19, 16, 18, 17]
   p_wave(P0, normal, _), equal(P0, R0),
   p_wave(P1, normal, R0), qrs(R1, abnormal, P1).
class(normal) :-        %[0, 0, 0, 17, 4], [18, 19, 18, 1, 13]
   p_wave(P0, normal, _), qrs(R0, normal, P0),
   p_wave(P1, normal, R0), qrs(R1, normal, P1),
   p_wave(P2, normal, R1), qrs(R2, normal, P2),
   p_wave(P3, normal, R2), qrs(R3, normal, P3), p_wave(P4, normal, R3).
class(pvc) :-           %[0, 0, 0, 0, 17], [18, 19, 18, 18, 0]
   p_wave(P0, normal, _), qrs(R0, normal, P0),
   p_wave(P1, normal, R0), qrs(R1, normal, P1),
   qrs(R2, abnormal, R1), rr1(R1, R2, short).
```

**Fig. 4.** Rules induced for a learning experiment on 5 classes

## 4 Results

The first goal of the experiments was to test whether understandable and useful arrhythmia specifications could be learnt from temporal data coming from example ECGs. A second goal was to assess the flexibility of using a declarative bias for imposing desirable properties such as readability or robustness on induced concepts. For instance, inducing the shortest clauses can be achieved by imposing only one cardiac cycle. This should bring efficiency to recognition as such rules specify less events to be recognized. Inducing longer rules enhance readability since a phenomenon regularity may be easier to assessed. A bias imposing several cycles, e.g. three or four, would be used to this purpose.

**Inducing rules for five arrhythmias**
Figure 4 displays the rules obtained from ICL when imposing one mandatory cardiac cycle and four optional ones. Those rules produce the shortest chronicles which are expected to enable early detection. To each rule is associated the number of examples covered by this rule in each class (respectively bigeminy, lbbb, mobitz2, normal and pvc) and the number of examples covered by its negation. For example, the list `[13,0,0,0,0]` associated to the first rule for bigeminy in figure 4 means that this rule covers 13 positive examples from class bigeminy, and none from the classes lbbb, mobitz2, normal and pvc.

Though only one cycle was mandatory, every rule states constraints on at least two cycles. Two types of temporal constraints are used: sequential con-

**Table 1.** Learning 5 classes: statistics of 10-fold cross-validation

| Set | Acc | TrueTot | FalseTot | TrAcc | Correct*Incorrect/class # |
|---|---|---|---|---|---|
| 1 | 1.000 | 10 | 0 | 0.989 | [1,1,5,1,2] * [0,0,0,0,0] # |
| 2 | 1.000 | 10 | 0 | 0.989 | [1,2,2,2,3] * [0,0,0,0,0] # |
| 3 | 1.000 | 10 | 0 | 1.000 | [3,2,2,1,2] * [0,0,0,0,0] # |
| 4 | 1.000 | 10 | 0 | 1.000 | [2,4,2,0,2] * [0,0,0,0,0] # |
| 5 | 1.000 | 10 | 0 | 0.989 | [2,1,2,2,3] * [0,0,0,0,0] # |
| 6 | 1.000 | 10 | 0 | 0.989 | [3,0,2,3,2] * [0,0,0,0,0] # |
| 7 | 0.900 | 9 | 1 | 1.000 | [1,2,0,5,1] * [0,0,0,1,0] # |
| 8 | 1.000 | 10 | 0 | 0.989 | [2,1,3,2,2] * [0,0,0,0,0] # |
| 9 | 1.000 | 10 | 0 | 0.989 | [2,4,0,1,3] * [0,0,0,0,0] # |
| 10 | 1.000 | 10 | 0 | 0.989 | [3,3,2,2,0] * [0,0,0,0,0] # |
| Tot: | 9.900 | 99 | 1 | | |

Accuracy: 0.990 (+/-0.030) (Training set Accuracy: 0.992 (+/-0.005))

straints between events by means of the third argument of `p_wave` and `qrs` predicate literals and temporal constraints on intervals by means of predicates `pr1` and `rr1` which appear to be the most used by specialists. Two rules were necessary for mobitz2. This arrhythmia can be characterized by the episodic absence of a ventricular contraction. It is sometimes accompanied by a right bundle branch block (rbbb) provoking an enlarged QRS. This was the case for some of the examples of this class. The two rules that were obtained reflect this fact: in the first one the QRS are normal whereas in the second one the QRS are abnormal and then denote a joint rbbb.

**Validation**

Table 1 gives the statistics obtained after a 10-fold cross-validation on learning 5 classes. 10% of the examples were left out for test in each round. The column TrAcc gives the training accuracy and the column Acc gives the test accuracy for each round. 99.2% and 99% global accuracy was obtained for training and test respectively. These results are very good and show that accurate definitions may be induced from complex data.

The rules learnt in the previous experiments were also assessed by specialists from a qualitative point of view. Though sometimes they were surprised by some definitions which did not correspond to the general definition they were used to, they rated all the rules as being correct and relevant.

## 5 Conclusion

This paper has presented an application of ILP techniques to the acquisition of a set of high-level temporal patterns (or chronicles) characterizing cardiac arrhythmias. The main novelty in this application is the fact that we are dealing with temporal and structured data. The ultimate goal is to get a chronicle base which is used by a chronicle recognition tool to analyse, in an on-line monitoring context, an ECG signal and detect cardiac disorders. A description of the whole project can be found in [2]. A set of real recorded ECG signals, taken from the MIT database, has been preprocessed by a signal processing algorithm into a symbolic representation and constitute the training base.

We focus in this paper on the experimentation we did with ICL [12] and we demonstrate the interest of using a declarative bias as DLAB. According to the properties that are looked for, such as readability or robustness, different biases have been experimented and result in different sets of rules.

Two main issues are currently investigated: the first one is to cope with multiple sources of information (multichannels and multisensors). This means a new learning phase in order to get a set of chronicles able to take into account not only the temporal aspect of each signal but also the relationships existing among these different signals. The second issue concerns active cardiac devices which rely on leads located in both ventricles. These new devices can tackle both rhythmic and hemodynamic disorders but the signatures are still poorly known. We are currently experimenting our learning module on these data in order to exhibit such signatures.

## References


1. I. Bratko, I. Mozetic, and N. Lavrăc. *Kardio: A Study in Deep and Qualitative Knowledge for Expert Systems.* MIT Press, 1989.
2. G. Carrault, M.-O. Cordier, R. Quiniou, M. Garreau, J.-J. Bellanger, and A. Bardou. A model-based approach for learning to identify cardiac arrhythmias. In *Proc. of AIMDM'99*, LNAI, vol. 1620. Springer Verlag, 1999.
3. C. Dousson. Crs: Chronicle recognition system. `http://crs.elibel.tm.fr/`, 2001.
4. C. Dousson, P. Gaborit, and M. Ghallab. Situation recognition: representation and algorithms. In *Proc. of 13th IJCAI*, Chambéry, France, 1993.
5. A I. Hernández, G. Carrault, F. Mora, G. Passariello, and J. M. Schleich. Multisensor fusion for atrial and ventricular activity detection in coronary care monitoring. *IEEE Trans. on Biomedical Engineering*, 1999.
6. G. Kókai, Z. Alexin, and T. Gyimóthy. Analyzing and learning ecg waveforms. In *Proc. of ILP'96*, pages 152–171, 1996.
7. W. Van Laer, L. De Raedt, and S. Dzeroski. On multi-class problems and discretization in inductive logic programming. In *Proc. of ISMIS97*, LNAI, vol.1325. Springer-Verlag, 1997.
8. N. Lavrăc, I. Kononenko, E. Keravnou, M. Kukar, and B. Zupan. Intelligent data analysis for medical diagnosis: Using machine learning and temporal abstraction. *AI Communications*, 11(3-4):191–218, 1998.
9. G.B. Moody and R.G. Mark. The MIT-BIH arrhythmia database on cd-rom and software for use with it. In *Computers in Cardiology 1990*, pages 185–188. IEEE Computer Society Press, 1990.
10. S. Muggleton. Inductive logic programming: issues, results and the challenge of learning language in logic. *Artificial Intelligence*, 114(1-2):283–296, 1999.
11. C. Nédellec, C. Rouveirol, H. Adé, F. Bergadano, and B. Tausend. Declarative bias in inductive logic programming. In L. de Raedt, editor, *Advances in Inductive Logic Programming*, pages 82–103. IOS Press, 1996.
12. L. De Raedt and W. Van Laer. Inductive constraint logic. In *Proceedings of the 5th Workshop on Algorithmic Learning Theory*, LNAI, 1995.

# Efficient Cross-Validation in ILP

Jan Struyf and Hendrik Blockeel

Katholieke Universiteit Leuven, Dept. of Computer Science,
Celestijnenlaan 200A, B-3001 Leuven, Belgium
{Jan.Struyf, Hendrik.Blockeel}@cs.kuleuven.ac.be

**Abstract.** Cross-validation is a technique used in many different machine learning approaches. Straightforward implementation of this technique has the disadvantage of causing computational overhead. However, it has been shown that this overhead often consists of redundant computations, which can be avoided by performing all folds of the cross-validation in parallel. In this paper we study to what extent such a parallel algorithm is also useful in ILP. We discuss two issues: a) the existence of dependencies between parts of a query that limit the obtainable efficiency improvements and b) the combination of parallel cross-validation with query-packs. Tentative solutions are proposed and evaluated experimentally.

## 1 Introduction

Cross-validation is a technique used in many different machine learning approaches, such as instance based learning, artificial neural networks or decision tree induction, to tune parameters, select relevant features or to estimate predictive accuracies. Running an $n$-fold cross-validation consists of partitioning the data set $D$ into $n$ subsets $D_i$ and then running the given learning algorithm $n$ times, each time using a different training set $T_i = D - D_i$ and a different validation set $D_i$.

An obvious disadvantage of performing cross-validation is the computational overhead of running the learning algorithm $n$ times. This is a problem for ILP systems which are known to have high execution times. However, for some systems, this overhead can be reduced significantly. The training sets $T_i$ are highly similar. Indeed, each example from the original data set $D$ occurs $n - 1$ times as training example. Because of this similarity, redundant computations are performed in the different cross-validation runs. These redundancies can be removed by integrating the different runs into one single algorithm. This is shown in [4] for decision tree induction.

Similarities between the training sets are not the only kind of similarities that can cause an ILP system to do redundant computations. ILP systems typically search a large hypothesis space. This involves testing a huge number of first order logic queries on the training set. Most ILP algorithms search through the hypothesis space in a greedy manner. First order decision tree learners (TILDE [1], S-Cart [8]) for example consider refinements of the query from the previous

C. Rouveirol and M. Sebag (Eds.): ILP 2001, LNAI 2157, pp. 228–239, 2001.

level of the tree when selecting a query for a new node. A refinement of a query is obtained by extending it with new literals. This means that different refinements of the same query are highly similar (share literals). One can imagine that there will be redundant computations when testing these similar queries separately on the training set. It is shown in [2] that this kind of redundancies can be removed by integrating the similar queries in one so-called query-pack.

A first goal of this text is to discuss efficient cross-validation from an ILP point of view. We use decision tree induction to explain the concepts, but the method for efficient cross-validation can also be integrated in rule induction systems like FOIL [11] or Progol [9]. We discuss an important problem related to the fact that a query in a given node of a first order decision tree depends on the queries of higher level nodes. This query-dependency problem also occurs to some extent for rule induction. We show how the parallel cross-validation algorithm from [4] can be adapted to reduce the overhead caused by this problem. A second goal of this text is to investigate how the query-packs from [2] can be integrated in the parallel cross-validation algorithm.

This paper is organised as follows. Section 2 summarises logical decision tree induction, efficient decision tree cross-validation and query-packs. Section 3 discusses the query-dependency problem, shows how query-packs can be integrated in the parallel algorithm and suggests how the parallel algorithm can be modified for rule induction. Section 4 presents experimental results. We investigate the possible efficiency gain of combining parallel cross-validation with query-packs and the effect of the query-dependency problem. Section 5 states the conclusions.

## 2 Preliminaries

### 2.1 Logical Decision Tree Induction

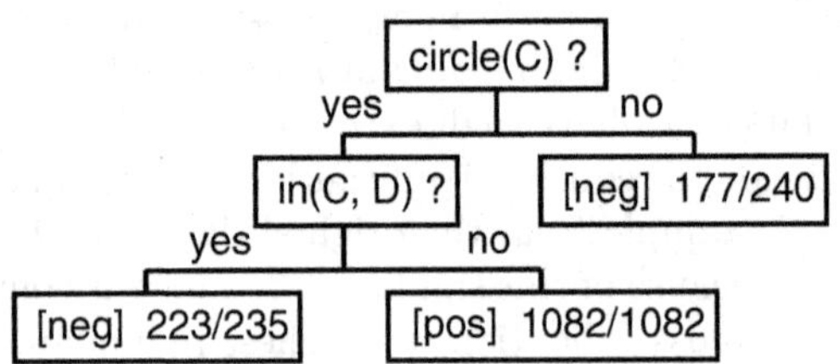


**Fig. 1.** A first order decision tree.

A first order decision tree [1] is a binary decision tree with conjunctions of first order literals in the nodes. The leaves contain class values in case of a classification task or (vectors of) real values in case of a regression task. An example tree grown on one of the Bongard data sets [6] is shown in Fig. 1. The prediction task for this set is classifying pictures containing circles, squares and triangles as positive or negative. We use the learning from interpretations setting [5] in which each example is given by a set of (Prolog) facts. Notice that it is not necessary to include a key variable in this setting.

First order decision trees are grown top down. The induction algorithm starts with the trivial query `true`. It then continues to add new nodes to the tree until a stop criterion is satisfied. The literal for a new node is selected by a greedy algorithm. It first generates refinements of the current query by extending it with new literals. In the Bongard example possible refinements of the query `circle(C)` are `(circle(C), triangle(D))`, `(circle(C), square(D))`, `(circle(C), in(C,D))`, ... The algorithm computes a quality measure such as information gain [10] for each refinement. The refinement that maximises this quality is used to create the new node.

### 2.2 The Parallel Algorithm

1. $(q^*, Q^*)_{0..n} = (none, -\infty)$<br>
2. **for each** refinement $q$<br>
3.     $S^D_{0..n} = 0$<br>
4.     **for each** $i \in 1 \ldots n$<br>
5.         **for each** $e \in D_i$<br>
6.             update_statistics($S^D_i$, $q(e)$, $e$)<br>
7.     $S^D = \sum_{i=1}^{n} S^D_i$<br>
8.     $S^T_{0..n} = S^D - S^D_{0..n}$<br>
9.     **for each** $i \in 0 \ldots n$<br>
10.         $Q =$ compute_quality($S^T_i$)<br>
11.         **if** $Q > Q^*_i$ **then** $(q^*, Q^*)_i = (q, Q)$<br>
12. **for each** *different* $q^* \in \{q^*_i\}$<br>
13.     partition $D_i$ according to $q^*$

**Fig. 2.** Parallel cross-validation.

As explained briefly in the introduction, decision tree cross-validation involves growing $n$ different trees, each on a slightly different training set $T_i = D - D_i$. Because the training sets $T_i$ are highly similar, one can expect that the trees will be highly similar too, especially near the root. The parallel algorithm [4] shown in Fig. 2 exploits this similarity while growing $n+1$ different trees at once. One tree for each cross-validation fold and one tree grown on the whole data set $D = T_0$. We call this set of $n+1$ trees the cross-validation forest. The algorithm keeps track of a tuple $(q^*, Q^*)_i$ (Line 1) for each tree of the forest. The first component of this tuple, $q^*$, is the best query found so far and the second component, $Q^*$, is $q^*$'s quality. In each iteration another refinement $q$ is evaluated on the data (Lines 3 - 10). Line 11 updates $(q^*, Q^*)_i$ if $q$ is better than $q^*_i$.

Lines 3 - 6 compute statistics $S_i^D$ for query $q$ on each set $D_i$ of the cross-validation partition. Because these sets are disjoint, the query is evaluated only once on each example from $D$. To estimate the quality $Q$ (Line 10) we need statistics $S_i^T$ on the training sets $T_i$, which are derived from the previously calculated $S_i^D$ (Line 7 - 8). This step is only possible if the statistics are additive, meaning that $S^{A_1 \cup A_2} = S^{A_1} + S^{A_2}$ if $A_1 \cap A_2 = \emptyset$. Each statistic $S$ is a tuple with two components $PS$ and $NS$. The positive component $PS$ is updated if $q(e)$ succeeds (Line 6) and the negative component $NS$ is updated if $q(e)$ fails.

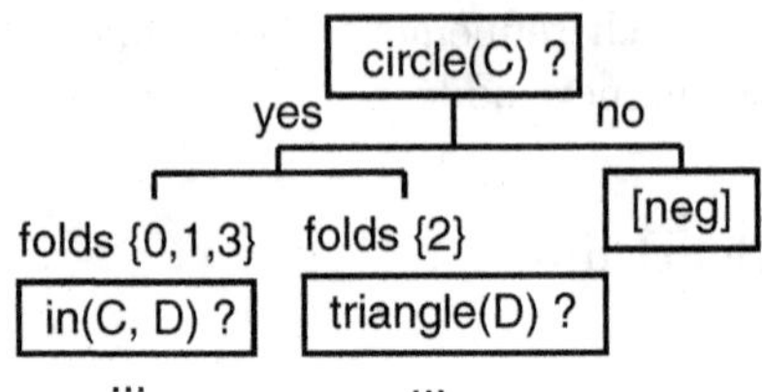


**Fig. 3.** A 3-fold cross-validation forest.

The last two lines of the algorithm update the nodes of the forest. A forest is not really a set of disjoint trees, there is some amount of sharing between the trees. The trees continue to share nodes as long as the same query $q^*$ is selected for each tree. A group of trees or a single tree can be split off from the forest if the algorithm selects a different $q^*$ for this group. An example forest is shown in Fig 3. At level two the tree for training set $T_2$ is split off from the forest and stops sharing computations.

It is shown in [4] that the speedup factor $T_{\text{serial}}/T_{\text{parallel}}$ is given by ($t_r(i)$ is the average time for growing one level of a single tree from $D$ and $f(i)$ is the average number of tree-groups that have been split off in the forest):

$$\frac{n \cdot t_r(1) + n \cdot t_r(2) + n \cdot t_r(3) + \ldots}{t_r(1) + f(1) \cdot t_r(2) + f(2) \cdot t_r(3) + \ldots} \tag{1}$$

Because tree-groups usually split off at lower levels of the forest, where only a few examples are left, speedup is in most cases quite good.

### 2.3 Query-Packs

Figure 4 shows refinements for the query `circle(C), in(C,D)`. The parallel algorithm considers each of these refinements if it has to select the best query for the left - left subtree of the Bongard forest from Fig. 3. All these refinements have the first two literals in common and executing these queries separately on the training set will cause redundant computations. By integrating the queries in a query-pack [2] as shown in the right part of Fig. 4, this redundancy can be removed.

A query-pack is a tree structure with literals or conjunctions of literals in the nodes. Each path from the root to some node represents a conjunctive query. Decision tree query-packs can be compared to brooms. The current query, its length being proportional to the current tree depth, forms the stick of the broom. It is shown in [2] that the speedup factor $T_{\text{sequential}}/T_{\text{pack}}$ ranges from 1 to $\min(c+1, b)$ where $b$ is the branching factor of the pack and $c$ is the ratio of the computational complexity in the shared part over the complexity in the non-shared part. Because a broom has a long shared part and a high branching factor, one can expect high speedups.

```
circle(C), in(C,D), triangle(D)
circle(C), in(C,D), square(D)
circle(C), in(C,D), circle(D)
circle(C), in(C,D), triangle(E)
circle(C), in(C,D), square(E)
circle(C), in(C,D), circle(E)
circle(C), in(C,D), in(D,E)
...
```

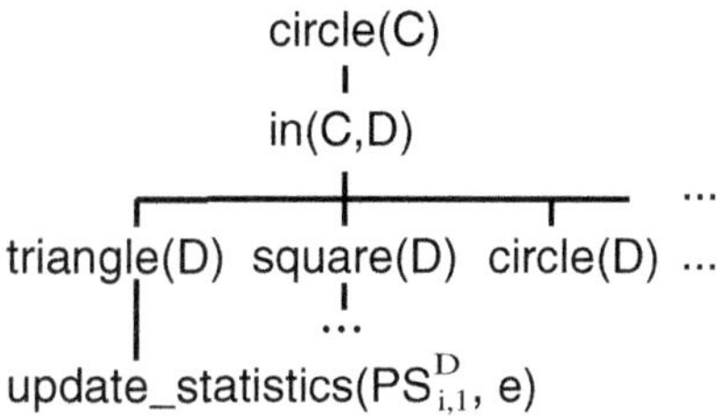

**Fig. 4.** A query-pack.

Note the similarity between a query-pack and a cross-validation forest. The structure and the basic idea are the same but the goals are different. A cross-validation forest represents the shared part of similar decision trees and a query-pack represents the shared part of similar queries.

## 3 Parallel Cross-Validation in ILP

In this section we introduce the query-dependency problem and show how the query-packs from the previous section can be integrated in the parallel cross-validation algorithm. We discuss the latter in the context of first order rule and constraint induction systems.

### 3.1 The Query-Dependency Problem

In the parallel algorithm from [4] sharing of computations stops once a group of folds is split off from the main forest. In the propositional case, it is relatively easy to share computations between different fold groups. For ILP systems this is more difficult because of the query-dependency problem. In this section we discuss this query-dependency problem and show how the parallel algorithm can be improved to allow sharing of computations among different fold groups.

Consider again the example forest from Fig. 3. Let $G^1$ be the group for folds {0,1,3} and $G^2$ the group for fold {2}. The best query for $G^1$, $q^1 =$ `(circle(C), in(C,D))`, differs from the best query for $G^2$, $q^2 =$ `(circle(C), triangle(D))`.

Although $q^1$ and $q^2$ are different it is likely that the partitions $(D^+, D^-)^1$ and $(D^+, D^-)^2$ they induce have a large overlap ($|D^{1+} \cap D^{2+}| \gg 0$). This is because $q^1$ and $q^2$ both are best queries on a similar data set.

Suppose that the partitions are similar. We now move to the next level of the forest and evaluate all refinements of $q^1$ on $D^{1+}$ and all refinements of $q^2$ on $D^{2+}$. This does not involve redundant computations because the refinements of $q^1$ are all different from the refinements of $q^2$. This is because the refinements of $q^1$ contain the literal `in(C,D)` and the refinements of $q^2$ contain the literal `triangle(D)`. This effect, to which we referred in the introduction as the query-dependency problem, does not occur for a propositional decision tree learner because this kind of system does not have variables that link tests from different levels of the tree.

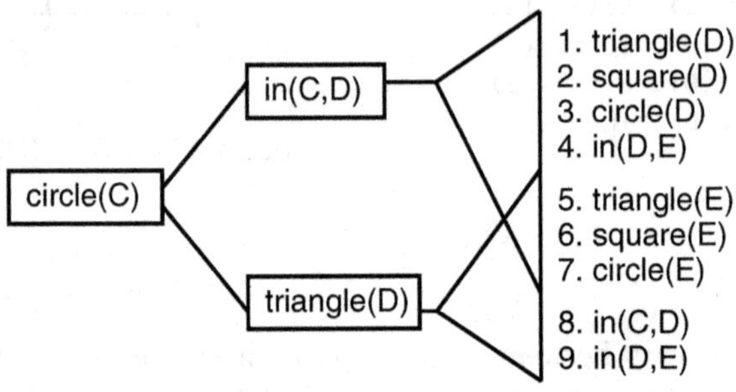


**Fig. 5.** Overlapping refinements.

Figure 5 shows all refinements for $q^1$ and $q^2$. Each refinement is a conjunction of 3 literals. The first literal is always `circle(C)`, the second either `in(C,D)` or `triangle(D)`. For the last literal we have three different cases: it occurs only in $q^1$'s refinement set (literals 1 - 4 in Fig. 5), it occurs only in $q^2$'s refinement set (8 - 9) or it occurs in both sets (5 - 7). The last case is of course the most interesting. Is it possible to remove the second literal and gain efficiency by evaluating refinements 5 - 7 only once instead of twice on the data?

Smartcall [3] is a query transformation that removes literals from a clause which are known to succeed. It first partitions the query in equivalence classes. Two literals are in the same class if they share (indirectly) variables. Refinement 5 of $q^1$ for example, can be partitioned in two classes $C_1 = \{$`circle(C)`, `in(C,D)`$\}$ and $C_2 = \{$`triangle(E)`$\}$. The literals in $C_1$ are known to succeed because they were used to partition the data at a higher level of the tree. We remove $C_1$ from the query and obtain `triangle(E)`.

Smartcall removes the first two literals of refinements 5 - 7 for both $q^1$ and $q^2$. This is shown on the left side of Fig. 6. The rectangle represents the overlap of the refinement sets in the vertical dimension and the overlap of the example sets in the horizontal dimension. If the overlap is big in both dimensions then we can expect a high speedup by evaluating overlapping queries only once on the intersection of the example sets. Remember that the overlap of the example sets is large if similar queries are selected in a higher node of the tree. The overlap in the refinement sets is large if Smartcall can remove the crucial literals. Notice that propositional tests can always be removed because they do not introduce new variables.

Although we have considered only two groups $G^1$ and $G^2$, everything said in this section can be generalised to $k > 2$ groups. One problem is that the intersection of the refinement sets and the intersection of the example sets is smaller. We solve this by adding groups using a greedy algorithm until the number of examples in the intersection drops below a given threshold.

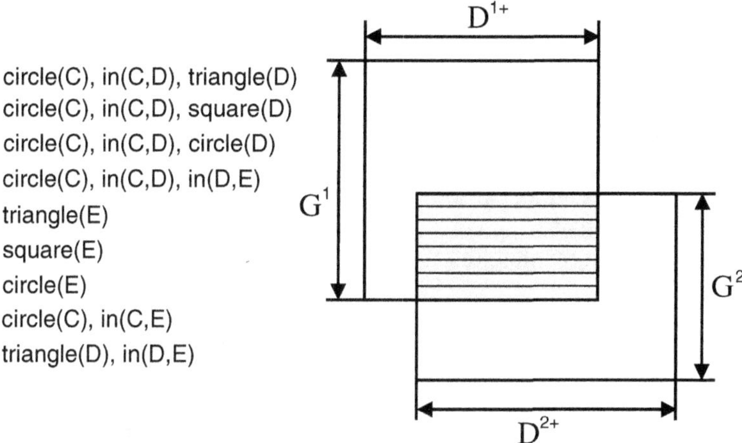


**Fig. 6.** Overlapping refinements and data sets.

Another problem we did not discuss so far is the problem of anti-similar queries. Suppose that we have a classification task with two classes *pos* and *neg*. If query $q_1$ moves almost all positive examples to the left and query $q_2$ moves almost all positive examples to the right then we have anti-similar queries. The extreme case is that $q_1 = \neg q_2$. This problem can be solved by making sure that the left subtree always covers the most positive examples. We swap the left and right subtree if this is not the case. A similar approach can be used for regression (put the set with the lowest mean on the left) or for classification problems with more than two classes (impose an artificial order on the classes and put the set with the smallest most frequent class on the left).

### 3.2 Combination with Query-Packs

Figure 7 shows the parallel cross-validation algorithm adapted to use query-packs. Line 3 of the adapted algorithm creates the pack $\mathcal{Q}$ and returns the number of queries in the pack (i.e. the pack size) $s$. Lines 4 - 6 evaluate the pack on the data. Because the query-pack integrates $s$ different refinements, we have to keep track of a $(n+1) \times s$ statistic matrix. The rows of this matrix correspond to the different trees in the forest and the columns correspond to the different queries in the pack.

1. $(q^*, Q^*)_{0..n} = (none, -\infty)$<br>
2. refine_and_compile_pack($\mathcal{Q}$, $s$)<br>
3. $PS^D_{0..n,1..s} = 0$<br>
4. **for each** $i \in 1 \ldots n$<br>
5.     **for each** $e \in D_i$<br>
6.         execute_pack($\mathcal{Q}$, $PS^D_i$, $e$)<br>
7. $PS^D = \sum_{i=1}^{n} PS^D_i$<br>
8. $PS^T_{0..n} = PS^D - PS^D_{0..n}$<br>
9. **for each** $j \in 1 \ldots s$<br>
10     $q =$ get_from_pack($\mathcal{Q}$, $j$)<br>
11.     **for each** $i \in 0 \ldots n$<br>
12.         $NS^T_{i,j} = TS^T_i - PS^T_{i,j}$<br>
13.         $Q =$ compute_quality($TS^T_i$, $PS^T_{i,j}$, $NS^T_{i,j}$)<br>
14.         **if** $Q > Q^*_i$ **then** $(q^*, Q^*)_i = (q, Q)$<br>
15. **for each** *different* $q^* \in \{q^*_i\}$<br>
16.     partition $D_i$ according to $q^*$

**Fig. 7.** Packs version of the parallel algorithm.

The leaves of the pack contain `update_statistic` functions (See Fig. 4). These functions update the positive component $PS^D_{i,j}$ of the statistics $S^D_{i,j}$ for each query $q_j$ in the pack. Updating the negative component of $S^D_{i,j}$ is not possible with the pack representation discussed in Section 2.3. However, $NS^T_{i,j}$ can be calculated indirectly, by introducing total statistics $TS^D_i$ and $TS^T_i$. Total statistics are equal for all refinements $q_j$ and can be computed from the data before the parallel algorithm is started. The negative component $NS^T_{i,j}$ can be derived using the equality $TS^T_i = PS^T_{i,j} + NS^T_{i,j}$ (Line 12). The rest of algorithm is similar to the version without packs (See Fig. 2).

### 3.3 Rule Induction

Although we focused on decision tree induction, almost everything said so far also applies to top down rule induction (e.g. FOIL [11], Progol [9]) and to top down constraint induction (e.g. ICL[7]). A top down rule induction system tries to cover all positive examples by learning a disjunction of conjunctive rules. Each time a new rule is learned, the systems removes the covered positive examples from the data set and tries to learn a next rule until all positive examples are covered or no more good rules can be found. To learn one rule, the system starts from the most general rule `true` and keeps adding the best literal according to some quality measure as long as the rule's quality improves.

We can use the ideas from the parallel decision tree cross-validation algorithm to build a parallel rule cross-validation algorithm. This parallel rule cross-validation algorithm builds a tree that represents the shared part between rules for different folds. If one or more folds select a different literal then the rule for this group of folds is split off from the main tree and forms a new branch. This can be compared to the cross-validation forest from Section 2.2. As long as a group of folds remains together, computations can be shared by evaluating the rule for this group on the disjoint sets $D_i$ and not on the overlapping training sets $T_i$.

If it is possible to use the Smartcall query transformation (i.e. if the positive examples that are not covered by the current rule are removed each time a new literal is added) then it is also possible to share computations between different branches of the rule tree in a similar way as discussed in Section 3.1.

Before a rule induction system starts to learn a new rule, it removes all positive examples covered by the previous rule. As long as the same rules are selected for different folds of the cross-validation (i.e. the tree has no branches) the same examples are removed from the data set $D$ and $D$ remains equal for all folds. If fold $i$ selects a different rule then different examples will be removed from $D$ and the data set for fold $i$ will differ from the data sets of the other folds. If we partition $D$ in $(D^s, D^1 \ldots D^n)$, where $D^s$ contains the shared examples and $D^i$ contains the examples for fold $i$ not in $D^s$, then it is possible to share computations over $D^s$.

Progol uses one of the positive examples $e$ to constrain its hypothesis space $H$ to a space $H_e$ which only contains hypotheses more general than $e$. After that, it performs an exhaustive search in $H_e$ looking for the rule that maximises a quality measure called compaction. When running an n-fold cross-validation, each fold will select a different example $e_i$ but some of the hypothesis spaces $H_{e_i}$ will be equal. This means it is possible to remove redundancies among folds that share the same $H_e$.

## 4 Experimental Results

For our experiments we implemented the different cross-validation optimisations discussed in this text as a module of TILDE, the first order decision tree learner from the ACE data mining tool[1] [2].

We compare execution times of a 10-fold run for serial (no optimisations), serial + query-packs, parallel, parallel + intersection (share computations among different groups of trees) and finally parallel cross-validation + query-packs. The data sets used are:

- The simple (SB) and complex (CB) Bongard data set [6] (this set was also used as running example in this text). SB contains 1453 examples with a

[1] ACE is available for academic purposes upon request. `http://www.cs.kuleuven.ac.be/~dtai/ACE/`

simple underlying theory, CB contains 1521 examples with a more complex theory.
- A subset (ASM) of 999 examples sampled from the "Adaptive Systems Management" data set, kindly provided to us by Perot Systems Nederland.
- The Mutagenesis (Muta) data set [12], an ILP benchmark (230 examples).

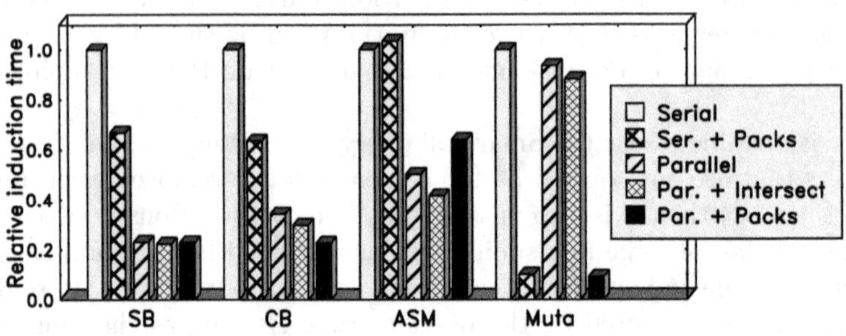


**Fig. 8.** Different cross-validation optimisations (time relative to serial 10-fold).

As can be seen in Figure 8, Table 1 and Table 2,[2] the results are not uniform for all data sets. This is because we deliberately selected different types of data sets. For SB all parallel algorithms perform more or less the same. The intersection algorithm does not perform better because no groups are split off from the forest. The packs version does not perform better because the queries are too short to have many literals in common. CB is the least surprising data set: some groups are split off from the forest and the queries become longer. The ASM data set contains many propositional numeric attributes. The combination of the parallel algorithm with intersection performs well on this data set because it has a lot of propositional attributes that can be removed by Smartcall. One problem is that intersecting refinement sets (using a hash tree) and example sets (sorted lists) is still rather slow in our implementation. Query-packs perform very bad on ASM because the pack has a high branching factor (it contains a huge number of tests comparing numeric attributes to each of their discretised values). The time necessary for compiling a pack depends on the pack size. Near the leaves this compilation time dominates the execution time which is linear in the number of examples. The Mutagenesis data set is not suited for parallel cross-validation because some queries, generated near the leaves of the forest, dominate the total execution time [4] (this happens when the algorithm looks for circular substructures in the molecules). Query-packs on the other hand perform very well for Mutagenesis (10 times faster). This is because query-pack execution shares computations among the different refinements of this few complex queries.

[2] The timings are faster comparing to [4] because we have ported the statistics code from Prolog to C++.

**Table 1.** Timings (seconds) comparing parallel to serial cross-validation (10-folds), once with packs disabled and a second time with packs enabled.

| **SB** | Packs off | Packs on | |
|---|---|---|---|
| Serial | 16 | 11 | 1.5× |
| Parallel | 3.6 | 3.5 | 1.0× |
| | 4.4× | 3.1× | |
| **CB** | | | |
| Serial | 24 | 15 | 1.6× |
| Parallel | 8.2 | 5.4 | 1.5× |
| | 2.9× | 2.8× | |

| **ASM** | Packs off | Packs on | |
|---|---|---|---|
| Serial | 4100 | 4300 | 0.95× |
| Parallel | 2100 | 2600 | 0.81× |
| | 2.0× | 1.7 × | |
| **Muta** | | | |
| Serial | 5000 | 500 | 10× |
| Parallel | 4600 | 450 | 10× |
| | 1.09× | 1.11× | |

**Table 2.** The effect of sharing computations between different fold groups (10-folds, times in seconds).

| | SB | CB | ASM | Muta |
|---|---|---|---|---|
| Parallel | 3.6 | 8.2 | 2100 | 4600 |
| Intersect | 3.5 | 7.1 | 1710 | 4400 |
| | 1.03 × | 1.15× | 1.22× | 1.05× |

## 5 Conclusions

We discussed two optimisations specific to ILP for the parallel decision tree cross-validation algorithm proposed in [4]. The first one was intersecting refinement and example sets to be able to share computations between different fold groups of the cross-validation forest. The second one was integrating query-packs in the parallel algorithm.

One possible improvement is to implement the combination of the two optimisations discussed in this text: parallel cross-validation with query-packs and intersection. In order to implement this, one would need an equivalent to Smartcall for query-packs. This is future work.

It became clear from the experiments that different optimisations work well for different data sets. The more optimisations that are integrated in a learning system, the more difficult it is for an end-user to know which optimisations are suited for his particular data set. Maybe it is possible to use meta-learning to decide which optimisations have to be used for a given set.

We also discussed how the ideas from the parallel decision tree cross-validation algorithm can be used to devise a parallel rule or constraint induction cross-validation system.

## Acknowledgements

The authors are a research assistant, respectively post-doctoral fellow, of the Fund for Scientific Research of Flanders (Belgium). They thank Perot Systems Nederland / Syllogic for providing the ASM data. The cooperation between Perot Systems Nederland and the authors was supported by the European Union's Esprit Project 28623 (Aladin).


## References


1. H. Blockeel and L. De Raedt. Top-down induction of first order logical decision trees. *Artificial Intelligence*, 101(1-2):285–297, June 1998.
2. H. Blockeel, B. Demoen, L. Dehaspe, G. Janssens, J. Ramon, and H. Vandecasteele. Executing query packs in ILP. In J. Cussens and A. Frisch, editors, *Proceedings of the 10th International Conference in Inductive Logic Programming*, volume 1866 of *Lecture Notes in Artificial Intelligence*, pages 60–77, London, UK, July 2000. Springer.
3. H. Blockeel, B. Demoen, G. Janssens, H. Vandecasteele, and W. Van Laer. Two advanced transformations for improving the efficiency of an ILP system. In *10th International Conference on Inductive Logic Programming, Work-in-Progress Reports*, pages 43–59, London, UK, July 2000.
4. Hendrik Blockeel and Jan Struyf. Efficient algorithms for decision tree cross-validation. In *Proceedings of ICML-2001 - Eighteenth International Conference on Machine Learning*. Morgan Kaufmann, 2001. To appear.
5. L. De Raedt and S. Džeroski. First order *jk*-clausal theories are PAC-learnable. *Artificial Intelligence*, 70:375–392, 1994.
6. L. De Raedt and W. Van Laer. Inductive constraint logic. In Klaus P. Jantke, Takeshi Shinohara, and Thomas Zeugmann, editors, *Proceedings of the Sixth International Workshop on Algorithmic Learning Theory*, volume 997 of *Lecture Notes in Artificial Intelligence*, pages 80–94. Springer-Verlag, 1995.
7. L. De Raedt and W. Van Laer. Inductive constraint logic. Unpublished, 1995.
8. Stefan Kramer. Structural regression trees. In *Proceedings of the Thirteenth National Conference on Artificial Intelligence*, pages 812–819, Cambridge/Menlo Park, 1996. AAAI Press/MIT Press.
9. S. Muggleton. Inverse entailment and Progol. *New Generation Computing, Special issue on Inductive Logic Programming*, 13(3-4):245–286, 1995.
10. J. Ross Quinlan. *C4.5: Programs for Machine Learning*. Morgan Kaufmann series in machine learning. Morgan Kaufmann, 1993.
11. J.R. Quinlan. Learning logical definitions from relations. *Machine Learning*, 5:239–266, 1990.
12. A. Srinivasan, S.H. Muggleton, M.J.E. Sternberg, and R.D. King. Theories for mutagenicity: A study in first-order and feature-based induction. *Artificial Intelligence*, 85(1,2), 1996.

# Modelling Semi-structured Documents with Hedges for Deduction and Induction

Akihiro Yamamoto[1,3], Kimihito Ito[1], Akira Ishino[2], and Hiroki Arimura[2,3]

[1] MemeMedia Laboratory, Hokkaido University
N 13 W 8, Sapporo 060-8628 JAPAN
{yamamoto, itok}@meme.hokudai.ac.jp
[2] Graduate School of Information Science and Electrical Engineering
Kyushu University
Hakozaki 6-10-1, Fukuoka 812-8581, JAPAN
{ishino, arim}@i.kyushu-u.ac.jp
[3] "Information and Human Activity", PRESTO
Japan Science and Technology Corporation (JST)

**Abstract.** Semi-structured documents are now commonly used for exchanging information. The aim of this research is to apply deductive and inductive reasoning to semi-structured documents. From our observation that first-order terms are inadequate for modelling semi-structured documents, we model them with hedges. After defining semi-structured documents and hedges so that they can contain logical variables, we introduce hedge logic programs, in which every argument of an atom is a hedge. We give a method for transforming hedge logic programs into original logic programs. We also give an algorithm for computing minimal common anti-unifications of hedges, with aiming inductive reasoning of hedge logic programs from sets of semi-structured data.

## 1 Introduction

Semi-structured documents are now commonly used for exchanging information. HTML and XML are most famous languages in which flat text documents are marked up into semi-structured ones. In exchanging information we firstly define types of data and then represent a method of transforming a type of data into another type of data. It is well-known that logic programs are useful in both of the activities. Moreover, inductive logic programming techniques could contribute to automate them. In this paper we investigate how to treat semi-structured documents in logic programming. We also give a fundamental result for inductive reasoning of logic programs from sets of semi-structured documents.

Some logic programming systems, e.g. Pillow [5], have already support the treatment of semi-structured documents. They model semi-structured documents with first-order terms, but as explained in this paper, such modelling causes problems. Instead of using first-terms, we propose to adopt *hedges* [6].

C. Rouveirol and M. Sebag (Eds.): ILP 2001, LNAI 2157, pp. 240–247, 2001.

```
<TABLE>
  <TR><TD>John Doe</TD><TD>34</TD><TD>John.Doe@foo.com</TD></TR>
  <TR><TD>Bob Smith</TD><TD>29</TD><TD>Bob.Smith@foo.com</TD></TR>
  <TR><TD>Alice Miller</TD><TD>26</TD>
                                 <TD>Alice.Miller@foo.com</TD></TR>
</TABLE>
```

**Fig. 1.** An example of a semi-structured document

Hedges are sometimes called forests [11] or ordered forests [1]. Some previous research [4,9,10] has shown that hedges are adequate for modelling semi-structured documents.

In the following section we explain that modelling semi-structured documents with first-order terms is inadequate in logic programming. Then we formally define semi-structured documents and hedges so that they can contain logical variables. In Section 3 we introduce logic programs in which hedges are used as arguments of atoms. We give a method for transforming such hedge logic programs into original logic programs with keeping their procedural semantics based on SLD-resolution. In Section 4, we give an lca (least common anti-unification) algorithm for two hedges in some class, with aiming inductive reasoning of hedge logic programs from sets of semi-structured data. In the last section hedge logic programming is compared with other types of extension of logic programming.

Because of the limit of space, precise discussion including the proofs of a theorem and lemmata is omitted in this paper. It will be given in a forthcoming full paper.

## 2 Semi-structured Documents and Hedges

Let us consider a semi-structured document $d_1$ displayed in Fig. 1. We put some spaces and newlines for readability. By using the tag names TABLE, TR and TD as function symbols, the document $d_1$ could be represented in a first-order term

$$
\begin{aligned}
t_1 \;=\; & \texttt{TABLE(TR(TD(John Doe),TD(34),TD(John.Doe@foo.com))} \\
& \quad \texttt{TR(TD(Bob Smith),TD(29),TD(Bob.Smith@foo.com)),} \\
& \quad \texttt{TR(TD(Alice Miller),TD(26),TD(Alice.Miller@foo.com)))}
\end{aligned}
$$

As is well-known, the document $d_1$ is for representing a table in HTML which can have arbitrary numbers of rows marked-up with <TR> and </TR>. This means that the arity of the function symbol TABLE in $t_1$ may vary.

A problem is caused by the variation of arities of function symbols, when we define the type of $t_1$ with a logic program. Since there is no bound of the numbers of arities of the function symbol TABLE, we have to prepare infinitely many clauses:

$$\text{is\_table}(\texttt{TABLE}(x_1)) \leftarrow \text{is\_column}(x_1)$$

$$\text{is\_table}(\texttt{TABLE}(x_1, x_2)) \leftarrow \text{is\_column}(x_1), \text{is\_column}(x_2)$$

$$\text{is\_table}(\texttt{TABLE}(x_1, x_2, x_3)) \leftarrow \text{is\_column}(x_1), \text{is\_column}(x_2), \text{is\_column}(x_3)$$

$$\ldots$$

We cannot replace all of the clauses with a clause $C_1 = \text{is\_table}(\texttt{TABLE}(x)) \leftarrow \text{is\_column}(x)$ though only one DTD rule `<!ELEMENT TABLE (TR)+>` is sufficient to represent the type which $d_1$ belongs to. This shows that first-order terms are not adequate for modelling semi-structured documents. If we use hedges as arguments of atoms in logic programs, the clause $C_1$ is enough in the definition of the type of table documents.

Now we formally define semi-structured documents and hedges with context free grammars. We represent a grammar with a tuple $G = (V, T, R, S)$, where $V$ and $T$ are finite sets of non-terminal symbols and terminal symbols respectively, $R$ is a set of production rules, and $S$ is the start symbol. The set $R$ is allowed to have infinitely many rules.

Let $N$ and $\Sigma$ be mutually disjoint sets. Each element in $N$ is called a *name*. For every name $n$ we prepare a pair of new symbols $b_n$ and $e_n$, which are respectively called a *start-tag* and an *end-tag*. The set of start-tags (end-tags) is denoted by $B_N$ ($E_N$, resp.). We also prepare a set $X$ of *logical variables* (or *variables*) so that semi-structured documents and hedges can be used in logic programs.

**Definition 1.** A *well-formed pattern* over $(\Sigma, N, X)$ is a word in the language $L(G_W)$ generated by a context-free grammar $G_W = (V_W, T_W, R_W, S)$, where $V_W = \{S\} \cup \{T_n \mid n \in N\}$, $T_W = \Sigma \cup X \cup B_N \cup E_N$, and

$$\begin{aligned} R_W = \ & \{S \to \epsilon\} \cup \{S \to SS\} \cup \{S \to T_n \, ; \, n \in N\} \\ & \cup \{T_n \to b_n S e_n \, ; \, n \in N\} \cup \{S \to c ; \, c \in \Sigma \cup X\} \end{aligned}$$

A *well-formed document* is a well-formed pattern without any logical variables. The set of well-formed patterns over $(\Sigma, N, X)$ is denoted by $\mathcal{W}(\Sigma, N, X)$.

In XML the set $N$ is a subset of $\Sigma^+$ defined according to the specification (`http://www.w3.org/XML/`), and $b_n$ ($e_n$) is a string <$n$> (</$n$>, resp.).

**Definition 2.** A *hedge* $h$ over $(\Sigma, N, X)$ is defined inductively as follows:

1. The empty string $\varepsilon$ is a hedge.
2. A terminal symbol $c \in \Sigma$ is a hedge.
3. A logical variable $x \in X$ is a hedge.
4. If $n \in N$ is a name and $h$ is a hedge, then $n(h)$ is a hedge.
5. If $h_1$ and $h_2$ are hedges, then a concatenation $h_1 h_2$ is a hedge.

A hedge without any logical variables is called a *ground hedge*. The set of hedges over $(\Sigma, N, X)$ is denoted by $\mathcal{H}(\Sigma, N, X)$. For a hedge of the form $n(h_1 \cdots h_m)$ $h_1, \cdots, h_m$ are called *siblings*.

We often write $(h_1 \cdots h_m)$ for a hedge $h_1 \cdots h_m$ ($m \geq 0$) for readability, though this pair of parentheses without any name is not a part of syntax.

We define a grammar $G_H = (V_W, T_W, R_H, S)$ where $V_W$ and $T_W$ are same that used in $G_W$, and $R_H$ is obtained by replacing each rule of the form $T_n \to b_n S e_n$ with $T_n \to n(S)$. It is easily checked that the word accepted by $G_H$ is a hedge in $\mathcal{H}(\Sigma, N, X)$, and any hedge in $\mathcal{H}(\Sigma, N, X)$ is accepted by $G_H$. Moreover, directly from the definition of $G_W$ and $G_H$, every well-formed pattern $w$ can be translated into exactly one hedge $hdg(w)$, and conversely, every hedge $h$ can be translated into exactly one well-formed pattern $w$ such that $h = hdg(w)$.

*Example 1.* The hedge $hdg(d_1)$ is obtained by removing all commas from $t_1$.

## 3 Deductive Reasoning on Hedges

Let $\Pi$ be a set of predicate symbols, with each of which a natural number arity is associated. We define an atom as an expression of the form $p(h_1, h_2, \ldots, h_n)$ where $p \in \Pi$, $n$ is the arity of $p$, and $h_i \in \mathcal{H}(\Sigma, N, X)$ for every $i = 1, 2, \ldots, n$. Definite clauses and goal clauses are defined with such atoms in the same manner as in the original logic programming. A *hedge logic program* is a finite set of definite clauses.

We use SLD-resolution for the execution of hedge logic programs. We have to take it into consideration that there is no mgu (most general unifier) of two hedges in general. This problem is solved by assuming some restriction to the occurrences of variables in definite clauses and goal clauses. An example of such restriction was given in [3].

*Example 2.* Let $P_1$ be a hedge logic program

$$\left\{\begin{array}{l} trans(x, y) \leftarrow t(x, y) \\ t(\mathtt{TABLE}(x), \mathtt{TABLE}(y)) \leftarrow s(x, y) \\ s((\mathtt{TR}(x\, \mathtt{TD}(z))\, y), (\mathtt{TR}(\mathtt{TD}(z))\, w)) \leftarrow s(y, w) \\ s(\varepsilon, \varepsilon) \leftarrow \end{array}\right\}$$

and $G_1$ a goal clause $\leftarrow trans(hdg(d_1), x)$, where $d_1$ is the well-formed document in Fig. 1. By an SLD-refutation of $P_1 \cup \{G_1\}$ we obtain an answer which substitutes the variable $x$ in $G_1$ with a hedge

```
TABLE(TR(TD(John.Doe@foo.com))
      TR(TD(Bob.Smith@foo.com))
      TR(TD(Alice.Miller@foo.com)))
```

Each hedge is regarded as a congruence class of first-order terms, under an equality theory representing associative law for catenation and idempotence of the empty hedge. Based on this fact we give a method with which every hedge logic program can be transformed into an original logic program using lists with function symbols $[\,]$ and $[\,|\,]$, and an auxiliary relation *append*, .

**Definition 3.** For a hedge $h \in \mathcal{H}(\Sigma, X, N)$, we inductively define a first order term $\alpha(h)$ and a sequence of first-order atoms $\beta(h)$ as follows:

1. $\alpha(\varepsilon) = [\,]$ and $\beta(\varepsilon) = \phi$.

2. For a constant $c \in \Sigma$ $\alpha(c) = [c]$ and $\beta(c) = \phi$.
3. For a variable $x \in X$ $\alpha(x) = x$ and $\beta(x) = \phi$.
4. If $h = n(h_1)$ for some name $n \in N$, then $\alpha(h) = \alpha(n(h_1)) = n(\alpha(h_1))$ and $\beta(h) = \beta(h_1)$.
5. If $h = h_1 h_2$, then $\alpha(h) = y$ and $\beta(h) = \mathit{append}(\alpha(h_1), \alpha(h_2), y), \beta(h_1), \beta(h_2)$ where $y$ is a fresh variable.

Each of $\alpha$ and $\beta$ can be easily extended to a function on atomic formulas. For a definite clause $C = A_0 \leftarrow A_1, \ldots, A_k$ of a hedge logic program $P$, we define

$$\pi(C) = \alpha(A_0) \leftarrow \alpha(A_1), \ldots, \alpha(A_k), \beta(A_0), \beta(A_1), \ldots, \beta(A_k)$$

and we define $\pi(P) = \{\pi(C) \mid C \in P\}$.

**Lemma 1.** *Let $P$ be a hedge logic program, and $G$ be a goal clause. Then there is an SLD-resolution for $P \cup G$ iff there is an SLD-resolution $\pi(P_H) \cup P_{append} \cup \pi(G)$, where $P_{append}$ is a logic program defining the predicate append.*

*Example 3.* A definite clause $p(x \, \texttt{<TD>}(y) \, z) \leftarrow q(x), r(y), q(z)$ in a hedge logic program is translated to a first-order definite clause

$$p(w) \leftarrow q(x), r(y), q(z), \mathit{append}(x, [td(y)], u), \mathit{append}(u, z, w)$$

## 4 Inductive Reasoning on Hedges

In this section, we give an anti-unification algorithm for hedges. For a hedge $p$, we define the size of $p$, denoted by $\mathit{size}(p)$, by the total number of symbols in $\Sigma \cup X \cup N$. Note that we allow the empty substitutions.

**Definition 4.** Let $p, q$ be hedges. If there exists some substitution $\theta$ such that $p\theta = q$ then $p$ is *more general than* $q$ and written $p \geq q$. If $p \geq q$ but $q \not\geq p$ then $p$ is *properly more general than* $q$ and written $p > q$. If $p \geq q$ ($p > q$), then $p$ is a *generalization* of $q$ (*proper generalization* of $q$). If $p \geq q$ and $q \geq p$ then we $p$ is *equivalent to* $q$ and written $p \equiv q$.

**Definition 5.** For a hedge $h$, we define the *language* of $h$ by the set $L(h) = \{g \mid h\theta = g,\ g \text{ is a ground hedge, } \theta \text{ is a substitution}\}$ of ground hedges obtained by substituting ground hedges for the variables in $h$.

Clearly, $p \equiv q$ if and only if $p$ and $q$ are obtained from each other by renaming variables. Furthermore, if $p \geq q$ then $\mathit{size}(p) \leq \mathit{size}(q)$ holds.

There are no unique least common anti-unification (lca) or the least general generalization (lgg) for hedges. Thus, we define below a weaker notion of mca.

**Definition 6.** Let $q_1, q_2$ be hedges. A *common generalization* of $q_1$ and $q_2$ is a hedge such that $p \geq q_i$ for every $i = 1, 2$. A *minimal common anti-unification* (mca) of $q_1$ and $q_2$ is a common generalization $p$ of $q_1$ and $q_2$ such that $p \not> p'$ for any common generalization $p'$ of $q_1$ and $q_2$.

There are exponentially many mca's of a given pair of hedges, while there is the unique lca for first-order terms. It will be difficult to compute *all* of the mca of a given pairs of hedges. Thus, we will concentrate on the problem of finding one of the minimal anti-unifications for simple subclass, called simple hedges.

**Definition 7.** A hedge $v$ is *simple* if $v$ has mutually distinct logical variables and any set of siblings contains at most one logical variable.

*Example 4.* Let $\Sigma = \{a, b, c\}$, $X = \{x, y, z, \ldots\}$, and $N = \{f, g\}$. Then, $h_1 = (a\ x\ f(y\ g(b)))$, $h_2 = (g(f(x)\ f(y)\ f(z)))$ and $h_3 = (x\ f(y\ f(a\ z)))$ are examples of simple hedges. On the other hand, the hedge $h_4 = (a\ x\ f(b)\ y\ a)$, $h_5 = (x\ f(x))$ and $h_6 = (g(f(x)\ f(x)))$ are not simple because $h_4$ contains $x, y$ among siblings, and $h_5$ and $h_6$ contain repeated occurrences of $x$.

A key of our anti-unification algorithm for hedges is a search operator called the *refinement operator* defined as follows, which are used to search all hedges from general to specific.

**Definition 8.** A substitution $\theta$ for a hedge $p$ is called *simple* if $\theta$ has one of the following forms: (i) $x := x\, n(y)$, (ii) $x := n(y)\, x$, (iii) $x := y\, c$, (iv) $x := c\, y$, and (v) $x := \varepsilon$, where $n \in N$ is a name, $c \in \Sigma$ is a letter, $x \in var(p)$ and $y \in var(p)$ are variables appearing and not appearing in $p$, respectively.

**Definition 9.** For simple hedges $p, q$, if there exists a simple substitution $\theta$ such that $p\theta = q$ then we write $p \Rightarrow q$. We denote by $\overset{+}{\Rightarrow}$ and $\overset{*}{\Rightarrow}$ the transitive closure and the reflexive transitive closure of $\Rightarrow$, respectively. If there exists a sequence $p_0 = p \Rightarrow p_1 \Rightarrow \cdots \Rightarrow p_n = q$ $(n \geq 0)$, where $p_i$ $(1 \leq i \leq n)$ of simple hedges then we write $p \overset{n}{\Rightarrow} q$. This sequence is called a *derivation sequence* for $p \overset{*}{\Rightarrow} q$.

**Definition 10.** Let $p, q_1, q_2$ be simple hedges. Then, we define the set $\rho(p, q_1, q_2)$ of immediate refinement of $p$ by

$$\rho(p, q_1, q_2) = \{p' \mid p' \text{ is a simple hedge}, p \Rightarrow p', p' \geq q_1, p' \geq q_2\}$$

**Lemma 2.** *For any simple hedges $p, q_1, q_2$ such that $p \geq q_i$ for every $i = 1, 2$, the set $\rho(p, q_1, q_2)$ is of cardinality $5n$, of polynomial size, and $O(n^2)$ time computable, where $n = size(p)$. Furthermore, it is decidable in $O(n^2)$ time to check whether $\rho(p, q_1, q_2)$ is empty.*

In Fig. 2, we present an efficient algorithm for computing one of the simple mca's of a given pair of hedges.

**Theorem 1.** *For any pair of simple hedges $q_1, q_2$, the algorithm AU of Fig. 2 computes one of the minimal anti-unifications of $q_1$ and $q_2$ in time $O(n^3)$, where $n = size(q_1) + size(q_2)$ is the total input size.*

**Algorithm** $AU(q_1, q_2)$
**Input:** Simple hedges $q_1, q_2$.
**Output:** Finding a mca of $q_1, q_2$ within simple hedges.
$p := x$;
**while** $\rho(p, q_1, q_2) \neq \phi$ **do begin** /* Apply refinement operator */
  Select any $p' \in \rho(p, q_1, q_2)$;
  $p := p'$;
**end**;
**output** $p$;

**Fig. 2.** A polynomial time algorithm for computing a minimal common anti-unification

```
<TABLE>
  <TR><TD>Forecast for 04.22</TD><TD>Tokyo</TD><TD>Strasbourg</TD></TR>
  <TR><TD>Today</TD><TD>Sunny</TD><TD>Rain</TD></TR>
  <TR><TD>Tomorrow</TD><TD>Partly Cloudy</TD><TD>Showers</TD></TR>
</TABLE>

<TABLE>
  <TR><TD>Forecast for 04.23</TD><TD>Tokyo</TD><TD>Strasbourg</TD></TR>
  <TR><TD>Today</TD><TD>Cloudy</TD><TD>Showers</TD></TR>
</TABLE>
```

**Fig. 3.** Two well-formed documents for anti-unification

*Example 5.* Let us consider the well-formed documents in Fig. 3 which describe weather forecast. After transforming them into hedges and then $AU$ outputs a hedge $h$ which is a minimal anti-unification. The well-formed pattern $w$ in Fig. 4 satisfies $h = hdg(w)$.

This example shows that anti-unification extracts a common structure of given semi-structured documents as a hedge pattern, which is general enough to be used in hedge logical program as the arguments of some predicates.

## 5 Concluding Remarks

Hedges are used for various technologies for semi-structured documents, especially XML documents. A type definition languages is developed based on automata (regular expressions) on hedges [10]. In LMX [8] transformation of types can be represented as hedges. We are now confirming that hedge logic programs cover roles of these languages. For deductive databases of XML documents, forestlog [10] is proposed based on hedges. The usage of hedge logic programs in forestlog is quite different from ours because it adopts the $T_P$ operator.

Some researchers has proposed to model semi-structured documents with data structure other than hedges. Thomas [12] developed a Prolog program package for representing a semi-structured document as a feature structure. However feature structures cannot keep the order of contents in a semi-structured doc-

```
<TABLE>
  <TR><TD>Forecast for 04.2x</TD><TD>Tokyo</TD><TD>Strasbourg</TD></TR>
  <TR><TD>Today</TD><TD> y</TD><TD>z</TD></TR>
  w
</TABLE>
```

**Fig. 4.** An output of the anti-unification algorithm

uments. Grieser et al. [7] proposed to apply EFSs [2] to semi-structured documents. Since EFSs regard a semi-structured document as a string of symbols, they need some techniques for distinguishing names and terminal symbols. One of such a technique is introducing negation in EFSs as in [7]. Another technique is employing type definitions in EFSs. The full-paper version of this extended abstract will show the relation between typed EFSs and hedge logic programs.

## References


1. T. R. Amoth, P. Cull, and P. Tadepalli. Exact Learning of Tree Patterns from Queries and Counterexamples. In *Proceedings of COLT '98*, pages 175–186, 1998.
2. S. Arikawa, T. Shinohara, and A. Yamamoto. Learning Elementary Formal Systems. *Theoretical Computer Science*, 95(1):97–113, 1992.
3. H. Arimula and T. Shinohara. Inductive Inference of Prolog Programs with Linear Data Dependency. In H. Jaakkola, H. Kangassalo, T. Kitahashi, and A. Markus, editors, *Information Modelling and Knowledge Bases V*, pages 365–375. IOS Press, 1994.
4. G. J. Bex, S. Maneth, and F. Neven. A Formal Model for an Expressive Fragmanet of XSLT. In J. W. Lloyd et al., editor, *Proceedings of CL 2000 (LNAI 1861)*, pages 1137–1151. Springer, 2000.
5. D. Cabeza, M. Hermenegildo, and S. Varma. The Pillow/CIAO Library for INTERNET/WWW Programming using Computational Logic Systems. In R. A. Kowalski and Bowen K. A., editors, *Proceedings of the JICSLP'96 Post-Conference Workshop on Logic Programming Tools for INTERNET Applications*, 1988.
6. B. Courcelle. On Recognizable Sets and Tree Automata. In M. Nivat and H. Ait-Kaci, editors, *Resolution of Equations in Algebraic Structres.* Academic Press, 1989.
7. G. Grieser, K. P. Jantke, S. Lange, and B. Thomas. A Unifying Approch to HTML Warapper Representation and Learning. In *Proceedings of the Third International Conference on Discovery Science (LNCS 1967)*, pages 50 – 64, 2000.
8. H. Maruyama, K. Tamura, and N. Uramoto. *XML and Java : Developing Web Applications.* Addison-Wesley, 1999.
9. M. Murata. Transformation of Documents and Schemas by Patterns and Contextual Conditions. In *Proceedings of Document Processing '96 (LNCS 1293)*, pages 153 – 169, 1997.
10. M. Murata. Data model for Document Transformation and Assembly (Extended Abstract). In *Proceedings of Document Processing '98 (LNCS 1481)*, pages 140 – 152, 1998.
11. M. Takahashi. Generalizations of Regular Sets and Their Application to a Study of Context-Free Languages. *Information and Control*, 27:1–36, 1975.
12. B. Thomas. Intelligent Web Querying with Logic Programs. In *Proceedings of the KI'98 Workshop on Interface Systems in Knowledge-based Systems*, 1998.

# Learning Functions from Imperfect Positive Data

Filip Železný

Center for Applied Cybernetics, Czech Technical University
Prague, Czech Republic

**Abstract.** The Bayesian framework of learning from positive noise-free examples derived by Muggleton [12] is extended to learning functional hypotheses from positive examples containing normally distributed noise in the outputs. The method subsumes a type of distance based learning as a special case. We also present an effective method of outlier-identification which may significantly improve the predictive accuracy of the final multi-clause hypothesis if it is constructed by a clause-by-clause covering algorithm as e.g. in Progol or Aleph. Our method is implemented in Aleph and tested on two experiments, one of which concerns numeric functions while the other treats non-numeric discrete data where the normal distribution is taken as an approximation of the discrete distribution of noise.

## 1 Introduction

Most of noise-handling techniques in machine learning are suited for the type of errors caused by wrong classification of training examples into classes, e.g. true or false. In a powerful family of ML methods such as ILP, which uses a Turing-equivalent representation to produce hypotheses and can therefore hypothesise about complicated input-output relations (e.g. functions), the role of *noise in attributes (arguments)* has been recognised [1,7] but rarely attempted to h andle. Moreover, we are not aware of a system which would directly exploit the knowledge of a particular noise-distribution in arguments, despite the fact that Bayesian and distance-based techniques - which have recently been paid a lot of attention in ILP [6,8,3,16,15] - can very well serve for this purpose.

We want to test the hypothesis that by exploiting the knowledge of a particular noise-distribution in the data (though it may hold only approximately) we may outperform standard noise-handling techniques. In the next section we shall see how to optimally (in the Bayes sense) learn functions with unknown domains and normally-distributed noise in the output arguments. The outstanding role of the normal noise-distribution has been extensively justified in many sources (see e.g. [2]) namely on the basis of the central limit theorem. We implemented the method in the ILP system Aleph. Section 3 describes an effective outlier-identification technique applicable in the clause-by-clause theory-construction performed by this system, modified as to follow the guideline developed in Section 2.

In the experimental part (Section 4), we first test our method on artificial data. In particular, we learn numeric functions representable by a one-clause

C. Rouveirol and M. Sebag (Eds.): ILP 2001, LNAI 2157, pp. 248–259, 2001.

Prolog program. This experiment will comply with the conditions of *U-learning* [14] and the noise will be exactly normal. We shall then also try to slightly relax the conditions of U-learning. The second experiment will be based on English verb past tense data. These data have functional, discrete and non-numeric character. The output argument will be damaged by altering a certain number of characters in the word and the continuous normal distribution of noise will only be approximated. This kind of errors simulates the one encountered in literal data digitisation by e.g. OCR systems or human transcription. The predictive accuracy of the resulting multi-clause theory will be significantly improved by the outlier-identification technique described in Section 3. Section 5 concludes.

## 2 Bayesian Framework

A standard approach to learn functions from positive data in ILP makes use of the closed-world assumption (CWA). Using CWA, we substitute negative examples necessary in the normal ILP setting e.g. by an *integrity constraint* which falsifies all hypotheses which yield the output $\boldsymbol{out_h}$ for an input $\boldsymbol{in}$, such that there exists a positive example $e(\boldsymbol{in}, \boldsymbol{out_e})$ and $\boldsymbol{out_e} \neq \boldsymbol{out_h}$. But CWA clearly cannot be used if the output part of examples contains noise.

Another common drawback of functional learners is that they get no information from the distribution of values in the input parts of the presented positive examples. To get a rough idea how such information could be used, imagine that we are learning scalar functions on the integer (sampling) interval $\langle -10; 10 \rangle$. Assume that the current hypothesis space is $\{equal(in, out), sqrt(in, out)\}$ and we get two positive examples $e(0,0)$ and $e(1,1)$. Then both hypotheses are consistent with the exa mples but $sqrt/2$ has higher posterior probability (in the Bayes sense) since it is less general (defined only for non-negative inputs).

Both of these problems will be treated in the following framework embedded in the Muggleton's U-learning scheme of learning from positive data [12]. For ease of insight we shall formalize it for numeric data to later easily generalize for non-numeric data in the experimental part of the text.

Let $I$ be a finite set, if $f$ and $g$ are (real) functions on a superset of I then the *Euclidean distance* between $f$ and $g$ on $I$ is

$$\mathcal{E}(f(I), g(I)) = \sum_{i \in I} (f(i) - g(i))^2 \tag{1}$$

The normal distribution $N_{\mu,\sigma}(x)$ with *mean* $\mu$ and *standard deviation* $\sigma$ is given as

$$N_{\mu,\sigma}(x) = \frac{1}{\sigma\sqrt{2\pi}} \exp -\frac{(x-\mu)^2}{2\sigma^2} \tag{2}$$

Let ***bold*** characters denote vectors, their elements being addressed by the lower index. The *instance space* $X$ will be the Cartesian product of the sets of possible inputs $I$ and outputs $O$. An instance (example)[1] $e \in X$ is then given by the

[1] We reserve plain characters for vector examples and mappings to improve readability.

input part $\boldsymbol{in}(e) \in I$ and output part $\boldsymbol{out}(e) \in O$. These parts are in general vectors of $|\boldsymbol{in}|$ and $|\boldsymbol{out}|$ elements, respectively. A (functional) *hypothesis* $H$ on the instance set $X = I \times O$ is a tuple $\langle H_d \subseteq I, h : H_d \rightarrow O \rangle$. $H_d$ is the *domain* of $H$ and $H_c = \{e \in E | \boldsymbol{in}(e) \in H_d\}$ is the *coverage* of $H$. $H$ is said to be *consistent with* $e \in X$ if $\boldsymbol{in}(e) \in H_d$, $H$ is *consistent* (with $E$) if it is consistent with all $e \in E$. The mapping (such as $h$) corresponding to a hypothesis (such as $H$) will be always denoted by lowering the case and by $h_j(.)$ we shall denote the $j^{th}$ element of $h(.)$.

Given a probability distribution $D_I$ on the input space and assuming mutual independence of outputs, we can express the distribution of the conditional probability on the instance space under the condition of validity of a hypothesis $H$ as

$$\begin{aligned} D_{X|H}(e) = D_{X|H}(\boldsymbol{in}(e), \boldsymbol{out}(e)) = D_{I|H}(\boldsymbol{in}(e)) D_{O|H,\boldsymbol{in}(e)}(\boldsymbol{out}(e)) = \\ = D_{I|H}(\boldsymbol{in}(e)) \prod_{j=1}^{|\boldsymbol{out}|} D_{O|H,\boldsymbol{in}(e)}(\boldsymbol{out}_j(e)) \end{aligned} \tag{3}$$

$D_{X|H}(e)$ is zero if $e$ is not consistent with $H$ since then $D_{I|H}(\boldsymbol{in}(e)) = 0$. Otherwise, $D_{I|H}(\boldsymbol{in}(e))$ can be expressed as

$$D_{I|H}(\boldsymbol{in}(e)) = \frac{D_I(\boldsymbol{in}(e))}{D_I(H_d)} \tag{4}$$

and the conditional probability on the outputs will express our assumption of normally distributed error with standard deviation $\sigma_j$ in the $j^{th}$ output argument

$$D_{O|H,\boldsymbol{in}(e)}(\boldsymbol{out}_j(e)) = N_{h_j(\boldsymbol{in}(e)),\sigma_j}(\boldsymbol{out}_j(e)) \tag{5}$$

Given a *prior probability* distribution on hypotheses $D_H$, a target hypothesis $H^*$, a set of examples $E = e_1, e_2, ..., e_m$ selected by $m$ statistically independent choises from $D_{X|H^*}$, the posterior probability of a hypothesis $H$ consistent with $E$ can be found by applying the well-known Bayes rule and Eqs. 3,4,5 as

$$\begin{aligned} P(H|E) = P(H|e_1, e_2, ..., e_m) = D_H(H) D_X^{-1}(E) D_{X|H}(e_1, e_2, ..., e_m) = \\ = D_H(H) D_X^{-1}(E) \prod_{i=1}^{m} \left[ D_I^{-1}(H_d) D_I(\boldsymbol{in}(e)) \prod_{j=1}^{|\boldsymbol{out}|} N_{h_j(\boldsymbol{in}(e)),\sigma_j}(\boldsymbol{out}_j(e_i)) \right] \end{aligned} \tag{6}$$

To choose the most-promising hypothesis, we want to maximise $P(H|E)$ w.r.t $H$. We shall take logarithms of both sides of this equation (to maximise $\ln P(H|E)$) and for this sake we disassemble the rightmost side into several terms. First, it is argued in [12] that $D_H$ should be expected to obey

$$\ln D_H(H) = -size(H) const_N \tag{7}$$

where $size(H)$ measures the number of bits necessary to encode the hypothesis $H$ and $const_N$ is a normalising constant ensuring that $\sum_H D_H(H)$ sums to one; this constant is neglectable when maximising $\ln P(H|E)$. Following the same source, $\prod_{i=1}^{m} D_I^{-1}(H_d) = D_I^{-m}(H_d)$ can be identified as

$$\ln D_I^{-m}(H_d) = -m \ln gen(H) \tag{8}$$

where $gen(H)$ is the *generality* of $H$ (i.e. the portion of the input space covered by $H_d$). The term $\ln\left[D_X^{-1}(E)\prod_{i=1}^{m} D_I(\boldsymbol{in}(e_i))\right] = const_1$ is constant for all hypotheses, so it can be neglected when maximising $\ln P(H|E)$. Finally it holds

$$\begin{aligned} &\ln\prod_{i=1}^{m}\prod_{j=1}^{|\boldsymbol{out}|} N_{h_j(\boldsymbol{in}(e_i)),\sigma_j}(\boldsymbol{out}_j(e_i)) = \\ &= \ln\prod_{i=1}^{m}\prod_{j=1}^{|\boldsymbol{out}|}\frac{1}{\sigma_j\sqrt{2\pi}}\exp-\frac{(\boldsymbol{out}_j(e_i)-h_j(\boldsymbol{in}(e_i)))^2}{2\sigma_j^2} = \\ &= -m\sum_{j=1}^{|\boldsymbol{out}|}\ln(\sigma_j\sqrt{2\pi}) - \sum_{j=1}^{|\boldsymbol{out}|}\frac{1}{2\sigma_j^2}\sum_{i=1}^{m}(\boldsymbol{out}_j(e_i)-h_j(\boldsymbol{in}(e_i)))^2 \end{aligned} \tag{9}$$

The term $-m\sum_{j=1}^{|\boldsymbol{out}|}\ln(\sigma_j\sqrt{2\pi}) = const_2$ does not depend on the hypothesis and can be neglected when maximising $\ln P(H|E)$. Combining Eqs. 7-9 and considering Eq. 1 we arrive to the fact that to maximise $\ln P(H|E)$ we need to maximise the function $f_E(H)$ (w.r.t. consistent hypotheses $H$)

$$f_E(H) = -m\ln gen(H) - size(H) - \sum_{j=1}^{|\boldsymbol{out}|}\frac{1}{2\sigma_j^2}\mathcal{E}(\boldsymbol{out}_j(E), h_j(\boldsymbol{in}(E))) \tag{10}$$

which can be simplified if there is only one output argument as

$$f'_E(H) = -m\ln gen(H) - size(H) - \frac{1}{2\sigma^2}\mathcal{E}(out(E), h(\boldsymbol{in}(E))) \tag{11}$$

The first two terms in $f_E(H)$ or $f'_E(H)$ express a generality - size tradeoff derived by Muggleton [12] for the case of learning classification hypotheses from noise-free positive data. In our case of learning functional hypotheses from data with normal output noise, we have instead arrived to a generality - size - Euclidean distance tradeoff, where generality is measured on the input space (function domain) and the output-distance term is weighted by the inverse value of the *variance* $\sigma^2$. This is natural: the more noisy (more deviated) are the outputs in the examples, the more it makes sense to decide rather by the input domain data (by measuring the generality on the input domain) and prior hypothesis probability (reflected by the size term) and vice-versa.

In the following we shall concentrate on single-output hypotheses and therefore maximise $f'_E(H)$. Thus the assumption of statistically independent outputs is no longer needed.

## 3 Outlier Identification

In a hypothesis constructed by an ILP system (ordered set of Prolog clauses $C^1, ..., C^n$), one example may be consistent with more than one clause. Although we are learning functional hypothesis, we do not require consistency with at most one clause, since this would too much constrain the learning algorithm. Instead, we shall *interpret* the Prolog program functionally, i.e. as[2]

[2] The standard Prolog `once/1` predicate returns only the first-found answer whatever may be the number of solutio ns.

`once(target_predicate(`$\boldsymbol{inputs}, OUTPUT$`))`. Accordingly, we define the *reduced domain* and *reduced coverage* of a clause $C^n$ as $C^n_{rd} = C^n_d \setminus \cup_{k=1}^{n-1} C^k_d$ and $C_{rc} = \{e \in E | \boldsymbol{in}(e) \in C_{rd}\}$.

To select a hypothesis by maximising $f'_E(H)$ we need to have at hand a set of candidate hypotheses. But in a typical ILP system, hypotheses are constructed clause-by-clause, therefore [12] proposes estimates of the value $gen(H)$ and $size(H)$ based on $|C^n_d|$, $gen(H^n)$, $gen(H^{n-1})$ and $size(C^n)$ where $H^n = \{C^1, ..., C^n\}$ (i.e. $H^{n-1}$ is the already-constructed partial hypothesis and $C^n$ the currently added clause) and $H$ is the final hypothesis. In an analogical spirit, if $|C^i_{rc}|^{-1}\mathcal{E}(out(C^i_{rc}), c^i(\boldsymbol{in}(C^i_{rc})))$ (the average distance of the output of $C^i$ from individual examples on its domain $C^i_{rd}$), is approximately equal for all clauses $C^i$ in the final hypothesis $H$, we may make the following estimation[3]

$$\mathcal{E}(out(E), h(\boldsymbol{in}(E))) \approx \frac{|E|}{|C^n_{rc}|}\mathcal{E}(out(C^n_{rc}), c^n(\boldsymbol{in}(C^n_{rc}))) \tag{12}$$

Let the function $f^e_E(C^n)$ denote the estimate of $f'_E(H)$ determined by substituting the size, generality and distance terms by their estimates described in [12][4] and the estimate in Eq. 12, respectively. The clause $C^n$ that maximises $f^e_E(C^n)$ will then be added to the current hypothesis $H^{n-1}$.

In the clause-by-clause functional hypothesis construction, we are no longer learning optimally (as by Eq. 11). The algorithm maximising $f^e_E(C^n)$ for each added clause has a greedy character and we can use the following heuristic to improve the clause ordering: If there exists a clause with good accuracy on (low output-distance from) a large part of the example set but poor accuracy on a few exceptions (outliers), then this general clause should be preceeded with a more special clause 'handling' these exceptions. Together with the *once*−interpretation, this strategy will produce a form of a specific-to-general decision list, whose advantage to functional representation has been argued in [10].

To attain such clause-ordering, we use the 'degree of freedom' given by the seed-example selection in ILP systems like Aleph [5] and Progol [11]. In these systems, the seed-example is selected randomly or in the presentation order and used for the construction of a *bottom clause* which is then suitably generalised. The idea of our method is that we direct the seed-example selection as to first choose (and cover) those examples that are outliers to some potentially good clause. To protect efficiency, we shall avoid backtracking (deleting previously constructed clauses) .

During the computation of $f^e_E(C^n)$ for each candidate clause $C^n$, we also evaluate the function $Hope_E(C^n) = max_{O \subset E}(f^e_{E\setminus O}(C^n))$ which yields the highest evaluation potentially reached by $C^n$ if some example subset $O$ (outliers) were avoided, i.e. covered by some previous clause. Evaluating $f^e_{E\setminus O}(C^n)$ for every $O \subset E$ would be intractable, but we can avoid it by first sorting the examples $e \in C^n_{rc}$ decreasingly by the value $(out(e) - c^n(\boldsymbol{in}(e)))^2$, i.e. by their contribution

[3] Remind that $c^n$ is the mapping corresponding to the hypothesis $C^n$.

[4] Where $|C^n_{rc}|$ is taken instead of $|C^n_c|$ denoted as $p$ in [12].

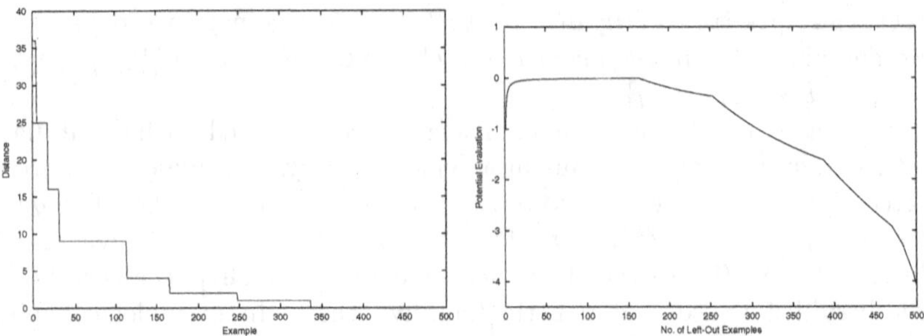


**Fig. 1.** Outlier Identification in English past tense data with noise variance 0.3. The left diagram shows the decreasing output distance contribution of each of 500 examples w.r.t the clause `past(A,B):-split(B,A,[e,d])`. The right diagram plots for each example $e_i$ the potential evaluation of the clause if $\{e_1, ..., e_i\}$ were avoided from the clause's domain. This potential evauation reaches its maximum for example no. 165. Examples 1-165 are thus considered outliers.

to the distance $\mathcal{E}(out(C^n_{rc}), c(\boldsymbol{in}(C^n_{rc})))$ (see Eq. 1). Then outliers are identified by successively replacing examples in this order from $C^n_{rc}$ into the (initially empty) set $OL$. The set $OL$ which maximises $f^e_{E\backslash OL}(C^n)$ during this cycle is taken as the outlier set and it then holds that $f^e_{E\backslash OL}(C^n) = max_{O\subset E}(f^e_{E\backslash O}(C^n))$. To roughly see why, note that by exchangin g any example $e_1$ from $OL$ with any example $e_2$ from $C^n_{rc}\backslash OL$, obtaining $OL_{alt} = \{e_2\}\cup OL\backslash\{e_1\}$, the generality and size estimates in the function $f^e$ maintain the same value and the distance term remains the same or grows as the contribution of $e_1$ to the Euclidean distance is the same or smaller than that of $e_2$ (due to the precomputed decreasing order). Therefore $f^e_{E\backslash OL_{alt}}(C^n) \leq f^e_{E\backslash OL}(C^n)$. Fig. 1 shows an ex ample of outlier identification in the English past tense data domain (Section 4.2).

In the learning algorithm, each example in $E$ is assigned a *selection-preference* value, initiated to zero. For every evaluated candidate clause $C^n$ with outliers $OL$, the current selection-preference value of each example $e \in OL \subset E$ is updated by adding a value increasing with the *Hope* of $C^n$. When selecting the seed-example, the example with maximum selection-preference value is chosen[5]. This way, examples that are outliers of high-*Hope* clauses will be covered in the earlier stages of hypothesis construction. Typical for the described method as implemented in Aleph is that at one stage a clause with high *Hope* is evaluated, rejected due to outliers, which are then forced to be covered. When the same clause is evaluated newly (as a result of a newly selected seed example), it is accepted since its outliers are already covered. It is the multiple evaluation of one clause intrinsic to the *cover algorithm* of Aleph that enables us to implement the method without backtracking. The only (slightly) superlinear computational overhead introduced by the technique is the sorting of examples by their contribution to the Euclidean distance.

[5] In the first step, before generating any clause, the seed example is chosen randomly.

# 4 Experiments

## 4.1 Learning Numeric Functions

In the first experiment, we want to identify numeric functions composed of the four elementary functions $\{\ln(x), \sin(x), \cos(x), x+y\}$ by one Prolog clause. The hypothesis bias is limited by the maximum composition depth 4. There are 425 functions in this hypothesis space assuming commutativity of addition [4]. As *background knowledge*, the learning system uses the Prolog definitions of the elementary functions (e.g. `ln(X,Y):-X>0, Y is log(X)`). To comply with the framework o f U-learning, we repeatedly perform the learning process with a target hypothesis chosen with a probability exponentially decreasing with the size of its Prolog notatiton. The following table lists the used set of target functions, their input domains within the chosen sampling interval of integers $\langle -10; 10\rangle$ for example presentation, and their prior probabilities[6].

| Target Function | Domain $\in \langle -10; 10\rangle$ | Prior Probability |
|---|---|---|
| $\ln(x)$ | $\langle 1; 10\rangle$ | $1/2 * c_n$ |
| $\ln(\sin(x))$ | $-10, \langle -6; -4\rangle, \langle 1; 3\rangle, \langle 7; 9\rangle$ | $1/4 * c_n$ |
| $\cos(x) + \ln(\cos(x))$ | $\langle -7; -5\rangle, \langle -1; 1\rangle, \langle 5; 7\rangle$ | $1/8 * c_n$ |
| $\ln(\sin(x) + \cos(x))$ | $\langle -7; -4\rangle, \langle 0; 2\rangle, \langle 6; 8\rangle$ | $1/16 * c_n$ |

Examples are presented in the form `e(input,output)` from equal probability distribution on the input domain and the output value is distorted by normal noise. We test three learning methods. BL denotes the Bayesian technique developed in Section 2. DBL is a simpified BL, where size and generality of hypotheses are ignored when maximising $f'_E(H)$, i.e. we ignore the information in the input domain data distribution and in the prior hypothesis probability distribution. We thus reason only on the basis of the output distance and so DBL corresponds to a simple kind of distance based learning. The last tested method is based on a simple classical manner of treating noise in real values in ILP: the standard Aleph (Progol) algorithm of learning from positive data is used, but we introduce a predicate `close/2` as part of the background knowledge, such that `close(A,B)` is true if the values in `A` and `B` differ by less than 10%. The learner may thus identify e.g. $\ln(x)$ from noisy-output data by the clause `e(A,B):-log(A,C),close(C,B)`.

Considering Fig. 2, BL clearly outperforms the other two methods, i.e. the exploitation of the generality and size measures proves useful (compare with DBL) as well as the exploitation of the Eucledian distance measure derived from the normal noise distribution (compare with `close/2`). Relaxing the U-learning conditions by presenting target hypotheses in equal probabilities makes the difference btw. BL and the other methods smaller, but not significantly.

[6] $c_n$ is a normalising constant

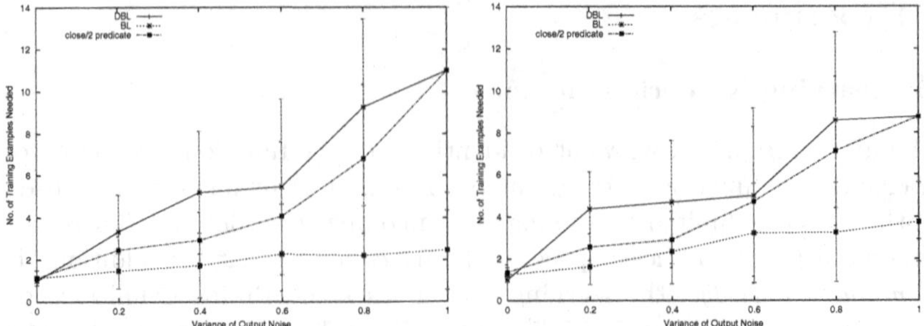


**Fig. 2.** Learning Numeric Functions. The left diagram shows the minimum number of examples each of the tested methods needed to correctly identify the target function with growing variance in the output noise. For each method and each value of variance the experiment was repeated 20 times, the average result is plotted with standard deviation in the measurement points. The right diagram reflects a similar experiment where, however, the prior hypothesis probabilities were not respected, i.e. the targ et hypotheses were presented with equal probability.

## 4.2 Learning English Past Tense Rules

The second experiment is based on 1392 tuples of English verbs and their past tenses. Learning rules of English past tense by a multi-clause Prolog program has been studied with noise-free data [9,13]. The background knowledge contains the predicate `split/3` which splits a word into a prefix and suffix (e.g. `split([m,a,i,l,e,d],[m,a,i,l],[e,d])`; see [9] for typical hypotheses constructed by ILP in this domain. Unlike the noise-free experiments, in our case the output argument is distorted by altering a number of characters in the word such that the probability of $n$ wrong characters decreases exponentially with $n^2$ to approximate the normal distribution. Following is an example of 5 data with noise.

```
past([m,e,e,t],[m,e,t]).
past([m,i,n,i,s,t,e,r],[m,i,n,i,s,t,w,r,e,d]).
past([n,e,c,e,s,s,i,t,a,t,e],[n,e,c,q,s,s,i,y,a,t,e,d]).
past([o,b,s,e,r,v,e],[o,b,s,e,r,v,e,d]).
past([o,c,c,u,r],[o,c,c,u,r,r,e,f]).
```

The normal probability distribution was discretised in such a way that for $\sigma = 1$, the majority of examples contained at least one error, i.e. in the language of binary classification most of the presented positives were actually negatives.

We compare our method with the standard algorithm of Progol (Aleph) whose performance is good on the noise-free past tense data [13].[7] The integrity constraint (see Section 2) used in [13] to substitute negative examples cannot

[7] Progol was only outperformed by the method of *analogical prediction* whose application scope is rather specialised.

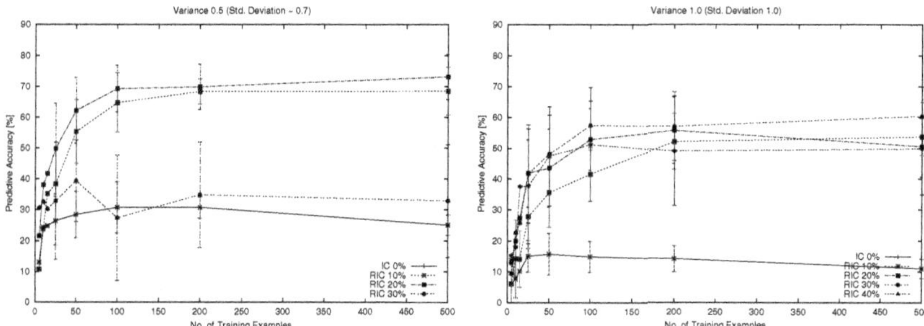


**Fig. 3.** Learning past tense rules with RIC's for two values of output noise variance. The training sets are selected randomly from the past-tense database and contain successively 5, 10, 15, 20, 50, 100, 200 and 500 examples; the testing set for measuring the predictive accuracy is always composed of 500 examples not including any of the training example. For each training set volume and each tested tuning of RIC, the experiment was repeated 20 times and the average value with its standard deviatio n is plotted.

work in the noisy domain but we may use a *relaxed integrity constraint* (RIC) which falsifies h ypotheses giving wrong outputs for a certain minimum percentage of examples. The question which percentage (tolerance) should be allowed for which level of noise (variance) is solved empirically in a preliminary comparative experiment of RIC's tuned to 0%, 10%, 20%, 30% and 40% of tolerance, shown in Fig. 3.

We shall use the Progol (Aleph) algorithm with the best performing RIC for each variance (tolerance 20% for $\sigma^2 = 0.5$, 30% for $\sigma^2 = 1$) to compete with our method, which will first be simplified in the following ways. First, we require that any resulting hypothesis must yield some output for any input word, i.e. the generality of all acceptable hypotheses is identical. We therefore consider the generality term in $f'_E(H)$ constant. Next, we limit the hypothesis bias by a maximum *variable d epth* [11] and within this bias we have no reason to expect that prior hypothesis probability decreases with the hypothesis size, i.e. the size term is also considered constant. Since only the output distance term (measured as squared Hamming distance[8]) is then maximised, we refer to this simplified method as distance-based (DBL).

---

[8] E.g. the distance of the hypothesis output [a,b,c] from the example outputs {[a,b,x], [a,x]} would be $1^2 + 2^2 = 5$ because the first example differs from [a,b,c] in one corresponding character and to compare two lists of different length s we add a suffix to the shorter with characters considered mismatches, i.e. the second example is taken as [a,x,x]. In the normal noise distribution definition we accordingly measure the Hamming distance instead of the subtraction $(x - \mu)$ (see Eq. 2). Such defined distance measure is natural in the experimented domain and different definitions may be suitable in other domains.

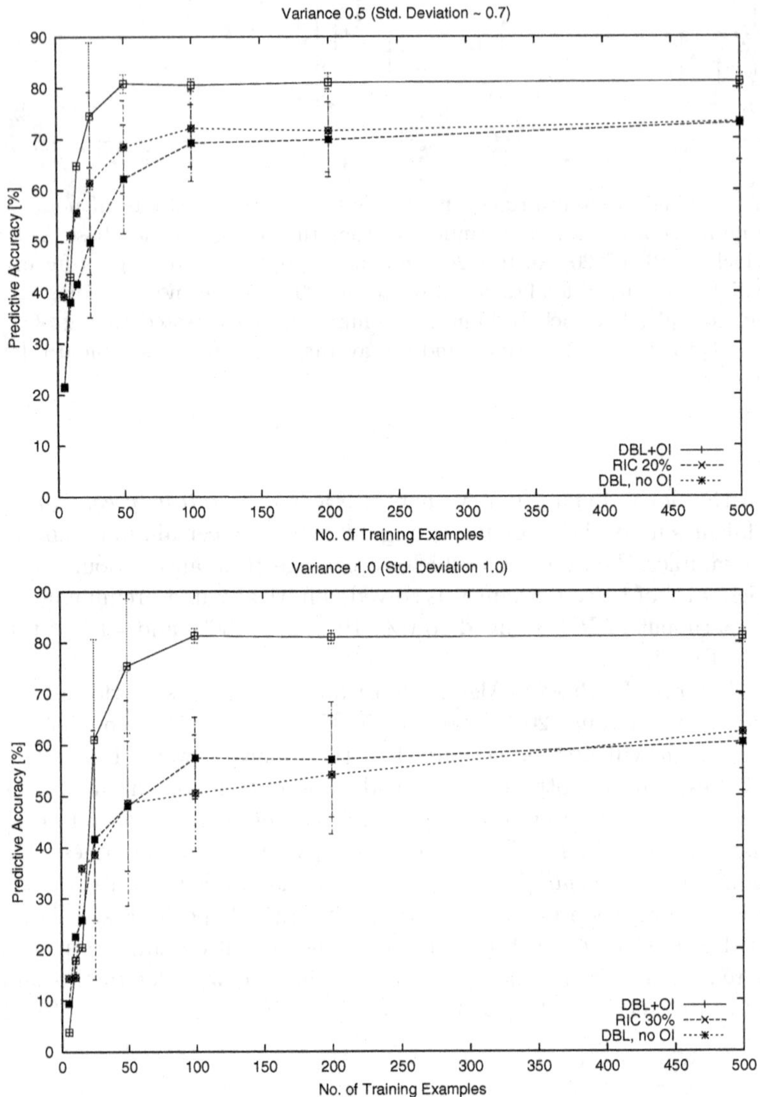


**Fig. 4.** Learning past tense with RIC, DBL and DBL+OI. The experimental setup is identical to the previous experiment (Fig. 3), from which the best performing RIC was taken for comparision.

As we are learning a multi-clause hypothesis, the outlier identification (OI) technique (Section 3) may be used. The performance of the three methods (Aleph with RIC, DBL and DBL+OI) is shown in Fig. 4 for two levels of noise.

We observe that the DBL method alone is comparable with the best-tuned integrity constraint. However, with RIC we need to first determine (e.g. empirically) a good value of tolerance, otherwise the performance may be very poor (Fig. 3). This is not necessary with DBL. Note also that to maximise $f'_E(H)$ the DBL learner does not need to know the value of the noise variance if the size and generality terms are considered constant. We also observe that outlier identification greatly improves the predi ctive accuracy of the multi-clause hypothesis constructed with DBL and we think this would be the case with any functional data with a high percentage of exception-items, as English past tense. Note also that the integrity constraint method cannot be further improved with OI, since the OI technique is directly based on the distance measure.

## 5 Conclusions and Future Work

We have illustrated how the exploitation of the knowledge of a particular noise distribution in training data arguments can be utilized to outperform classical noise-handling techniques. Using a Bayesian framework for optimal learning of functional hypothesis in the presence of normal noise, we also exploit the knowledge of the prior hypothesis probability and its generality on the input domain of the learned function. The advantage of exploiting all these properties was shown in a function-learning experim ent.

We implemented the method in the ILP system Aleph and for the clause-by-clause construction of hypotheses guided by this method we proposed a heuristic technique which forces outliers to be covered first so that general clauses can be accepted in the later stage of the clause-by-clause hypothesis construction. This ordering of clauses improves the predictive accuracy of the final hypothesis interpreted functionally, e.g. by the Prolog `once/1` predicate. This was illustrated in an experiment with a high percentage of exceptional examples. The technique does not introduce backtracking into the learning algorithm.

Our future work will focus on proving a bound of expected error related to the deveoped Bayesian learning with noise, similar to the one shown for the noise-free data case in [12]. Next, we want to extend the framework to non-functional hypotheses learning from data with normal noise in arguments.

### Acknowledgements

The experimental part of this work was conducted during the author's stay in LORIA, France - special thanks go to Amedeo Napoli and Hacene Cherfi. Thanks as well to Ashwin Srinivasan and Steve Moyle for feedback concerning positive-only learning as implemented in Aleph, and to the careful ILP'01 reviewers. The author is supported by the Ministry of Education of the Czech Republic under Project No. LN00B096, and by the project IST-1999-11.495 Sol-Eu-Net.

## References

1. W. Emde and D. Wettschereck. Relational instance-based learning. In L. Saitta, editor, *Proceedings of the 13th International Conference on Machine Learning*, pages 122–130. Morgan Kaufmann, 1996.
2. V. V. Fedorov. *Theory of optimal experiments.* Academic Press, 1972.
3. Peter A. Flach and Nicolas Lachiche. Decomposing probability distributions on structured individuals. In Paula Brito, Joaquim Costa, and Donato Malerba, editors, *Proceedings of the ECML2000 workshop on Dealing with Structured Data in Machine Learning and Statistics*, pages 33–43, Barcelona, Spain, May 2000.
4. http://labe.felk.cvut.cz/vzelezny/howmanyfunctions.pl.
5. http://web.comlab.ox.ac.uk/oucl/research/areas/machlearn/Aleph/aleph.html.
6. Kristian Kersting and Luc De Raedt. Bayesian logic programs. In J. Cussens and A. Frisch, editors, *Proceedings of the Work-in-Progress Track at the 10th International Conference on Inductive Logic Programming*, pages 138–155, 2000.
7. N. Lavrač, S. Džeroski, and I. Bratko. Handling imperfect data in inductive logic programming. In L. De Raedt, editor, *Advances in Inductive Logic Programming*, pages 48–64. IOS Press, 1996.
8. Eric McCreath and Arun Sharma. ILP with noise and fixed example size: A bayesian approach. In *IJCAI*, pages 1310–1315, 1997.
9. R.J. Mooney and M.E. Califf. Induction of first–order decision lists: Results on learning the past tense of English verbs. *Journal of Artificial Intelligence Research*, 3:1–24, 1995.
10. R.J. Mooney and M.E. Califf. Induction of first-order decision lists: Results on learning the past tense of English verbs. In L. De Raedt, editor, *Proceedings of the 5th International Workshop on Inductive Logic Programming*, pages 145–146. Department of Computer Science, Katholieke Universiteit Leuven, 1995.
11. S. Muggleton. Inverse entailment and Progol. *New Generation Computing, Special issue on Inductive Logic Programming*, 13(3-4):245–286, 1995.
12. S. Muggleton. Learning from positive data. In S. Muggleton, editor, *Proceedings of the 6th International Workshop on Inductive Logic Programming*, volume 1314 of Lecture Notes in Artificial Intelligence, pages 358–376. Springer-Verlag, 1996.
13. S. Muggleton and M. Bain. Analogical prediction. In S. Džeroski and P. Flach, editors, *Proceedings of the 9th International Workshop on Inductive Logic Programming*, volume 1634 of Lecture Notes in Artificial Intelligence, pages 234–244. Springer-Verlag, 1999.
14. S. Muggleton and C.D. Page. A learnability model for universal representations. In S. Wrobel, editor, *Proceedings of the 4th International Workshop on Inductive Logic Programming*, volume 237 of GMD-Studien, pages 139–160. Gesellschaft für Mathematik und Datenverarbeitung MBH, 1994.
15. S-H. Nienhuys-Cheng. Distance between herbrand interpretations: A measure for approximations to a target concept. In S. Džeroski and N. Lavrač, editors, *Proceedings of the 7th International Workshop on Inductive Logic Programming*, volume 1297 of Lecture Notes in Artificial Intelligence, pages 213–226. Springer-Verlag, 1997.
16. J. Ramon and L. De Raedt. Instance based function learning. In S. Džeroski and P. Flach, editors, *Proceedings of the 9th International Workshop on Inductive Logic Programming*, volume 1634 of Lecture Notes in Artificial Intelligence, pages 268–278. Springer-Verlag, 1999.

# Author Index